Reflexivity and Criminal Justice

Sarah Armstrong • Jarrett Blaustein • Alistair Henry
Editors

Reflexivity and Criminal Justice

Intersections of Policy, Practice and Research

palgrave
macmillan

Editors
Sarah Armstrong
Department of Sociology
University of Glasgow
Glasgow, United Kingdom

Alistair Henry
Law School
Old College
Edinburgh, United Kingdom

Jarrett Blaustein
Menzies Building
Monash University, School of Social Sciences
Clayton, Australia

ISBN 978-1-137-54641-8   ISBN 978-1-137-54642-5   (eBook)
DOI 10.1057/978-1-137-54642-5

Library of Congress Control Number: 2016956650

Cover illustration: Dmitriy Abramov / Alamy Stock Photo

Printed on acid-free paper

This Palgrave Macmillan imprint is published by Springer Nature
The registered company is Macmillan Publishers Ltd.
The registered company address is: The Campus, 4 Crinan Street, London, N1 9XW, United Kingdom

Acknowledgements

We would like to thank Richard Sparks and his co-investigators from the ESRC project 'Crime Control and Devolution: Policy-Making and Expert Knowledge in a Multi-Tiered Democracy' for affording us the opportunity to collectively reflect on the intersections between policy, practice and research during a seminar that was held at the University of Edinburgh in December 2013. It was at this event that the idea for this volume was born. We would also like to thank our mentors and colleagues, both past and present, and of whom there are too many to acknowledge individually, for helping us to develop our awareness of the importance of reflexivity in the context of criminological research. We are grateful to Dominic Walker, Jules Wilan, Josie Taylor and the production team at Palgrave for their ongoing patience and support and we would like to thank all of the authors who feature in this volume for their bold and thoughtful contributions.

Contents

Contributors

Harry Annison is Lecturer at the School of Law, Southampton University. His primary research interest is penal politics and policymaking. His articles have been published in *Theoretical Criminology, the Journal of Law and Society* and elsewhere. He is the author of *Dangerous Politics: Risk, Political Vulnerability, and Penal Policy* (2015).

Sarah Armstrong is Director of the Scottish Centre for Crime and Justice Research. Her research concerns prisons and punishment policy and practice including an ESRC funded research project called 'Ethnography of Penal Policy'.

Bilel Benbouzid is Assistant Professor of Sociology at the University of East Paris (UPEML). Prior to this he was a postdoctoral researcher at Center for Sociological Research on Law and Criminal Justice Institutions (CESDIP) and he holds a Ph.D. in Sociology from the University of Lyon. His research interests are in the area of science and technology (STS), sociology of statistics and the status of knowledge in crime prevention policy.

Jarrett Blaustein is Lecturer in Criminology at Monash University. He is the author of *Speaking Truths to Power: Policy Ethnography and Police Reform in Bosnia and Herzegovina* (2015) and has published his research in the *European Journal of Criminology, Policing & Society* and *Theoretical Criminology*.

Mary Bosworth is Professor of Criminology at the University of Oxford where she is Director of the Border Criminologies research group. She is also, concurrently, Professor of Criminology at Monash University, Australia. Mary has published widely on issues to do with race, gender and incarceration, including, most recently the first national study of life in British immigration removal centres: *Inside Immigration Detention* (2014).

Graham Ellison is Reader in Criminology in the Institute of Criminology and Criminal Justice, School of Law, Queen's University Belfast. His main area of research lies in the fields of police and policing, particularly in divided societies such as Northern Ireland. Latterly his research has focused on international policing and the policing and regulation of commercial sex. He is the co-author of *Globalization, Police Reform and Development: Doing it the Western Way?* (with Nathan Pino) and *Policing in An Age of Austerity: A Neocolonial Perspective* (with Mike Brogden). He has just completed a British Academy/Leverhulme Trust funded study into the policing and legal regulation of commercial sex in four European cities.

Elaine Fishwick is a Sydney-based researcher, writer and academic scholar of social policy, criminology and human rights. From 1988 until 2010 Fishwick was a member of a rights based community advocacy organisation in New South Wales called the Youth Justice Coalition (YJC), which has provided her with practical experience of the policy making process. Fishwick is also a co-author, with Leanne Weber and Marinella Marmo, of *Crime, Justice and Human Rights* (2014) and co-editor of the soon-to-be-released *Routledge International Handbook of Criminology and Human Rights*.

Christopher Harding is Professor of Law in the Department of Law and Criminology at Aberystwyth University, with research and teaching interests in the international and European dimensions of crime, crime control and criminal justice, with a particular interest in the criminalisation of business cartels and the emergent regime of EU criminal law.

Alistair Henry is Senior Lecturer in Criminology at Edinburgh University. He is an Associate Director of the Scottish Institute for Policing Research and is co-chair of the European Society of Criminology's Policing Working Group. He has published on issues of policing, community safety, knowledge exchange and negotiated orders.

Andrew M. Jefferson is a prisons researcher at Danish Institute Against Torture (DIGNITY), specializing in the ethnographic study of prisons and prison reform processes in the global south. He works at the intersection between activism and research on justice, human rights and confinement. Jefferson is the author (with Liv Gaborit) of *Prisons and Human Rights: Comparing Institutional Encounters* (Palgrave Macmillan).

Blerina Kellezi is Lecturer in Psychology at Nottingham Trent University. Her research investigates how people deal with and are affected by extreme life events like war, dictatorship, torture and immigration detention. She is particularly interested in the role of social identities, appraisal, social support, inter-group conflict, and transitional justice on well-being.

Anita Lam is Associate Professor of Criminology at York University. She is the author of *Making Crime Television* (2014). Her research examines representations of crime across various forms of media.

Karen Lumsden is Senior Lecturer in Sociology at Loughborough University. She is the author of *Boy Racer Culture: Youth, Masculinity and Deviance* (2013) and *Reflexivity: Theory, Method and Practice* (forthcoming), and co-editor of *Reflexivity in Criminological Research: Experiences with the Powerful and the Powerless* (Palgrave Macmillan, 2014). Karen's articles have appeared in many journals including *Sociology, Qualitative Research, Policing & Society* and *Mobilities*. An ethnographer of crime and deviance, her research interests also include policing, car culture, youth, and social media.

Lesley McAra is Professor of Penology at the University of Edinburgh, School of Law. She is Co-Director (with Susan McVie and David Smith) of the Edinburgh Study of Youth Transitions and Crime, a longitudinal programme of research on pathways into and out of offending for a cohort of around 4,300 young people. She also has been pioneering methods of co-production and exploring the role of the performance arts in promoting community safety and well-being.

Ruari-Santiago McBride is a post-doctoral researcher at the University of Witwatersrand, Johannesburg. His current research interests include the bio-politics of personality disorder, the reordering and disordering of prisoner sub-jectivities, policy ethnography, the history of therapeutic communities, gender non-conformity, and heteronormativity. He likes to cycle, garden and protest.

Kelly J. Stockdale is Lecturer in criminology at Northumbria University. Her doctoral thesis explored the implementation of restorative justice across a police force. She has over ten years' experience working in the criminal justice system, working in various tactical and strategic roles as a police intelligence analyst.

Emma Williams is Programme Director for the Policing BSc at Canterbury Christ Church University and also works on the MSc and MA programmes. She previously worked as a principal researcher at The Metropolitan Police Service and the Ministry of Justice. Emma has worked on numerous research projects in policing including; policing and sexual violence, public confidence and policing, intervention evaluations and the CJS Reform Programme. She is specialised in operational research and ensuring that learning from research is developed into practical solutions for the police organisation.

Dominic Wood is Head of the School of Law, Criminal Justice and Computing at Canterbury Christ Church University. He was a founder of the Higher Education Forum for Learning and Development in Policing and its Chair from 2009–2014. He has developed and led numerous academic programmes designed for serving police officers over the past 20 years and has contributed to all nine editions *Blackstone's Student Police Officer Handbook*.

List of Figures

1

Impact and the Reflexive Imperative in Criminal Justice Policy, Practice and Research

Sarah Armstrong, Jarrett Blaustein, and Alistair Henry

This volume grows out of two parallel but distinct developments in social science research that affect the way researchers study and seek to have an impact in the areas of crime and criminal justice. These are the increasing acceptance and practice of (some form of) reflexivity in social science research, on the one hand, and, on the other, the changing context of research itself. On the latter point, we note that criminologists working across different jurisdictions are experiencing heightened pressures to render their research relevant and appealing to external audiences. These pressures are linked in part with the fact that governments in Australia, the UK and the USA (along with other countries) are increasingly keen to

S. Armstrong (✉)
University of Glasgow, Glasgow, UK

J. Blaustein
Monash University, Melbourne, Australia

A. Henry
University of Edinburgh, Edinburgh, UK

© The Author(s) 2017
S. Armstrong et al. (eds.), *Reflexivity and Criminal Justice*,
DOI 10.1057/978-1-137-54642-5_1

ensure that their investment in the higher education sector is delivering 'value for money'. This implies that research and teaching activities that are government-funded must increasingly align with, or at least demonstrate alignment with, what these governments define as the public interest. In Australia, for example, the Australian Research Council, which is responsible for administering public research funding, has identified a list of nine strategic 'Science and Research Priorities' to organise funding of 'support for science and research on the most important challenges facing Australia' (developed partly from a 2014 white paper 'Boosting the commercial returns of research'; see ARC 2016). With the possible exception of 'cybersecurity', none of these strategic priorities appear to be directly relevant to criminology or indeed, the social sciences. The specified research priorities relate primarily to what are known as 'STEM' subjects (Science, Technology, Engineering and Medicine), thereby prioritising an increasingly narrow set of subjects and research methodologies that reflect a pragmatic and in our view myopic governmental understanding of what constitutes societal value.

This growing emphasis on pragmatism further implies that universities as the institutional sites within which much of what constitutes criminological research today takes place are also expected to operate efficiently. Notions of accountability, and more specifically financial accountability (Power 1999), thus constitute powerful discursive mechanisms that ultimately contribute to the legitimation of an overarching programme of public divestment from the higher education sector. Politicians are prone to justifying these cuts by invoking the language of austerity. Some academics have come to associate contemporary discourses of austerity with a wider neoliberal project, one that is generally cited as a threat to the future of the sector and the pursuit of independent academic inquiry. A recent and influential paper notes that the high productivity and compressed time frames of the 'neoliberal university' create isolating and divisive work conditions, further undermining critical and independent research agendas (Mountz et al. 2015).

No longer able to rely primarily on government investment as a primary source of research income, universities have also started placing greater emphasis on the need for academics to assume the role of research entrepreneurs. The STEM subjects are perhaps ideally placed to develop lucrative partnerships with industry, but the social sciences are not immune to this development. Researchers from all disciplines are facing pressures to market their work to prospective research partners (read: funders) as well as users spanning the public, private and third sectors. Many academic criminologists along with their counterparts from other disciplines have vocally opposed these managerial pressures and expressed concerns about the implications of research commodification with respect to academic autonomy. For criminologists, the preservation of academic autonomy is especially crucial due to the discipline's historical legacy as a technology of governmental control (Foucault 1980) and our recognition of the risk that policy makers and practitioners may utilise our concepts, data and theoretical constructs to justify coercive practices or unjust policies, impinge upon the rights and freedoms of vulnerable individuals and groups, and potentially even generate harms (Cohen 1988). The intersections that exist between criminological research, policy and practice might therefore be characterised as ethical minefields.

Ironically, while the political and institutional environment in which research takes place is becoming more instrumental and less well funded, criminology as a discipline is flourishing. This is evident from the growth of undergraduate and postgraduate degree programmes and jobs across Europe and North America. Our sense is that this is due, at least in part, to the field's relative strength in arguing for its own relevance and importance given the perennial policy fixation on questions of crime and security in these regions. Of course, this is not to take away from the excellence of much criminological research. Indeed, what has been particularly marked in the past 20 years has been the field's enriching pluralism and the ability to support so many research traditions and perspectives (Loader and Sparks 2011; Bosworth and Hoyle 2011). While some criminologists have characterised this trend as disciplinary fragmentation, broken into 'independent', 'critical' and 'administrative' schisms (Young 1986; Ericson and Carriere 1994; Hough 2014), we tend to side with commentators who see pluralisation as a process of mutual enrichment because it implies that criminology is no longer, if it ever truly were, tied to its originating thinkers and disciplinary influences. Criminologists today not only draw on the methods of but also have important things to say to and are taken seriously by historians, sociologists, geographers, philosophers, political scientists, economists, cultural theorists and more.

In addition to looking outward for inspiration, criminologists increasingly are looking inward, critically and reflexively scrutinising their own field and the research that is produced through it. While there remains in some corners an impulse towards particular strands of scientific (and particularly medicalised or psychologised) methods and models like the experiment (of which even medical researchers are increasingly critical and sceptical), post-positivist, reflexive engagement has become ever more of an explicit topic as recent criminological texts attest (see, e.g. Lumsden and Winter 2014; Bosworth and Hoyle 2011). It is our contention then that the concept of reflexivity provides a valuable resource for navigating the practical and ethical dilemmas posed by our changing research environment. And in this, we believe the volume offers a new and important contribution for thinking about reflexivity and its potential to illuminate the nature of the social, of which researchers, universities, policy processes and makers are a part. Specifically, all the contributors to this book are grappling in different ways not only with how to employ notions of research in particular projects but also with how we might engage wider political, economic and social contexts of the worlds that both researcher and researched occupy. Criminal justice and academic settings are increasingly governed through the same technologies of measurement and performance—how do we begin to document, analyse and make sense of this? We argue that criminologists must be sensitive to how structural and cultural conditions within the higher education sector have come to influence the questions we seek to explore and the methods and collaborative research partnerships we draw upon to do so. Hence, reflexivity is conceived in this book as not only a way of approaching the encounter of researcher and researched but also, as our subtitle states, a way of centring and exploring the intersection of policy, practice and research.

In this chapter, we set out some of the dynamics in the research environment that require us to think through and expand upon ideas of reflexivity as a problem not only for research but also for policy and practice in criminal justice. First, we discuss the current context of criminal justice research and review key aspects of the reflexivity concept as these have arisen in social science debates so far. We then present a reworked notion of reflexivity, incorporating both its potential and its challenges, that can be employed to develop insights on the interconnected areas of criminal justice research, policy and practice. Throughout our discussion, we refer to the ways in which the contributors to this volume themselves are engaging the notion of reflexivity. Though each chapter provides its own examples of and stance towards reflexivity, this book overall makes the case for an expansion of a criminological agenda in which the processes, objects and actors often treated as 'backstage' to the analysis of crime and punishment join the conventional objects of analysis front and centre.

The Current Context of Criminal Justice Research

Criminological research is inherently political because 'crime', its object of study, lacks a fixed reality. It is a social construction, the contours of which vary across time and jurisdiction and which are in part shaped, validated or reconfigured by the work of criminologists, albeit not in isolation (Maguire 2012). Indeed, the representations of crime and order made by political actors, criminal justice institutions, third sector and campaigning organisations and, of course, the mass media probably play a more crucial role in framing public, and criminological, understandings of the 'crime problem' than does academic research. This implies that criminological research has never had anything approaching a monopoly over criminal justice discourse and 'crime talk' (Garland and Sparks 2000: 2–5).

Up until the 1970s, in the UK and the USA at least, crime was largely viewed by political elites and parties as a technical administrative matter with, to contemporary eyes, surprising levels of party political consensus over its management (Loader 2006). However, from then on, crime control came to play important roles in shaping both party political debate (Downes and Morgan 2012) and the very public sensibilities to which such debates speak (Garland 2000; Simon 2007). Crime and its control became increasingly salient in state claims to sovereignty and authority (Garland 1996), even eclipsing broader public service and welfare rationales for action, becoming the driver of policy initiatives in wider fields including education, family law, child welfare and housing (Simon 2007; Crawford 1998). All of this meant that criminological research, where it even tried to engage with criminal justice policy and practice, tended to do so within a highly politicised, oft contested and thus notably emotional sphere of public policy, a sphere which, as already noted, was crowded with other powerful actors, vested interests and alternative representations. Many developments have taken place subsequently thus complicating and showing the evolution of this well-rehearsed history of the politics of crime control in the UK and the USA. We focus on a few such developments here in order to sketch what we see as the main features of the current context within which criminological research gets done.

Shifting Grounds of Concern

Downes and Morgan (2012) argue that the days of intense partisan criminal justice politics may be on the wane, going as far as to suggest that the governing through crime agenda may currently be 'debased currency' (2012: 203). Perhaps in the aftermath of global recession, crime control has played a less decisive role in post-2008 elections and there is, for the moment, considerable agreement across political parties on key areas of criminal justice, in particular around 'volume crime' and its management through adaptive or 'dispersed' strategies that look beyond criminal justice institutions themselves for solutions (Downes and Morgan 2012: 183). Rather, they argue that much public debate about crime control in the UK (though one might consider the Black Lives Matter movement in the USA in a similar vein) has coalesced around specific scandals, only some of which, such as the 2011 urban disorders in England, have really sparked the kinds of demonising rhetoric that had characterised much crime talk in recent years (2012: 201–203). Whether this will present a more welcoming climate for deliberation around criminological research in the longer term remains to be seen (see, e.g. Brown et al. 2015). Also counter to this optimism, it might be argued that it is the terms and focus of contestation that have shifted (as well as multiplied, hybridised and pluralised) targets of othering and stigmatisation, and in the present moment, it appears that migration flows and terrorism have emerged as potent rallying points for fear and reactionism. As Mary Bosworth and Blerina Kellezi note in their chapter to this volume, reactions against migration have produced an entirely new system of control and detention that should be of interest to criminologists. They narrate the emotional toll of these new forms of the carceral, not only on the confined but also on the researcher as well, employing a reflexive lens to suggest how these sites cannot be equated simply with imprisonment, presenting distinct logistical, affective and intellectual challenges for researchers.

Criminal Justice Policy Research

There are already quite extensive literatures on the various components of the criminal justice system. What has been rather less developed is research more explicitly focused on criminal justice policy itself: the actors involved, the roles of expert knowledge within it and the processes through which it takes shape (Newburn and Sparks 2004). There are some notable exceptions (inter alia, the work of Paul Rock; Armstrong 2010; Annison 2015; Blaustein 2015; Morrison and Sparks 2015; Souhami 2007; McAra 2005, 2016; Jones and Newburn 2002); however, the lack of attention to policy is becoming, particularly in the context of a research agenda premised on some notion of 'impact', an increasingly glaring lapse in criminological scholarship, a gap this volumes aims partly to fill. Armstrong and Lam's chapter, for example, argues there is a 'double absence' of policy in criminological research, suggesting scene-thinking as a way of bringing policy into the same frame as the core criminological issues of 'the street'.

Institutional Funding Regimes, Impact and Knowledge Exchange

Right from the formation, in the UK, of the Cambridge Institute of Criminology and the Home Office Research Unit, the ways in which criminological research has been institutionally supported and funded have drawn a critical eye (Garland 2002; Martin 1988). Where funding becomes an issue, the priorities and focus of the funders play an important role in shaping a priori assumptions about what the problems of the day are, the preferred methods for investigating them and the main channels through which research is disseminated. They might be said to play a key, even a defining, role in determining what the contours of a discipline is, although in criminology the support of independent universities, and criminology's ongoing expansion as a discipline within them, has historically ensured that funders have enjoyed no such monopoly. Two relatively recent and interrelated developments in the institutional support and funding of criminological research invite consideration of the extent to which we can take for granted the independence of universities, or at least treat universities as places where researchers are entirely free to develop their own agendas. These include the aforementioned 'impact' agenda (in the UK and Australia) and a growing emphasis on 'knowledge exchange'.

In the UK research impact is defined and promoted through nationally organised and compulsory assessment of research activity (most recently in the 2014 Research Excellence Framework, or REF), and it will be incorporated into the Excellence in Research for Australia evaluation in 2018. Such benchmarking exercises are used, along with assessments of the quality of research work in general, to determine levels of research funding that academic departments in universities receive, meaning that impact represents an important determinant of the very viability of these departments. Impact in the context of the 2014 UK REF was defined as leading to worthwhile effects on policies and practices in the wider social world. Impact case studies required individuals to demonstrate how their academic work underpinned documentable change. Of course, there remains an element of debate and contestation about the impact agenda and the extent to which its requirements are in fact feasible aspirations for researchers (see, Stella 2014), or whether they demand uncomfortable over-claiming and time scales. Impact therefore represents an important theme for a number of contributors featured in this volume. For example, Elaine Fishwick's chapter notes that real and positive change can be achieved through research but suggests the paths of this are so unpredictable and circuitous that complexity theory is necessary for analysing them. Similarly, Lesley McAra's chapter argues that pathways to impact are cultivated and navigated over years and decades, time frames which are less amenable to the rapid documentation and measurement sought by universities to evidence their institutional success.

Related to the impact agenda is a growing emphasis on knowledge exchange, a concept that we do not wish to discredit but rather subject to analytical scrutiny. Knowledge exchange came late to criminology, being much more developed in medicine and nursing for example, and underpins the evidence-based policy and practice (EBPP) agendas, also representing a field of research in its own right. Earlier variants tended to assume that research was a kind of commodity to be packaged and disseminated for unidirectional transfer to those for whom it would be useful. This simple understanding of how research knowledge might come to influence policy or practice was quickly challenged as more nuanced understandings of the complexities and partiality of the process emerged (Henry and Mackenzie 2012; Nutley et al. 2007). The evolution of terminology from 'knowledge transfer' to 'knowledge exchange' attempted to reflect the ideal, if not always the reality, that practice should also be influencing research. 'Knowledge exchange' often is treated as a universally positive value and practice, and we note that it more properly refers to particular developments (such as EBPP as noted) and should be analysed more in terms as a movement, with a particular history and set of actors and forces in the same way as we might do with 'what works'. This is not to suggest that sharing knowledge is not beneficial to research or those that it affects or is based on, but that it has come to take on a particular set of meanings and modes of documentation (Rappert 1999). This bears directly on the next point.

Collaborative research associations between universities, practitioners and policy makers Undoubtedly related to the particular understanding of knowledge exchange and impact as salient for 'research users' has been the growth of formalised collaborative associations between universities, practitioners and policy makers whereby longer-term relationships and more direct collaboration on the research process are envisaged between them. Perhaps the best known in the UK criminology is University College London's Jill Dando Institute of Security and Crime Science which, as well as including government as a partner, also seeks to involve criminal justice organisations and the commercial sector. Bilel Benbouzid's chapter in this volume describes the founding of the Jill Dando Institute, and how a disagreement over statistical modelling, combined with the divergent missions of a crime science centre and solely university based research, led to distinct statistical models of repeat victimisation. More recently, the N8 Research Partnership in England has established a Policing Research network that involves eight university collaborators, government, Police and Crime Commissioners, police services and partner organisations with relevant interests. Indeed, the editors of this collection have affiliations with similar enterprises in Scotland, including the Scottish Centre for Crime and Justice Research (SCCJR), a collaboration between the Scottish Government, the Scottish Higher Education Funding Council and four Scottish Universities; and the Scottish Institute for Policing Research (SIPR), a collaboration between Police Scotland, the Scottish Police Authority and 13 Scottish Universities. Other collaborations have emerged or are emerging around the world including the Centre for Evidence-Based Policy in the USA and the now defunct Centre for Excellence in Policing and Security in Australia. In many Northern European countries (Norway, the Netherlands and Finland, e.g.), police colleges for the education and professional development of police officers have university status and are staffed by research-active academics, in contrast to the approach in the UK documented by Wood and Williams in this volume whereby academics contribute to police education in a more piecemeal fashion. Like funding regimes, these institutional reconfigurations of the places within which research gets done have the potential to profoundly shape criminology and criminal justice for the better (e.g. by supporting more appreciative, engaged, sensitive to practice) or for the worse (e.g. by contributing to less independent, critical and theoretically sophisticated forms of scholarship; or, by imposing 'Northern' understandings of good research and policy onto 'Southern' subalterns, see Blaustein in this volume). The global dimensions and implications of 'collaboration' should not be overlooked as potential sites of critical inquiry: one of the editors of this book, recently returned from a trip to Hong Kong with the aim of negotiating university-to-university partnerships, was struck by the frequency of 'global branding' as part of the language of exchange as well as standards of quality (with UK academics hired as consultants to provide REF-like reviews of departments in Asian universities).

Changes to the institutional landscape of criminology thus span a wide and evolving range of developments, from criminology being a niche interest conducted in support of criminal court and prison processes (Garland 2002) to the establishment of specialist sites of criminological expertise as in the aforementioned Cambridge Institute of Criminology and the Home Office Research Unit (Martin 1988), or in the work of Chicago School scholars (to give a US example), to the expansion of criminology within the (increasingly globalised) university sector, to the formation of partnership arrangements between statutory agencies and universities (Henry 2012). Where criminology gets done and under what institutional arrangements shapes its character, its relationship to power, and the problems and challenges to which it directs its gaze.

In the present volume, both Alistair Henry and Karen Lumsden pay particular attention to the challenges and possibilities of academic–practitioner collaboration. Henry focuses on the potential (and limitations) for such institutional arrangements to contribute to the cultivation of reflexivity towards the research process amongst practitioners themselves. Lumsden interrogates her experiences of 'doing' reflexivity within this kind of setting, paying particular attention to the 'public engagement/public criminology' dimensions of such endeavours (see also, Loader and Sparks 2011).

Summing up, the current context of criminological and criminal justice research thus far described is complicated, characterised by reconfigured zones of political contestation (more global phenomena on the fringes of traditional criminology), new fields of inquiry (policy making itself) and an emergent institutional landscape of resourcing, assessment and collaboration. Accordingly, we argue that a reflexive disposition is likely to assist in the negotiation of this terrain, but before elaborating on this, it is necessary to consider how the concept of reflexivity is commonly understood within the social sciences by accounting for its sociological origins.

Reflexivity: Some Starting Points

Reflexivity in social science research involves researchers recognising the fact that their insights about social worlds and processes (as socially constructed, and mediated by tensions and intersections between agency and structure) also apply to themselves, the social worlds of the academy and to their own work (see Alvesson and Skoldberg 2009). As such, it is a critique of the myth of positive science and its claims to objectivity and autonomy. According to this myth, social science is done to the world, rather than constructed through and negotiated with it. Reflexive insight challenges truth claims and sees research as interpreting the world through collaboration with it, collaboration that inevitably also changes the world (Law and Urry 2004). Hence, it is something to be taken seriously, particularly in the criminal justice field where state power is exercised in its most extreme forms and where research contributes so substantially to the social construction and definition of the very 'problems' to which it purports to attend. These understandings have come to influence the study of reflexive methodologies in the context of criminological research (see Lumsden and Winter 2014) as well as the discussions of how criminal justice research intersects with policy and practice which feature in this volume. This warrants a brief review of their historical development in the discipline of sociology, specifically in relation to influential work of Alvin Gouldner and Pierre Bourdieu, both of whom are referenced by a number of contributors to this volume.

Calls for a 'reflexive sociology', that is, a mode of sociological inquiry that seeks to account for how researchers influence and are influenced by the production of scientific and cultural knowledge, can be traced back to the work of the late Alvin Gouldner (1970). Knowledge, according to Gouldner (1970), consists of both 'information' and 'awareness'. Whereas Gouldner believed that positivists have a tendency to reduce their conception of knowledge to the former, his reflexive sociology posits that 'the inquiring subject and the studied object are seen not only as mutually interrelated but also as mutually constituted' (Gouldner 1970: 493). It is therefore the social scientist's awareness of their relationship to the object of their study and of the fact that this relationship is a product of their both personal and professional circumstances which prompts Gouldner

(1970: 491) to characterise reflexive sociology as a 'moral sociology' rather than one which purports to be 'value-free' (Id.). Indeed, the values of social scientists and the disciplinary and institutional cultures which they inhabit are deeply embedded within information with the effect that information cannot be described as 'neutral' (Gouldner 1970: 494).

As a 'moral' enterprise, reflexive sociology can be described as embodying two key transformative dimensions: self-transformation and social transformation. Self-transformation is linked with the pursuit of and revelation of self-awareness. It is the acknowledgement that the social scientist 'cannot know others unless he [sic] also knows his intentions toward and his effects upon them; he cannot know others without knowing himself, his place in the world, and the forces – in society and in himself – to which he is subjected' (Gouldner 1970: 497). Social transformation refers to the wider field of knowledge production and accounts for altering definitions of what constitutes valid knowledge, the purposes for which it is sought, and perhaps the means by which it is utilised. For Gouldner, this meant contesting the hegemonic tendencies of Western sociology that he argued were guided largely by positivist aspirations of controlling the social world through the disembodied production of objective knowledge. Gouldner (1970: 504) thereby positions the reflexive sociologist as a partisan, that is, a political being who embraces reflexive sociology as a 'work ethic' that 'affirms the creative potential of the individual scholar'.

Influential in a formative sense, with respect to the subsequent popularisation of critical and reflexive, approaches to sociology and criminology (see, e.g. Taylor et al. 1973), Gouldner's work has also been the subject of criticism within the discipline of sociology. Notably, Hammersley (1999) describes Gouldner's calls for reflexive sociology as a form of 'moral gerrymandering', criticising those who advocate a 'value-free' sociology yet presenting his own prescription for reflexive sociology as 'embodying universal human values, and therefore as not in need of sociological explanation' (Hammersley 1999: para. 2.3). In other words, Gouldner is argued by Hammersley (1999: para. 2.3) to 'present himself as operating in the realm of freedom' while simultaneously reducing the actions and mentalities of those he challenges to functions of cultural, institutional, structural and ideological influences and constraints. Hammersley questions whether sociology as a discipline has, or indeed should have, a privileged role in generating knowledge that dictates social action. Rather, he suggests that 'social action involves contexted processes of interpretation…[which] rely on diverse forms of knowledge…rather than being the "application" of a body of general knowledge or even of a method' (Hammersley 1999: para. 3.7). On the basis of these critiques, Hammersley (1999: para. 4.1) argues against the practice of formulating 'grand conceptions of sociology's roles' adding that 'reflexivity cannot provide the basis for specifying the mission or the method of sociology'. Accordingly, his contention is that sociological analysis should limit itself to comparatively 'modest' descriptive and explanatory aims and take 'no account of whether we believe what we are studying is good or bad' (Hammersley 1999: para. 4.5).

The Gouldner and Hammersley debate offers one useful springboard for thinking through reflexivity. Rather than seeing this as presenting a binary choice between different versions, we see an evolving understanding of how the researcher begins to account for herself and understand her role in a field of study. These themes arise as well in feminist epistemologies which similarly challenge the ideas of value-free knowledge and objectivity. A feminist reflexive stance acknowledges the researcher's position as 'normative and interested' (Cuthbert forthcoming: 2, citing Marshall 2008: 688); at the same time, it encourages vigilance of the risks of ideological imperialism and universalism. Indeed, feminist (and queer) theory are underused resources in criminology, often limited (ironically and mistakenly) to areas of research cordoned off as 'feminist' and typically limited to explicit studies of gender. Cuthbert's (forthcoming) discussion of feminist epistemology and methods establishes these as having long adopted positions that reflexive criminological work is only now beginning to engage. This includes the recognition that knowledge is always situated (Haraway 1988); that critical research should 'account for the conditions of its own production' (Stanley 1990: 13) and that researchers should be willing to open themselves up to their participants (Cuthbert, forthcoming, citing Reinharz 1992).

Pierre Bourdieu's work also has proven influential in terms of shifting the gaze of Western sociologists inward, that is, by prompting them to consider their status as 'cultural producers of knowledge'. Like Gouldner,

Bourdieu advocated a 'sociology of sociology' (quoting Bourdieu in Wacquant 1989: 33) which actively encouraged its academic practitioners to engage in 'self-analysis' by considering their epistemological orientation and discursive influences in relation to their positioning within particular fields of knowledge production. It is Bourdieu's emphasis on locating oneself within a field as opposed to a particular profession or institutional or structural configuration that distinguishes his call for reflexive sociology from that of Gouldner. This distinction is important because it recognises that one's discipline and indeed the higher education sector constitute structuring mechanisms in their own right (see Stella 2014; Mountz et al. 2015). For Bourdieu's reflexive sociology then, the boundaries of the field of knowledge production appeared to coincide with the boundaries of the university as the social institution ascribed this unique societal function.

As noted previously, however, the university today finds itself continuously prompted to reassert its value as a public good worthy of public expenditure. It must do so by demonstrating its ability to generate research and pedagogical practice of relevance to different 'users' spanning the public, private and third sectors. Bourdieu's vocabulary for understanding this reflexive praxis remains especially relevant because it can accommodate a plurality of knowledge producers representing different institutional positions. Furthermore, against the backdrop of impact, knowledge exchange and academic–practitioner collaboration described at the beginning of this chapter, reflexive sociology establishes the foundations of an important ethos for recursively moderating one's contributions to the production of knowledge as well as for regulating the manner by which such knowledge is disseminated and adopted as a result of our contact with empowered spaces or positions in these fields.

Reflexive Criminology?

Reflexivity has very much arrived as a dimension of social-scientific thinking and practice, even though it took a little longer for the concept to gain a foothold within criminology, at least explicitly. The chapters that follow cumulatively explore, from varying perspectives, the work that criminologists do and the conditions under which they do it, the nature of the research process and the institutions which shape it, for better or worse. We believe that the chapters featured in this volume represent timely and important contributions to an ongoing dialogue about the purpose and value of criminological research but we acknowledge that these issues have long been focal points for critical criminologists who take issue with the collusive, repressive and anti-intellectual origins of the discipline (see, e.g. Heidensohn 1968; Cohen 1988).

We note however that one effect of the particular forms of critical criminology that have emerged has been to discourage exploration of areas and involvement with actors perceived to be the source of oppressive and anti-intellectual impulses in criminology. So criminologists study drug users and drug dealers but not civil servants working on harm-reduction strategies. Co-production is enthusiastically pursued with young people but not with statisticians. Studying and working *with* practitioners, and particularly policy makers, remain, despite the impact agenda, ingredients of a spoiled identity for the criminologist. The contributors to this volume go against this grain. Each has spent considerable time studying, working with, and even trying to change, crime and justice policy and practice through research. Their collective contribution lies in illuminating the ways in which criminological research intersects with, constituting and being constituted by, the fields of criminal justice policy and practice that it studies.

We argue that reflexivity reveals much about the complex, sometimes messy, reality of the research process, allowing for more credible, transparent and modest engagements across research, policy and practice. In this section, we discuss the key points and values of reflexivity for criminal justice researchers, attempting to show how such an orientation in social research can widen and deepen our understanding of the world. However, we have no intention of promoting a 'reflexive criminology' uncritically. We recognise that there are risks of reflexivity as well as particular pathologies and discuss these as well. The aim of this concluding substantive section is to begin developing a clearer sense of how criminologists adopt and might develop reflexive approaches, leaving the rest of the chapters in the book to show how different scholars are 'doing' reflexivity rather than simply 'being' reflexive (Mauthner and Doucet 2003).

An important insight of the reflexivity literature is that researchers are complex persons who are themselves, in all this complexity, part of the research process, whether they like to acknowledge it or not. Biographical details and demographic characteristics of the researcher (such as age, race, gender and class) shape and frame their work—from their choices of topics and questions, to methodological preferences and skills, to how they interpret the worlds they study and to how they themselves are interpreted by people in that world. These choices might also be informed by more particular aspects of personal lives and histories (whether a parent, a survivor of trauma, a victim of crime or an ex-offender, e.g.). Across different reflexive stances is shared a sense that choice of discipline, methods and subfields will have been guided more or less consciously by these factors and related/subsequent preferences (personal, political and professional). Many of the contributors to this volume therefore have decided to incorporate autobiographical details into their discussions of the methodological and practical challenges and prospects inherent to doing research in the sphere of criminal justice. Christopher Harding, for example, uses his chapter in this volume to provide an autobiographical discussion of the role that researchers play in constituting and validating narrative constructions of their 'outlaw' subjects by drawing on his own biography in academia and history of researching cartels.

In short, the researcher is as much of a social construct as any social world or practice that she might hope to study. Scientific rationality and method make claims to distance and rigor but ultimately do not separate researchers from the world or its influence that would secure them clear objective independence and claims to the 'truth'. Increasing articulation of and reflexivity around issues of biography and standpoint is therefore also one of the promising dimensions of reflexive, credible and modest research. Being reflexive about one's position in relation to a field means making transparent and holding oneself to account for choices right through the process—from picking topics, designing, doing and interpreting the research and disseminating it. Such a disposition exposes research as always already a negotiated, collaborative and political encounter with the world, not a disembodied, technical process done to it. For example, Ruari McBride's contribution to this volume shows his own gradual awareness of how certain terms, which he himself used, came to construct particular identities of people as 'offenders'. If taken seriously, this urges researchers to think about their responsibilities—to those that they research, to the potential effects of both the process and the findings, to the implications for policy and practice and to the integrity of their own scholarship and the discipline within which they work. Reflexivity as recognition of standpoint therefore improves transparency around the position of the researcher in shaping the process, in foregrounding this position and the responsibilities that flow from it. It also has the potential to cultivate a disposition of responsibility towards research participants and potential users. This is, of course, easier said than done, as Kelly Stockdale's contribution shows, exploring the idea that standpoint in relation to research is itself not static and is in fact often re-negotiated within specific encounters and towards different audiences in the research process (and see, Goffman 1959).

Reflexivity also attunes the researcher to the fact that the field is not an objective given, but is emergent through the activities of the actors (including researchers) who animate it, and responsive to the research process itself (Bourdieu and Wacquant 1992). It gives emphasis to the idea that the researcher may not know in advance the important questions to be explored, and that it is through appreciation of the local contexts of a field of research and how it is understood by actors within it that they might emerge. This is well understood within reflexive approaches to fieldwork—including much ethnography and collaborative approaches such as participatory action research or 'critical friend' research, where researchers are embedded in and responsive to the worlds that they study (Case and Haines 2014). The promise of such approaches is that the researcher becomes curious about elements of the field hitherto unknown, and open to challenging their own a priori assumptions about it and through engagement with it.

We note that while reflexive research is often associated with particular methodological approaches, such as ethnography or qualitative work more generally, that this is not a necessary association. Consider the quantitative research of Duguid and Pawson (1998) evaluating what works in prison education through a quasi-experimental study design and involving a sample of over 600 men. The authors openly describe their orientation to the research as 'hopeful' (Duguid and Pawson 1998: 473) rather than neutral and disinterested. And, in finding that prison education correlated with reduced recidivism, they qualify this by asking: 'But do we have the patience to give nondirective programs such as education time to do their work? And do we have the humility necessary to accept that we can neither diagnose with precision nor prescribe with surety?' (Duguid and Pawson 1998: 492). Appreciation of local contexts and possessing a genuine curiosity, modesty and openness to the world and how it works are values that can be expressed in and enhance any research regardless of method (see also Blaustein 2014: 311). Reflexivity, in other words, is a perspective rather than a (prescription of) method (and see Reinharz 1992).

Reflexivity thus conceived entails respect for participants and users of research as active collaborators in the process. Of course, they may not be collaborators who share the researcher's understanding of research or their particular disciplinary frames of reference for interrogating the world. But instead of relegating such differences to being the voices of an unenlightened 'other' a reflexive disposition encourages engagement with and deliberation around them as potentially productive elements in the research process. It encourages taking such different perspectives on more explicitly and not reifying the researcher's voice above all others. This is absolutely not to suggest that a reflexive researcher would not challenge other perspectives including those of the powerful (in fact we very much view this as a responsibility). Rather, a respectful and diplomatic acknowledgement of other perspectives on research is a promising starting point for cultivating an understanding of research and the process of doing research, more a means for prompting informed deliberation about criminal justice problems, and less as instrumental answers to them. Indeed, Alistair Henry's chapter suggests deliberation is a more promising long-term aspiration for academic–practitioner collaborations with the police than instrumental goals that target immediate and functional outcomes.

An important component of research diplomacy is modesty and humility about both our skills and status as 'experts', 'scientists' and 'researchers' and about what our research accounts are. Social scientists and bodies of research evidence do not necessarily have 'the answers', or 'the only answers'. To this effect, Jarrett Blaustein's chapter argues that undertaking ethical criminological research 'abroad' necessitates a continuous recognition of the identity that may be conferred upon even an inexperienced researcher as an expert, and the structural asymmetries that both motivate and flow from this. Andrew Jefferson's chapter also raises the problem of the 'other' in a global sense, arguing that reflexivity arises on a different scale where those researchers from the 'developed' North travel and 'share expertise' with those in the 'developing' South.

Embracing complexity and resisting pressures to reduce our findings to appealing and digestible narratives (pressures that we associate, at least in part, with the continued development of a performance management and impact culture in the higher education sector) is also an important element of doing criminology reflexively. This implies that individual pieces of research, and certainly bodies of research, often have complex, partial and sometimes contradictory or unwelcome messages to convey. These messages are not easily collapsed into the sound bites that research users might be looking for. Rather than trying to provide these sound bites with the aim of securing 'impact' for particular pieces of research, a reflexive disposition encourages caution around this, a caution all the more profound because researchers do enjoy a privileged status, and their accounts can play important roles in validating practice or constructing social problems. A more credible dialogue around research is one that is diplomatic in the face of alternative perspectives, and modest about the claims of research to having the 'right answer'. As with a diplomatic disposition, a more modest reflexive disposition would be one that saw both the engagement and collaboration around doing research and the dissemination of research findings and outputs as more about the cultivation of informed deliberation about criminal justice policy and practice, where research is but one kind of evidence. Indeed, a key theme of Lesley McAra's chapter is to question the extent to which researchers have power over the pathways to impact (or not) that their work takes. Her chapter practices humility, even when writing about a research programme that came to have substantial impact on national policy; it reminds us to be careful of what we wish for.

While we recognise the merits of collaborative and diplomatic approaches to undertaking research reflexively with criminal justice policy makers and practitioners, we recognise that sensitivities to the researched and to research audiences are not alternatives to critical research. Rather, we argue that reflexive approaches are promising precisely because they can foster more credible critique through the dispositions just discussed. The credibility stems from the appreciation of policy and practice worlds and contexts, and the modest status and claims of research. However, reflexive research, in emphasising the layers of interpretation at the heart of the process, also does not see research as the simple holding up of a mirror to the world through which it records and in so doing validates its 'reality'. The opposite is very much the case. Attentiveness to the lived and negotiated contexts of social worlds and the complex and contested realities within them is to look beneath their surface, to differentiate between what people say and what they do and to view critically what current practice or experience is, its rationale and meaning for those involved. Graham Ellison's chapter gives a powerful account of his experience conducting and disseminating research about sex-work practices in Northern Ireland. He is quite open in sharing the personal fallout for himself of intervening in such a politically and morally contested domain, and provocatively makes an argument about the politics of evidence and how research is used, ignored and vilified as part of this. Criminal justice processes have the capacity to exclude, label and coerce and Ellison's work displays how policy processes do as well. Ruari McBride's chapter makes this point as well, and he shows with some poignancy how processes of exclusion might themselves look and feel benign. A reflexive reading of both these chapters renders them as studies in how researchers themselves produce the fields they study and can become complicit in certain disheartening and disempowering practices (of policy, practice and research) without or despite realising this.

Conducting research on the powerful remains a marginal interest in criminology, and research *with* the powerful even more so. It is our view that conducting research with the powerful is compatible with a reflexive understanding of the co-production of knowledge as long as the researcher retains the capacity to uncover and offer challenge. That capacity, or assumptions about it, often relate to the actual and perceived independence of the researcher in relation to their powerful collaborator, a theme that animates many of the contributions to this volume. At the same time, it offers new opportunities for and contexts of research. Exposing the fine-grained dynamics of power that shape practices 'on the street' has been a central and important focus of criminology; equally important and bringing its own particular challenges is a focus on practice 'in the suites' of the powerful. Harry Annison's chapter reveals that civil servants who were involved in the drafting of a profoundly draconian UK sentencing law were thoughtful, ambivalent, professional and open. Access to these standpoints is crucial for understanding the development and implementation (and possibly reform or repeal) of policy and was achieved here through a collective enterprise between researcher and researched.

Keeping to our promise not to promote reflexivity uncritically, we note some particular risks and pathologies of the reflexive practices we have just touted. A posture of humility and recognition of relative power differences might lead to passiveness, an unwillingness to develop bold claims or to intervene. Rejection of a positivistic and singular notion of the truth undermines all claims, levelling research as just one more opinion about the world. If every actor's perspective matters, what right does the researcher have to evaluate and criticise any particular one? Acknowledgement of the researcher's biography and standpoint presents its own set of concerns. Not least of these is solipsistic navel gazing, where considerations of self in the research process overshadow attentiveness to the field, its complexity, and the fact that some things will not be visible through a particular standpoint's gaze. Moreover, the recognition of standpoint may establish new hierarchies of research power and legitimacy. Here, the researcher becomes the source of validation of his or her own accounts and arguments, one's biographical 'bias' reified as qualification to speak, and authenticity replacing but having the same imperialistic tendencies as 'neutrality'. This can lead to positions just as entrenched and as ideological as those based upon competing claims of positivist method and epistemology. Another concern in focusing on biographical reflexivity is to overstate the power of the researcher's own intentions and contribution. The biographical lens obscures the wider conditions of research, that we have taken care to point out throughout the discussion, involving a knowledge and political economy beyond the control of any individual (Rappert 1999). We might also question the extent to which we are even fully aware of and in control of our own research intentions and contribution, as wider forces undergird the conditions in which these are formed.

Because we conceive of reflexivity as an orientation to and practice of research, and to the world, that is consonant with post-positivist and feminist epistemologies, we do not deny in blanket terms or seek to refute these concerns. We accept these and would aim to resolve and mitigate them through the strategies that we describe earlier in the discussion as the beneficial features of reflexivity: open-mindedness, transparency and modesty. We need to accept that working 'reflexively' may open our eyes to seeing how neutral legal and scientific language is deeply raced and sexed, but blind us from seeing other forms of oppressive and obscuring practices. For example, the term 'neoliberalism' appears in a number of chapters, and one might question how empirically clear and critically examined this concept is in particular usages. Standpoints are included as core elements in many of the chapters, and the reader can decide for herself whether this is harnessed effectively to display the nature and course of research or whether particular voices and views are therefore silenced. Many of the chapters reflect on or explicitly describe working relationships between researchers and practitioners or policy makers. The telling of these stories should offer enough detail to gain a sense of whether critical distance was maintained and insights were achieved. A reflexive turn does not do away with concepts of research integrity or rigour, but seeks to unpack the ways these are socially, and politically, constructed. Where positivist scientific method measures its results through the minimisation or even elimination of bias, a reflexive perspective demands the clarification of the biases that are part of all research processes.

In gathering these diverse contributions together in one volume, we are 'doing' reflexivity, by showing the many ways people are engaging the concept in their own work. That is, we would not wish to promote the idea that there is one way of getting reflexivity 'right'; reflexivity cannot be a universalistic, self-satisfied and untouchable notion. A plurality of approaches, which broadly share and practice the values we have discussed above, are the broad tent in which many might gather. We believe the chapters in this volume showcase deeply interesting and important explorations of the questions, situations and relationships that feature in contemporary criminology and criminal justice.

In concluding this introduction, we would like to note some themes and features of the chapters which can develop our thinking and practice of reflexivity in the context of criminology. Collectively, these raise the questions and issues of the kind of conversation we would like to stimulate. First is the range of ways reflexivity is defined and harnessed in individual chapters, with the authors herein employing the term in multiple, multilayered and even, across chapters, potentially competing ways. A number of chapters offer useful typologies and extensive reviews of the concept as it has emerged in the social sciences. For some, it is tied to the idea of *reflective* practice and research (Stockdale), aimed at supporting reflective practitioners (Wood and Williams) organisations (Jefferson) and relationships (Henry). This work treats researchers as practitioners of a kind as well, which enables the role of the researcher in policy and practice development to become part of the core object of study. Other chapters take reflexivity as an opportunity to grapple directly and critically with the politics of knowledge and power in criminal justice (McBride) as well as (Ellison) policy processes. Sometimes questions of politics require attention to mundane, background issues of a technical nature, like the organisation of a statistical category (Armstrong and Lam) or the modelling disagreements of two criminological camps (Benbouzid). Reflexivity, here, invites attention to the details of practices that do not on their face appear political. Other contributors practice reflexivity in detailing the affective dynamics and consequences (Bosworth and Kellezi, Fishwick) of the often tough, and complex, research and policy environments of criminological researchers. Reflexivity is also put to excellent use 'studying up', making visible the people (Annison) and the shifting power dynamics in research on powerful organisations (Lumsden), or the ethics and possibilities of studying 'over there' (Blaustein). Finally, reflexivity, alternately, offers a channel for the biographical, where the researcher's own narrative is paired with the trajectory of a research project (Harding).

In addition to the many ways reflexivity is being defined and practiced, a second area of interest are the kinds and range of theoretical and methodological resources drawn on by individual authors. While many refer to specific debates and elaborations of reflexivity in the work of Bourdieu, Gouldner, Hammersley, Burawoy, or long-standing influences in criminology such as Foucault, Bauman and Goffman, additional thinkers and fields include Paulo Friere, complexity theory, Donald Schön, Interpretive Policy Analysis, Science and Technology Studies, John Dryzek. Reflexivity has meant casting the net wider to include not only subjects that have been at the fringe of criminology, such as policy makers and university research structures; it has also meant looking to other disciplines for tools and inspiration. Contributors to this volume move well beyond criminology's favoured fields of sociology, law, social work and psychology to draw on work in education, politics, anthropology, public administration and more. Through notions of reflexivity, the scholars in this collection are introducing the language of emancipation, social justice, solidarity and democratic deliberation into the conversation. This has the potential to increase the ambition and critical scrutiny of research impact agendas, allowing for critical debates to emerge about supporting research that genuinely promotes positive change in the world.

A Brief Note about the Structure of This Volume

The book is organised into three cross-cutting themes that loosely correspond to the three parts of this book. These allow the reader to focus on a particular major theme in approaching the volume, though all chapters overlap in these themes to some extent. The parts are as follows:

1. *Reflexive Approaches to Criminal Justice Policy Research*: Each of these chapters has at its heart a specific policy development that serves as an opportunity to conduct a detailed, theory-rich approach that makes sense of them. They include Imprisonment for Public Protection sentences in England and Wales (Annison); juvenile justice policy in New

South Wales, Australia (Fishwick); the 'mentally disordered offender' category in Northern Ireland (McBride), reform of short prison sentences in Scotland (Armstrong and Lam); and statistically modelling repeat victimisation in England and Wales (Benbouzid).

2. *Collaboration and Knowledge Exchange in Practice:* The chapters in this section focus on examples of engagement in different contexts between researchers, practitioners and policy makers. They thoroughly address the challenges and potential of collaboration, sometimes specifically in the context of knowledge exchange and impact, but also more generally for conducting research. They range in area and jurisdiction to include youth justice policy in Scotland (McAra); police-academic collaborations in Scotland (Henry) and England (Lumsden); academic involvement in professional education of police in England (Wood and Williams); and working with Home Office and Immigration Removal Centre staff to research the experiences of detained migrants in the UK (Bosworth and Kellezi).

3. *Positionality, Power and the Reflexive Imperative:* This section comprises chapters that highlight, among other things, lessons and insights of researcher positionality. These include absent presences in biographies of researcher and researched in studying anti-cartel regulation across Europe (Harding); the blurring of professional and ad hominem critique in passing a zero tolerance policy on sex work in Northern Ireland (Ellison); navigating insider–outsider status in researching a police force in Northern England (Stockdale); reflecting on tensions in the mission versus sustainability issues of an anti-torture organisation based in Denmark (Jefferson); and using the experience of being a 'Northern' researcher in the Global 'South' to reflect on the ethics of engagement and the possibility of a civic criminology (Blaustein).

References

Alvesson, M. and Skoldberg, K. (2009) *Reflexive Methodology: New Vistas for Qualitative Research* (2nd edn), London: Sage.

Annison, H. (2015) *Dangerous Politics: Risk, Political Vulnerability, and Penal Policy,* Oxford: Oxford University Press.

Armstrong, S. (2010) 'Prison Prisms: Policy's Objects in Scottish Penal Reform', Conference paper, Interpretive Policy Association, Grenoble, France (July). URL (accessed 14 May 2016): http://www.researchcatalogue.esrc.ac.uk/grants/RES-000-22-2881/read.

Australian Research Council (ARC) (2016) 'Science and Research Priorities', Website. URL (accessed 14 May 2016): http://www.arc.gov.au/science-research-priorities.

Blaustein, J. (2014), 'Reflexivity and Participatory Police Ethnography: Situating the Self in a Transnational Criminology of Harm Production'. In K. Lumsden and A. Winter. (eds.) *Reflexivity in Criminological Research: Experiences with the Powerful and the Powerless*, Basingstoke: Palgrave Macmillan: 301–312.

Blaustein, J. (2015) *Speaking Truths to Power: Policy Ethnography and Police Reform in Bosnia and Herzegovina*, Oxford: Oxford University Press.

Bosworth, M. and Hoyle, C. (2011) *What is Criminology?*, Oxford: Oxford University Press.

Bourdieu, P. and Wacquant, L. (1992) *Invitation to a Reflexive Sociology*, Chicago: The University of Chicago Press.

Brown, D., Cuneen, C., Schwartz, M., Stubbs, J. and Young, C. (2015) *Justice Reinvestment: Winding Back Imprisonment*, Basingstoke: Palgrave.

Case, S. and Haines, K. (2014) 'Reflective Friend Research: The Relational Aspects of Social Theory'. In K. Lumsden and A. Winter (eds), *Reflexivity in Criminological Research: Experiences with the Powerful and the Powerless*, Basingstoke: Palgrave Macmillan: 58–74.

Cohen, S. (1988) *Against Criminology*, London: Transaction Publishers.

Crawford, A. (1998) *Crime Prevention and Community Safety: Politics, Policies and Practices*, London and New York: Longman.

Cuthbert, K. (forthcoming) *Exploring the gendered experiences of those who do not feel sexual attraction, and those who choose not to be sexually active*, Doctoral dissertation, University of Glasgow, manuscript on file with the editors.

Downes, D. and Morgan, R. (2012) 'Overtaking on the Left? The Politics of Law and Order in the "Big Society"'. In M. Maguire, R. Morgan and R. Reiner (eds.) *The Oxford Handbook of Criminology*, 5th edn, Oxford: Oxford University Press: 182–205.

Duguid, S. and Pawson, R. (1998) 'Education, Change, and Transformation: The Prison Experience', *Evaluation Review* 22(4): 470–495.

Ericson, R.V. and Carriere, K. (1994) 'The Fragmentation of Criminology'. In D. Nelken (ed.) *The Futures of Criminology*, London: Sage: 89–109.

Foucault, M. (1980) *Power/Knowledge: Selected Interviews and Other Writings, 1972–1977*, Brighton: Harvester Press.

Garland, D. (1996) 'The Limits of the Sovereign State: Strategies of Crime Control in Contemporary Society', *British Journal of Criminology* 36(4): 445–471.

Garland, D. (2000) 'The Culture of High Crime Societies: Some Preconditions of Recent Law and Order Policies', *British Journal of Criminology* 40(3): 347–75.

Garland, D. (2002) 'Of Crimes and Criminals: The Development of Criminology in Britain'. In M. Maguire, R. Morgan and R. Reiner (eds), *The Oxford Handbook of Criminology*, 3rd edn, Oxford: Oxford University Press: 7–50.

Garland, D. and Sparks, R. (2000) 'Criminology, Social Theory and the Challenge of Our Times'. In D. Garland and R. Sparks (eds.), *Criminology and Social Theory*, Oxford: Oxford University Press: 1–22.

Goffman, E. (1959) *The Presentation of Self in Everyday Life*, London: Penguin Books.

Gouldner, A.W. (1970) *The Coming Crisis of Western Sociology*, London: Heineman Educational Books Ltd.

Hammersley, M. (1999) 'Sociology, What's It For? A Critique of Gouldner', *Sociological Research Online* 4(3): no page numbers.

Haraway, D. (1988) 'Situated Knowledges: The Science Question in Feminism and the Privilege of Partial Perspective', *Feminist Studies* 14(3): 575–599.

Heidensohn, F. (1968) 'The Deviance of Women: A Critique and an Inquiry', *The British Journal of Sociology* 19(2): 160–175.

Henry, A. (2012) 'Situating Community Safety: Emergent Professional Identities in Communities of Practice', *Criminology and Criminal Justice* 12(4): 413–431.

Henry, A. and Mackenzie, S. (2012) 'Brokering Communities of Practice: A Model of Knowledge Exchange and Academic-Practitioner Collaboration Developed in the Context of Community Policing', *Police Practice and Research* 13(4): 315–328.

Hough, M. (2014) 'Confessions of a Recovering "Administrative Criminologist": Jock Young, Quantitative Research and Policy Research', *Crime Media Culture* 10(3): 215–226.

Jones, T. and Newburn, T. (2002) 'Policy Convergence and Crime Control in the USA and the UK: Streams of Influence and Levels of Impact', *Criminal Justice: The International Journal of Policy and Practice* 2(2): 173–203.

Law, J. and Urry, J. (2004) 'Enacting the Social', *Economy and Society* 33(3): 390–410.

Loader, I. (2006) 'Fall of the "Platonic Guardians"', *British Journal of Criminology* 46(4): 561–586.

Loader, I. and Sparks, R. (2011) *Public Criminology?*, London: Routledge.

Lumsden, K. and Winter, A. (2014) *Reflexivity in Criminological Research: Experiences with the Powerful and the Powerless*, Basingstoke: Palgrave Macmillan.

Maguire, M. (2012) 'Criminal Statistics and the Construction of Crime'. In M. Maguire, R. Morgan and R. Reiner (eds), *The Oxford Handbook of Criminology*, 5th edn, Oxford: Oxford University Press: 206–244.

Marshall, Y. (2008) 'Archaeological possibilities for feminist theories of transition and transformation', *Feminist Theory*, 9(1): 25–45.

Martin, J.P. (1988) 'The Development of Criminology in Britain, 1948–1960', *British Journal of Criminology* 28(2): 35–44.

Mauthner, N. and Doucet, A. (2003) 'Reflexive Accounts and Accounts of Reflexivity in Qualitative Data Analysis', *Sociology* 37(3): 413–431.

McAra, L. (2005) 'Modelling Penal Transformation', *Punishment and Society* 7(3): 277–302.

McAra, L. (2016) 'Can Criminologists Change the World? Critical Reflections on the Politics, Performance and Effects of Criminal Justice', *British Journal of Criminology*, first published online March 11, 2016 doi: 10.1093/bjc/azw015.

Morrison, K. and Sparks, R. (2015) 'Research, Knowledge and Criminal Justice Policy: The Scottish Experience'. In H. Croall, G. Mooney and M. Munro (eds.), *Crime, Justice and Society in Scotland*, London: Palgrave.

Mountz, A., Bonds, A., Mansfield, B., Loyd, J., Hyndman, J., Walton-Roberts, M., Basu, R., Whitson, R., Hawkins, R., Hamilton, T, Curran, C. (2015) 'For Slow Scholarship: A Feminist Politics of Resistance through Collective Action in the Neoliberal University', *ACME: An International E-Journal for Critical Geographies* 14(4, August): 1235–1259. URL (accessed 14 May 2016): http://ojs.unbc.ca/index.php/acme/article/view/1058.

Newburn, T. and Sparks, R. (2004) *Criminal Justice and Political Cultures: National and International Dimensions of Crime Control*, Cullompton: Willan.

Nutley, S., Walter, I. and Davies, H.T.O. (2007) *Understanding Evidence: How Research can Inform Public Services*, Bristol: The Polity Press.

Power, M. (1999) *The Audit Society: Rituals of Verification*, Oxford: Oxford University Press.

Rappert, B. (1999), 'The Uses of Relevance: Thoughts on a Reflexive Sociology', *Sociology* 33(4): 705–723.

Reinharz, S. with Davidman, L. (1992) *Feminist Methods in Social Research*, New York and Oxford: Oxford University Press.

Simon, J. (2007) *Governing Through Crime: How the War on Crime Transformed American Democracy and Created a Culture of Fear*, Oxford: Oxford University Press.

Souhami, A. (2007) *Transforming Youth Justice: Occupational Identity and Cultural Change*, Cullompton: Willan.

Stanley, L. (1990) 'Feminist Praxis and the Academic Mode of Production: An Editorial Introduction'. In L Stanley (ed.) *Feminist Praxis: Research, Theory and Epistemology in Feminist Sociology*, London: Routledge: 3–19.

Stella, F. (2014) 'Engaging with "Impact" Agendas? Reflections on Storytelling as Knowledge Exchange'. In Y. Taylor (ed.) *The Entrepreneurial University: Engaging Publics, Intersecting Impact*, Basingstoke: Palgrave Macmillan: 105–124.

Taylor, I., Walton, P. and Young, J. (1973) *The New Criminology: for a Social Theory of Deviance*, London: Routledge and Kegan Paul.

Wacquant, L. (1989) 'For a Socio-Analysis of Intellectuals: On Homo Academicus', *Berkeley Journal of Sociology* 34: 1–29.

Young J. (1986) 'The Failure of Criminology: The Need for a Radical Realism'. In R. Matthews and J. Young (eds.) *Confronting Crime*, London: SAGE Publications.

Part 1

Reflexive Approaches to Criminal Justice Policy Research

2

Interpreting Influence: Towards Reflexivity in Penal Policymaking?

Harry Annison

Introduction

The shift in the nature and effects of penal policymaking in the UK from the 1970s to the present day is a well-told tale, to the extent that it can effectively be told in a series of shorthand phrases: the 'fall of the Platonic guardians' (Loader 2006); the 'rise of the public voice' (Ryan 2004); and the increasing centrality of 'penal populism' (Pratt 2007), leading to a penal arms race (Lacey 2008) within a 'culture of control' (Garland 2001). These criminological accounts tend to cast the majority of policy-makers—or at least political actors—as cynical and non-reflexive about the effects of their policymaking efforts. Even those who do not cast policymakers in such terms suggest that this is the instrumentally rational response to the broader political climate.

The research on which this chapter draws was supported by an Economic and Social Research Council 1+3 Studentship (grant ES/GO10307/1). Thanks to John Boswell, Ian Loader and the editors for comments on earlier drafts. The usual disclaimers apply.

H. Annison (✉)
School of Law, Southampton University, Southampton, UK

© The Author(s) 2017
S. Armstrong et al. (eds.), *Reflexivity and Criminal Justice*,
DOI 10.1057/978-1-137-54642-5_2

This chapter explores the contribution to be made by interpretive political analysis (IPA) in understanding the extent to which participants in penal policymaking can be considered to be reflexive. Further, it considers the extent to which IPA might facilitate the improvement of reflexivity amongst penal policymakers. Relevant forms of reflexivity are first set out. Research conducted for the monograph *Dangerous Politics* (Annison 2015) is then drawn upon in order to explore this issue empirically. In closing, the potential value of IPA to the improvement of penal policymaking, via a promotion of individual and collective reflexivity, is discussed.

Reflexivity

We can begin, as Holland does, with the Oxford English Dictionary definition:

> *Reflexivity.* Social Sciences. Applied to that which turns back upon, or takes account of, itself or a person's self, especially methods that take into consideration the effect of the personality or presence of the researcher on the investigation. (Oxford English Dictionary, quoted in Holland 1999: 464)

The discussions of reflexivity drawn on below tend to derive from considerations of scholarly practice. As will become clear, here they are being applied to policy participants and their activity. For the purposes of this chapter, we can distinguish three forms of reflexivity, which I term 'occupational', 'holistic' and 'collective'.

The first speaks to what Gouldner describes as the need to 'acquire the ingrained *habit* of viewing our own beliefs as we now view those held by others' (Gouldner 1971: 490, emphasis in original). In this respect, Holland similarly speaks of a mode of reflexivity that involves the recognition that one's 'own, necessarily limited construct systems [are] being used to appraise the construct systems of other people' (Holland 1999: 465). Researchers are encouraged not to become fixed within one perspective but to use paradigms (e.g. law, sociology, liberalism, Marxism) 'against each other to highlight contradictions and conflicts of viewpoint' (Holland 1999: 475). These remarks speak to researchers' *work*—the need, in other words, for occupational reflexivity. This discussion is equally applicable to policymakers—are they self-aware about the context in which they operate, their beliefs and actions, and the inherent partiality of their commitments and understandings?

The second term, holistic reflexivity, is used here to denote the promotion by Gouldner and others of a reflexivity that goes beyond professional activity. Gouldner argued that reflexivity requires not merely a detailed scrutiny of how to work but 'how to *live*' (Gouldner 1971: 489, emphasis in original). We are compelled, from this view, to consider the researcher's role and social position, and how this relates to the processes and products of their work. Central, therefore, is consideration of 'the *relationship* [reflexivity] establishes between being a sociologist and being a person' (Gouldner 1971: 494, emphasis in original).[1] There is no prima facie reason that these considerations should not apply equally to policymakers. Indeed, such questions have been addressed, at different levels of abstraction, in my own work (Annison 2014a; 2014b) and by scholars including Bauman (1989), Barker and Wilson (1997), Carlen (2008) and Fielding (2011).

Third, collective reflexivity is used to denote the 'journey from the individual level to the social level', leading in the psychological context from 'individual distress into a social context of action' (Holland, 1999: 476). Pierre Bourdieu, a leading proponent of reflexive sociology, argues:

> [Reflexive] sociology frees us by freeing us from the illusion of freedom, or, more exactly, from the misplaced belief in illusory freedoms. Freedom is not something given: it is something you conquer – collectively. (Bourdieu 1990: 15)

In considering a collective notion of reflexivity, we can usefully draw on Wagenaar et al.'s (2015) discussion of recursive collaboration. It seeks

---

[1] There are echoes here of Howard Becker's famous call to sociologists to identify 'whose side we are on' (Becker 1967).

to promote 'a continuous and interlocking cycle of perspectives' (Ansell 2011: 104), in order to generate a useful 'tension between top-down and bottom-up organizations' (Ansell 2011: 107). We will return to this approach in greater detail below. Presently, we can turn to my own research on penal policymaking, and the insights it may provide into the reflexivity (or otherwise) of policymakers in the penal field.

Interpreting Penal Policymaking

> *Researcher (HA)*: Minister wants this scheme, which appears to have problems that we can't predict the right people and it's going to cause all kinds of problems –

> *Former Home Office official*: And on the history of these kinds of things it fails –

> *HA*: and on justice, fairness, on those sorts of levels it fails. Essentially everything we've seen happen was predictable. Well and it sounds like, predicted?

> *Official*: Absolutely.

> *HA*: So the interesting question for me there is –

> *Official*: Why did it happen then?

Significant developments in penal policy constitute a valuable 'way in' to understanding the beliefs and practices that underpin penal policymaking. One such development in the UK is the Imprisonment for Public Protection (IPP) sentence of the Criminal Justice Act 2003. It was a life sentence in all but name, focused on potential future offending as opposed to past behaviour (Annison 2015: see Chap. 1). Convicted individuals identified as 'dangerous' at point of sentencing found themselves serving an indeterminate prison sentence remaining in prison until the Parole Board was persuaded that it was no longer necessary for the protection of the public that he or she remained confined.[2] It has proved to be one of the most important developments in British sentencing law and penal policy in recent decades. Its effects have been dramatic, with over 8200 IPP sentences imposed from April 2005 to September 2012 (Ministry of Justice 2013).[3] As of March 2015, over 4600 of those sentenced to IPP remained in custody (Prison Reform Trust 2015). It exemplifies the dramatic rise of preventive sentencing and risk-oriented penal policy (Ashworth and Zedner 2014).

My research, published as *Dangerous Politics* (Annison 2015), provides a detailed analysis of the politics and policymaking processes that shaped the creation, contestation, amendment and ultimate abolition of the sentence; what I term the IPP story. While a key goal was historical reconstruction, the research went beyond this, utilizing the IPP story as a window into British penal politics and policymaking in the early twenty-first century. Those seeking a comprehensive account of these events and their broader relevance should consult this source.

The research was underpinned by an IPA framework. This approach concentrates on meanings and beliefs, understanding change as the 'result of people's ability to adopt beliefs and perform actions through a reasoning that is embedded in the tradition they inherit' (Bevir and Rhodes 2006: 5). In contrast to approaches that draw on rational choice models, or focus on institutions, broad cultural shifts or economic substructures as the drivers of change, IPA approaches utilize frameworks that place 'conscious, reflexive and strategic' actors at their centre (Hay 2002: 127).[4] To explore these beliefs and practices, 63 interviews were conducted with current and former ministers, civil servants, senior judges, representatives

---

[2] Relevant offenders must have committed one of 153 'specified offences' and be considered by the trial judge to pose a 'significant risk to members of the public of serious harm occasioned by the commission by him of further specified offences': s225(1)(b) Criminal Justice Act 2003.

[3] The sentence was abolished in November 2012 by the Legal Aid, Sentencing and Punishment of Offenders Act 2012.

[4] For a detailed and incisive survey of interpretive approaches, see Wagenaar (2011).

of Inspectorates, penal reform groups, unions, members of the House of Commons and Lords and others (see Annison 2015: Appendix I).

We can now examine the lessons my interpretive analysis of the IPP story provide about the extent to which policymakers can be considered to be 'reflexive', in the various ways implied by that term.

Signs of Reflexivity in Penal Policymaking?

One initial point must be noted here. In any research drawing on oral history, two processes (at least) may be indicated: first, *reflection* on the policymaking processes after the event; and second, the exercise of *reflexivity* in the moment of policymaking. In practice, these indications may often be interwoven; the distinction will be returned to in the conclusion.

Occupational Reflexivity

An initial indication of the openness by policymakers to reflect upon their beliefs, practices and actions is provided by the acceptance or otherwise of requests to engage with the research for *Dangerous Politics*. The traditional opacity of the civil service to the outsider, coupled with the commonplace lack of clarity (to the outsider and even 'insiders') about which policy participants were in fact centrally involved with specific developments means that any quantitative measure of policymaker engagement would be of little utility. The majority of respondents who declined to meet pointed to their lack of involvement with the relevant events. A few individuals simply never responded. However, most of the policy participants contacted were open to engaging with the research, fitting interviews within their pressurized schedules.

Policymakers' openness to research interviews, and their conduct within the interviews, supported Dexter's observation that many senior professionals have a strong 'taste for self-analysis' (Dexter 2006: 41–2). In response to my interest in their world (my appearance as an 'understanding stranger': Dexter 2006: 41), the majority of interviewees appeared to make considerable efforts not only to answer specific questions but also to locate these within a broader discussion of the nature of their role, the institutional or cultural context in which they operated and the ways in which they considered this to influence their activities. For example, Parliamentary Counsel carefully explained the nature of their role and the benefits and disbenefits that flow from the deliberate policy of avoiding subject specialism (see Page 2009).

Similarly, peers patiently explained the respectful traditions of the House of Lords, the pragmatic issue of debate scheduling and the effect of these factors on the manner in which policies were challenged:

> If you raise a serious concern, then the minister will take the time to meet with you. If you're not happy he will speak with you at length (peer, notes from unrecorded interview).
>
> You need a tactical approach to amendments, "picking one's battles". If one can get an amendment in before around 7pm, and ensure that enough cross-benchers are in the chamber, then there is a good chance of getting it through. (peer, notes from unrecorded interview)

Further, civil servants at all levels presented considered reflections on their own actions and on the broader context in which they operated. For example, one civil servant reflected on the disruptions to the 'well-oiled machine'—the workings within and between government departments—in the wake of the installation of the Conservative–Liberal Democrat coalition government, and its implications for penal policy-making (Annison 2015: Chap. 7).

Some civil servants were forthcoming about the incentive structures within the civil service (see Page and Jenkins 2005), and the implications of this for policy outputs:

> [The system] relies on generalists being able to be on top of the law, [have] an understanding of offender management, and [have] an understanding of risk. That is a big ask of anyone. (civil servant)

In terms of the broader context, civil servants reflected that:

Thirty years ago you'd have a green paper, a white paper, a length of time where proposals were worked through, more thought given to it and then legislation. Things don't work like that anymore. The timescales are truncated. It's very much a culture of, "We must do this, we must do it quickly and we must do it now". (civil servant)

Concerns about the political climate and its effects on policymaking were most prevalent:

The debate just gets ramped up and ramped up. And you see what happens when [then] current Justice Secretary [Ken Clarke] tries to bring some balance or tries to have a debate about it. It is absolutely toxic. (civil servant)

Some policy participants were frustrated by the apparent rigidity of politicians' beliefs and the resulting framing of policy problems:

Over-simplification has very far-reaching consequences. I don't doubt the sincerity of the desire [to better protect the public from violent individuals] but there was a lack of thinking-through. (Inspectorate representative)

However, a senior civil servant echoed many of those interviewed in reflecting on the limitations that the 'toxic' context placed upon political actors: 'If you stand up and say, "I'm thinking I might, perhaps, maybe, do this", you will get shredded' (civil servant). These reflections on policymaking do suggest, but are perhaps not conclusive proof, of the exercise of reflexivity during moments in the IPP story.

One minister did admit to what he now characterized as 'naivety'; another was clear about the failures in the policymaking process and their part in those processes.[5] Politicians, as we might expect, robustly defended their actions and motives. One politician closed the research interview by stating that, despite the many problems caused by the IPP sentence (which they recognized), 'the answer isn't to do nothing [in relation to dangerous offenders]… If I've saved one life, I'm happy with that'.

---

[5] See, for example, Blunkett's public admission of regret in relation to the IPP sentence (Conway 2014).

Does this suggest a resistance to a deeper consideration of the ethical dimensions of particular outputs resulting from their work? It is to this ethical dimension that we can now turn.

Holistic Reflexivity

> The delivery of pain, to whom, and for what, contains an endless line of deep moral questions. (Christie 1994: 187)

It is perhaps in this section that the findings must be most tentative. It is unlikely, but not impossible, that a relatively short discussion with policymakers about a specific policy development would result in a detailed reflection upon the relationship between their work and their broader conceptions of how to practise a 'good life'. However, by complementing analysis of the interview data with contextual information on policy participants, we can make some limited observations.

First, it is important to recognize the considerable commitment made by many policy participants to their work. In different ways and perhaps for different reasons, significant time and energy is expended by political actors, civil servants, penal reformers and many others involved in the development and contestation of criminal justice policy. Consider, for example, the sustained work and considered reflections of the following policy participants: former Home Secretary David Blunkett (Blunkett 2006); former Chief Inspectors of Prisons Lord Ramsbotham (Ramsbotham 2003) and Dame Anne Owers (Edemariam 2009); and penal reformer Juliet Lyon (Arnand 2014).

Many officials were open about the ethical dimension of their activities, and the context in which they operated. One former civil servant painted a troubling picture in recalling a discussion between himself and colleagues regarding the limits of their subservient role. He quoted a colleague thus:

> 'You [would] have to be given an instruction [by a minister] that is immoral as it were, seriously immoral, not just you don't agree with it. [If] you're being told to gas people or something, then of course your

obligation is not [to do it].' But other than that, the whole of the Civil Service is schooled to the idea that ministers get what they want. (Home Office official)

Often, early discussion of the policymaking process and the instrumental thinking involved therein was followed, as the interview developed, by reflections on the ethical dimensions of their work. Contrast the two following quotes, from the same civil servant involved in the development of the Criminal Justice Bill in 2001–2003:

> The Lords were very worrying, because you need a lot of consent. The really tough people are those in the Lords speaking on principle, it is much harder to deal with them. The House of Commons is easier, because you can guillotine things and there is the party discipline there. (civil servant, notes from unrecorded interview)
>
> It was a fantastic achievement to get it done [the Bill passed]. But I'm not proud of it in terms of what it did, the effects it had on people. (civil servant, notes from unrecorded interview)

We see here two possible conceptions of 'success' in play: first, as an act of procedure, an instrumental concern; and second, as a substantive measure having real impact on individuals' lives.

The following statement, made at a gathering of senior policymakers in the teeth of an acute crisis in prison capacity (see Annison 2015: Chap. 6), reveals the interplay between personal ethics and professional responsibilities:

> I believe that the most critical problem to be addressed … is the consequences of the IPP sentence. And I speak, I'm not sure in what capacity I speak there… a human being? (senior policy participant, Chatham House Rule event, 2010)

Penal reformers expressed admiration for then Justice Secretary Ken Clarke's willingness to risk sustaining deep political damage in the course of seeking to abolish the IPP sentence. The reflection by one civil servant that '[he is] coming to the end of his career, so he just does what he thinks is right rather than thinking about his job prospects' (MoJ official) is perhaps as telling for what it suggests about the ministerial status quo, as for what it tells us about Clarke's own ethical stance.

Collective Reflexivity

Clear distinctions between the consideration of individual and collective reflexivity are difficult to maintain when faced with the 'attractive mess' of interview reflections (Ritchie and Lewis 2003: 202). In many cases, discussion of individual frustrations with the political context was married with reflections on its implications for the prospects of an improved penal policymaking process. These reflections were generally predicated upon a desire for a more deliberative politics, a better 'penal democracy' (Dzur 2014); one in which 'we design institutions, structure processes and develop support systems to make it easier for people to engage', to 'have a say' (Stoker 2006: 14).

In discussing the exclusionary nature of much penal policymaking, one interviewee, a close observer of civil servant activity, provided the following reflections:

> Ministers [did not want] to be disagreed with. And basically the role of the civil service was simply to do what it was told. And…people learn. It's like having an electric fence around a field. You rapidly learn what hurts and what's pointless. (policy participant)

This was also raised by those subject to this context, with one senior civil servant giving media influence as a pertinent example:

> I mean, how many laws have we got with dead children's names associated with it, because of campaigns by the *Mail* or the *Sun*? And some lunches with Rebekah Brooks and the Prime Minister have resulted in changes in penal policy. I mean that couldn't be any more exclusionary, because the civil service isn't even involved at that point until a decision's been made and they say, 'Go and implement X'. (civil servant)

Concern was also raised at the established patterns of working within the Ministry of Justice (MoJ), and their deleterious effect upon a more open, deliberative politics of criminal justice within, let alone beyond, the department:

> When you have a sentencing discussion with the Secretary of State, who's in the room? You have the sentencing team, a good bunch of generalists. You'll have probably one lawyer from the Government Legal Service...who likely has never been a practitioner... The only person in the room who will understand offending behaviour will be [a senior representative of] NOMS... *Never* do we have in the room a psychologist or someone who understands risk. (civil servant)[6]

> Everything was done in very small circles. (civil servant)

Further, the relatively short period of time spent in the MoJ, not only by ministers and their special advisers but also by many civil servants, was considered to be another factor that militated against collective reflexivity.

> All the main actors are in [the department] for a very short period, but they can be very influential when they're in it. (civil servant)

We have seen in this section reflections upon penal policymaking, which also suggest—though do not conclusively evidence—a level of reflexivity among at least some respondents. What was equally clear was the view, among many respondents, that the practices of policymaking could be considerably improved, in a manner that could be conceived of as facilitating a greater level of reflexivity in day-to-day policymaking. We can now consider the potential value of IPA for the understanding, and thereby the improvement, of penal politics.

---

[6] NOMS, the National Offender Management Service, is responsible for prisons and oversees probation services in England and Wales.

Interpreting and Influencing Penal Policymaking?

Scholarly interpretations of penal policymaking might be of utility for the improvement of penal policymaking in (at least) two ways, which we can term 'evidential' and 'collaborative'. As regards the former, interpretive accounts may support policy participants in understanding their practices, the beliefs and traditions that they draw upon when carrying out their policymaking functions. It might support, in other words, efforts at individual *post hoc* reflexivity (i.e. reflection), which might lead to greater reflexivity during future policymaking processes.[7]

As regards the latter, the role of interpretive scholars and those utilizing interpretive accounts may be more active. Interpretive scholars might act in collaboration with policy participants during the course of research projects, to test developing interpretations and potentially thereby to improve the policymaking process under consideration. They might also collaborate with policy participants after completion of research, using their accounts as a means by which prospective reforms—and the means by which they might realistically be achieved—can be considered.

The Evidential Role

As I have indicated above, many of those interviewed for my own research presented observations that suggested a considerable degree of occupational reflexivity. Perhaps there is therefore nothing further for interpretive researchers to add. However, the strength of interpretive scholarly accounts is their ability to draw together, interweave and contrast the different perspectives of those engaged in a particular policymaking process. We can demonstrate this briefly by summarizing my account of the creation of the IPP sentence, by the 2001–2005 Labour government.[8]

---

[7] As will become clear, this conception of 'evidence' is importantly distinct from that generally promoted by those operating within an 'evidence based policy' paradigm.

[8] For a full discussion, see Annison (2015).

I found that some politicians were populist, in the sense of cynically shaping their policy goals in light of their likely electoral effects. However, what was more striking, given the theoretical dominance of ministers in the British constitutional structure, was the extent to which politicians and civil servants were so 'very concerned about managing public opinion' (political adviser) that many policy participants acted as if they were subservient to the public voice. I was presented with a paradoxical situation in which the penal policymaking process was generally exclusionary, secretive and driven by a very small number of individuals, but where many of the relevant policymakers spoke as if they were being driven along by forces outside of their control: the rise of the public voice.

It also became clear that despite the Labour government's continual chafing against legal constraints (Stevens 2002), legally trained civil servants—in the form of Parliamentary Counsel, government lawyers and other legally trained officials—remained central in shaping policies such as the IPP sentence. While officials sought faithfully to bring into being the sentence desired by the Secretary of State and his ministerial team, it was taken as a given that human rights considerations, coupled with a more general sense of British fairness (a sense of 'how we do things', as one official put it), set the parameters. Systems of civil detention were being introduced in several Australian states and parts of the USA around the time of the creation of the IPP sentence (Brown 2011; McSherry and Keyzer 2011). Such measures were introduced to achieve the same stated policy goal: protecting the public from dangerous offenders. However, this type of post-sentence preventive detention was immediately discounted:

> The idea that you go along to a prisoner and say, "you look dangerous", without him having [committed a further offence], and giving him a longer sentence – you need some kind of legal justification. (sentencing official)

This episode hints at the various traditions in play. Political actors tended to be motivated by the dominant Third Way political tradition; senior civil servants relied upon the Westminster tradition to guide their actions, acting 'as if the 19th century liberal constitution [still] sets the rules of the political game' (Rhodes 2013: 487). Legally trained officials drew upon liberal legal traditions in seeking to implement the wishes of their political masters. These interacted with other considerations of the time, such as Prime Minister Tony Blair's keen interest in Home Office affairs and an unbridled tabloid media's efforts to harry ministers of the day, to guide the government's agenda. The Iraq War loomed large in the background.

Such an account, summarized here in brief, adds depth and precision to critiques of populist politicians as the source of inadvisable reforms. This 'evidential' role, as I have termed it, is an important contribution that interpretive accounts can make both for academic and policymaker communities. There remains much scope for further scholarly analysis of the processes by which penal policy is generated.

Further, such accounts may help us to understand why the 'civil service reform syndrome' persists (Hood and Lodge 2007). Why do reform initiatives based on concerns about the lack of 'joined-up policymaking' or 'a civil service cut off from private sector insight' (see Rhodes 2013) 'come and go, overlap and ignore each other, leaving behind residues of varying size and style'? (Hood and Lodge 2007: 59). Perhaps this is because reformers tend to carry with them assumptions that are inappropriate: for example, that financial incentives (or indeed disincentives) will improve civil servant output; that competition is a universal motivator; and that clear lines of accountability are essential. Their envisaged policymakers are ideal-typical rational actors, basing their policies on precise calculations of evidence and available resources (Rhodes 2013).

The interpretive account presented in *Dangerous Politics* points to the unwillingness by key policymakers to consult practitioners and recognized experts in the field of risk, notwithstanding its centrality to their stated goal (the identification and management of convicted offenders who posed 'a significant risk of serious harm' to members of the public). This was supported by traditions that fostered the development of policy within small, relatively isolated, groups of generalist civil servants and political actors. Ministerial misreadings of the punitive bent of the average Crown Court judge, as opposed to the more liberal traditions generally shared by the senior judiciary (Annison 2014a) represented another failure to draw upon 'softer', but no less important, forms of evidence in the development of this indeterminate sentence.

This is not to argue that an uncritical adoption of 'evidence based poli-cymaking' would have improved the situation.[9] Rather, what is made clear is that the IPP policy process failed on its own internal logic (a risk-based sentence developed without detailed understanding of how this would relate to current risk-based practice). An interpretive analysis of the policymaking process provides insights into why this was the case. Second, an interpretive account provides an important, and distinctive, evidential resource for policymakers which may be well placed to inform future practice.

The Collaborative Role

The discussion so far suggests that the primary function of interpretive accounts may be to urge caution, to point out problems and to hold back impatient reformers. Its presentation of 'thick descriptions' (Geertz 1983) of the life worlds under consideration may tend to support proposals for 'incremental change over more ambitious schemes' (Rhodes 2013: 489). However, might interpretive scholars, or others utilizing their accounts, play a more active role in policymaking reform? Can it contribute to the improvement of penal policymaking by fostering ongoing collective reflexivity, one that looks backwards but also encourages an alternative mode of practice moving forwards?

The fostering of collective reflexivity might occur within (and between) policymaker organizations. It could also be conceived more broadly, involving the public more closely in policy decisions as proponents of deliberative politics would propose (Dzur 2012). The desire to bring the public more centrally into the policymaking process was expressed by some policymakers involved with the IPP story:

> Holding a national conversation – how do we engage people in this topic? Because as we all know, a lot of the rhetoric around offenders, around law and order, gets very shrill, at least at the headline level. Once you get below that you can start to have a more considered debate. (policy participant, Chatham House rule event, 2010)

---

[9] On this point, see Loader and Sparks (2010: Chap. 5).

Some believed that other, less dramatic, changes were desperately needed, in order to promote the productive interplay of distinctive viewpoints:

> [Some would rightly ask,] 'Why don't we have police officers seconded into policy teams? Why don't we have policy teams where the people you'll rely on to implement it are actually part of the policy development?' That hasn't generally happened. (former civil servant)

An important example of the collaborative role that might be played by interpretive researchers in facilitating the development of individual/collective reflexivity, and thereby policy reform, is the work of Hendrik Wagenaar. With a number of colleagues and over a number of years, he has sought to utilize interpretive research—both during the research phase and following publication of findings—in support of what he terms 'recursive collaboration' (Wagenaar et al. 2015). The researchers 'test' their interpretations of policy activity with policymakers and practitioners. This encourages organizational representatives to articulate 'norms and values in a cross sector collaborative setting' (Vos and Wagenaar 2014). Accurate accounts of beliefs and practices are assembled and practical challenges that these present to policymakers are identified. Vos and Wagenaar argue that such an approach is capable of fostering 'a collective orientation towards a new, morally grounded, order' (Vos and Wagenaar 2014). It can enable actors 'to create a relatively durable community that is action oriented and that is in sustained interaction with opponents' (Wagenaar et al. 2015: 112).

A pertinent example is Wagenaar and colleagues' work with organizations engaged in the Dutch *veiligheidshuis* ('Safety House') initiative, an effort better to address treatment-resistant serious habitual offenders (Wagenaar et al. 2015). This scheme was intended as a collaborative innovation, bringing together (and reliant upon) 'a network of key partners: police, municipality, district attorney, youth services, social psychiatry, and criminal justice' (Wagenaar et al. 2015: 115).

There were significant challenges in bridging the contrasting 'care' and 'justice' logics that were in operation. Social workers and criminal justice practitioners were working to different priorities, based on different starting assumptions. Wagenaar and colleagues studied the practices engaged in by the practitioners. They communicated initial findings in a series of workshops, encouraging the participating practitioners to reflect on the findings and to propose the revision or refinement of these scholarly interpretations (Wagenaar et al. 2015: 118). This allowed both researchers and participants 'collaboratively [to] learn about the meaning a case has for the service providers and the values that are at stake' (Wagenaar et al. 2015: 118).

Wagenaar and colleagues argue that by exploring and detailing the competing logics, values, practices and structures of the 'care' and 'justice' realms, this model of action-oriented interpretive policy analysis supported dramatic improvements in the functioning of a specific initiative. Simply putting the relevant organizations together was not enough. What was required was practitioners 'working together *in practice* and reflecting on experiences', supported by a reflexivity fostered by the interpretive research. This was argued to create an atmosphere 'where experiences could be transformed into opportunities and where on-going learning could take place in the interaction between management and practitioners of the different fields' (Wagenaar et al. 2015: 129–30).

In a similar manner, particular developments in penal policy could be utilized as prompts for collaborative learning at a local or national level. Policy participants could come together to reflect upon particular case studies of, for example, the development of sentencing policy or prison planning. Different perspectives could be presented and debated. The understanding of policymaking roles could be examined, along with the practical implications of current understandings. Pragmatic difficulties faced by policymakers could be brought out into the light and addressed as prompts for collaborative responses.

By exposing entrenched positions, by problematizing settled assumptions around policymaking, there may be potential for the *post hoc* reflection demonstrated in many of the research interviews to be fostered within the policymaking processes more generally. At its best, this may serve to generate more effective, and even more just, penal policy.

Some would go further and suggest that these collaborative efforts should place 'informed societal debate' as a central goal (Loader 2010: 91), with open and inclusive public engagement 'an integral part of a framework that fosters the right kind of criminal justice dialogue' (Dzur 2012: 115). Arguments for the development of a 'continuous, detailed dialogue between policymakers and the public' (Johnstone 2000: 172), would likely be welcomed by some policy participants; others may be troubled by the potential damage caused to existing (elite) practices (Rhodes 2013: 485–488).

Conclusion: Prospects and Limits

This chapter has considered the ways in which policy participants might be considered to be 'reflexive', and to what extent the research conducted for *Dangerous Politics* suggests this presently to be the case. We have also seen that there is some evidence to suggest that many policy participants are prone to engage in sustained reflection upon their professional activities. What is less clear is whether this reflexivity is 'operationalized' (forms a central part of day-to-day practice) or whether it is primarily experienced as a 'higher level', *post hoc* activity. Policymakers also face significant impediments. Their analysis of the context in which they operate, examined above, poses challenges for the improvement of penal policy-making, in terms of both process and outcome.

While Rhodes, Wagenaar and others have made a convincing case for the utility of interpretive research in supporting the development of more reflexive policy reform, substantial challenges remain. These include issues of time, relationships, access and relevance. As Rhodes notes, 'observation in the field is time-consuming [for researchers] and fits uncomfortably if at all with the demands of politicians and administrators alike' (Rhodes 2013: 492). As demands on researchers and policymakers ever-increase, the prospects for sustained, empirically grounded IPA appear somewhat bleak. Further, elite policymakers have considerable power to grant, or refuse, access. They can make or break work that seeks to explore their beliefs and practices. If access is achieved and maintained, sustaining an outsider status (not 'going native'), while developing a strong relationship with research subjects, is a considerable challenge.

As regards relevance—being 'perceived by a non-academic as usefully worth reading or listening to' (Parsons 2015: 152)—if findings fail to conform to expectations held by senior policymakers about the causes of problems and their solutions, they may be dismissed as 'irrelevant or disruptive' (Sillitoe 2006: 14). Such research may further 'bring the social technologist notion of what a social scientist is...into question' (Geertz 1983: 35). Interpretive scholars must be cautious about their claims and the limitations of their position as academics (Parsons 2015), but they can potentially play an important role by:

> Speaking (caveated) truth to power; destabilizing complacent, ideologically blinkered politics; and pushing people to problematize their political views and strategies more profoundly. (Parsons 2015: 163)

Research, on this view, does not provide a 'right answer' to be uncritically applied. Rather, it serves to open up different perspectives; it facilitates a more deliberative, a more reflexive, policymaking process.

The problems bedevilling penal policymaking—grand schemes, poor implementation, damaging unintended consequences and so on—have refused to go away. Interpretive approaches, which analyse the beliefs and practices that underpin penal policymaking, and encourage policy participants to share perspectives within and beyond relevant organizations, have the potential to make an important contribution to the development of what Loader and Sparks have termed a 'better politics of crime and its regulation' (2010: 117). For as Parsons argues:

> People who fail to perceive the operative norms, identities, cultural practices and other social constructs within an arena are likely to misunderstand it and fail to achieve their goals, whatever they may be. (Parsons 2015: 162)

References

Annison, H. (2014a) 'Interpreting the Politics of the Judiciary: The British Senior Judicial Tradition and the Pre-emptive Turn in Criminal Justice', *Journal of Law and Society* 41(3): 339–366.

Annison, H. (2014b) 'Weeding the Garden: The Third Way, the Westminster tradition and Imprisonment for Public Protection', *Theoretical Criminology* 18(1): 38–55.

Annison, H. (2015) *Dangerous Politics*, Oxford: Oxford University Press.

Ansell, C. K. (2011) *Pragmatist Democracy: Evolutionary learning as public philosophy*, Oxford: Oxford University Press.

Arnand, A. (2014) 'Anita Arnand talks to Juliet Lyon', *One to One*. London: BBC.

Ashworth, A. and Zedner, L. (2014) *Preventive Justice*, Oxford: Oxford University Press.

Barker, A. and Wilson, G. K. (1997) 'Whitehall's Disobedient Servants? Senior Officials' Potential Resistance to Ministers in British Government Departments', *British Journal of Political Science* 27(2): 223–246.

Bauman, Z. (1989) *Modernity and the Holocaust*, Cambridge: Polity.

Becker, H.S. (1967) 'Whose Side Are We On?', *Social Problems* 14(3): 239–247.

Bevir, M. and Rhodes, R.A.W. (2006) *Governance Stories*, London: Routledge.

Blunkett, D. (2006) *The Blunkett Tapes: My Life in the Bear Pit*, London: Bloomsbury.

Bourdieu, P. (1990) *In Other Words: Essays Towards a Reflexive Sociology*, Cambridge: Polity.

Brown, M. (2011) 'Preventive Detention and the Control of Sex Crime: Receding Visions of Justice in Australian Case Law', *Alternative Law Journal* 36: 10–16.

Carlen, P. (2008) 'Imaginary Penalities and Risk-Crazed Governance'. In P. Carlen (ed.) *Imaginary Penalities*, Cullompton: Willan Publishing: 1–25.

Christie, N. (1994) *Crime Control as Industry: Towards GULAGS, Western style*, London: Routledge.

Conway, Z. (2014) *David Blunkett 'Regrets Injustices' of Indeterminate Sentences*. Available at: http://www.bbc.co.uk/news/uk-26561380

Dexter, L.A. (2006) *Elite and Specialized Interviewing*, Colchester: ECPR.

Dzur, A. (2012) 'Participatory Democracy and Criminal Justice', *Criminal Law and Philosophy* 6: 115–129.

Dzur, A. (2014) 'An Introduction: Penal Democracy' *The Good Society* 23(1): 1–5.

Edemariam, A. (2009) 'Saturday Interview: Anne Owers', *The Guardian*. Manchester/London: Guardian News Media.

Fielding, N.G. (2011) 'Judges and Their Work', *Social & Legal Studies* 20(1): 97–115.

Garland, D. (2001) *The Culture of Control: Crime and Social Order in Contemporary Society*, Oxford: Oxford University Press.

Geertz, C. (1983) 'Blurred Genres'. In C. Geertz (ed.) *Local Knowledge*, New York: Basic Books.

54   H. Annison

Gouldner, A. (1971) *The Coming Crisis of Western Sociology*, London: Heinemann.
Hay, C. (2002) *Political Analysis*, Basingstoke: Palgrave.
Holland, R. (1999) 'Reflexivity', *Human Relations* 52(4): 463–404.
Hood, C. and Lodge, M. (2007) 'Endpiece: Civil Service Reform Syndrome – are we Heading for a Cure?', *Transformation* Spring: 58–59.
Johnstone, G. (2000) 'Penal Policy Making: Elitist, Populist or Participatory?', *Punishment and Society* 2(2): 161–180.
Lacey, N. (2008) *The Prisoners' Dilemma: Political Economy and Punishment in Contemporary Democracies*, Cambridge: Cambridge University Press.
Loader, I. (2006) 'Fall of the 'Platonic Guardians': Liberalism, Criminology and Political Responses to Crime in England and Wales', *British Journal of Criminology* 46(4): 561–586.
Loader, I. (2010) 'Is it NICE? The Appeal, Limits and Promise of Translating a Health Innovation into Criminal Justice', *Current Legal Problems* 63(1): 72–91.
Loader, I. and Sparks, R. (2010) *Public Criminology?*, London: Routledge.
McSherry, B. and Keyzer, P. (2011) *Dangerous People: Policy, Prediction and Practice*, Hove, East Sussex: Routledge.
Ministry of Justice. (2013) *Offender Management Statistics (Quarterly) – October to December*. London: Ministry of Justice.
Page, E.C. (2009) 'Their Word is Law: Parliamentary Counsel and Creative Policy Analysis', *Public Law* 4: 790–811.
Page, E.C. and Jenkins, W. (2005) *Policy Bureaucracy: Government with a Cast of Thousands*, Oxford: Oxford University Press.
Parsons, C. (2015) 'Constructivism and Interpretive Approaches: Especially Relevant or Especially Not?'. In G. Stoker, B.G. Peters and J. Pierre (eds.) *The Relevance of Political Science*, London: Palgrave: 148–168.
Pratt, J. (2007) *Penal Populism*, London: Routledge.
Prison Reform Trust. (2015) *Bromley Briefing Autumn 2015*. London: Prison Reform Trust.
Ramsbotham, D. (2003) *Prisongate*, London: Free Press.
Rhodes, R.A.W. (2013) 'Political Anthropology and Civil Service Reform: Prospects and Limits', *Policy & Politics* 41(4): 481–496.
Ritchie, J. and Lewis, J. (2003) *Qualitative Research Practice: a Guide for Social Science Students and Researchers*, London; Thousand Oaks, Calif.: Sage Publications.
Ryan, M. (2004) 'Red Tops, Populists and the Irresistible Rise of the Public Voice(s)', *Journal for Crime, Media and Conflict* 1: 1–14.

Sillitoe, P. (2006) 'The Search for Relevance: A Brief History of Applied Anthropology', *History and Anthropology* 17(1): 1–19.

Stevens, R. (2002) *The English Judges: Their Role in the Changing Constitution,* Oxford: Hart Publishing.

Stoker, G. (2006) *Why Politics Matters: Making Democracy Work,* Basingstoke: Palgrave Macmillan.

Vos, J. and Wagenaar, H. (2014) 'The Münchhausen Movement: Improving the Coordination of Social Services Through the Creation of a Social Movement', *The American Review of Public Administration* 44(4): 409–439.

Wagenaar, H. (2011) *Meaning in Action: Interpretation and Dialogue in Policy Analysis,* New York: ME Sharpe.

Wagenaar, H., Vos, J., Balder, C. and van Hemert, B. (2015) 'Overcoming Conflicting Logics of Care and Justice'. In A. Agger, B. Damgaard, A.H. Krogh and E. Sorenson (eds.) *Collaborative Governance and Public Innovation in Northern Europe.* Bentham Science Publishers.

3

When the Stars Align: Juvenile Justice Policy Reform in New South Wales

Elaine Fishwick

Introduction

> It's exactly like when the stars align. You just get moments in public policy
> and public debate when stars align and the right people and the right
> things start to happen – you can make leaps. Otherwise it's like pushing
> everything uphill. (Participant 6, an experienced third sector policy activist
> and now public servant)

This eloquent summary of what it is like to advocate for the rights of
young people in the policy process was made by a very experienced
policy advocate who was a participant in a recent research project that
I conducted, examining policy decision-making in the New South
Wales (NSW) juvenile justice system (Fishwick 2015). It describes the
moments when, constellations of conditions come together and create
the opportunity for progressive policy decisions to emerge. And, as the
quotation implies, these moments happen less often than those of us

E. Fishwick (✉)
Independent researcher and scholar, Sydney, Australia

© The Author(s) 2017
S. Armstrong et al. (eds.), *Reflexivity and Criminal Justice*,
DOI 10.1057/978-1-137-54642-5_3

involved in advocating for social justice would like. Consequently, I would argue, when they occur, it is important that we make the most of them. As a critical social scientist, who for many years was engaged in policy activism in the third sector, I completely understood where my interviewee was coming from and her words encapsulated the very reason why I was trying to understand how particular policy decisions were taken, in the hope that I could then work out how those advocating for young people's rights and interests could intervene even more effectively in the policy process. The study covered a specific period in NSW juvenile justice history 1990–2005 during which I was involved in campaigning for reform as both a researcher and advocate in the third sector (known as the non-government or not-for-profit sector in Australia). As I explain later, it was a very frustrating period in youth justice policy since it often felt like that just as we took one step forward in moving towards rights and social justice informed change, we were also being pulled backwards and sideways as we tried to defend the very positions we had just gained.

The discussion in this chapter draws on my research about this period in NSW history and incorporates a number of elements of reflexivity. The study itself, was borne out of my own praxis, that is, I wanted to make sense of my own experience of the policy process by providing myself with the analytical and theoretical space to examine what had happened and why. I also wanted to develop an analysis of the policy process that could contribute to the development of a more detailed understanding of policy in criminology and at the same time, provide a 'how to be a more effective policy advocate' guide for other policy players. There were autobiographical elements woven throughout the research as I thought through my own experiences and discussed policy events with other key players (see, on autobiography, Jewkes 2011). I also wanted the policy actors to think through what factors they considered were influential on decision-making and to reflect on their own role and those of others in making policy happen. My focus too, was on exploring the dynamic, reflexive relationships out of which decisions emerge (see also, Annison, this volume). In the end, it is people who make policy decisions, and people who implement them although, to paraphrase Marx, they do so 'not necessarily in circumstances of their own choosing'.

The discussion also highlights how my own multi-disciplinary background and my engagement with the key conceptual tools of complex realism (Byrne and Callaghan 2014), provided me with the theoretical capacity to explain the co-existence of order and disorder, the rational and serendipitous, the interaction of structure and agency out of which policies emerge in the youth justice field (see, e.g., Byrne and Callaghan 2014; Pycroft and Bartollas 2014 for an introduction to complexity theory in the social sciences and in criminal justice).

The discussion begins with an overview of the policy process in NSW from 1990 to 2005 that provided the impetus to my research and the need to look beyond criminology for developing an understanding of youth justice policy decisions. The discussion then moves on to provide a very brief overview of complexity theory before examining the research process and finally a snapshot of some of the findings from the project.

I hope that this analysis will help others with an interest in policy to develop more of an insight into the interwoven and often disordered nature of the policy world and how integral policy players are to the whole process.

Biography of a Research Project

As stated above, my research was prompted by my own experiences in the youth justice policy field and what appeared to me to be, the messy, often contradictory and serendipitous nature of decision-making in juvenile justice. I considered that there was a gap in knowledge and understanding waiting to be filled.

My involvement in youth justice policy began in 1988 when I became a founding member of a voluntary advocacy group called the NSW Youth Justice Coalition (YJC). I was active in this policy network until 2009. YJC is a community of lawyers, academics, youth workers and other individuals from non-government and government organisations interested in reforming juvenile justice and child welfare policy legislation and practices; in campaigning for children's and young people's rights, as well as advancing social justice for marginalised young people, in particular, Indigenous young people who are hugely over-represented in all aspects of the juvenile justice system especially detention (Australian Human Rights Commission 2014). At the same time as the YJC was being established, the United Nation's Convention on the Rights of the Child (CRC) was in the last stages of development; it was adopted in 1989 and signed and ratified by Australia in 1990. Naively, in retrospect, as members of the YJC, we believed that the Convention might offer a wealth of principled possibilities for governments to use as a tool for positive future reforms.

From its early days, the YJC and its members were, and continue to be, active stakeholders in all aspects of youth justice policy processes. We were collectively and individually key advocates in our epistemic communities and policy networks (Howlett and Ramesh 2003; Karstedt 2004). From the early days, YJC chose to concentrate its energies at the state level where we could have the most impact on juvenile justice law and policy reform, although we also kept our eyes on national and international reforms and movements. Our focus on the state level was mostly due to the fact that Australia has a federal government system and adult criminal and juvenile justice law and procedures are principally state and territory responsibilities.[1] Juvenile justice at the NSW level is a relatively discrete entity made up of specific child-focused legislation, a set of institutions such as children's courts, and detention centres and a juvenile justice department all of which are staffed by specialists such as children's magistrates, children's solicitors and juvenile justice officers. However, it does not completely stand alone, since it is policed by a generalist force with a small number of youth officers, where serious offences are dealt with in the adult criminal justice system, and broader legislation policy and procedures on bail and sentencing apply to under 18-year-olds (Youth Justice Coalition 1990).

One of the major achievements of the YJC in the late 1980s and early 1990s, emerged from a detailed consultative research project we conducted that engaged young people as active researchers and culminated in

---

[1] There are three levels of government—commonwealth, state/territory and local government. The states are Tasmania, South Australia, Western Australia, Queensland, New South Wales and Victoria and the territories are the Australian Capital Territory and the Northern Territory.

a detailed report *Kids In Justice: A Blueprint for the Nineties* (Youth Justice Coalition 1990). The report documented how the youth system in NSW was in disarray and failing young people. As a response to these findings, the report mapped out a series of recommendations for a holistic, coherent strategy for change (Youth Justice Coalition 1990). Supported by an active media strategy and intense lobbying by YJC members, the report became highly influential in policy discussions and debates relating to the reform of juvenile justice legislation in the early to mid-1990s. In 1997, after a series of deliberative policy processes initiated by government[2] and continued support from key policy players, including successive Attorneys-General and senior bureaucrats, the NSW government passed the *Young Offenders Act 1997* (see Bargen et al. 2005; Chan 2005). The legislation reflected many of the recommendations that were outlined in the *Kids In Justice Report* and introduced a range of graded diversionary strategies, policing initiatives and restorative justice-style conferencing, to establish what many saw to be an example of 'best practice' legislation (Chan 2005).

An independent Conferencing Directorate was established to administer youth justice conferencing and its first Director was in fact, a former member of the YJC. At the same time, a publicly funded Children's Legal Service was introduced as a section within the NSW Legal Aid Commission, providing free legal advice to children in police custody and representation to all children appearing in the Children's Courts on criminal matters.[3]

Yet, at the same time that these progressive reforms were introduced and policy agendas seemed to be informed by principles of diversion, rehabilitation, restorative justice and rights, a whole other stream of legislative and policy reforms emerged. They appeared to be hastily introduced and were overwhelmingly punitive, regressive and reactive. They were the kind of reforms that commentators have described as being informed by 'the politics of law and order' (Hogg and Brown 1998) or

---

[2] Juvenile Justice Advisory Council 1993; NSW Government 1996 NSW Parliament Legislative Council Standing Committee on Social Issues 1992 and 1996.

[3] The NSW Legal Aid Commission also funds a panel of expert children's solicitors who specialise in care and protection matters; they are community based and private practice solicitors. They have recently established a children's civil law section.

as 'moral panics' (Cohen 2002; Young 2009), that is, decisions driven by political expediency and media pressure. Before 2001, these kinds of changes were exemplified by the introduction of anti-gangs' legislation and street-sweeping local government initiatives in towns with high numbers of Indigenous young people (Fishwick 2015). However, it was in the wake of 9/11 and a series of local street disturbances that the government introduced even tougher public order legislation, as well as policing reforms that were characterised by some of the anti-terrorist, security and 'risk'-based discourses and practices found in many corners of the globe (Loughnan 2009; Zedner 2009).

In addition, from 1999 onwards, there was a constant stream of amendments to the *NSW Bail Act 1976*. Again, these seemed to be introduced in direct response to media scare stories about juvenile offending and as a consequence it was much harder for young people to be granted bail, and magistrates began to impose complex, confusing bail conditions that were subsequently closely policed (Stubbs 2010; Wong et al. 2010). As a result, despite an initial increase in the use of diversionary options and a drop in the number of children and young people in custody (Chan 2005), the rate of young people being put behind bars steadily rose, mostly for breaches of bail conditions. This affected Indigenous young people in particular and their rates of over-representation in detention rose dramatically (Stubbs 2010; Taylor 2009). The co-existence of different streams of policy agendas, options and practices in juvenile justice meant that by the tenth anniversary of the *Young Offenders Act 1997*, the system was clearly in a mess again and had lost its earlier strategic vision (Noetic Solutions 2010). For those of us who had worked so hard to develop a coherent system informed by research evidence, best practice, rights, principles of diversion, we could only look on with frustration and dismay as gourmet legislation and policy turned into a dog's breakfast.

Throughout this phase of policy change, I had been involved mostly as a volunteer in project managing research, conducting research, writing submissions to government, lobbying and networking and supporting other members of the YJC as they appeared in the media, acted as witnesses in government inquiries, and sat on key committees. I had come to know some of the key policy players working within the system and knew that personally and professionally, many of them held the same kinds of values about youth justice as those of us in the third sector and battled hard to resist the more regressive policy changes that had been proposed.

The whole situation made me curious about how decisions, which seemed so contrary and at times irrational, could come about. There seemed to be moments when policies were made on the run in the face of overwhelming evidence that they wouldn't work, yet they co-existed alongside well thought-out principled decisions. I decided to investigate the factors that shaped the policy decision-making process to understand how and why such a Gordian youth justice policy knot had become so tangled.

Analysing Policy

At the time I decided to develop the research project, I knew I needed to look to other disciplines outside of criminology to provide the conceptual policy analytical tools that I needed to fully explore the policy process. I was teaching criminology at a university in Sydney, but had previously taught law, social policy and human rights at different universities in the UK and Australia, and had a broad social science/law background. And, during my eclectic academic journey, I had also completed a Masters in Journalism and consequently had developed a good knowledge of media studies literature and its framework of understanding the role of media and policy, as well as the practical demands of both journalism and the communications industry. From this broad multi-disciplinary background, I was aware that there were significant gaps in criminological understanding of policy systems and processes.

I wasn't alone in this perception. In 2008, Frances Heidennsohn had remarked in a discussion of public criminology at the British Society of Criminology conference, 'I think we have fallen down, we have done very little work on examining the policy process' (Garside 2008: 5, quoting Heidensohn and cited in Fishwick 2015: 5). Barton and Johns (2013) in their work on policy and criminal justice have also drawn attention to the fact that policy understanding is relatively underdeveloped in criminology, and Jones and Newburn (2004) make the point that criminologists have tended to take the notion of policy for granted (Jones and Newburn

2004: 127). Further, as Newburn and Sparks (2004) state, the emergence of policy ideas is rarely the product of a process that bears any resemblance to a simple rational choice model they are more likely to be serendipitous and 'the product of messy compromises and uneasy and temporary alliances and exigencies' (Newburn and Sparks 2004: 12). Other commentators have highlighted these themes of messiness in relation to youth justice, for example, John Muncie (2009) discusses the co-existence of competing, contradictory and often conflicting discourses, rationales and strategies of justice. Likewise, Fergusson, in his analysis of discourse and youth justice, explores the vicissitudes of the policy process; arguing that youth justice policies during the Major, Thatcher and Blair governments in the UK, 'were a melting pot of contradictions, ideas and ideologies' (Fergusson 2007: 179). My aim was to bring these insights together to develop an empirical analysis of the policy process in NSW within a critical theoretical framework.

I had come across the work of John Kingdon (2003)[4] whose writing on policy streams, policy entrepreneurs and the opening of policy windows as opportunities to achieve change provided me with the more nuanced understanding of the dynamics of the policy process that I was searching for. What I wanted to do was blend this knowledge together in a way that could develop a coherent narrative about what appeared to be a relatively incoherent system, and which could provide me with a way of applying that understanding to future policy activism. I began my research hoping that there would be a theoretical epiphany that would emerge out of the research itself. And, in the end, it was a chance (indeed serendipitous) comment of an interviewee that led me to read about complexity theory and to discover its capacity to shed light on my own observations and the findings that were emerging from the qualitative data. There is not enough room in this chapter to really do justice to the breadth of approaches that come within the purview of complexity theory but the following section provides a quick overview of its key concepts.

---

[4] Kingdon (2003: 2) argues that policy development is not always a neat, staged sequential, rational process. Policy streams relating to agenda setting, options development and implementation co-exist and are populated by different groups of people. And, the flow of policy decisions is not always from the top-down it can flow from the bottom-up as well as horizontally and across streams.

Complexity Theory: Tools for Analysis

Complexity does not simply mean complicated. As Pycroft (2014) explains, complexity means 'woven or enmeshed' (Pycroft 2014: 21) and is concerned with looking at the dynamic reflexive nature of social phenomena. It was in fact a particular thread of complexity theory—complex realism—which resonated with my own world view since it engaged with critical social science, and social praxis, and understood that politics, research, theory and social action for justice were inextricably intertwined (Byrne 2011; Byrne and Callaghan 2014). This particular strand of complexity theory provided me with the tools to do just that.

A complexity approach argues that policy needs to be understood holistically since it emerges out of intersections of the macro and micro; structure and agency; order and chaos; of systems within systems in which the policy process is dynamic and ever-changing (Geyer and Rihani 2010). And, although policy systems may appear random when at first studied, ordering and patterning become observable and explainable (Pycroft 2014: 18). Due to the overlapping and nested nature of systems, they are interdependent so that actions in one sphere can have direct and indirect repercussions in another (Byrne 1998, 2011). Likewise, causality can run in all possible directions (Walby 2007). In this way, according to Pycroft:

> Interactions are non-linear in nature and can produce (unpredictable) or chaotic behaviour or outcomes that are not proportionate to inputs, so that small changes can have disproportionate effects. (Pycroft 2014: 23)

Chaos and disorder in complexity theory are terms used to describe how the constant motion and interaction of systems and individuals produce effects that are never entirely predictable since 'they may not coalesce in the same way and may have a whole range of intervening factors' (Byrne 2011: 22). It also accepts that unexpected events are intrinsic to society. There are disruptions to social equilibrium that can either bind systems together or radically alter them (Byrne 1998, 2011). However, the possibilities of change are not infinite or completely random or totally unpredictable because systems are bounded by tradition and shaped by broader historical pathways (Byrne and Callaghan 2014).[5] As Callaghan (2008) argues, systems, their culture, relations and processes are characterised by 'negotiated order' where there is a process of constant renegotiation by the policy actors who inhabit them. And further, structured relations of power set some of the boundaries of interaction. Callaghan states:

> structure is important because it sets the position from which individuals negotiate and in turn gives their negotiations a patterned quality, but these products are historically and temporally shaped, always open to review and revision. (Callaghan 2008: 45)

This is a point echoed by Henry and McAra who argue that negotiated order in criminal justice is characterised by the 'interconnectedness of individuals, communities, institutions, regimes and politics' (2012: 342; see also, McAra and McVie 2012). In complexity theory then, the actions of individuals are important and must be taken into consideration in analyses of policy (Callaghan 2005). According to Pycroft, 'as individuals we are constitutive components of the various systems…that we live and work in, whether we are conscious of it or not' (2014: 15). A complexity approach can explain then, 'how people work within relatively permanent structures in the daily process of making and remaking the social world' (Callaghan 2008: 408). For Byrne and Callaghan (2014), the work of Pierre Bourdieu on habitus and doxa provides the kind of conceptual tools necessary for understanding the reflexive interaction of the individual and the systems in which they work (see Bourdieu 1977; Bourdieu and Wacquant 1992). There are also other constraints on systems, organisations and individuals that determine the boundaries of what is possible. In complexity theory the study of institutions and organisations[6] and their day-to-day values, routines and practices are important factors to take into consideration for understanding the emergence of policy decisions.

---

[5] Like the depiction of history as subjunctive in Alan Bennett's (2004) *The History Boys*, history is seen in complexity theory as a series of moments of possibilities and it is the intersection of multiple factors that affects the choice of what is on offer.

[6] The revival of the study of institutions in public policy provides an example of this; see McKay et al. (2010) and Considine (2005) for a discussion of 'New Institutionalism'. See also Wacquant (2011) on institutions and criminology.

Reflexivity in Research Method

The rationale for the research was in part driven by my own praxis and a desire to think through a phase in policy history in which I had played a small part. I wanted to not only make sense of the policy process itself but also learn from the experience and develop a practical understanding of how decisions happened in order to be a more effective advocate in the future. For those of us who identify as critical criminologists Van Swaaningen reminds us that we social justice and human rights are key principles underpinning our work, and we should endeavour to ensure that social justice is adapted to 'present-day cultural, political and socio-economic constellation[s]' (Van Swaaningen 1999:19). I too wanted my research to be the basis for change.

In order to get the kind of detail of how policy was made in practice, the role of agency and the impact of individuals in the policy process, I designed a qualitative retrospective study that drew on the knowledge and experience of key policy players and incorporated my own reflections on what I had seen and experienced. This approach is summarised succinctly by Callaghan (2005) who states:

> people do know a lot about why they do things, they are reflexive about their world, they subject their own experiences and motivations to examination. Social research seeks to render the taken-for-granted reflexive and through the comparison of different styles and experiences, to gain access both to the ways in which people articulate things for themselves and to those elements which are pre-conscious and tacit. (Callaghan 2005: 12–13)

I conducted 19 in-depth, open-ended interviews with experienced policy makers and commentators. Before doing the interviews, I had examined a range of official documentary sources from the period as well as my own personal archives (there are advantages of being a hoarder) in order to not only remind myself of the key policy events of the time but also provide me with the materials for documentary analysis. I asked individuals to reflect on their own role in the policy process as well as identifying other key policy players and their influence in the field. Interestingly, some of the interviewees stated at the beginning of our discussions that they were not sure they had anything to contribute to the research but, as the conversation continued, they provided countless illustrative examples about the day-to-day realities of policy decision-making. The insights that they brought to the discussion were so illuminating. They made me reappraise my own outlook and I began to realise how important emotions and relationships are in the policy process.

I did know some of the people that I interviewed but as it happened, many people didn't remember me. We had shared common experiences and therefore the interviews were essentially iterative, mutual, subjective explorations (Hollway and Jefferson 2013). Interviewing embodied a dynamic interaction of habitus and field between me and the research participants (Callaghan 2005).

A complexity approach is not concerned with discovering cause and effect type explanations but with pulling together detailed and qualitative narratives, and from these identifying patterns and commonalities as well as unexpected data developing an analytical understanding of 'what is, and how it has come to be' (Byrne 2011: 71). I followed up any policy issues or events, case studies that were mentioned by interviewees by conducting further research, locating media stories, contemporary commentaries, parliamentary records and relevant statistics. As Bartels and Richards (2011) point out, this kind of flexible approach is one of the benefits of qualitative work where researchers are:

> Free to capitalise on serendipitous occurrences such as the discovery of new sources of data…to follow up leads and explore themes that emerge unforeseen. (Bartels and Richards 2011: 7)

By allowing myself to be open to new ideas, I found a number of unexpected themes emerging from the data. As will be discussed below, the most striking of these were: the extent to which personalities, emotions and relationships have an impact on the course of policy; the contingent nature of the relationship between media, policy and politics; and the impact that routine has on decisions. The themes that emerged from the research process also indicated that decisions were influenced by a panoply of factors from the cataclysmic events of 9/11 to the buying of flowers for a Minister.

Reading the Stars

By being open to a holistic view of a dynamic policy process, coupled with my own and my interviewees' reflections on the policy process, I was able to see how the articulation of different structural, systemic and subjective factors at one particular historical moment can set the parameters in which policy windows open and shut as well as presenting boundaries to the range of options available for policy makers to pursue. I have discussed elsewhere (Fishwick 2015) the details of my research findings but in this penultimate section, I just want to provide an overview of the factors that have been important to me in understanding and appreciating the dynamics of the policy process.

It became clear that global and local international and domestic socioeconomic conditions framed the policy universe in which policy decisions in NSW were made. For example, from 1990, the ratification of the United Nations CRC by the Australian government required some action by Federal and state governments. Although, never fully adopted into domestic legislation (Tobin 2013), a number of its guiding principles were incorporated into legislation, policies and procedures, and certainly formed the basis of the YJC lobbying campaigns from 1989 onwards. Another key global event that had repercussions at the local level was 9/11, which shaped many of the changes in criminal justice, juvenile justice, policing and penality from 2001 onwards.

Contemporary policy systems are also influenced by their histories; they are path dependent (Byrne 2011). For example, contemporary social, economic, political and cultural relations; court systems and practices; policing and penality in NSW are shaped by the state's penal colonial heritage. We see the effects of neo-colonialism in the hyper-incarceration of Indigenous people and over-policing of many communities (see Blagg 2008; Cunneen et al. 2013; Hogg 2001). The constraints of neo-colonial conditions also explain why, despite numerous policy initiatives to address the over-representation of Indigenous young people in the court system and in juvenile detention, it is difficult, although not impossible for change to occur. From the perspective of a complexity framework, it may take a significant disruption to this particular policy equilibrium for the policy trajectory to change its course.

As discussed in the section above, in a federal system like Australia, the relationship between the three tiers of government and the delegations of powers, responsibilities and funding can create gaps and discontinuities in policy, and policy reverberations that have effects in other areas. As we know, crime is strongly linked to public and social policy so changes that occur outside the responsibility of the states can have a major impact on the incidence of crime and also on the capacity of juvenile justice to respond to crime. For example, reductions in funding for emergency accommodation for young people has had a major impact on them getting bail, especially since security of housing is a condition to be taken into consideration in bail determinations. An appreciation of the broader public policy and social policy fields, especially health, housing income security, care and protection means that as criminologists we can better understand why particular outcomes might be happening in juvenile justice and advocate for appropriate responses that lie outside of criminal justice policy domains.

Some of the key influences on the shaping of policy decisions are to be found in the everyday functioning of government, management and administration. Considine (2006) calls these the mundane or more 'routine' aspects of policy where the majority of policy activity takes place. Institutional life plays a significant role in establishing, what Mackay et al. (2010) call the 'the rules of the game', which include formal administrative and governance procedures as well as the values, beliefs and informal expectations of policy players. Kingdon (2003: 116) also argues that the bulk of policy activity especially the development of policy options, takes place in this more subterranean and mundane environment, a space he calls the 'policy primeval soup'. It is difficult to see these aspects of the policy process from the outside of political, government and bureaucratic systems, but my research revealed that these are highly influential in shaping policy decisions and provide many of the constraints and opportunities for what can be done and when. By concentrating too much on higher order official policy statements in official discourse, we miss the importance of these day-to-day routines on the evolution on policy agendas and options (see also Annison in this volume).

My research interviewees agreed that on occasions rational policy processes based on deliberation, research and evidence informed decision-making, embodied in the procedures of consultative committees, parliamentary inquires, law reform inquiries, government interdepartmental meetings and joint ministerial, departmental decisions, were ideal ways to make policy. However, they were seen to be cumbersome in practice. As the following statements demonstrate:

> The processes exist for good policy making and law reform to occur.... those processes are good processes because they are consulting with the relevant agencies and people. They take a holistic view so that they're looking for a consistent answer that works. (Participant 12)
> I've been in government now longer than I've been outside government. You do get a finer appreciation of it's frustratingly slow, but generally the quality of what comes out of the other end, if you do get your moment... is fantastic because you do get good reform and enduring reform and things that do make a big difference in people's lives. (Participant 6)

Decisions were more often driven by pragmatism, the necessities of politics and the desire not to lose power (French 2012). Especially, in the face of demands from angry constituents or when set against the moral authority of well-resourced policy lobbyists. As one interviewee highlighted in the face of what she called a 'firestorm' of public disturbances on the streets:

> I can't imagine an Attorney or Premier fronting a press conference saying, our response is to refer this matter to a general justice advisory council and they shall report to us. (Participant 17)

Policymakers reflected that there was an intersection of particular youth justice discourses with political, bureaucratic and professional interests. These not only provided the justifications for actions but also privileged the kinds of knowledge, research and evidence that were deemed to be the legitimate basis for decision-making. So, for example, in the early years of the 1990s, rights, diversion, rehabilitation and restorative justice dominated the policy landscape but by the late 1990s, a new managerialism and risk management paradigm began to permeate policy and practice responses to crime including policing, sentencing and program development for offenders. As one of my interviewees observed:

> If I was to reflect on that period, it felt like it [juvenile justice policy] went from being almost a really home spun, kid-centric social work oriented model for lack of a better term, to a site based at a distance, sterile, technologically driven, risk based. (Participant 17)

Although risk management and actuarial perspectives claim to be driven by the objective science and to be evidence based, interviewees felt that they were really ideologically driven and underpinned by neo-liberal agendas, shutting down alternative points of view. From the interviewees' perspective, policy choices led evidence rather than the other way round (see also Mosse 2004; Ransley 2011).

Academics were seen by interviewees to play only a minor role in the policy process. As Stevens (2010) and Chancer and McLaughlin (2007) have also found, academic criminologists were found to be too far removed from the practicalities of the everyday policy world, and too concerned with the intricacies of research evidence to be useful contributors to the policy process. Stevens (2010) provides excellent insights from his time working in the UK civil service on how strategically and persuasively argued policy points from staff were far more powerful in influencing senior bureaucrats than his own detailed policy proposals. This raises important issues for academics about the ways in which research is conducted and presented in terms of its potential to influence the policy process. From my own experience and that of the project's interviewees, it was when academics produced short, bullet-point fact sheets during election campaigns, or showed an understanding of the day-to-day world of politics or the public service and then over time developed strong alliances with key politicians and policy players, that they had the most influence.

Finally, one of the most interesting themes to emerge out of the research was the impact that individuals, emotions and relationships had on the decision-making process. For example, it became clear that it was the personal commitment of successive Attorney Generals to the principles and philosophies of the *Kids In Justice Report* and their standing in Cabinet that helped to drive the early legislative reforms through. I was provided with many anecdotes about both excellent and hopeless Ministers and Director Generals and the impact that they individually had on policy outcomes. Some ministers were seen to be really in tune with their policy responsibilities and to have the political skills to be able to represent their portfolio in Cabinet, whereas other Ministers were seen to have no clue whatsoever or simply didn't care about juvenile justice. These individuals were considered to be solely concerned with their political image and career advancement based on performance-based achievements. It was also made clear to me that the quality of relationships between Ministers and Director Generals had a direct influence on the quality of juvenile justice policy decision-making. In one instance, when that relationship deteriorated, both the Minister and the Director General began leaking stories to the press, which naturally had a detrimental effect on future policy productivity. In another situation, office gossip about a romantic relationship between a Director General and a Minister created an atmosphere of distrust about their decisions in the relevant Department.

The charisma and authority of individuals also affected the culture, philosophical outlook and practices of organisations. For example, the Director General of Juvenile Justice from the early 1990s until 2002 had a passionate commitment to rehabilitation, diversion and social justice. Once she left, it became much easier for other discourses and rationalities of juvenile justice such as risk aversion and containment to dominate the policy landscape. Similarly, in the NSW police, a senior officer had a huge influence in shifting police policies in relation to warnings, cautions and conferencing. As a high-ranking officer, with a strong working relationship with two police commissioners, she was able, by authority of her position and sheer force of character, to introduce changes to policy and procedures that ensured that diversionary schemes were valued and incorporated into the day-to-day practices of policing. Significantly, when this officer retired and a new commissioner was appointed, the commitment of police to diversion, conferencing and custody as an option of last resort began to fall away.

Individuals made important differences to policy outcomes in other ways. A skilled, experienced public servant was seen to be a strategic operator in selecting the 'right' members of a key committee in order to steer its decisions in a particular direction. As Colebatch (2006) reminds us, it is the particular mix of people at the policy table, not just the organisations they represent, that influence policy outcomes; he argues that if the same organisations were involved in policy decision-making but were represented by a different mix of individuals, then outcomes might vary. For example, I found that there were strong emotional bonds forged by some of the policy players working on one particular committee, which appeared to have a significant impact in setting policy agendas and pushing policy decisions in a particular direction. Indeed, the friendships forged during the life of that committee's work persist today.

During the research process, I also gained a much more nuanced understanding of the relationship between the media, politics and policy. From my interviews with media players, politicians and public servants, I came to see that there is a much more inconsistent, complicated dynamic at play than many criminological analyses allow.

The landscape of politics and policy has no doubt been shaped by the 24-hour news cycle, public relations and spin, and the investment of vast amounts of resources in media monitoring and government and departmental media units (Lee and McGovern 2013). Yet, from my research, the capacity of the media to influence the policy agenda was highly contingent and shaped by an ever-changing relationships between politicians, public servants and different media forms.[7] In the early days of the Labor government, led by a former journalist—Premier Bob Carr, the government's media strategy was well developed, ministers were ready to defend the government's position and people who understood public policy were in charge of their media and communications teams. In this way, the government directed the media spin cycle. However, I was repeatedly told by interviewees that as the Labor government began to run out of ideas by the late 1990s, and key experienced media and communications staff left, and Ministers including successive Attorney Generals resigned, the situation deteriorated. As one of my interviewees told me, it came to a situation where there was 'little policy substance

---

[7] The research period predated the surge in social media and no doubt the landscape has changed since.

behind media statements' resulting in a situation where the 'the spin and the reaction pushes policy rather than the other way round' (Participant 8). In these circumstances, she argued, policy becomes inconsistent and underdeveloped as the media gain the upper hand 'because you're still in that little abusive relationship cycle but you're not the abuser anymore, you're actually being abused' (Participant 8). Policy decision-making becomes shaped by how the policy will sell to the media and also by the objective of maintaining good relations with those sections of the media that are seen to have populist credentials, rather than due to the integrity of the decision.

It is still important to remember that not all media-driven campaigns become automatically embedded in policy and legislative reforms. For example, the balance of power in the two NSW houses of parliament in the 1990s was held by a small number of progressive independent politicians who played an important part in amending or blocking more law and order style proposals. Skilled lobbyists like the YJC, also used their own media skills and lobbying techniques to change the course of policy decisions.

Conclusion

> In social science, reflexivity is not a decorative device, a luxury or an option ... Rather it is an indispensable ingredient of rigorous investigation and lucid action. (Wacquant 2011: 239)

My search for understanding and explanation of how youth justice policy developed in NSW led me on a journey imbued with reflexivity. From the impetus for the project, which was borne out of my own praxis, through adopting a theoretical approach which has complex dynamic interaction as a fundamental feature, via qualitative iterative research, to my discovery and acceptance of the importance of personalities, emotion, friendships (and enmities) in the policy process. All of these factors came together to provide me with a richer, deeper understanding of decision-making.

By engaging empirically in understanding policy in action, we build up criminological knowledge of the policy process and contribute to the emerging literature in criminology concerned with policy, such as the recent work of Hobbs and Hamerton (2014). By integrating the experiences of those who have been involved in the field, as this volume is doing, our understanding is deepened and our capacity to engage more effectively in policy is enhanced.

References

Australian Human Rights Commission (AHRC) (2014) *Social Justice and Native Title Report 2014,* Aboriginal and Torres Strait Islander Social Justice Commissioner https://www.humanrights.gov.au/social-justice-and-native-title-reports accessed March 2015.

Bargen, J., Clancey, G. and Chan, J. (2005) Development of the Young Offenders Act. In J. Chan (ed) *Reshaping Juvenile Justice: The New South Wales Young Offenders Act 1997,* Sydney: Sydney Institute of Criminology.

Bartels, L and Richards, K. (2011) The Story Behind the Stories: Qualitative Criminology Research in Australia. In L Bartels and K. Richards (eds) *Qualitative Criminology Stories from the Field,* Sydney: Hawkins Press: 1–10.

Barton, A. and Johns, N. (2013) *The Policy Making Process in the Criminal Justice System,* Abingdon: Oxon.

Bennett, A. (2004) *The History Boys,* London: Faber & Faber.

Blagg H. (2008) *Crime, Aboriginality and the Decolonisation of Justice,* Sydney: Hawkins Press.

Bourdieu, P. (1977) *Outline of a Theory of Practice,* Cambridge: Cambridge University Press.

Bourdieu, P. and Wacquant, L. (1992) *An Invitation to Reflexive Sociology,* Chicago: University of Chicago Press.

Byrne, D. (1998) *Complexity Theory and Social Science,* London: Routledge.

Byrne, D. (2011) *Applying Social Science: The Role of Social Research in Politics, Policy and Practice,* University of Bristol, Bristol: The Policy Press.

Byrne, D. and Callaghan, G. (2014) *Complexity Theory and the Social Sciences: The State of the Art,* London: Routledge.

Callaghan, G. (2005) 'Accessing Habitus: Relating Structure and Agency Through Focus Group Research' *Sociological Research Online* 10(3). URL (accessed Dec. 2009): http://www.socresonline.org.uk/10/3/callaghan.html

Callaghan, G. (2008) 'Evaluation and Negotiated Order: Developing the Application of Complexity Theory', *Evaluation* 14(4): 399–411.

Chan, J. (2005) Implementation of the Young Offenders Act. In J. B. L. Chan (ed.) *Reshaping Juvenile Justice: the New South Wales Young Offenders Act 1997*, Sydney: Sydney Institute of Criminology: 25–46.

Chancer, L. and McLaughlin, E. (2007) 'Public Criminologies: Diverse Perspectives on Academia and Policy', *Theoretical Criminology* 11(2): 155–173.

Cohen, S. (2002) *Folk Devils and Moral Panics*, London: Routledge.

Colebatch, H.K. (2006) Mapping the Work of Policy. In H. K. Colebatch (ed.) *Beyond the Policy Cycle*, Sydney: Allen & Unwin: 1–19.

Considine, M. (2005) *Making Public Policy: Institutions, Actors, Strategies*, Cambridge: Polity.

Cunneen, C., Baldry E., Brown D., Schwartz M., and Steel, A. (2013) *Penal Cultures and Hyper-incarceration: the Revival of the Prison*, London: Ashgate.

Fergusson, R. (2007) 'Making Sense of the Melting Pot: Multiple Discourses in Youth Justice Policy', *Youth Justice* 7(3): 179–194.

Fishwick, E. (2015) '*When the Stars Align*': Decision-making in the NSW Juvenile Justice System 1990–2005. PhD Thesis, University of Sydney.

French, R.D, (2012) 'The Professors on Public Life', *The Political Quarterly* 83 (3): 532–540.

Garside, R. (2008) 'Criminal Justice Matters' Panel Discussion on *Influencing Policy*, British Criminology Conference (July), University of Huddersfield.

Geyer, R. and Rihani, S. (2010) *Complexity and Public Policy: A New Approach to 21ˢᵗ Century Politics, Policy and Society*, Abingdon: Routledge.

Henry, A. and McAra L. (2012) 'Negotiated Order: Implications for Theory and Practice in Criminology', *Criminology and Criminal Justice* 12 (4): 341 -345.

Hogg, R (2001) 'Penality and Modes of Regulating Indigenous Peoples in Australia' *Punishment and Society* 3(3): 355–379.

Hogg, R. and Brown, D. (1998) *Rethinking Law and Order*, Sydney: Pluto Press.

Hobbs, S. and Hamerton, C. (2014) *The Making of Criminal Justice Policy*, London: Routledge.

Hollway, W. and Jefferson, T. (2013) *Doing Qualitative Research Differently: Free Association, Narrative and the Interview Method*, 2ⁿᵈ Edition, London: Sage.

Howlett, M. and Ramesh M. (2003) *Studying Public Policy: Policy Cycles and Policy Subsystems*, Oxford: Oxford University Press.

Jewkes, Y. (2011) 'Auto-ethnography and Emotion as Intellectual Resources: Doing Prison Research Differently', *Qualitative Inquiry* 18 (1): 63–75.

Jones, T. and Newburn, T. (2004) The Convergence of US and UK Crime Control Policy: Exploring Substance and Process. In Newburn, T. and Sparks, R. (eds.) *Criminal Justice and Political Cultures: National and International Dimensions of Crime Control*, Cullompton: Willan Publishing: 123–144.

Juvenile Justice Advisory Council of NSW (1993) *Future Directions for Juvenile Justice in New South Wales*, Green Paper February. Sydney, NSW Government Press.

Karstedt, S (2004) Durkheim, Tarde and Beyond: The Global Travel of Crime Policies in Newburn. In T. Newburn and R. Sparks (eds.) *Criminal Justice and Political Culture: National and International Dimensions of Crime Control*, Cullompton: Willan Publishing: 16–29.

Kingdon, J. (2003) *Agendas, Alternatives and Public Policies*, 2nd Edition, New York: Longman.

Lee, M. and McGovern, A., (2013) *Policing and the Media: Public Relations, Simulations and Communications*, London: Routledge.

Loughnan, A. (2009) 'The Legislation We Had to Have? The Crimes (Criminal Organisations Control) Act 2009 (NSW)' *Current Issues in Criminal Justice* 20(3): 457–465.

Mackay, F. Kenny, M., Chappell, L. and Donnelly, N. (2010) 'New Institutionalism Through a Gender Lens: Towards a Feminist Institutionalism?' *International Political Science Review* 31(5): 573–588.

McAra, L. and McVie, S. (2012). 'Negotiated Order: The groundwork for a theory of offending pathways', *Criminology and Criminal Justice* 12 (4): 347–375.

Mosse, D. (2004) 'Is Good Policy Unimplementable? Reflections on the Ethnography of Aid', *Policy and Practice Development and Change* 35(4): 639–671.

Muncie, J. (2009) *Youth & Crime*, London: Sage.

Newburn, T. and Sparks, R. (2004) Criminal Justice and Political Cultures. In T. Newburn and R. Sparks (eds.) *Criminal Justice and Political Cultures: National and International Dimensions of Crime Control*, Cullompton: Willan: 1–15.

Noetic Solutions Pty Ltd (2010) *A Strategic Review of the New South Wales Juvenile Justice System*, Canberra: Noetic Solutions Pty.

Pycroft, T. (2014) Complexity Theory: An Overview. In T. Pycroft and C. Bartollas (eds) *Applying Complexity Theory: Whole Systems Approaches to Criminal Justice and Social Work* Bristol: Policy Press: 15–38.

Pycroft, T. and Bartollas, C. (eds) (2014) *Applying Complexity Theory: Whole Systems Approaches to Criminal Justice and Social Work*, Bristol: Policy Press.

Ransley, J. (2011) From Evidence to Policy and Practice in Youth Justice. In A. Stewart, T. Allard and S. Dennison (eds) *Evidence Based Policy & Practice in Youth Justice*, Annandale: The Federation Press: 225–241.

Stevens, A. (2010) 'Telling Policy Stories: An Ethnographic Study of the Use of Evidence in Policy-making in the UK' *Journal of Social Policy* 40(2): 237–255.

Stubbs, J. (2010) 'Re-examining Bail and Remand for Young People in NSW', *Australian & New Zealand Journal of Criminology* 43(3): 485–505.

Taylor, N. (2009) 'Juveniles in Detention in Australia 1981–2007', *AIC Reports* Monitoring Reports No. 5 Canberra, Australian Institute of Criminology.

Tobin, J. (2013) Children's Rights in Australia: confronting the challenges in Gerber. In P. & M. Castan (eds) *Contemporary Perspectives on Human Rights Law in Australia,* Sydney: Lawbook Co. Thomson Reuters: 275–300.

Van Swaaningen, R. (1999) 'Reclaiming Critical Criminology: Social Justice and the European Tradition', *Theoretical Criminology* 3(1): pp. 5–28.

Wacquant, L. (2011) 'From "Public Criminology" to the Reflexive Sociology of Criminological Production and Consumption A Review of Public Criminology? by Ian Loader and Richard Sparks London, Routledge 2010', *British Journal of Criminology* 51: 438–448.

Walby S. (2007) 'Complexity Theory, Systems Theory, and Multiple Intersecting Social Inequalities', Philosophy of the Social Sciences December 37(4): pp. 449–470.

Wong, K., Bailey, B. and Kennedy, D.T. (2010) *Bail Me Out: NSW Young People and Bail,* Sydney: Youth Justice Coalition and Public Interest Advocacy Centre.

Young, J. (2009) 'Moral Panic: Its Origins in Resistance, Ressentiment and the Translation of Fantasy into Reality', *British Journal of Criminology* 49(1): 4–16.

Youth Justice Coalition (1990) *Kids In Justice: A blueprint for the nineties,* Sydney: Law & Justice Foundation NSW.

Zedner, L. (2009) *Security,* London: Routledge.

4

Towards Hope, Solidarity and Re-humanisation

Ruari-Santiago McBride

Introduction

In the UK, as elsewhere, researchers of criminal justice policy and practice are enmeshed in a web of neoliberal political dogma, economic austerity and a drive towards evidence-based policy and practice. Their activities and outputs have become embroiled in a political project that promotes cost-effectiveness and cost-efficiency over all other principles, seeks to dramatically reduce public expenditure by promoting privatisation and attempts to depoliticise government decision-making through the application of scientific evidence. They are increasingly pushed towards conducting evaluative research *for* policy rather than carrying out critical investigations *of* policy. In this neoliberal ecology, it is essential that researchers practice reflexivity, which is defined here as a critical process of self-examination and contextual contemplation that enables introspective reflections on the personal biases and structural influences that shape the activities of criminal justice researchers.

R.-S. McBride (✉)
University of Witwatersrand, Johannesburg, South Africa

© The Author(s) 2017
S. Armstrong et al. (eds.), *Reflexivity and Criminal Justice,*
DOI 10.1057/978-1-137-54642-5_4

In examining researcher reflexivity, I draw on the writings of Loïc Wacquant and Paulo Freire. I argue that researcher reflexivity presents an opportunity to ask critical questions about how criminal justice research, policy and practice are linked to wider forms of social insecurity and precariousness; founded on dehumanising discourses; and rely on a naïve understanding of researcher objectivity. In making this argument, I reflect on my subjective experiences of investigating personality disorder policy and practice within the criminal justice system, and so provide the reader with clear examples of the utility of reflexivity. In conclusion, I suggest reflexivity, if conducted collectively, can provide the basis for emancipatory acts that promote solidarity between researchers and socially marginalised groups; re-humanise criminal justice discourses; and radically reimagine the future direction of criminal justice policy and practice.

Neoliberal Criminal Justice Policy and Practice

Since the 1980s neoliberal forms of governance have become the norm within post-industrial nation states, such as the USA and the UK. At the heart of this neoliberal political project is the aim of reducing public expenditure while simultaneously creating new profit-making industries. This strategy, which aims to consumerise and marketise public services, has involved incremental organisational reforms that have streamlined managerial control, promoted performance orientated goals and situated cost-efficiency and cost-effectiveness as the principle aims of public policy (see Davies 2003; Deem and Brehony 2005; Pollitt 2003; Randle and Brady 1997). Following the 2008 global banking crisis, countries around the world have experienced economic recession, and, with a popular mandate or otherwise, embarked upon policies of austerity in an attempt to reduce public spending. A consequence of this has been significant reductions in government expenditure on public services and the subsequent acceleration of their privatisation. Government institutions created, in theory at least, 'for the public good', are increasingly subjected to market standards as well as deregulated 'for private profit'. A corollary of this process of marketisation and privatisation has been consumerisation, whereby citizens with rights have been repositioned as consumers with choice. This has fed into the increasing individualisation and responsibilisation of social issues, with policy problems framed as matters of individual rather than collective responsibility.

The UK's criminal justice system instantiates these neoliberal principles in action. Since the 1980s, criminal justice agencies have been restructured along managerial lines in an attempt to improve efficiency and reduce expenditure (see Boin et al. 2006; McEvoy 2001; Mennicken 2013). Within this context risk has become the key organising principle of criminal justice policy and practice, as is evident in the UK's risk-based sentencing framework whereby the length of prison sentences, parole decisions and release conditions are shaped by expert risk assessments (see Home Office 2002, 2005a, 2005b). The bureaucratic reliance on forensic risk assessments has enabled more pervasive and personal forms of discipline and punishment, such as targeted treatments and direct case management (Maurutto and Hannah-Moffat 2006). The risk-centric nature of UK's culture of control (Garland 2001), in turn, is linked to the increasing psychologisation of 'criminality', which is founded on a presumed link between cognitive faults and 'criminal behaviour'. Subsequently, cognitive behavioural techniques have become the hegemonic mode of 'offender rehabilitation' (Pilgrim 2011). These developments have helped to individualise 'crime' and divorce it from conditions of endemic social insecurity and precariousness. The primary goal of criminal justice agencies continues to be rehabilitation, but few policymakers or practitioners take, or have, the time to reflect on the social circumstances to which people are being rehabilitated.

A side project of neoliberalism has been a purposeful attempt to depoliticise public policy and practice (see Bourdieu and Wacquant 1999). In the UK, this is most clearly palpable in the drive towards evidence-based policy and practice. 'Evidence-based' is an increasingly normative neologism that suggests that government policy and practice should be based on objective, unbiased scientific evidence and thus be apolitical (see HM Government 2012). The evidence-based dictum has generated a new economy around policy and practice-orientated research that has been institutionalised within academia through the UK's Research Excellence Framework's impact factor (see also the Introduction and Blaustein in this volume). As a result, the livelihoods of criminal justice researchers are institutionally bound to the imperative of generating policy/practice relevant evidence. Within the current ecology of neoliberal penality, it is essential that these researchers pause to reflect on the political economy surrounding the production, circulation and consumption of criminal justice knowledge.

Reflexivity in Criminal Justice Research

Loic Wacquant (2001, 2002, 2008, 2009, 2011) has been at the forefront of critically investigating the relationship between neoliberalism and trends in penality in the USA. His approach has built upon the work of other critical scholars, such as Foucault (1977, 1991) and Garland (2001), who moved their analysis beyond understanding 'crime' and 'criminal behaviour' in an attempt to understand how post-industrial criminal justice systems operate as dispersed, yet interconnected, webs of discourses and practices that discipline, regulate and control undesirable social groups. Wacquant has shown how neoliberal policies within the USA have led to the simultaneous erosion of welfare provisions, widening social inequality and expansion of criminal penality (2011: 438). A consequence of this has been the dramatic rise in the US prison population, with 'the land of the free' becoming home to largest number of imprisoned people in the world. By the end of 2014, over 1.5 million people reside in state and federal custody (Bureau of Justice Statistics 2015). This upward surge in prison detention is mirrored in the UK where the prison population rose by 41,800 between June 1993 and June 2012 to over 86,000 (PRT 2013). Wacquant has argued that the criminal justice system does not simply function to protect the public, but to discipline members of the working class, warehouse disruptive elements of the population and, in turn, reaffirm governmental authority. Wacquant's research is reinforced by a study conducted in the UK that shows people who are sent to prison are likely to be poor, undereducated, unemployed and suffering from emotional and psychological distress; and that prison is more likely to exacerbate this social disadvantage rather than ameliorate it (see Social Exclusion Unit 2002).

Wacquant (2011) has highlighted the need to lay bare the political economy of criminological knowledge through reflexive research practice. For Wacquant, researcher reflexivity entails empirical analysis of the institutional and structural conditions under which criminal justice research is funded and conducted, how it is deployed and by whom, and to its ideological underpinnings and effects. This expansive project requires that researchers situate their research, as well as themselves, within the social field of power and appreciate the authority of academic, bureaucratic, political and journalistic institutions and actors. For researchers working in post-industrial nation states, this requires reflexive engagement with the neoliberal ecology within which research is produced, validated and appropriated (or ignored) (Wacquant 2011: 442). The aim of this *reflexive sociology of criminological knowledge* is to create a vision that will transform modern penality and move towards remedying the institutional problems perpetuated by neoliberal public policy (Wacquant 2011: 445–6). In this regard, Wacquant suggests reconceptualising and reframing criminal justice research away from criminology (the science of crime) towards a civic social science of justice (the study of justice). This semantic shift redirects the aim of research practice *away* from disciplinary isolation and the intellectual separation of crime from its social, political and cultural determinants, and *towards* a focus on the extra-penological significance of crime and extra-criminological functions of punishment. Wacquant's provocation, then, is to see reflexivity as part of a grander project of radically transforming the way justice is thought about, discussed and practiced.

In his call for the development of a civic social science of justice, Wacquant (2011) describes three forms of researcher reflexivity: (a) *egological reflexivity*, which focuses on the person of the researcher; (b) *textual reflexivity*, which focuses on the politics of the language and rhetoric; and (c) *epistemic reflection*, which focuses on the context of social science knowledge production. All three forms of reflexivity are essential if researchers, in collaboration with others, are to contribute to the radical re-imagination of criminal justice policies and practices. In this respect, the legacy of Paulo Freire (1971, 1994, 2014) provides insight into the value of reflexivity as a process of re-knowing the self in order to recreating society.

Freire's project was pedagogical and set within the context of post-colonial and dictatorial Brazil where poverty was endemic. Inspired by other revolutionary thinkers such as Fanon (1961 [1974]), Freire recognised that education could both be a tool for oppression, used both to further subjugate people to the interests of powerful social elites, and as a means to overcome oppression, used to liberate people from subjugation. For Freire, enabling reflexivity was central to realising the liberating potential of education. He felt that acquiring skills and consuming knowledge was not enough, and that a person must be able to critically reflect on knowledge so that they can understand themselves, their position within the social order and consider difficult existential questions, such as *what is justice?* Reflexivity, Freire (2014) argued, is thus a lifelong process that involves re-knowing the self, questioning how we may act (inadvertently, or otherwise) to dehumanise and oppress others as well as acting to achieve a more just social order.

This understanding of reflexivity is a positive one. It directs researchers investigating criminal justice policy and practice to (a) challenge fatalism and promote hope among socially oppressed groups; (b) challenge dehumanising rhetoric and promote humanising discourses; and (c) challenge individualism and promote social solidarity. In this light, reflexivity becomes a process of subjectivity that propels researchers to participate in meaningful social action, both as part of and beyond their research activities. Researcher reflexivity thus must be more than a form of intellectual masturbation that decries the social and political abuses of researchers and their research. Instead, it should be a process of deep personal introspection that results in a re-knowing of the self, which, in turn, stimulates direct actions that challenge the injustices of neoliberal penal policies and practices and contributes to a positive re-imagination of what justice can be.

Researcher Positionality

Egological reflexivity centres on the *person of the researcher* and how his or her biography, identity, social standing and experiences impact the research process. This form of reflexivity, particularly when published as text, is in danger of being considered academic navel-gazing (see also, Introduction). However, to say reflexivity should not be concerned with the biographic idiosyncrasy of the individual researcher, as Bourdieu did (Wacquant 1989), or to pathologise it, as Wacquant (2011) has by labelling it narcissistic, is problematic; for to do so denies the relevance of criminal justice researchers' class, skin colour, ethnicity, gender identity, sexuality and/or religion as significant determinants within the research process. Combined, these overlapping factors shape a researcher's identity and thus *positionality*, which is defined as a person's position within the historically situated and culturally specific social field in which research takes place. I argue, however, reflecting on positionality does not need to be a self-indulgent endeavour; rather it has the potential to enable researchers to appreciate their own privileges and thus produce awareness of their own inherent prejudices.

Reflecting on positionality is inevitably an introspective process that involves critical self-questioning of normative assumptions and perceptions by acquiring new knowledge from a wide array of conflicting sources. Engaging in such a process does not necessarily have to be a psychoanalytical process, but it does rely on an understanding that we are all *uncompleted beings* with the capacity for re-knowing who we are as active agents within a community of beings (Freire 2014). Reflecting on positionality can thus be a transformative experience that alters the researcher's world view and unquestioned assumptions. Practicing reflexivity can therefore enable criminal justice researchers to enter the research field with fresh perspectives and to act in counter-normative ways. From this understanding, if criminal justice researchers were to collectively reflect on their positionality it would support the re-imagination of the reality of criminal justice research, policy and practice.

Let me 'navel gaze'. When beginning my PhD research (2011–14) into personality disorder policy and practice within Northern Ireland's criminal justice system, I had relatively little experience of criminological or penological issues. Having read key sociological texts, such as *Discipline and Punishment* (Foucault 1977) and *Asylums* (Goffman 1961), I approached the field of research with a critical mentality, viewing prisons as total institutions and mental health policy as a means to manage and regulate deviant bodies who challenged the moral order. Using my privileged status as a (white, male, British, heterosexual) graduate student researcher, I was able to gain access to a prison mental health day centre as an art facilitator (see Browne and McBride 2015). Working as an art facilitator, rather than purely as a researcher, I assumed that I would be able to engage with the structurally disempowered men I encountered in the day centre in an equitable manner. Instead of simply interviewing prisoners and extracting the information I required, I presumed that by drawing, painting and moulding clay with them I would be able to engage in mutually beneficial dialogue. I believed this approach would enable me to use my privilege to gain fresh insights into the reality of prison life, which would in turn enable me to critique and progressively transform mental health policy and practice inside prisons, while prisoners would benefit from personal insights. This would in turn enable them to reflect on and understand their situation better. The evocative artwork that was produced was later displayed in multiple public exhibitions. I supposed exhibiting the artwork would help raise public awareness of the emotional and psychological challenges prisoners face.

As this unfolded over time, I continually reflected on the legitimacy of my assumptions. I came to appreciate that my research, like all prison research, involves an asymmetry of power relations, which is likely to benefit the researcher and institutional actors more than prisoners. The prisoners who participated in the art project may have gained some temporary solace, but it is unlikely that their lives significantly changed for the better as a result. On the other hand, facilitating the art project contributed to the propulsion of my academic career and the careers of certain institutional actors. The art exhibitions, meanwhile, provided good PR for the prison service. However, rather than being weighed down by these self-critical insights, I used them to inform the direction of my research at a later stage. Consequently, instead of collaborating with the probation service in a similar venture, I chose to engage with a group of former prisoners working to establish their own peer-support service. This enabled me to avoid issues of collusion with 'the system' and to use my positionality to bolster the capacity of a grassroots initiative. This process of reflexivity, thus, afforded me with the opportunity to contribute, in a small way, to the mobilisation of former prisoners who were engaged in transforming justice at a local level.

Reflecting on positionality, as I have just done, enables researchers to probe their privileges and the uncritical assumptions they may hold. Inherent power dynamics shape all social science research, due to researchers' collective status as powerful experts with an objectifying gaze vis-à-vis research participants' status as objects and subjects of scientific knowledge and practice (see Wacquant 1989). Within the field of criminal justice policy and practice, this hierarchy can be compounded by intersectional issues of class, ethnicity and gender. Without reflecting on positionality, researchers are in danger of hiding their privilege and acting paternalistically (Macedo 2014). Consequently, researchers can inadvertently, or otherwise, act to support oppressive power relations within society. Ultimately, reflecting on positionality requires researchers to ask themselves: *for what am I in favour and for what am I against?* Answering such questions requires researchers to accept that research into criminal justice policy and practice is never a neutral endeavour, but a process implicated within an institutional power matrix. Coming to terms with this predicament empowers researchers to consciously locate themselves within the neoliberal economy penality and, potentially, to challenge it.

Political Poetics

Textual reflexivity, Wacquant (2011) points out, requires considering the politics embedded in language. This involves critically examining the words used by researchers when disseminating findings; policy-makers when drafting policy documents; and practitioners in everyday situations. It requires researchers to look beyond the explicit meanings of words and consider their political ramifications. The importance of this form of reflexivity is founded in the assumption that language is fundamental both in the communication of human experiences and in structuring the possibilities of human subjectivities. Charting how language use develops over times enables us to understand how commonly used words that appear neutral at a given historical moment are in fact laden with political inferences that shape how people think about, discuss and act towards particular groups of people. Textual reflexivity is vital for researchers working in the field of criminal justice as it promotes awareness of the symbolic functions of the language used to craft penal policies and the ways in which institutional discourses shape the experiences of those within the criminal justice system.

Textual reflexivity was an important part of my approach to doctoral research into personality disorder policy and practice. It is common for people diagnosed with a psychiatric condition and found guilty of a criminal offense to be classified as a mentally disordered offender, or referred to in everyday prison discourse as an MDO. I came to understand this acronym, and the term, as labelling: a classification process that dehumanises people by reducing the richness of their life experiences into an administrative shorthand. For people labelled as an MDO their personal identity is erased, their biography annihilated and the structural conditions in which they grew up and lived exorcised. The use of MDO is therefore not neutral but highly political. On an individual level, it simultaneously pathologises and criminalises a person: stigmatising them as a person of low moral worth. On a collective level, it creates an imagined *risky* group of people: legitimising the development of enhanced institutional security regimes. In short, I came to perceive MDO as a dehumanising label with the potential to restrict autonomy and freedom. Recognising the oppressive extra-criminological functions of MDO enabled me to avoid using the label uncritically while designing my research, collecting and analysing my data, and when disseminating my research. Instead I used phrasing that was more accurate and humanistic, although slightly cumbersome, such as *prisoner diagnosed with personality disorder* or *former prisoners suffering emotional and/or psychological distress.* Such phrasing recognises that people can be in, or have gone through, the criminal justice system and simultaneously, or subsequently, experience 'mental health issues' without conflating these two distinct facets of a person's life. Textual reflexivity thus allowed me to critically probe a dominant discourse and to choose whether to comply or resist its normative assumptions.

If researchers undertake textual reflexivity and critically engage with the language of criminal justice policy and practice they can actively challenge dehumanising discourses. It requires researchers to pay attention to political implications of linguistic nuances and to how, within documents and across institutional spaces, different words and phrases are used to discuss the same phenomenon. Textual reflexivity attunes us to the divergent perspectives and experiences of justice. It pushes us not to uncritically use politically potent terms and phrases, such as 'risky', 'dangerous' and 'mentally disordered', without attempting to decode their symbolic associations. Ultimately, the practice of textual reflexivity by researchers drives us to ask ourselves a series of critical questions (see de Oliveira 2014). *In whose interests does the language I use favour? Does the language I use dehumanise those in contact with the criminal justice system? And, does the discourse of criminal justice institutions erode hope and promote fatalism among people within the criminal justice system?* By asking these questions, criminal justice researchers will be able to positively transform how we speak about justice and support the development of a re-humanising justice discourse. We may be more inclined to talk about social justice, rather than criminal justice; about hope, rather than risk; and about solidarity, rather than individualism. Over time, such reflection may support the development of a new reflexive discourse that can provide the foundation for re-imagining how we conceptualise and practice justice.

One way in which this is already happening is through the emergence of 'convict criminology' in both the USA and UK, which, as the name suggests, is a new school of thought made up of criminologists who have been convicted of a crime (see Ross and Richards 2003). Reacting to their collective dissatisfaction with the misrepresentation of 'convicts' within mainstream criminology, the media and elsewhere, convict criminologists are embarking on a collective, critical and reflexive process that seeks, among other things, to develop a new vocabulary. This aims to challenge existing definitions within criminal justice policy and practice and present new ways forward. Learning from, and working with, convict criminologists will enable other criminal justice researchers to contribute to this intellectual revolution.

Situated Research

Beyond egological and textual reflexivity, Wacquant (2011) calls for researchers to practice *epistemic reflexivity* and dissect the social conditions in which modern criminal justice research is produced, disseminated and consumed. This is perhaps the most challenging form of reflexivity to act on, as researchers are limited in their capacity to exert power over how the knowledge they produce is used. Nevertheless, epistemic reflexivity is at the core of Wacquant's call to develop a reflexive sociology of justice and penality. A difficult and time-consuming process, it requires researchers to locate their research within the current neoliberal ecology of criminal justice policy and practice, which nudges researchers to conduct research that has a social impact and contributes to the development of evidence-based policy and practice.

With its roots in medical and health sciences, the drive towards evidence-based policy normatively suggests that the solutions to criminal justice problems can be best developed if underpinned by rigorous scientific research. It thus contributes to a mythological hierarchy of methods that situates positivistic research using quantitative methods as the gold standard and positions interpretative research using a qualitative research design as mere background information (Petticrew and Roberts 2003). Consequently methodologies that claim to be objective and apolitical have become the most influential among policymakers. In line with neoliberal principles, research that seeks to identify the most cost-effective and efficient solutions to criminal justice policies in a supposedly unbiased manner, for example, randomised-control trials and systematic reviews, has been institutionally positioned as superior to methods that aim to deconstruct and contextualise social issues that have become criminal justice problems. This reflects an assumption among certain academics and policymakers that positivistic knowledge, which claims universality and independence from context and political relations, is the most valuable and thus has a greater social impact. Within the neoliberal academy, in which researchers increasingly have to defend their jobs and the relevance of their research (Hall and Page 2015), this link among methodology, epistemology and value has taken on a new significance; it shapes budget allocations, influences academic appointments and informs overall judgement of a researcher's career and entire academic disciplines (see Raffaetà and Ahlin 2015).

A significant strand of intellectual enterprise, namely constructionist, post-structural and postmodern thought, rejects the possibility of objectivity. Within this perspective research can never be neutral—no matter how far we try to distance ourselves from the object of study—as all research questions can be understood to be historically determined, a product of a theoretical gaze and thus are inherently shaped, either explicitly or implicitly, by a political bias (Freire 2014). As Bourdieu (cited in Wacquant 1989: 34) has noted: 'All research is bias, as soon as we observe the social world we introduce our perception of it'. This point is particularly salient for researchers working in the domain of criminal justice policy and practice. The evolution of the discipline of criminology, for example, long claimed to be the objective study of crime, is associated with the political desire to develop panoptical modes of surveillance for deviant subpopulations (Turner 1997). Far from being apolitical, certain forms of criminological research, such as classic and administrative criminology, have historically been implicated in the governmental regulation of problematic citizens (see Foucault 1991). Given this, it is essential that criminal justice researchers today reflect on the current institutional imperative to contribute to evidence-based policy and practice. It requires us to ask: am I conducting research *for* policy or *of* policy? While this may be a simplistic dichotomy, which negates the potential of researchers to do both—conduct critical research of as well as for policy—it nevertheless provides researchers with an important reflexive platform for designing their research.

When designing my doctoral research into mental health policy and practice in the criminal justice system, I decided to conduct research *of* policy and practice using a qualitative research design. For data collection, I drew from proponents of policy and political ethnography (see Schatz 2013; Shore and Wright 2011; Yanow 2011) who investigate policy and the way it 'creates links between agents, institutions, technologies and discourses and brings all these diverse elements into alignment' (Shore and Wright 2011: 11). This approach led me to focus my investigation on personality disorder policy and practice within the criminal justice system, rather than 'personality disordered offenders'. Consequently, the focus was on institutional discourses and practices, not personality faults and interpersonal dysfunctions. As a result, I immersed myself into the policy field; conducted participant-observation in diverse institutional spaces; interviewed a heterogeneous range of actors who made up the policy network; and gathered policy documents that were authoritative and guided institutional action. When analysing the data gathered, I drew from proponents of critical discourse analysis (see Mayr 2008; van Dijk 2003) to investigate the discursive construction of personality disorder as a policy problem and process of power that operated to marginalise certain perspectives, whitewash professional tensions and promote a policy narrative in line with the British Governments agenda of introducing authoritarian legal reforms. This research strategy meant not attempting to objectively analyse personality disorder as a pathological characteristic of a deviant sub-population, but critically investigate personality disorder policy as a technology of governance linked to broader shifts in mental health and penal policy. In so doing, the research design did not support the de-politicisation of the UK government's regulation of personality disorder. Instead, I sought to politicise it by investigating how personality disorder was used to legitimise the introduction of a risk-centric sentencing framework and to legitimise increasingly punitive practices of micro-surveillance within prisons.

Reflecting on the politics of methodological choice, Denzin (2014: 99) has argued that it is the role of researchers to help promote solidarity among oppressed members of society, to struggle alongside socially marginalised groups and to help resist forms of oppression. In this regard, he has called for research to be based on the moral principles of respect, care, equity, empathy and fairness (2014: 105). Denzin also advocates Bloom and Sawin's (2009) ethical research agenda, which (a) places the voices of the oppressed at centre; (b) works to reveal sites of change and activism; (c) aims to provide help; (d) works to affect and critique social policy; and (e) requires the researcher to make changes to the self and serve as a model for wider social change. Together, I argue, these provide a strong moral and ethical framework for the development of a reflexive research agenda beyond the institutional directive to conduct research with a social impact that contributes to evidence-based policy and practice. Within the realm of criminal justice, this research framework would encourage researchers to investigate the complex web of relations among institutional policies, spaces and practices, political doctrine, the experiences of people, the development of discourse and action overtime, and the self (see Lumsden and Winter 2014). This reflexive research agenda would benefit from a transdisciplinary approach (Nicolescu 2002, 2008), which recognises the strengths and limitations of different research traditions and attempts to combine them to the fullest effect. A transdisciplinary approach would provide a platform of open dialogue between the social sciences and humanities regarding justice and penality. Fostering interchange across and beyond individual disciplines, on an equal basis, could help to move researchers away from the blind drive to cost-effectiveness and efficiency and to refocus on promoting social justice and challenging social inequality. Thus greater critical reflection on how dominant political values shape current research goals and methodological choices can push us to ask: *What knowledge am I producing? What ends will this knowledge serve?* Taking the time to answer these questions will help promote a critical consciousness among researchers of justice and penality that rejects the fallacy of objectivity, and reorientates researchers' energy towards an ethical-socio-political research agenda that maintains methodological rigor.

Conclusion

I have argued that researchers should practice reflexivity so that they can conduct investigations with a clearer understanding of for who and to what ends they are conducting their research. Reflecting on positionality should lead many researchers to empathise with those oppressed by the criminal justice system and show solidarity with those who experience social insecurity and precariousness. *True solidarity* requires engaging in actions that support people so that they will not need future assistance (de Oliveira 2014: 77). At the local level, researchers can forge links with grassroots activists and use their social privilege to help build the capacity of actors engaged in justice and penal reform. At the national level, researchers can assist the mobilisation of dispersed networks of grassroots activists who share similar goals of penal reform. At the international level, researchers can use their institutional affiliations to facilitate discussions and debates across national borders. Initiatives in this vein have already taken place through the Convict Criminology movement. This network of former prisoners-cum-criminologists and allied researchers is working to challenge problematic criminal justice policies as well as develop peer-support programmes for prisoners seeking to attain university degrees in criminology in the UK and USA. By building local capacity, developing national networks and generating international dialogue, these reflexive researchers are supporting the development of new understandings about justice and penality, redefining criminal justice problems and, in turn, creating new strategies that oppose the pervasiveness of neo-liberal penalism.

I have argued that it is essential for researchers of justice and penality to reflect on the dehumanising potential of their own language as well as that of criminal justice policy; and, argued that such language reproduces exclusionary and marginalising practices. Taking this forward, researchers, in collaboration with grassroots activists, must work to re-humanise how we communicate about people within the criminal justice system, particularly people entangled within the prison system. This will require researchers to appreciate the symbolic capacity of language and how words shape experiences. There is a clear imperative to move beyond objectivist risk-based penal discourses that focus on individual responsibility, as well as the current fetishisation of cost-effectiveness and efficiency within policymaking. Researchers should talk more about issues of subjectivity by foregrounding personal and emotional experiences, cultural specificities and social nuances, and to exploring the application of alternative policy values such as respect, care, equity, empathy and fairness.

In re-humanising justice discourses, researchers must also consider who has access to the knowledge they produce, consider publishing in non-academic platforms and write in an accessible manner. Following this, alternative media, such as art, poetry, drama and film, should be considered valid and valued among criminal justice researchers. By moving beyond words and academic texts, researchers can allow the knowledge they produce to be consumed by a larger, lay audience, and to be used for public education.

Transforming how society discusses criminal justice matters. In co-developing a humanistic justice discourse, researchers can act to change the reality of neoliberal penality by supporting the development of counter-hegemonic criminal justice narratives. In this way, not only can they promote critical and ethical research practice, but also critical consciousness among the general population.

My final argument is anchored on the need for researchers to reflect on how they frame and carry out their research. If they do not, researchers run the risk of merely providing answers to policymakers' questions and thus becoming subservient to political authority. Instead of being consumed with future decision-making, researchers can problematize the reality of criminal justice policy and prompt policymakers and practitioners to ask internal questions. By disseminating counter-normative narratives within policy arenas, such as consultations, policy forums and parliamentary proceedings, and participating in training, researchers can encourage policymakers and practitioners to practice critical reflection themselves. Furthermore, researchers can realise a fuller civic role by actively lobbying politicians. In this regard, recognising the historically contingent nature of society and its organisation should not be a mere academic exercise. Rather, appreciation of the inherent changeability of things should drive researchers to engage in personal growth and promote social transformation (Freire 2014). Criminal justice researchers should thus use their privileged position in society to support participatory and direct democracy as well as challenge unfair policies and practices. In this way, they can reject neutrality yet still legitimately promote decriminalisation and decarceration.

References

Bureau of Justice Statistics (2015) *Prisoners in 2014*, Washington: BJS.

Bloom, L. R. and Swain, P. (2009) 'Ethical Responsibility in Feminist Research: Challenging Ourselves to do Activist Research with Women in Poverty', *International Studies of Qualitative Studies in Education* 22: 333–51.

Boin, A., James, O., and Lodge, M. (2006) 'The New Public Management "Revolution" in Political Control of the Public Sector: Promises and

Outcomes in Three European Prison Systems', *Public Policy and Administration* 21(2): 81–100.

Bourdieu, P. and Wacquant, L. (1999) 'On the Cunning of Imperialist Reason', *Theory Culture and Society* 16(1): 41–58.

Browne, B. C. and McBride, R. (2015) 'Politically Sensitive Encounters: Ethnography, Access and the Benefits of "Hanging Out"', *Qualitative Sociology Review* 10(4): 35–48.

Davies, B. (2003) 'Death to Critique and Dissent? The Policies and Practices of New Managerialism and of "Evidence-Based Practice"', *Gender and Education* 15(1): 91–103.

Deem, R. and Brehony, K. J. (2005) 'Management as Ideology: The Case of "New Managerialism" in Higher Education', *Oxford Review of Education* 31(2): 217–235.

Denzin, N. K. (2014) The Importance of Pedagogy of Solidarity. In P. Freire, A. M. A. Freire, and W. de Oliveira (eds.) *Pedagogy of Solidarity*, California: Left Coast Press.

de Oliveira, W. (2014) For a Pedagogy of Solidarity. In P. Freire, A. M. A. Freire, and W. de Oliveira (eds.) *Pedagogy of Solidarity*, California: Left Coast Press.

Fanon, F. (1961 [1974]) *The Wretched of the Earth*, Middlesex: Penguin Books.

Foucault, M. (1977) *Discipline and Punish: The Birth of the Prison*, New York: Random House.

Foucault, M. (1991) Governmentality. In G. Burchell, C. Gordon and P. Miller (eds.) *The Foucault Effect: Studies in Governmental Rationality*, Hemel Hempstead: Harvester Wheatsheaf.

Freire, P. (1971) *Pedagogy of the Oppressed*, New York: Continuum Press.

Freire, P. (1994) *Pedagogy of Hope*, New York: Continuum Press.

Freire, P. (2014) Pedagogy of Solidarity. In P. Freire, A. M. A. Freire, and W. de Oliveira (eds.) *Pedagogy of Solidarity*, California: Left Coast Press.

Garland, D. (2001) *Mass Imprisonment: Social Causes and Consequences*, London: Sage.

Goffman, E. (1961) *Asylums: Essays on the Social Situation of Mental Patients and Other Inmates*, London: Penguin.

Hall, M.C. and Page, S. J. (2015) 'Following the Impact Factor: Utilitarianism or Academic Compliance?' *Tourism Management*, htt://dx.doi.org/10.1016/j.touman.2015.05.013

HM Government (2012) *The Civil Service Reform Plan*, London: HM Government.

Home Office (2002) *Justice for All*, London: Home Office.

Home Office (2005a) *Forensic Personality Disorder: Medium secure and Community Pilot Services*, London: Home Office.

Home Office (2005b) *Dangerous and Severe Personality Disorder (DSPD): High Secure Services for Men*, London: Home Office.

Lumsden, K. and Winter, A. (Eds.) (2014) *Reflexivity in Criminological Research: Experiences with the Powerful and Powerless*, New York: Palgrave Macmillan.

Macedo, D. (2014) Re-imaging Freire Beyond Methods. In P. Freire, A. M. A. Freire, and W. de Oliveira (eds.) *Pedagogy of Solidarity*, California: Left Coast Press.

Maurutto, P. and Hannah-Moffat, K. (2006) 'Assembling Risk and the Restructuring of Penal Control', *British Journal of Criminology* 46: 438–54.

Mayr, A. (2008) *Language and Power: An Introduction to Institutional Discourse*, London: Bloomsbury Publishing.

McEvoy, K. (2001) *Paramilitary Imprisonment in Northern Ireland: Resistance, Management and Release,* Oxford: Oxford University Press.

Mennicken, A. (2013) '"Too Big to Fail and Too Big to Succeed": Accounting and Privatisation in the Prison Service of England and Wales', *Financial Accountability & Management* 29(2): 206–26.

Nicolescu, B. (2002) *Manifesto of Transdisciplinarity*, New York: SUNY Press.

Nicolescu, B. (2008) *Transdisciplinarity: Theory and Practice*, New York: Hampton Press.

Petticrew, M. and Roberts, H. (2003) 'Evidence, Hierarchies, and Typologies: Horses for Courses', *Journal of Epidemiology and Community Health* 57(7): 527–9.

Pilgrim, D. (2011) 'The Hegemony of Cognitive-Behaviour Therapy in Modern Mental Health Car', *Health Sociology Review* 20(2): 120–32.

Pollitt, C. (2003) *The essential Public Manager,* Buckingham: Open University Press.

Raffaetà, R. and Ahlin, T. (2015) 'The Politics of Publishing: Debating the Value of Impact Factor in Medical Anthropology', *Anthropology and Medicine* 22(2): 202–205.

Randle, K. and Brady, N. (1997) 'Further Education and the New Managerialism', *Journal of Further and Higher Education* 21(2): 229–39.

Ross, J. I. and Richards, S. C. (2003) *Convict Criminology*, Belmont, CA: Wadsworth.

Schatz, E. (2013) *Political Ethnography: What Immersion Contributes to the Study of Power*, Chicago: University of Chicago Press.

Shore, C. and Wright, S. (2011) Conceptualising Policy: Technologies of Governance and the Politics of Visibility. In C. Shore, S. Wright and D. Però (eds.) *Policy Worlds: Anthropology and the Analysis of Contemporary Power*, New York: Berghahn Books.

Social Exclusion Unit (2002) *Reducing Re-offending by Ex-prisoners*, London: Social Exclusion Unit.

Turner, B. S. (1997) From Governmentality to Risk: Some Reflections on Foucault's Contribution to Medical Sociology. In A. Petersen and R. Bunton (eds.) *Foucault, Health and Medicine*, London and New York: Routledge.

van Dijk, T. A. (2003) The Discourse-Knowledge Interface. In G. Weiss and R. Wodak (eds.) *Critical Discourse Analysis: Theory and Interdisciplinarity*, Basingstock: Palgrave.

Wacquant, L. (1989) 'Towards a Reflexive Sociology: A workshop with Pierre Bourdieu', *Sociological Theory* 7(1): 26–63.

Wacquant, L. (2001) 'The Penalisation of Poverty and the Rise of Neo-liberalism', *European Journal on Criminal Policy and Research*, 9(4): 401–12.

Wacquant, L. (2002) 'The Curious Eclipse of Prison Ethnography in the Age of Mass Incarceration', *Ethnography* 3(4): 371–97.

Wacquant, L. (2008) *Urban Outcasts: A Comparative Sociology of Advanced Marginality*, Cambridge: Polity.

Wacquant, L. (2009). *Punishing the Poor: The Neoliberal Government of Social Insecurity*, Durham and London: Duke University Press.

Yanow, D. (2011) 'A policy ethnographer's reading of policy anthropology'. In Shore, C., Wright, S. and Pero, D. (eds.) *Policy Worlds: Anthropology and the analysis of contemporary power*. New York, NY: Bergahn Books, Pp. 300–314.

Wacquant, L. (2011) 'From "Public Criminology" to the Reflexive Sociology of Criminological Production and Consumption: A Review of Public Criminology? By Ian Loader and Richard Sparks', *British Journal of Criminology* 51: 438–48.

5

Policy as a Crime Scene

Sarah Armstrong and Anita Lam

Mark worked in a McDonald's once but has no job now. He is not very close to any family and has no specific plans for his future. He is only 19, though, and who knows how he might develop. Katrina is 29, a decade older than Mark. She has two children; her four-year old has major sight and hearing impairments as well as a lung problem, and she has spent more time in hospitals than she cares to recall. Her parents are getting older, and one of them recently had a stroke, which is a source of deep stress for her. She is very close to her family and anxious to be with them.

Mark and Katrina have as much in common as two people who might find themselves in a supermarket at the same time. Perhaps there are predictable similarities: maybe they live in the same neighbourhood as the shop. Perhaps there are random ones like sharing a birthday. But while Mark and Katrina might otherwise pass each other on the street without stopping, they have been brought together and constituted as part

S. Armstrong (✉)
University of Glasgow, Glasgow, UK

A. Lam
York University, Toronto, Canada

© The Author(s) 2017   **101**
S. Armstrong et al. (eds.), *Reflexivity and Criminal Justice*,
DOI 10.1057/978-1-137-54642-5_5

of a single population.[1] They are both prisoners serving sentences of six months or less. While people in prison by definition have shared interests and needs and in that sense might be considered to form a group, whether or not they know each other or would choose each other's company, it is not only the fact of their confinement that draws them together. An ongoing policy drive in Scotland (as in many other places) aims to reduce the use of short prison sentences, and is targeting in particular those serving six months or less (Scottish Government 2015; Scottish Prisons Commission 2008). By drawing a circle around people serving a particular sentence, a policy process has also constituted them as an empirical phenomenon—that is, as a distinct entity that has particular origins, traits and needs. This chapter is about how policy does not simply target particular actors and social situations but participates in making them as well. By exploring this process in action through a case study of penal policy, it hopes to demonstrate the need to study policy in criminology as part of a core research programme, where policy is as much a frontline field of inquiry as street corners and jail cells. And just as the state of research on these latter sites of action has advanced significantly, so too could studies of policy be nurtured, by developing a greater capacity for critical and reflexive engagement, and deploying a wider and more inspired range of theories and methods than is currently the case (though, for inspiration, see chapters by Fishwick and McBride in this volume).

We develop this project, and model one approach to reflexivity, by conceiving of policy as a crime scene. One reason we adopt 'scene thinking' is because scenes, unlike sites, are not specific places, but instead comprise a set of spaces, affects, materials and discourses that together form a distinctive arena of action and culture (Straw 2001). This troubles conventional understandings of policy as a discrete and durable entity made in one place and delivered to another in the attempt to change behaviour (Gordon et al. 1977), reflecting instead the ways that policy can be observed constantly on the move, forming and reforming, contributing to, constituting and being constituted by the spaces and discourses it travels through (Clarke et al. 2015). The crime scene metaphor also is useful

---

[1] Mark and Katrina are pseudonyms of participants in a research project on 'users' views of punishment (see Armstrong and Weaver 2010, 2013).

because it situates policy at the centre of investigation; policy scenes ought to be as thoroughly investigated and scrutinised as crime scenes themselves. Like detectives tasked with inspecting, probing and exploring the construction of crime scenes, we turn the same kind of penetrating gaze onto policy itself. Yoked to an exercise in reflexive and critical questioning, we additionally ask what role criminology plays in producing and reacting to policy, particularly policy's constructions of crime.

Like other kinds of 'scientific facts' (Latour and Woolgar 1986), 'crime' is itself produced by the very processes that claim to discover and study it. 'Crime' then is at least partially produced by academic criminology, and academic criminologists have positioned themselves as legitimate producers of expert knowledge on crime, criminality and criminal justice. Yet academic criminology has had little occasion to be reflexive—that is, occasion to study and analyse the conditions of its own production of knowledge in order to overcome, change or critique them (Bourdieu 2004, and see, Chapter 1 in this volume). Indeed, criminologists rarely examine the conditions that underlie the production of academic criminological knowledge. Perhaps this is related to some criminologists' reticence to answering questions about the discipline itself, as such questions are not seen as intellectually stimulating, or worthy of criminologists' time and commitment (Bosworth and Hoyle 2011: 8–9). The pursuit of such reflexive questions about the criminological field, however, is of pressing importance when it comes to explaining why criminologists have often disregarded policy settings out of hand as uninteresting and empirically irrelevant cultural sites for inquiry, despite the fact that these settings produce knowledge, facts and subjects about the 'crime problem' that have a profound impact on the production of academic criminology. The knowledge products of policy processes become data for empirical investigations; they become the categories through which academic criminologists think; they serve as fuel for critical interrogation and inquiry; they produce the phenomena and actors that provide the criminological field's raison d'être.

This chapter is organised as follows. First, we identify and discuss a double absence of policy in criminology, meaning a general lack of criminological research which directly engages policy, and, where research does address policy, treating it unproblematically as a given, a black box into which evidence is fed (or not) and from which good ideas and practices emerge (or not). We then introduce our approach to policy as a crime scene, drawing from some of the literature on 'scene thinking'. This assists in the broadening out of conventional definitions of policy. We believe the scene frame assists centring policy allowing one to tackle its complexity as product, generator and setting of social and cultural processes. Finally, we bring this frame to bear on a case study of penal policy, specifically policy and reform on short prison sentences. Here we return to Mark and Katrina: in their role as subjects of penal policy, they become data doubles (Haggerty and Ericson 2000) coming to have a double presence, as real people confined in physical prisons and as part of an imaginary of a punishment problem that policy exists to solve.

Policy's Double Absence

Policy is missing in two ways in criminology. First, though with important qualifications, it is missing as a central topic of study. One qualification to this is the incorporation of criminal justice itself as an area of research alongside research on crime, which has led to a focus on the administrative and political processes through which justice actors and institutions govern and control others, and therefore on the policies which enable or constrain them. For example, drug policy, sentencing policy and victims policy are now a part of the criminological research agenda at least to the extent that research on drugs, sentencing and victims generally makes some reference to the policy context of these fields. Another qualification is the intensification of pressure, as in the UK's 'research impact' agenda, for researchers to demonstrate the importance of their work in terms of how directly it influences policy and practice. While such developments mean that policy is never far from view in criminological research, it is rarely the sole subject of research itself. It is something that research might inform, but not part of the empirical world under study.

A second way in which policy is missing in criminology, ironically, is in research on policy. Where policy is the topic of study, the focus tends to be on content and outcomes rather than processes, and the analysis tends to adopt a rationalist and instrumentalist perspective (as criminologists have observed, e.g., Newburn 2003). That is, research addresses how well policy achieves (or does not achieve) its aims, what its unintended consequences have been, who its winners and losers are. But within this approach to policy, there remains, to quote Harding in this volume, a 'hollow space'. What is policy? Who are its actors, and what are its lives and loves (Riles 2005)? How does it do its work, and what does this work consist of? What are its inner workings and politics, its particular resources and constructions of the world? These are the sorts of questions that criminologists apply to phenomena from drug dealers to courts and prisons but rarely to the processes through which drugs are criminalised and courts and prisons organised. Policy is 'black boxed', treated as a given like an independent variable, and thus 'no longer open for debate' (Riles 2005: 999, n84; Latour 1987).

One senses that the double absence of policy in criminological research arises not from its lack of relevance or potential to contribute to central questions for the discipline but due to other causes. We posit one of these causes as the troubled relationship the field has long had with the state, arising from the assumption that the relationship between state and academia is a parasitic, one-way relationship. In a sharply worded argument, Hope and Walters (2008: 23) called upon academic criminologists to boycott government research because the government 'manipulates or cherry-picks criminological knowledge and produces distorted pictures of the "crime problem"' for political gain. Academic legitimacy, they argue, must not be granted to such a corrupt process. To dissociate academic knowledges from its potential corruption and contamination by the state, criminologists have tended to conceive of academic and policy sites of criminological production as distinct, bounded realms that ought to remain separate from each other. This conceptual separation between academic criminology and policy is tied to the field's overall attempt at establishing itself as a properly scientific discipline, distinct from the institutions and impulses of governance which initially sustained it. We can see academic criminology's resistance to policy settings in reflections on the field's increasing fragmentation (Bosworth and Hoyle 2011; Ericson and Carriere 1994) and pluralism (Loader and Sparks 2011), which build on accounts of the development of the discipline along the lines of two particular knowledge projects (Garland 2002): a governmental project where research is used to more efficiently administer justice through more effective policies directed at the management and control of certain populations; and an etiological project where inquiry is aimed at explaining the root causes of crime. While these two projects can converge, they have often been placed in competition with one another in a zero-sum game of knowledge production and legitimation. Although we can trace the governmental and policy project back to the origins of the discipline (Garland 2002), it—now often rearticulated as 'administrative criminology'—has been currently constructed as a 'pejorative label' (Clarke and Felson 2011: 25). Few, if any, academic criminologists would locate their work under this category precisely because it comes with an implicit stamp of disapproval from colleagues (Cullen 2011; Hough 2014). Even though administrative criminology is a fuzzily and nebulously defined site with boundaries that have increasingly blurred with those of mainstream criminology (O'Malley 1996) and critical criminology (Pavlich 2000; Rock 1994), it currently provides both academic and critical criminologies with a chief 'sparring partner' (Young 1986: 7) and binary opposite. As an imagined site of knowledge production, administrative criminology appears as a monolithic strawman, supporting the boundary work (Gieryn 1983) and occasional evangelising (Carlen 2011) of otherwise fragmented academic criminologies. That is, the boundaries of academic criminology, in both its mainstream and critical modes, have been erected to legitimate (and represent their own activity as) knowledge produced independent of politics and the market, in an attempt at sealing off such knowledge production from policy processes.

Where Is Policy?: Scene Thinking

If policy is not 'black boxed' nor accepted unquestioningly as a durable thing, then its boundaries cannot be sealed, nor should they be by criminologists who cling to a notion of particular knowledges as independent and pure (and see, Chapter 1). This leaves us with several questions to resolve about policy: what is it, how might one engage it, and just as pertinent, *where* is it? The question of 'where' emerges once we stop treating the meaning and actors of policy as self-evident. If we cannot assume it is an object with sealed boundaries, the where becomes a central aspect of interrogation. Critical policy scholars attempt to do this by moving beyond 'a conception of policy as [a thing that moves] horizontally, across sites, and vertically from policymaking centres to "implementation" on the front line [towards envisioning] "the life of social policy – a process rather than a thing – as complex and convoluted, tracing and leaving traces of meaning and power as it travels across sites and through persons"" (Clarke et al. 2015: 9–10, quoting Kingfisher 2013). Far from being fixed, policy settings refuse to fit into the neat boundaries of a circumscribed arena of action, where there are clear delineations of a beginning and end. Even policy's products escape attempts to bind them to specific places and institutions, as policies and policy knowledges can travel from local sites of production within the closed corridors of bureaucracy to international, public arenas for discussion and back again. To capture the messiness and amorphous nature of policy settings and their products, we speak of and target policy not as a discrete site, but rather as a scene. In so doing, we explicitly treat policy like any other object of cultural analysis, as the concept of 'scene' has been primarily used to analyse cultural phenomena ranging from popular music scenes (e.g. Bennett 2004; Bennett and Peterson 2004; Shank 1994), youth subcultures (e.g. Bennett 1999; Glass 2012) and urban life (e.g. Boutros and Straw 2010; Irwin 1977). Policy, often assumed to encompass the technical activities of bureaucrats, then is placed on the same analytic footing as hip, effervescent and exciting cultural scenes, and consequently presumed to be as interesting and disruptive a phenomenon. We recognise the need to do something to entice the criminologist into studying what feels distant in space and meaning from the visceral excitement of the street and its gangs. Moreover, like Riles (2005: 985), we hope to 'bring the technical into view not as an effect or a byproduct, a tool of more important agents and forces, but as the protagonist of its own account'.

Our turn toward scene thinking aligns with the ways in which 'policy worlds' have been conceived in anthropology and interpretative political science. Specifically, the term 'policy worlds' implies that policies should not be considered essentialised or bounded entities, but rather as migrating windows onto political processes, in which multiple actors, agents, ideas and technologies interact at different sites, in order to create or consolidate new rationalities of governance and regimes of knowledge and power (Shore et al. 2011: 2). Such a processual perspective opposes the conventional practitioner perspective, which casts policy in terms of an 'authoritative instrumentalism'. That is, practitioners tend to assume that policies are objective entities that exist 'out there' as the product of decisions made by some visible, rational authority to solve a particular problem. Like the notion of 'policy worlds', we introduce the idea of 'policy scenes' to counteract presumptions that policy processes are best described as linear, hierarchical and logical. Like policy worlds, policy scenes are similarly anti-essentialising, flexible entities with elastic and fluid boundaries.

As Will Straw (2001) has argued, 'scene' is a slippery concept in cultural analysis because it has been called upon to perform multiple tasks, describing unities of highly variable scale and scope that range from local clusters of activity to practices scattered across the globe. Some of these unities are bound to specific local places, while others are loosely grouped together only through a hazy coherence between sets of practices, affinities and tastes. For example, when cultural studies scholars have examined music scenes, the term 'scene' has been applied to designate the following phenomena: (1) the recurring congregation of people at a time and place (e.g. a specific bar or café), or in Bruno Latour's (1987, 2005) terms, a point of assembly, such as a laboratory or centre of calculation, for multiple and diverse actors to do transformative work; (2) the movement of people and products along streets or strips between different spaces of congregation, or in more Foucauldian terms, the migration of techniques into new contexts and settings; and (3) all the other spatially dispersed places and activities, such as social media promotion or journalistic coverage of a music scene, that surround and support a particular cultural affinity or preference. In short, scenes can simultaneously characterise collectivities, spaces of assembly, workspaces of transformation, spaces of travel and circulation, and ethical and mediated worlds (Straw 2015). Moreover, 'scenes' might not name a thing or a phenomenon at all. Instead, Woo, Rennie and Poyntz (2015: 292) insist that 'scene' is an orientation to things, or a way of seeing the world. Specifically, scene thinking represents a decision to treat a set of individuals, institutions and practices as if they constitute a scene. Arguably, this is what members themselves do, sweeping discrete people, places, events and artefacts up into what comes to be called a scene. Focusing on the scene switches figure and ground, bringing taken-for-granted conditions of possibility to the fore. In the hands of different analysts, these might include spaces, organisations and infrastructures; affects, emotions and structures of feeling; or routes, networks and practices that make a particular scene part of the texture of a place. But to identify any or all of these as constitutive features of a scene sensitises us to the ways they provide the setting for action.

Following Woo et al. (2015), we think through policy scenes as slippery settings for action that sweep together a range of spaces, actors and materials, all the while producing 'crime' and its actors through a particular set of practices and affinities across different institutional sites. Policy scenes have a messy indeterminacy, but give coherence to something that might otherwise have an amorphous and relatively unbounded shape. The concept of 'thinking through' is also instructive particularly when it comes to analysing the production of policy because it urges us to reject the impulse to turn an analysis of policy into an examination of policymakers, a studying up exercise limited to the places where elites work. When policy itself is centred as the thing to be explained, it requires 'studying through'—that is, following a 'process of political transformation through space and time' (Wright and Reinhold 2011: 101). From the outset, then, while policymakers are part of the policy community so, too, are the people whose lives will be regulated through policy change.

Policy as Crime Scene: The Case of Penal Reform

Katrina and Mark were two of 22 people interviewed for a 2010 research project on those serving a short prison sentence in Scotland.[2] At the time they were in prison, the Scottish Government was pursuing major changes in sentencing policy as part of a larger drive to address chronically high and rising imprisonment rates in this part of the UK.[3] A nationalist Government had come into power in 2007, placing a high priority on criminal justice reform, partly as the arena in which it would sharply delineate its differences from prior UK and Scottish governments. In contrast to the direction of prison policy in England and Wales at this time, Scotland

---

[2] http://www.sccjr.ac.uk/projects/user-views-of-punishment/
[3] Scotland has a separate criminal legal and justice system, including a separate prisons service and structure.

adopted an explicitly reductionist and sceptical attitude towards prison, framing high prison populations not as evidence of effective crime control but as a symptom of civic failure. One of the Government's first acts in the area of justice policy was to pull out of advanced contract discussions to build new privatised prisons, reversing the pro-privatisation stance of the previous administration (Mulholland 2007). The new Government positioned Scotland as part of a network of small, welfarist northern European nations: 'The Government refuses to believe that the Scottish people are inherently bad or that there is any genetic reason why we should be locking up twice as many offenders as Ireland or Norway' (MacAskill 2007). It appointed an independent Scottish Prisons Commission in 2007, composed of justice officials and civic leaders, and charged it with gathering evidence and views to '[c]onsider how imprisonment is currently used in Scotland and how that use fits with the Government's wider strategic objectives'.[4] These are the key elements of the penal policy scene in Scotland in the latter part of the 2000s, which we analyse as follows.

An expansive and diffuse list of 'drivers' of prison growth emerged over the Commission's seven months of deliberations. These included rising rates of recalling people on parole to prison and disproportionate growth in the number of women in prison (SPC 2008). However, even before any evidence had been gathered by the Commission, short prison sentences were identified as a key issue of concern, raised in the Cabinet Secretary of Justice's speech launching the Commission: 'The Scottish Prison Service's ability to work with serious offenders…is being compromised by having to deal with the churn created by a large number of short sentences' (MacAskill 2007). This context further sets the scene where penal policy coagulated a series of long running debates and perspectives about the 'prison problem' in Scotland. Thus, it offers a discrete opportunity to engage with policy as a scene and to explore its cultural dynamics and reverberations.

A brief reflection on method: Sarah was engaged in this policy scene as both a researcher *of* it, and a researcher *in* it (see also Blaustein 2015). She along with another academic acted as an informal adviser to the Prisons Commission, supporting their gathering and analysis of evidence during 2008. Following on from this, an Economic and Social Research Council

---

[4] http://www.gov.scot/About/Review/spc/About [accessed 16 December 2015].

(ESRC) research grant funded her for two years to conduct an 'ethnography of penal policy' in which the aftermath of the Commission's work was followed through numerous sites from civil servant offices to conferences to prison wings. The methodological orientation drew on work by anthropologists of policy (Shore and Wright 1997; Strathern 2000) and increasingly Science and Technology Studies (STS) research, particularly on governance (Riles 2005, 2006; Davis et al. 2012; Engle Merry et al. 2015; Star 1999). At the same time, she remained a researcher in a criminological centre conducting Government-contracted and independent work on the criminal justice system of Scotland and employing conventional methods of qualitative and quantitative research. This gives a sense of the points of access to the scene, but also demonstrates the fluidity of roles of a single researcher, and the entanglement of roles generally in criminal justice research. At different points, the researcher may act as administrative criminologist, critical criminologist, autoethnographer or activist. This opens up, though not within the space constraints of this chapter, the need to question and explore the sharp division often claimed to mark the boundary between academic and critical criminology (as modes of independent knowledge production) on one side, and administrative criminology (knowledge production often characterised as reactive and compliant) on the other.

In all the sites that made up this particular policy scene, the prisoner, unsurprisingly, was the focus of attention. However, and also unsurprisingly, no prisoners or prisoner groups were invited to formally participate in the Commission process, or in the legislative process that eventually produced the policy instruments to implement reform (see also Blaustein, this volume). This raised a question for us about how prisoners, or any target population, can achieve presence in the policy processes that concern them. Put another way, how are actors located in different parts of a policy scene brought into conversation or made visible to each other? This is not just an issue about the spatial distance between a prison where prisoners live, and a Government office where civil servants draft bills. There are also social, material and cultural distances to overcome. People confined in prison and the managers and policymakers who govern the conditions of their confinement use different vocabularies, have different understandings of punishment and different reasons for their involvement in penal policy. They also have varying levels of access to technologies of communication and means of representation.

We want to isolate two modes of representation, or techniques of presence, that operated in this policy scene, both related to the issue of short prison sentences. The first is statistical information as a way of documenting the reality of prison, and the second is a research project on 'user views of short sentences' that made Mark, Katrina and a number of others visible in this policy scene. As noted, short sentences were identified at the outset as a problem and therefore became a focus for developing recommendations. Although short prison sentences have been viewed as undesirable since the nineteenth century (Faraldo Cabana 2015), what kinds of problems do short prison sentences cause? The conventional critique is that a short spell in prison offers insufficient opportunity either to inflict enough pain to deter, or enough time to trigger long-term rehabilitation: 'It could hardly be clearer that short-term imprisonment fails to end criminal careers' (SPC 2008: 39). The Prisons Commission further commented that the prevalence of short prison sentences constituted a 'problematic and largely unnecessary use of prison' (Id.: 13). The quantitative reality of a prison problem rooted in short sentences was focused on one key statistic: the percentage of prison sentences handed down by courts that were for six months or less. At the time of the Commission's role in prison policy, this figure was 83 % (SPC 2008: 13). That is, fewer than two in ten prison sentences pronounced in Scotland were for longer than six months, a statistic which was felt to establish a powerful and self-evident case of the overuse of short sentences. This rested on two premises: first, that the uncontested proper use of prison is as a place of confinement exclusively for those who commit such serious and violent crimes that they must be kept away from society for a substantial period; and second, a spell of imprisonment for less than a minimal period (typically one year[5]) is pointless, offering no likelihood either of punishment or rehabilitation.

The 83 % figure visibilised the problem of short sentences as the behaviour of courts, positioning the cause of short sentences as sentencers

---

[5] This latter assumption was often stated and referred to unproblematically in various policy reform conversations throughout the period of the penal policy ethnography, as noted down several times in field notes.

themselves. This is evident in the Policy Memorandum to legislation fol-lowing from the Commission's work, which stated that the objective of the law would be to 'ensure appropriate use is made by courts of short term cus-todial sentences' (Scottish Parliament 2009: 12). At this point in the policy scene's attempt to make sense of the short prison sentence, a crucial shift in representation occurred. To substantiate the effectiveness of the alternative to short prison sentences, expanded use of community-based sanctions, policymakers needed to know about the short-sentenced population. Who were the people on short sentences? What were their needs, and what kind of penal interventions would they respond to? Thus, a problematic sys-tem practice was turned into a problematic empirical population—the six-months-or-less prisoner. Although a shared length of sentence is a thin basis for group identity, it nevertheless usefully coordinated the organization of a variety of information and perspectives circulating in the policy scene. For example, the wrongness of putting people in prison for short periods was established by aggregating information about prisoners' backgrounds, such as the prevalence of drug and alcohol problems as well as difficult personal histories (Fig. 5.1). Such information aimed at concatenating a group that was 'troubled and troubling rather than dangerous' (SPC 2008: 2).

Although the graphic includes statistics about prisoners regardless of sentence length, this data was deployed in arguments for reducing or

Compared to the general population, prisoners are:	In respect of their basic skills:
• 13 times more likely to have been in care as a child	• 8 out of 10 have the writing skills of an 11 year old
• 10 times more likely to have been a regular truant from school	• 65% have the numeracy skills of an 11 year old
• 13 times more likely to be unemployed	• 5 out of 10 have the reading skills of an 11 year old
• 2.5 times more likely to have a family member who has been convicted of a criminal offence	• 7 out of 10 have used drugs before coming to prison
• 6 times more likely to have been a young father	• 7 out of 10 have suffered from at least two mental disorders
• 15 times more likely to be HIV positive	• 2 out of 10 male prisoners have previously attempted suicide
	• 37% of women prisoners have attempted suicide
• For younger prisoners aged 18-20 these problems are even more intense; their basic skills, rates of unemployment and previous levels of school exclusion are a third worse even than those of older prisoners	

Fig. 5.1 Excerpted graphic from the Scottish Prison Commission (2008) report, on prisoners' backgrounds

eliminating the use of imprisonment only for those serving the shortest sentences. Hence, through statistical documentation, six-months-or-less prisoners were fleshed out by their histories of deprivation and trauma (which provided evidence of both a cause of their imprisonment and its unfairness) and were foregrounded and connected to each other, allowing the substance abuse issues, marginalisation and victimisation of other kinds of prisoners, or of people not in prison, to fade into the background. Short prison sentences were linked to and gradually conflated with 'the least well off communities in Scotland' (SPC 2008: 16). In this way six-months-or-less prisoners were constructed as a distinct group based on shared characteristics, needs and social deprivation characteristics of postcode areas. The more those in the policy scene dwelled on the characteristics and needs of this population, the more real its existence, and therefore presence, seemed to be.

The presence and participation of prisoners in this policy process through the abstract forms of reports and statistics materialise them as particular kinds of analytical objects. As a policy object, the prisoner is created not only by a particular mode of presence, but also by a set of absences—absences in terms of other ways of participating, of 'realities that are necessarily absent, that cannot be brought to presence' (Law and Singleton 2005: 12). Abstract representations of prisoners are one iteration of a pattern of presences and absences. The processing and segregation of prisoners through their statistical invocations allowed for the specification of what increasingly came to be thought of as a natural object: the six-months-or-less prisoner. By contrast to other abstract formations of prisoners or prisons, the eligibility of this prisoner within policy deliberations was justified by the degree to which it seemed able to explain penal expansion. Bringing this group into presence, however, simultaneously rendered absent and implicitly constructed other kinds of presence/absence binaries. For example, lifers were denied presence as a 'driver' of penal expansion despite constituting a growing part of the prison population as well (from 11 % of the prison population in 2002 to 13 % in 2012, Scottish Government 2012), and whose increase was having a bigger impact on population expansion due to the longer time they spend in prison. The lifers' absence also implied their lack of eligibility to be a part of penal reform, serving to construct and legitimate prison as a place for long-term institutionalisation. At the same time, people in prison were categorically constructed as serious/not serious or dangerous/

not dangerous according to their length of time in it, translating a problem of (squeezed penal) space into a problem of (sentenced) time.

Already we are hoping to suggest that what might be dismissed as the sterility of statistics and the exclusion of 'real' bodies in policy, as compared to, say, traditional prison ethnography, is more complicated and carries its own consequences for constituting the physical reality of imprisonment. The presence of abstract and quantified prisoners in this site of the policy scene was no less real for not involving actual bodies. This abstract prisoner, in other words, was not a mute stand-in for a prisoner living somewhere else, but its 'data double' (Haggerty and Ericson 2000: 613, quoting Poster 1990). Data doubles involve 'the multiplication of the individual, the constitution of an additional self' that 'ostensibly refer[s] back to particular individuals, [but] transcends a purely representational idiom' (Haggerty and Ericson 2000: 613–4). The data double transforms 'the body into pure information, such that it can be rendered more mobile and comparable' (Haggerty and Ericson 2000: 613). In this case, individuals about whom little is known became a coherent group who would be expected to have similar needs and behavioural responses that could be addressed through the same policy instruments. Hence the data double creates a more manageable population for policy than the physical prisoners spread across the country. The six-months-or-less prisoner fixed in the cells of a spreadsheet could be tracked and followed from year to year and therefore used as a marker of the reform's success or failure in a way it would have been physically impossible to follow the real prisoners who turnover in their dozens on a daily basis.

Direct involvement and observation of a moment in a policy scene, as in this case study, allows one to detail the 'discursive and material practices through which people create the regularized patterns which both enable and constrain them' (Shore et al. 2011: 7). In 2009–10, Sarah and another colleague sought to gather the views of the people who would be affected by changes to short sentences. This research (Armstrong and Weaver 2010) was set within a wider turn towards including user voices in policy processes, a shift encouraged by Scottish Government officials. Enter Mark, Katrina and 20 other people in prison and a further 13 serving community sentences. Despite being asked questions focused on their experiences and views of sentences, prison and the criminal justice system, many of these research informants spontaneously opened up about their lives, particularly relating to issues of family, hope and hopelessness, jobs and substance abuse issues. So talk about self and talk about system were intermingled in interview transcripts, and our attempt to include voices on the *experiences of punishment* was dominated by *biographical accounts of the punished*. Perhaps this is not surprising in that the biographical—particularly the life history—is a genre that our informants were required to practice endlessly through their involvement in criminal justice activities (by social workers, lawyers, courts and risk assessors).

Interviewer: What Would You Say the Impact of Your Prison Sentence Has Been?

Respondent: Chhhhhhuh, don't know it's just, it gets me fucked with the missus. *[Are there any positives of prison?]* I've got two weans one with the missus and another, one up here, mah step wean but I brought her up. Just a [??], just pure nuts going on out there now. So I'd rather be in here because [of] all the social workers (unpublished interview transcript excerpt).

Interviewer: Have You Been on Remand Before?

Respondent: [Pause] uh yeah, em I've got a wee bit of a problematic relationship with my parents? Em and I come from a really, really strict background and me and mah dad have had some conflict before. And um he's got me charged with breach of the peace; it's just 'cause and it's just his way of annoyin' me. When more often than not he should be the person done for breach of the peace (unpublished interview transcript excerpt).

It can be seen here that not only were problems of prison articulated from the top, in elite policy settings, as problems of prisoners, but also prisoners themselves were articulating prison in terms of their personal lives and backgrounds. By supplying to the policy scene such personal stories, our research tended to confirm and give life to six-months-or-less prisoners as an empirical phenomenon. 'User voices' in research are always mediated; in this case they were mediated through the way we designed, carried out and disseminated our research. The 35 people who participated in the research were 35 specimens establishing the natural existence of a population, a species to be discovered rather than made. At the end of the user views of punishment project, we prepared two long research reports which attempted to convey some of the qualifications, reflections and complications of the work, findings that resisted explanation in terms of people with drug problems, family support desires and habitual offending (http://www.sccjr.ac.uk/projects/user-views-of-punishment/), the familiar narratives criminology ascribes to 'offenders'. However, in order for our work to be visible within our own institutional contexts—the university and the publish-or-perish imperative manifest in the UK through the Research Excellence Framework—we had to disseminate it in the recognised and validated form of the peer-reviewed journal article, a format which squeezes space for raising complications, hesitations and doubt (Armstrong and Weaver 2013).

In the translation from research report to peer-reviewed journal article, therefore, ambiguities, nuances and contradictions were lost, even though these would have challenged attempts to understand this set of research participants as a coherent social or even policy group. Some people we spoke to did not share the background commonly ascribed to those in prison, of being poor or uneducated. Some did not fit the policy construction that short sentences are a proxy for less serious offending patterns (a guard said in passing while a prisoner was about to be interviewed, alone in a room, 'You ok with sex offenders? He's got long-term previous…', field notes). While family contact has become a mantra in rehabilitation discourse, family for these research participants was as often the cause of problems including offending, as the alleviation of it; sometimes it was both (Armstrong and Weaver 2010). And finally, interviewees associated prison itself with both life changing and life stalling effects that complicated the presumption that short sentences were always and unconditionally useless, and that prison in longer doses might be helpful. Ironically, then, the premier knowledge product of independent academic research—the peer-reviewed journal article—facilitated the naturalisation of a statistical population into a real population. Meanwhile, the research report, the low-status knowledge product of administrative criminology, carried a message much more subversive and resistant to policy constructions.

The research on 'user views' received a great deal of attention and involved presentations to the Scottish Government and other organisations. In this way, Mark and Katrina came to have further presence, giving all but their real names to a policy process. Their stories told through our research could be bolted onto the technical policy instruments of legislation and subsequent policy programmes, in order to create an almost affective connection between policymakers and the troubled prisoner they sought to help. Here, Mark and Katrina are (re)produced in policy not only through the agency of statistical representation, but also through the humanistic representation of qualitative research as well as wider, longstanding debates about short sentences. At the same time, Mark and Katrina have also shaped policy, becoming, in a way, policymakers; their presence through research has reverberated back through other parts of the policy scene to influence subsequent waves of reform (Scottish Government 2015). Indeed, this assembled set of technicalities, stories and historical context creates a unified narrative establishing the need for policy and reform. Together, they overcome inconsistencies in any single part of the scene; for example, while one statistic became an important impetus for reform, others tended to diminish the relevance of short sentences as a driver of growth (these sentences actually account for a very small proportion of the prison population, meaning that reduction in the size of this group would not significantly affect the overall size of the prison population). Nor did the well-known but contrary experiences of admired comparators find its way into documentation: Norway's prison system overwhelmingly is used to confine people who are serving sentences of three months or less, challenging the entrenched logic that prison only 'works' when it has a minimum of a year to engage or punish a prisoner.

Conclusion

Approaching Scottish penal reform as a policy scene has allowed us to show how a particular prison sentence entered into a process, achieved reality and materiality through its transformation into a population and flowed through and around a site of elites and a site of policy targets, with both settings having transformative effects on understanding and acting on a particular issue.

Prisoner presence within policy is only one among an almost countless number of ethnographic opportunities to explore policy as a scene in which meanings (about crime, prison and punishment), desires (of prisoners and policymakers) and paths of action emerge and evolve. Its value here is to provide a brief example of how one might adopt an ethnographic and scene-thinking approach, particularly in sites which are marked by technical language, expert actors and heterogeneous spaces like conference rooms, prison cells and email. This in turn might help us better offers one of many possible alternate ways of escaping overdetermined and rational action models of policy analysis (and see, Fishwick's chapter in this volume) and thus understand, explain and avoid situations where policy often and confoundingly fails to achieve its aims or produces the opposite effect to what is desired. Indeed, this was the fate of the Scottish Prisons Commission: although it sought to reduce the prison population, its statistical construction of the 'prison problem' in terms of the needs of particular prisoners, was accompanied by a response that created new paths of state involvement in these prisoners' lives. Through creation of an expansive community sentence called Community Payback Orders, Scotland has witnessed the expansion of both the prison and community-sentenced population in the years following reform. However, we resist aggregating this case as just another example of a failed reform, or widened nets of social control, or proof of Foucault's (1977) claim that all attempts to reform the prison have the effect of expanding and legitimising it. To do so would be to practise one of the ways which criminology typically engages policy and which we criticise here—namely, the reflex to treat what has taken place as inevitable. These are the unexamined and asymmetric assumptions that an ethnographic investigation into policy scenes allows us to unpack.

References

Armstrong, S and Weaver, B. (2013) 'Persistent Punishment: User Views of Short Prison Sentences', *The Howard Journal* 52(3): 285–305.

Armstrong, S. and Weaver, B. (2010) *User Views of Punishment: The Comparative Experience of Short Prison Sentences and Community-based Punishments* (Research Report No. 04/2010), Glasgow: Scottish Centre for Crime and Justice Research.

Bennett, A. and Peterson, R.A. (eds.) (2004) *Music Scenes: Local, Translocal, and Virtual,* Nashville: Vanderbilt University.

Bennett, A. (1999) 'Subcultures or Neo-Tribes? Rethinking the Relationship Between Youth, Style and Musical Taste', *Sociology* 33(3): 599–617.

Bennett, A. (2004) 'Consolidating the Music Scenes Perspective', *Poetics* 32(3–4): 223–234.

Blaustein, J. (2015) *Speaking Truths to Power: Policy Ethnography and Police Reform in Bosnia and Herzegovina,* Oxford: Oxford University Press.

Bosworth, M. and Hoyle, C. (2011) *What Is Criminology?* Oxford: Oxford University Press.

Bourdieu, P. (2004) *Science of Science and Reflexivity,* Chicago: University of Chicago Press.

Boutros, A. and Straw, W. (eds.) (2010) *Circulation and the City: Essays on Urban Culture,* Kingston: McGill-Queen's University Press.

Carlen, P. (2011) 'Against Evangelism in Academic Criminology: For Criminology as Scientific Art'. In M. Bosworth and C. Hoyle (eds.) *What is Criminology?* Oxford: Oxford University Press: 96–108.

Clarke, R.V. and Felson, M. (2011) 'The Origins of the Routine Activity Approach and Situational Crime Prevention'. In F.T. Cullen, C.L. Johnson, A.J. Myer and F. Adler (eds.) *The Origins of American Criminology: Advances in Criminological Theory (volume 16),* New Brunswick, NJ: Transaction.

Clarke, J., Bainton, D., Lendvai, N., and Stubbs, P. (2015) *Making Policy Move: Towards a Politics of Translation and Assemblage,* Bristol: Policy Press.

Cullen, F.T. (2011) 'Beyond Adolescence-Limited Criminology: Choosing our Future – The American Society of Criminology 2010 Sutherland Address', *Criminology* 49(2): 387–330.

Davis, K., Fisher, A., Kingsbury, B. and Engle Merry, S. (eds.) (2012) *Governance by Indicators: Global Power through Quantification and Rankings,* New York: Oxford University Press.

Engle Merry, S., Davis, K. and Kingsbury, B. (eds.) (2015) *The Quiet Power of Indicators,* Cambridge: Cambridge University Press.

Ericson, R.V. and Carriere, K. (1994) 'The Fragmentation of Criminology'. In D. Nelken (ed.) *The Futures of Criminology,* London: Sage: 89–109.

Faraldo Cabana, E. (2015) 'A Certain Sense of Fairness? Why Fines Were Made Affordable', *European Journal of Criminology* 12(5): 616–631.

Foucault, M. (1977) *Discipline and Punish,* NY: Random House.

Garland, D. (2002) 'Of Crimes and Criminals: The Development of Criminology in Britain'. In M. Maguire, R. Morgan and R. Reiner (eds.) *The Oxford Handbook of Criminology*, 2nd edn, Oxford: Oxford University Press.

Gieryn, T.F. (1983) 'Boundary-Work and the Demarcation of Science From Non-Science: Strains and Interests in Professional Interests of Scientists', *American Sociological Review* 48(6): 781–795.

Glass, P.G. (2012) 'Doing Scene: Identity, Space, and the Interactional Accomplishment of Youth Culture', *Journal of Contemporary Ethnography* 41(6): 695–716.

Gordon, I., Lewis, J. and Young, K. (1977) 'Perspectives on Policy Analysis', *Public Administration Bulletin* 25(1977): pp. 26–35.

Haggerty, K.D. and Ericson, R.V. (2000) 'The Surveillant Assemblage', *British Journal of Sociology* 51(4): 605–622.

Hope, T. and Walters, R. (2008) *Critical Thinking about the Uses of Research*, King's College London: Centre for Crime and Justice Studies.

Hough, M. (2014) 'Confessions of a Recovering "Administrative Criminologist": Jock Young, Quantitative Research and Policy Research', *Crime Media Culture* 10(3): 215–226.

Irwin, J. (1977) *Scenes*, Beverly Hills, CA: Sage.

Latour, B. and Woolgar, S. (1986) *Laboratory Life: The Construction of Scientific Facts*, Princeton, NJ: Princeton University Press.

Latour, B. (1987) *Science in Action: How to Follow Scientists and Engineers Through Society*, Cambridge, MA: Harvard University Press.

Latour, B. (2005) *Reassembling the Social*, Oxford: Oxford University Press.

Law, J. and Singleton, V. (2005) 'Object Lessons', *Organization* 12(3): 331–355.

Loader, I. and Sparks, R. (2011) *Public Criminology?* London: Routledge.

MacAskill, K. (2007) *Debate on Penal Policy*, Speech, http://www.gov.scot/About/Review/spc/About/Review/penalpolicy [accessed 22 December 2015]

Mulholland, H. (2007) 'Scottish Executive Scraps Private Prison Plan', *The Guardian* (23 August); http://www.theguardian.com/politics/2007/aug/23/scotland.devolution [accessed 22 December 2015]

Newburn, T. (2003) *Crime and Criminal Justice Policy*, Harlow: Pearson Longman.

O'Malley, P. (1996) 'Post-Social Criminologies: Some Implications of Current Political Trends for Criminological Theory and Practice', *Current Issues in Criminal Justice* 8(1): 26–38.

Pavlich, G. (2000) *Critique and Radical Discourses on Crime*. London: Ashgate.

Riles, A. (2005) 'A New Agenda for the Cultural Study of Law: Taking on the Technicalities', *Buffalo Law Review*, 53: 973–1033.

Riles, A. (ed.) (2006) *Documents: Artifacts of Modern Knowledge,* Ann Arbor, MI: University of Michigan Press.

Rock, P. (1994) *History of Criminology*, Aldershot: Dartmouth.

Scottish Government (2012) Prison Statistics Scotland 2011/12, Statistical Bulletin CrJ/2007/7, Edinburgh: Scottish Government.

Scottish Government (2015) *Consultation on Proposals to Strengthen the Presumption against Short Periods of Imprisonment,* http://www.gov.scot/ Publications/2015/09/8223

Scottish Prisons Commission (SPC) (2008) *Scotland's Choice: Report of the Scottish Prisons Commission*, Edinburgh: Scottish Government.

Scottish Parliament (2009) Criminal Justice and Licensing (Scotland) Bill – POLICY MEMORANDUM, Stage 3 (5 March 2009). http://www.scottish. parliament.uk/S3_Bills/Criminal%20Justice%20and%20Licensing%20 %28Scotland%29%20Bill/b24s3-introdpm.pdf [accessed 22 December 2015].

Shank, B. (1994) *Dissonant Identities: The Rock 'n Roll Scene in Austin, Texas,* Hanover: Wesleyan University Press.

Shore, C. and Wright, S. (eds.) (1997) *Anthropology of Policy: Critical Perspectives on Governance and Power*, London: Routledge.

Shore, C., Wright, S. and Però, D. (eds.) (2011) *Policy Worlds: Anthropology and Analysis of Contemporary Power*, New York: Berghahn Books.

Star, S.L. (1999) 'The Ethnography of Infrastructure', *American Behavioral Scientist* 43(3): 377–391.

Strathern, M. (2000) *Audit Cultures*, London: Routledge.

Straw, W. (2001) 'Scenes and Sensibilities', *Public* 22/23: 245–257.

Straw, W. (2015) 'Some Things a Scene Might Be', *Cultural Studies* 29(3): 476–485.

Weaver, B. and Armstrong, S. (2011) *The Dynamics of Community-based Punishment: Insider Views from the Outside* (Research Report No. 03/2011), Glasgow: Scottish Centre for Crime and Justice Research.

Woo, B., Rennie, J. and Poyntz, S.R. (2015) 'Scene Thinking', *Cultural Studies* 29(3): 285–297.

Wright, S. and Reinhold, S. (2011) '"Studying Through": A Strategy for Studying Political Transformation'. In C. Shore, S. Wright and D. Pero (eds.) *Policy Worlds: Anthropology and Analysis of Contemporary Power*, New York: Berghahn Books: 86–104.

Young, J. (1986) The Failure of Criminology: The Need for a Radical Realism. In R. Matthews and J. Young (eds.) *Confronting Crime*, London: SAGE Publications.

6

Reflexivity in Statistics as Sociology of Quantification: The Case of Repeat Victimization Modelling

Bilel Benbouzid

In the criminological field, reflexivity in statistics often appears as a methodological problem. Most of the problems emanate from questions of 'measurement' and are mainly addressed in terms of 'reliability', 'bias', and 'error'. There is however another way of discussing quantification in social sciences, but it is rarely used in criminology: the sociology of quantification that invites a particular form of reflexivity. The basic premise of this sociology is that the statistic is not a simple realistic measurement operation, a reflection of reality, but a temporary adaptation to new 'ways of thinking about society and how to act on it' (Desrosières 2014). The interpretative framework proposed by this sociology may be summarized in two lines: to analyse the *convention* underlying the quantification of the social; and, simultaneously, to observe the uses of statistics and networks of actors linked to it. Thus, a sociology of social quantification must lie at the interface of scientific research practices and public policy issues. *To prove and to govern* (Desrosières, Ibid.) can be seen as two sides of the same operation: quantification.

B. Benbouzid (✉)
University of East Paris, Paris, France

S. Armstrong et al. (eds.), *Reflexivity and Criminal Justice*,
DOI 10.1057/978-1-137-54642-5_6

In this article we will focus on the demonstration of 'proof' in quantitative research in criminology showing that it is inseparable from the governance issue. In order to do so, we consider here a body of scientific work relating to a particular case: research on repeat victimization and the construction of predictive algorithms. This text corpus is interesting because it allows us to observe the social uses of various statistical techniques in the study of the same phenomenon. The analysis focuses on controversy in the interpretation of the results of statistical modelling of the distribution of victimization and the prediction of repeat victimization.

The controversy revolves around research on which two criminologists, Ken Pease and Tim Hope, worked together in the 1990s as part of a research team called the Quantitative Criminology Group (QCG), initially comprising three econometricians, Denise Osborn, Alan Trickett, and Dan Ellingworth, and three criminologists, Ken Pease, Graham Farrell, and Tim Hope. Their aim was to understand why a small number of victims suffer the most burglaries, and how processes of victimization are repeated in space and time. The controversy itself can be mapped as a *non-dialogue* around quantification that modelled repeat victimization. As the empirical data piled up, interpretations of the repeat victimization phenomenon increasingly weighed towards local experiments on a new form of time- and space-based situational crime prevention assisted by algorithms, known as predictive policing (Perry et al. 2013). Despite Tim Hope's many attempts to refute this interpretation, the idea that the best way of reducing delinquency was to use predictive policing (PROMAP and PREDPOL software) to protect victims gradually gained currency in public policies on security. The analysis of Tim Hope's critique enables us to see the political dimension of the statistical modelling of victimization.

The Interpretative Flexibility of Statistical Models

In the 1990s, the QCG embarked on a study of repeat victimization in support of prevention policy, but without a priori associating its research with any particular prevention model. The first step was to analyse data from victimization surveys, mapping the distribution of the probability of repeat victimization in the population. The researchers used fairly sophisticated statistical models (laws of distribution and hypotheses on random variables) to obtain an approximate mathematical description of the data. At the outset, the QCG first envisaged an exploratory analysis in which it sought to describe the differences of incidence of victimization in different geographical areas. It published its analysis in 'What is different about high crime areas?' (Trickett et al. 1992), now considered as a seminal article in repeat victimization research. In this article the authors applied a new conceptualization of the way of calculating the risk of victimization, by arithmetically linking the prevalence, incidence, and concentration (called vulnerability) of victimization in the formula:

$$\text{Incidence}^1 = \text{Prevalence} \times \text{Concentration}.$$

The aim was to understand the probabilistic distribution function underlying this arithmetical formula. By ordering the distribution of victimization by sector in deciles, the analysis showed simply that the relationship between prevalence and incidence (therefore concentration) varied according to the deciles and tended to increase considerably in the highest deciles: 20 % of residential areas accounted for half of the victims countrywide. To understand the law of probabilities underpinning this wide dispersion, the group carried out a simple statistical test: it compared the expected distributions of prevalence and incidence obtained according to a binomial law (a simple law that models repetitions of tests with binary results (victim or not) that are independent of one another). The group showed that the vulnerability observed in the sectors with the highest prevalence was much greater than that obtained with the simulation test (the simulated binomial law), that is, with a random distribution of victimization.

Hence, it concluded, victimization was not repeated randomly. It followed that it was probably better to focus the resources of prevention

---

[1] Incidence relates to the number of cases of victimization in a population over a specified period. Prevalence corresponds to the number of individuals who said they had been victims (at least once) during the observation period. Hence, the ratio of incidence over prevalence provides an indicator of the concentration of victimization in the population.

policies on a small number of victims on whom victimization seemed to be concentrated. But to be able to define more precisely how to go about doing so, the researchers needed to deepen their research on distribution, so as to understand why and how victimization was repeated and concentrated.

To explore the explanation of repeat victimization, Farrell and Pease (1993) put forward a dual hypothesis to account for the mechanism underlying victimization: the repeat victimization of a person or a home can be seen either as a *flag* signalling a relatively stable risk of victimization, or as an indication that the incidents of victimization *boost* the probability of the occurrence of subsequent incidents. Translated into statistical terms, the hypothesis of the flag is called risk heterogeneity, and that of the boost is said to be state-dependent.

These two hypotheses are very classical in econometric reasoning. They had already been put forward in the 1970s in the pioneering work of the British researcher Richard F. Sparks (Sparks et al. 1977). In his analysis of the data of local surveys on victimization, Sparks had first used Poisson's law of distribution, called the law of small probabilities, an ideal tool for applying the law of large numbers to a rare phenomenon such as victimization. This law, which states that 'for a rare event to occur, it generally takes the improbable conjunction of several factors, an unexpected series of strokes of fate' (Bouchaud 2013: 106), did not match the data from surveys on victimization. In this context the researchers spoke of 'overdispersion' of the distribution of victimization, the parameters of which can be added to the Poisson model to obtain a more satisfactory type of modelling called 'Poisson mixture'.[2] They first tried the most frequently used Poisson mixture, the negative binomial model. Rather than modelling a series of independent cases of victimization with a constant expectancy, the negative binomial model assumes that victimization occurs contagiously (boost) and/or in a heterogeneous environment (flag).

In the late 1970s the first modelling studies on victimization survey data showed that the negative binomial model was satisfactory for representing the distribution of victimization in the population. The explanation was given in terms of certain social groups' propensity to

---

[2] 'Mixed state' is a term used by statisticians for a combination of probabilities.

be victimized repeatedly, the idea of contagion being considered as irrelevant. In the mid-1990s, however, the two explanations seemed relevant and the QCG wanted to integrate into the same empirical examination what had until then been excluded: the statistical description of the shift from the state of non-victim to that of victim (first hurdle), and then from victim to repeated victim (second hurdle). What are the specific (individual and local) risk factors of the first hurdle and of the second one? What is the correlation between the first and second hurdle? To produce this type of model, the econometrics literature proposed a solution consisting of the elaboration of a dual system of simultaneous equations; one to represent the first hurdle, the other to represent the second. The idea behind using this model was taken from an analogy with how one might understand cigarette-smoking behaviour: knowledge about who does not smoke (identified in the first hurdle) is irrelevant to knowledge of the smoking behaviour of those who actually smoke. Without 'censoring out' the excessively redundant information that is available on non-smokers (especially if this group were in the majority), the factors associated with the smoking habits of the minority who actually smoked could be obscured (Hope 2015).

Nevertheless, the QCG researchers had three reasons for retaining knowledge of the first hurdle within the overall model, and not simply concentrating on modelling the frequency of crime victimization by itself: first, this strategy preserved information on the entire population, whether victim or not, which was the Group's main focus of investigation; second, since victimization was a rare phenomenon, it did not sacrifice the probably more reliable explanation of why people did *not* become victims to the perhaps more random set of possibilities as to why they did so repeatedly (Sparks 1981); and third, despite the evident desire to find out why some people became frequent victims while others did not, one still needed to know why they had become victims in the first place. In sum, the 'double hurdle' model seemed robust enough to cater for all these eventualities, even if it did perhaps overlook the very few extremely victimized victims (Hope 2015).

In 1996, based on an analysis of the British Crime Survey (BCS) using the double hurdle model, the QCG published the article 'Are repeatedly victimized households different?' (Osborn et al. 1996), which was a significant methodological step forward in research on the modelling of victimization. Its principal conclusion was that it was unable to identify any factor that was more significant than any other in explaining repetition. As one of the members commented, 'we inferred that we were not measuring any predictors that might distinguish repeat victims from victims in general which would have been different from those common to all victims and distinguished them from non-victims' (private discussion with Tim Hope 2014).

At the conclusion of this first modelling of the distribution as a whole, there remained considerable interpretive ambivalence: on the one hand, if repeat victims were no different from any other victims, then simply being a victim would be a good enough predictor of the likelihood of more frequent victimization; on the other hand, the absence of difference between any kind of victim implied that the most important difference to investigate was that between victims and non-victims. Depending on their theoretical stances, the erstwhile members of the QCG no longer shared the same hypotheses on the significance of the results obtained, and therefore began to pursue different research perspectives. On the one hand, Pease and Farrell, who were engaged in situational prevention, considered that the results were good enough to infer that the boost process was a sound explanation and therefore a good research route for the development of situational prevention. On this basis, Pease and colleagues embarked on a programme of research intended to inform crime prevention by investigating the repetitiveness of victimization. Focussing on the phenomenon of state dependency (the boost hypothesis), they tended to downplay the significance of risk heterogeneity (the flag hypothesis).[3]

In contrast, other members of the QCG considered that it was necessary to continue further with the analysis of the population distribution as a whole based on the flag hypothesis (Osborn and Tseloni 1998). For them, the boost effect was of less interest since it might be mostly a consequence of the flag hypothesis (Hope and Lab 2001). I now analyse these two different routes in turn.

---

[3] The heterogeneity route was not however ignored completely, especially in Ken Pease's collaborations with Andromache Tseloni (see Pease and Tseloni 2014).

Victimization Boosts Victimization: An Ideal Interpretation for Situational Crime Prevention (SCP)

In-depth analysis of boost mechanisms became a major research topic in situational crime prevention. From a situational crime prevention perspective, explaining a crime amounted to relating it to the behaviours of delinquents in the situation where they act, and to the target's vulnerability. Research on repeat victimization henceforth included situational crime prevention strategies into a complex and evolving space–time. It was from this perspective that Richard Townsley, Shane Johnson, and Kate Bowers, in close collaboration with Ken Pease, embarked on a series of studies in the early 2000s, at the newly created Jill Dando Institute of Crime Science (JDICS), England's first academic research and development laboratory entirely devoted to situational crime prevention.

To analyse the boost phenomenon in detail, researchers at JDICS sought to model the spatial-temporal dimension of repeat victimization.[4] The complex relations between time and space in the explanation of victimization had not yet been explored in any depth. Some minor studies had however already shown that victimization was not only repetitive but also apparently contagious (Anderson et al. 1995; Morgan 2000). This *near-repeat* phenomenon corresponded fairly well to the results of qualitative studies of burglars; burglars had told researchers that they regularly returned to burgle the same house when it was easy to burgle and they had not been able to take everything the first time around (Ashton et al. 1998). Burglars, moreover, operate within particular neighbourhoods that constituted their routine activity spaces, belonging to networks with whom they exchange information on the vulnerability of the targets detected in the reconnaissance stages. That is how victimization spreads in time and space.

The JDICS team of researchers wondered how to represent the spread of victimization in statistical terms, and how to identify the more or less repetitive spatial-temporal configurations on which prevention strategies

---

[4] On the origins of the spatial-temporal analysis of repeat victimization, see the article by Johnson et al. (1997).

could be built. To answer these questions they applied spatial analysis statistical tools—a standard reflex when one wishes to identify spatial-temporal concentrations of events. In particular, they were interested in Knox's spatial-temporal statistical test, well known for the analysis of contagion phenomena. Developed in the 1960s in an epidemiological research framework, Knox's test uses a Poisson test to determine whether the time-space distribution of events differs significantly from an independent, random distribution. This method was used to test the simultaneous existence of groups of victims in time and space—a statistical refinement that enables the spatial-temporal interdependence of crimes to be represented in the form of clusters. By inputting police statistics on the time and place of crimes, the researchers were able to use this test to model the way in which burglaries were repeated and spread by contagion.

Based on the Knox test, the researchers embarked on a series of studies on the communication of the risk of victimization. Townsley published one of the first articles on contagion, based on Knox tests, and proposed the notion of *infectious* burglaries (Townsley et al. 2003). In his PhD thesis he had already shown important elements of spatial-temporal analysis, such as the fact that the most unstable burglary hotspots corresponded largely to the addresses of repeat victims, whereas the most stable hotspots were linked more to aspects of the immediate social and physical environment. In his article on infectious burglaries, Townsley et al. pursued analysis of neighbourhood similarities, but showed this time that a first burglary increases the risk of another one following on a close target, provided that the new target has similar social and physical characteristics to the first.

Using the same Knox test, Kate Bowers and Shane Johnson showed that a first burglary increased the risk of a burglary in a 400-metreradius, in an estimated interval of one to two months (Bowers and Johnson 2005). They also showed that although the poorest areas are those with the most repeat victimization, clusters of burglaries in space and time are found more in the wealthiest areas. Hence, a burgled house next to a first burglary is far likelier to be burgled than a house situated a few metres away, especially during the first week after the first burglary.

Moreover, in the same street, burglaries are repeated on houses with the same architectural characteristics. In other words, a house with a different architectural layout in a street with identical houses can reduce the risk of being burgled.

Owing to the Knox test and temporal data geo-referenced on the scale of a street, the scientific discourse on repeat victimization gradually came to contain more and more details on the spatial-temporal boost process. But it was not enough for the researchers at JDICS to provide ever more detailed elements of analysis on the spatial-temporal dynamics of repeat victimization. The JDICS research policy was also to develop innovative technology to fight crime. How could the spatial-temporal analysis be used to devise prevention strategies? To answer this question, Pease joined with the Jill Dando researchers in the early 2000s, to develop an operational tool for crime prediction: Prospective Crime Mapping, known as PROMAP. It was based on the modelling of spatial-temporal changes in repeat victimization in a given area (Bowers and Johnson 2004). Their aim was to differentiate their work from the prediction of crime locations as it had been practised until then, that is, with calculation methods and hotspot representations (Weisburd et al. 2009). With the latter approach, simple representations of spatial concentrations of past burglaries (hotspots) were considered as good predictors of future crime. In contrast, the objective of PROMAP was not to map the past in order to reveal the future (the classical practice of hotspot policing), but rather to project from the present in order to anticipate future crimes.[5]

To switch from retrospective crime mapping to prospective mapping that located future risks, the researchers drew on smoothing methods ordinarily used in spatial analysis to find the nodal points on a map. To

---

[5] Because of their interest in promoting 'problem-oriented policing' based on situational and repeat victimisation prevention as a means of improving the effectiveness of policing in the UK, the JDICS researchers found themselves in competition with proponents of 'hotspots policing' based on the idea of increasing the deterrent effect of police patrols at known spatial clusters of crime. In particular, the appointment of Lawrence Sherman as Wolfson Professor of Criminology at the University of Cambridge had brought to Britain an energetic enthusiast not only for hotspot policing but also in using 'classic' prediction and experimental research methods to support it. This statistical orientation stood in marked contrast to the approach adopted by PROMAP.

generate a map on which hotspots could be detected, the cartographers projected a virtual grid with a regular mesh onto the study area. Over this they placed a circular mobile window with a fixed diameter which recorded the number of incidents (e.g. burglaries) in each cell of the grid. All these recordings enabled the researchers to calculate a level of density, called the risk intensity, for each grid, using a mathematical algorithm. Available methods for calculating the density abound in the literature (Kernel Density Estimation or KDE is one of the most sophisticated techniques). Pease and his colleagues drew on these methods but made a substantial change. Whereas the mathematical formulae used in hotspot policing to estimate the risks were parameterized on the basis of aesthetic considerations of mapped representations, with prospective mapping the idea was to integrate the formulae of criminological theories on contagion into the elements of parameterizing (Johnson et al. 2007, 2009). Thus, to predict crime, the researchers used the key results of research on repeat victimization: the risk of victimization spreads over 400 metres, with a higher risk for houses on the same side of the road, and over a period of two months.

The innovation of Pease and his colleagues lies in the translation of a criminological theory into the parameterizing of the mathematical algorithm that calculates the intensity of risks. Other parameterized elements can be integrated into mathematical models to weigh previous crimes, such as times of the day, days of the week, weather conditions, the topography of sites, and so on. The PROMAP algorithm can always be fine-tuned on the basis of more fundamental research on the spatial dynamics of victimization or nonparametric methods.[6]

---

[6] In its most rudimentary development phase, PROMAP enabled the police to patrol strategically and thus to optimize the deployment of increasingly scarce resources in the public service. But as ingenious and innovative as it may be, PROMAP was not given the funding needed to develop it, even though two police forces in England had tested the tool under local crime reduction programmes (Fielding and Jones 2012; Rowley 2013). By contrast, the PREDPOL software, of which the algorithm is very similar to that of PROMAP, but uses a nonparametric method, was immensely successful worldwide. In the USA, predictive policing has become a research field that has been abundantly funded by government over the past ten years (Perry et al. 2013).

Challenging the Boost Hypothesis: Understanding the Unequal Conditions of Access to Security

The publication of the article 'Are repeatedly victimized households different?' (Osborn et al. 1996) eventually triggered a full-blown controversy. Tim Hope, a co-author of the article, considered that the results of the modelling left in the dark many research questions that had been of no interest to Pease and his colleagues, who were more concerned with operational issues. Engaged in the promotion of social prevention of crime,[7] Hope was dissatisfied with Pease's interpretation and sought to push further the analysis of the distribution of victimization in the population.

The main traces of this critique are found in Hope and Trickett (2004a), but its outline was formalized in a 1995 paper written with Sandra Walklate.[8] Hope and Trickett (2004a) considered that too little analysis had been granted to the fact that far more non-victims were measured than victims (victimization is a rare phenomenon), and that the surveys showing the highest frequencies of victimization were the rarest. According to them, if one wanted to account for the over dispersion of distribution properly, one had to take into account not only the concentration of victimization on a small part of the population (the right-hand tail of the distribution curve), but also seek to explain the extreme con-

---

[7] What Tim Hope called 'social prevention' can refer equally to the 'community research' tradition, as well as to a sociological analysis of the contexts of implementation of security technologies. From this perspective, in the late-1980s he conducted a quasi-experimental evaluation of the effect of making neighbourhoods safe, under a programme for improving the living environment—the *Priority Estates Project Evaluation Study* (Foster and Hope 1993). The differences of approach taken by this study compared to the Kirkholt Project directly mirrored the divergence within government policymaking during the period from the early 1980s to the early 1990s; between crime prevention through 'community development' on the one hand, and situational crime prevention on the other.

[8] Tim Hope and Sandra Walklate, critical analysts of victimology, delivered a paper at the 1995 British Criminology Conference, in which they laid the foundations of a programme of deconstruction of the notion of repeat victimization. The same period also witnessed the critique of James Lynch and his colleagues who, based on longitudinal data from victimization survey in the USA, broadly challenged the boost hypothesis (Lynch et al. 1998).

centration of non-victimization on a very large portion of the population (left-hand tail of the distribution curve).

Hope and Trickett (2004a) first reasoned by simulation, based on equations of the bivariate probit model estimated by Osborn et al. (1996). They imagined three levels of probability of experiencing a first instance of victimization (p = 1 or 0.4 or 0.05). They used the bivariate probit model to simulate the probability of a subsequent victimization event, in relation to the three levels of risk, and deduced the probability of a subsequent victimization. For the least vulnerable people (p = 0.05), the risk of experiencing a first instance of victimization did increase the risk of a subsequent one substantially, as the boost hypothesis predicts. However, for people with an average risk of suffering a first instance of victimization (p = 0.4), the risk of experiencing a second one remained the same, and with the extreme hypothesis of 100 chances out of 100 (p = 1) of being victimized, the risk of a subsequent victimization appeared to decline. Second, by using a panel design, they then showed that most victims (not only people who had suffered a first instance of victimization but also those who had been multiply victimized) did not remain victims in the long term; on the contrary, they usually returned to the status of non-victims, although higher-level victims had a lower likelihood of reverting than did lower-level victims. Thus, Hope and Trickett (2004a) were able to demonstrate three key propositions: first, that the risk of repeat victimization was not equally distributed amongst the population but rather depended on the level of risk predictable a priori by exogenous risk factors such as area of residence and individual lifestyle (Osborn et al. 1996); second, that it was non-victims who were most likely to retain their (non)victimization status over time; and third, that the general tendency for the population, over time, was towards the cessation rather than the repetition of victimization. Each of these findings constituted a major challenge to the boost hypothesis.

Based on these results, Hope argued that the hypothesis of an increase in exposure to risk over time (the so-called 'boost') and related theories should be dropped, and that other interpretive frameworks of distribution of victimization in the population should rather be adopted. For his new framework of interpretation, Tim Hope drew on Giddens' theory of structuration, which was very popular in the 1990s (Bottoms and Wiles 1992). Giddens' notion of structuration refers to a set of rules and resources organized repetitively, updated and coordinated in the form of traces in actors' memories—in this case, in those of the victims. Most important is the focus on 'structures' rather than on epidemiological factors. This is how, according to Hope and Walklate, the notion of structure can be applied to conceptualize repeat victimization as 'one way of understanding the dynamism between, for example, the structural location of women (one way of understanding women's powerlessness, a defining characteristic of being a victim), and women's negotiation of their structural location (one way of understanding the term survivor)' (Hope and Walklate 1995).

To continue his research on repeat victimization, Hope explored the ways in which victims showed their competencies and oriented their behaviours based on their knowledge on how victimization took place. From this point of view, it was less risk that interested Hope than 'security' in the broad sense of the term, close to the concept of *ontological security* of the actor, defined by Giddens: How do victims explain their own vulnerability? What makes them review this explanation? How do they adapt? What are the conditions of this adaptation? What was important was to explore the structuration of safety—to find out how these private issues result in a public, social structure of risk and security (Hope and Karstedt 2003)—which led Hope towards developing a theory of *reflexive securitisation*.

By raising these questions, Tim Hope undertook research that radically turned the tide and paved the way for prevention policies that differed substantially from situational prevention (Hope 2001). There was thus a shift from the issue of the distribution of victimization to that of the distribution of reflexive securitization. Surveys on victimization provided abundant useful data on the consumption of security products and individuals' engagement in their own quest for security. Based on these data, Hope and Lab (2001) identified three forms of preventive actions that people engaged in to make their home environment safer: neighbourhood watch (all the activities related to reassuring themselves about their residential security, including marking property, telling neighbours when going on vacation, taking out home contents insurance, and keeping a watch in the neighbourhood), security technologies (e.g. alarms), and fortress security (everything pertaining to physical security related to the home).[9] The analysis of the data from surveys on victimization shows that the tendency to engage in these preventive actions is related not only to the perception of the risk of victimization (including past experience of victimization) but also possessing the economic and social capital necessary to ensure that this security is made available, so that the people who most readily take these security measures are those in the more privileged classes.

Among the security issues studied, neighbourhood watch initiatives have a particular status because they lie at the interface between public and private security services. By applying regression techniques to British Crime Survey data, Hope and Trickett (2004b) sought to show the determinants of participation in neighbourhood watches. One of the interesting results of their analysis showed that participation in collective security is closely linked to the sense of *neighbourhood reciprocity* and to the actors' involvement in other community activities. Hence, reflexive securitization depends as much on the actors' social resources as on their economic resources. Hope showed this repeatedly: in suburban residential areas, crime prevention is organized like a club, that is, a good that is shared yet exclusive. It was this notion of a club and the theory of reflexive security associated with it that enabled Hope to explain the hypothesis of immunity:

> The theory of reflexive securitisation would seem a plausible way of linking burglary victimisation and private security trends. The residential clubbing and consequent intensification of private security, may affect mid-range communities the most: very low crime communities have an excess of community over risk, and thus an excess of immunity; their investment in private security may be primarily symbolic. In contrast, high crime neighbourhoods have an excess of victimisation, which negatively affects trust and social capital formation [...] Some part of the decline in burglary may have been introduced asymmetrically into the trend by the socio-spatial distancing between victims and offenders brought about by the changing

ecology of tenure in the UK over the period [...] Thus, reflexive securitization may explain why the bulk of burglary reduction has come about through a reduction in prevalence, since a large number of erstwhile victims may have been removed from risk, and thus would be eligible no longer for selection as repeat or multiple victims. (Hope 2007: no page numbers)

By conceptualizing security as a mutualized good in his explanation of trends in crime against property, Tim Hope was better able to account for the role of non-governmental actors (citizens) in the social production of crime prevention and the relations they maintain with one another and other institutions (Hope and Karstedt 2003).

The disagreement between the immunity model and the boost model, related to two different conceptions of what produces security: 'the assumption of the immunity model is that *protection factors* actually say more about security than about the risk itself' (Hope and Trickett 2004a). According to Hope, crime prevention becomes a matter of detecting and predicting the disintegration of these factors of protection through an ever finer understanding of the unequal conditions of access to security.

Computational Turn in Victimization Research, But No Turn in Interpretation

Pease's prevention strategy (predictive policing) and Hope's conceptual innovation (reflexive securitization) were both based on ambivalent interpretations—respectively, the boost model and the immunity model—of statistical studies on the distribution of victimization in the population. They therefore had to carry out more fundamental research on this distribution. The advocates of situational crime prevention still had to solve the riddle of two explanations of repeat victimization that had never been untangled: *boost or flag*? As for the view represented by Hope, a comprehensive model still had to be found, that took into account the 'inflation of zero victimization', in order to account for the role of immunity in the distribution of victimization.

Hitherto, both sets of researchers had relied primarily on so-called *frequentist* statistical tools to build their models. Generally, they applied logistic regression econometric methods, with a view to isolating the effects of certain variables, the idea being to identify the separate influences of residential area versus household-level risk factors (Pease and Tseloni 2014; Hope and Lab 2001). Yet, this type of reasoning seemed to have reached its limits in the face of a number of persistent methodological problems. The two groups of researchers turned to other statistical techniques to further their analysis; for both groups, computational methods held out the most promise.

Jill Dando researchers investigated the social simulation techniques of Nigel Gilbert (1994) that had been taken up in all the social sciences from the early 1990s. Social simulation as defined by Gilbert interested Pease and his colleagues as it afforded the possibility of representing artificial social situations from which the researchers could observe spatial-temporal dynamics. Of the many simulation methods available, *multi-agent simulation* enabled them to push their analysis furthest. It afforded a high degree of flexibility in representing burglars, their behaviours and their interactions in an environment.

Multi-agent simulation enabled criminologists to represent an offender's behaviour by means of a computerized program. Pitcher and Johnson (2011) defined a multi-agent model offering a computer representation of burglars in the form of agents moving about in an environment consisting of targets (homes) whose attractiveness is both stable (depending on the situation) and changing (depending on the burglars' action). The burglars can see the attractiveness of a target and surrounding targets, and react according to that attractiveness. The rules defining the burglar's movement are translated into an algorithm. Once the algorithm is implemented, the researchers could execute the model by varying its dynamic and static aspect and thus simulate different configurations: heterogeneity of the risk, dependence on the event without heterogeneity of the risk, and heterogeneity of the risk with dependence on the event. After many experiments, they argued in favour of a boost hypothesis that differed from that of the 1990s. Whereas in the classical multivariate models there was always the possibility of having left out hidden variables that might explain repetition in terms of risk hetero-geneity, with their simulation the researchers showed that, on the con-trary, repeat victimizations could not be explained by the configuration of risk heterogeneity alone:

> In the introduction to this article, we discussed the possibility that observed space–time patterns of crime may be explained by a statistical artefact that occurs when results are aggregated for populations with very different risks (the flag account). However, the results of a series of simulations suggest that such models (as specified here) were insufficient and did not generate the types of pattern that are observed in real-world data [...] In contrast to the flag hypothesis, our results suggest that the boost account may offer a plausible explanation for why crime clusters in space and time. (Pitcher and Johnson 2011: 107)

The logic of statistical inference was reversed. It was a matter no lon-ger of measuring the gap between a statistical model and the empirical data collected from victims in large surveys on the population at large, but rather of evaluating the plausibility of the hypotheses concerning the mechanisms generating repetition. Whereas in statistical modelling, the theoretical models of the heterogeneity of risk and of event-dependence were centred on the intensity of relations between the variables, in social simulation studies these same models were centred on the plausibility of the mechanisms underlying repeat victimization. This new approach enabled Johnson and his colleague to show the interdependency between risk heterogeneity and event dependency in the explanation of repeat mechanisms. On this basis they inferred the importance of articulating conventional measures to reduce incidents (classical interventions in situ-ational crime prevention on immediate environmental factors) and pre-vention of repeat victimization (stopping contagion from an intervention toward repeat victims). The authors' interpretation of this 'fundamental' result still supported SCP.

At the same time, Tim Hope opened many methodological and epis-temological questions on quantification of repeat victimization (Hope 2007): first, the difficulty of deciding on the appropriate level (area or household?) for an observed effect—a problem known as *cross-level mis-*

specification; second, the problem of never knowing whether all the necessary and sufficient risk factors had been included—a problem known as *omitted variable bias*; and third, the ambiguity surrounding many of the significant risk factors—whether they were measuring security or risk, and why it was that variables separately indexing affluence and poverty should both appear as risk factors, contrary to theoretical expectations (Hope 2001). How can you group together and take into account in more detail the different components of the repeat phenomenon, without worrying about their observability, as the BCS data available were not longitudinal (Tim Hope could not directly account for the stochasticity of the process)?

To get around these difficulties, Hope sought a statistical technique that would enable him to estimate the most probable finite mixture of the heterogeneity in risk within the general population distribution of crime victimization. According to Hope, a good statistical technique to do so was *latent class analysis* (LCA) (Hope and Norris 2012).[10] LCA was not one of the statistical modelling methods that Hope had used before. As part of the family of classification methods, LCA serves to model relations between variables observed, and to postulate the existence of non-observable variables identified in the form of classes (or groups). It is unlike the hypothesis test method, which consists in posing the model a priori and in directly estimating its parameters using estimators calculated on the basis of observations. LCA, in contrast, is based on the specification of rival models which can be compared with each other in relation to several levels of adjustment. As LCA is a Bayesian-type[11] statistical technique, Hope saw it as an alternative to the frequentist statistics that he had been doing until then.

Why did Hope choose to turn towards another statistical approach? LCA would enable him to represent unobserved heterogeneity of the distribution of victimization in the population, which had not been accomplished before (cf. Tseloni 2006); and to develop a model consisting of

---

[10] Analysis was carried out on data sets derived from historic sweeps of the BCS and the Scottish Crime Victimization Survey (SCVS) (Hope and Norris 2012).

[11] Statistics textbooks describe LCA as a particular class of Bayesian networks because it represents relations of dependency in the group of variables studied (categories of crime and victim characteristics) in relation to a distribution of conditional probabilities associated with each variable.

a complex mixture of non-victims, multiple victims, repeat victims, and mono-victims, which, following Hope and Lab (2001), he believed was a more representative picture of the population's crime victimization experiences.[12]

The results of the LCA enabled Hope to classify victims in their most probable class, and to calculate the mean level of victimization suffered by the respondents in a particular class. Based on these results he identified three main classes of victim: non-victims, intermediate victims, and chronic victims.

Hope sought to model the distribution of each of these classes, based on the calculation of the probability of a respondent belonging to a class, according to the frequency of victimization. Respondents who had never been victims had a higher probability of being non-victims and a low probability of being intermediate victims. Only respondents with a high frequency of victimization belonged to the class of chronic victims. Moreover, the distribution of the probability of being a victim was heterogeneous for the two extreme classes (non-victims and chronic victims), whereas it was homogeneous for the intermediate class. Hope therefore wondered whether intermediate victims (which constituted a relatively large set) and chronic victims (which consisted of few victims but a very high level of victimization) might not pose etiological questions peculiar to them. LCA did not enable him to explore this further, but by raising this question Hope showed all the nuances that could still be brought to the modelling of the distribution of victimization. LCA enabled him to criticize the limited category of 'repeat victimization' by showing forms of distribution according to class. This supported the idea of a heterogeneous mixture of the distribution of victimization in the population.

The main contribution of LCA was that it enabled Hope to account for a general model of distribution. He showed that non-victimization had a strong influence on the general pattern of distribution. The class of non-victims accounted for 80 % of the population but only 20 % of victimization. The remaining 20 % of the population (intermediate and chronic victims) accounted for 80 % of the cases of victimization.

---

[12] Private discussion with Tim Hope in September 2014.

In sum, while the broad 80:20 inequality of the distribution persists, we can now see how that inequality is constructed out of a heterogeneous mixture of sub-distributions that lie between the two poles of maximum immunity and maximum exposure. (Hope 2015: 34)

Hope inferred that victimization could be predicted only on the basis of combined modelling of immunity and exposure to victimization risk. Immunity and exposure are two mutually interacting dimensions. But what was his intention when he showed that the general model of distribution of victimization could be conceptualized as propensities for immunity from and exposure to crime victimization, respectively? Hope explained his reasoning as follows:

In view of the nature of the distribution, non-victimization would appear to be a better predictor of non-victimization than would victimization be of victimization; in other words, long-run safety may be a more certain and reliable outcome for the general population than is the prospect of short-term, periodic risk. Of course, this is no consolation for the minority who, at any one time, suffer excessive victimization. It may be even more galling for them to know that a much larger proportion of their fellow citizens might be luxuriating in more than their 'fair share' of safety while they suffer more than their fair share of harm. (Hope 2015: 37–38)

While research on the prediction of victimization focuses only on a part of the distribution model (repetition of victimization in the population), Hope showed the importance of understanding the causes of the zero. He therefore challenged all the underpinnings of predictive policing. According to him, crime is a problem that can be understood only by looking at how immunity and chronicity are established in the population. This helps to explain Hope's complex proposition that has been ignored by all the advocates of situational crime prevention. Basing a public policy exclusively on the risk exposure model means disregarding the fact that the immunity of some is linked to the exclusion of others from security. It also means the failure to take timely and in-depth action to abate crime, and it prevents the protection of victims from being approached from a perspective of solidarity.

Conclusion

What does this examination of the controversy between Pease's group and Hope's, over the modelling of the distribution of victimization in the population, contribute? It enables us to go further than the methodological discourse of quantification. The main difference between them is their research approaches. Whereas Hope claims to do research for knowledge, Pease professes to do 'science in action' (which he calls *crime science*). Admittedly, Hope does pay far more attention to epistemological issues in the social sciences, whereas Pease's work corresponds to the engineering science tradition, with the aim of being useful, without ever examining the cognitive and political underpinnings of situational crime prevention. But this difference is debatable, for Hope also has a practical purpose in his research (he pleads for community social prevention), while Pease's group oscillates between ever more sophisticated research and the development of a practical solution. The difference between these two approaches is situated on the political order: Hope's hypotheses cannot be dissociated from a conception of public policy on security that is based on solidarity; those of Pease and his colleagues rest on a minimal (short public expenditures to protect victim) and short-term conception of public policy. We cannot fully understand the statistical debate without integrating the links between social quantification and governance of victim protection. We hope this sociology and social history of quantification models one way of being reflexive about statistics in criminology.

References

Anderson, D., Chenery, S., Pease, K. (1995) *Biting Back: Tackling Repeat Burglary and Car Crime*, London: Home Office.

Ashton, J., Brown, I., Senior, B., Pease, K. (1998) 'Repeat Victimisation: Offender Accounts', *International Journal of Risk, Security and Crime Prevention* 3(4): 269–279.

Bottoms, A. and Wiles, P. (1992) 'Explanations of crime and place', In D. Evans, N. Fyfe and D. Herbert (eds.), Crime, Policing and Place: Essays in Environmental Criminology, Abingdon, Oxon: Routledge, pp. 11–35.

Bouchaud, J-P. (2013) 'Les Lois des Grands Nombres'. In J.C. Zylberstein (ed.), *Histoire des nombres*, Paris: Editions Tallandier: 99–111.

Bowers, K.J., Johnson, S.D. (2005) 'Domestic Burglary Repeats and Space-Time Clusters: the Dimensions of Risk', *European Journal of Criminology* 2(1): 67–92.

Desrosières, A. (2014) *Prouver et Gouverner*, Paris: La Découverte.

Farrell, G. and Pease, K. (1993) 'Once Bitten, Twice Bitten: Repeat Victimization and its Implications for Crime Prevention', *Police Research Group, Crime Prevention Unit Paper n°46*, London: Home Office.

Fielding, M. and Jones, V. (2012) 'Disrupting the Optimal Forager: Predictive Risk Mapping and Domestic Burglary Reduction in Trafford, Greater Manchester', *International Journal of Police Science & Management* 14(1): 30–41.

Foster, J. and Hope, T. (1993) *Housing, community and crime: The impact of the Priority Estates Project.* Hope Office Research Study. London: HMSO.

Gilbert, N. and Doran, J. (1994) *Simulating Societies: The Computer Simulation of Social Phenomena*, London: UCL Press.

Hope, T. (2001) 'Community Crime Prevention in Britain: a Strategic Overview', *Criminology and Criminal Justice*, 1(4): 421–440.

Hope, T. (2007) 'Conceptualising the Trend in Burglary in England and Wales', Contribution au séminaire Atteintes aux biens, programme de coordination CRIMPREV du 6ème PCRD Assessing Deviance, Crime and Prevention in Europe, Bruxelles.

Hope, T. (2015) 'Understanding the Distribution of Crime Victimization Using "British Crime Survey" Data: An Exercise in Statistical Reasoning', *Oxford Handbooks Online: Criminology Criminal Justice*, New York: Oxford University Press.

Hope, T. and Karstedt, S. (2003) 'Towards a New Social Crime Prevention'. In H. Kury, J. Obergfell-Fuchs (eds.) *Crime Prevention: New Approaches*, Mainz, Weisse Ring: Verlag-GmbH: 461–489.

Hope, T. and Lab, S.P. (2001) 'Variation in Crime Prevention Participation: Evidence from the British Crime Survey', *Crime Prevention and Community Safety: An International Journal* 3(1): 7–21.

Hope, T. and Norris, P.A. (2012) 'Heterogeneity in the Frequency Distribution of Crime Victimization', *Journal of Quantitative Criminology* 29(4): 543–578.

Hope, T. and Trickett, A. (2004a) 'La Distribution de la Victimisation dans la Population', *Déviance et Société* 28(3): 385–404.

Hope, T. and Trickett, A. (2004b) 'Angst Essen Seele auf … but it keeps away the burglars! Private Security, Neighbourhood Watch and the Social Reaction to Crime, *Kölner Zeitschrift für Soziologie und Sozialpsychologie (Sonderheft)* 43: 441–468.

Hope, T. and Walklate, S. (1995) 'Repeat Victimization: Differentiation or Structuration?', Paper presented to the British Criminology Conference, Loughborough.

Johnson, S., Birks, D., McLaughlin, L., Bowers, K. and Pease, K. (2007) *Prospective Crime Mapping in Operational Context,* London: Home Office.

Johnson, S.D., Bowers, K., Hirschfield, A. (1997) 'New Insight into the Spatial and Temporal Distribution of Repeat Victimisation', *British Journal of Criminology* 37(2): 224–241.

Johnson, S., Bowers, K., Birks, D. and Pease, K. (2009) 'Predictive Mapping of Crime by ProMap: Accuracy, Units of Analysis, and the Environmental Backcloth'. In D. Weisburd (ed.) *Putting Crime in its Place,* New York: Springer: 171–198.

Lynch, J., Berbaum, M. and Planty, M. (1998) *Investigating Repeated Victimization with the NCVS.* Final Report for National Institute of Justice (Grant 97-IJ-CX-0027). Washington, DC: NIJ.

Morgan, F. (2000) 'Repeat Burglary in a Perth Suburb: Indicator of Short-Term or Long-Term Risk', *Crime Prevention Studies* 12: 83–118.

Osborn, D., Ellingworth, D., Hope, T. and Trickett, A. (1996) 'Are Repeatedly Victimized Households Different?', *Journal of Quantitative Criminology* 12(2): 223–245.

Osborn, D. and Tseloni, A. (1998) 'The Distribution of Household Property Crimes', *Journal of Quantitative Criminology* 14(3): 307–330.

Pease, K. and Tseloni, A. (2014) *Using Modelling to Predict and Prevent Victimization,* New York: Springer.

Perry, W.L., McInnis, B., Price, C.C., Smith, S.C. and Hollywood, J.S. (2013) *Predictive Policing: The Role of Crime Forecasting in Law Enforcement Operations,* Santa Monica, CA: Rand Corporation.

Pitcher, A. and Johnson, S.D. (2011) 'Examining Theories of Victimization Using a Mathematical Model', *Journal of Research in Crime and Delinquency* 48(1): 83–109.

Rowley C. (2013) A level 2 outcome evaluation of a police intervention aimed at reducing future burglary dwellings in the immediate vicinity of a burglary dwelling. Research Report. Cambridge, Institute of Criminology.

Sparks, R.F. (1981) 'Multiple Victimization: Evidence, Theory, and Future Research', *The Journal of Criminal Law and Criminology* 72(2): 762–778.

Sparks, R.F., Genn, H. and Dodd, D. (1977) *Surveying victims,* Chichester: Wiley.

Townsley, M., Homel, R. and Chaseling, J. (2003) 'Infectious Burglaries: A Test of the Near Repeat Hypothesis', *British Journal of Criminology* 43(3): 615–633.

Trickett, A., Osborn, D.R., Seymour, J. and Pease, K. (1992) 'What is Different About High Crime Areas?', *British Journal of Criminology* 32(1): 81–90.

Weisburd, D., Bernasco, W. and Bruinsma, G. (eds.) (2009) *Putting Crime in Its Place: Units of Analysis in Spatial Crime Research*, New York: Springer.

Part 2

**Collaboration and Knowledge
Exchange in Practice**

7

Criminological Knowledge and the Politics of Impact: Implications for Researching Juvenile Justice

Lesley McAra

Introduction

This chapter explores the politics of engaging in a research agenda aimed at maximising the impact of criminological knowledge on policy and practice. It is based on a case study of Scottish penal developments, with specific reference to the Edinburgh Study of Youth Transitions and Crime, a longitudinal programme of research which has had demonstrable influence on the nature and function of Scottish juvenile justice (and beyond) (Howard League 2013). The chapter builds on an article first published in the *British Journal of Criminology* (McAra 2016), which highlighted a major dissonance between policy discourse on youth crime in Scotland and the decision-making practices of key institutions within the juvenile and adult justice systems. In the article I concluded that, for maximum impact, criminologists needed to engage with and challenge both political and institutional practice: a multi-level approach to transformative action.

L. McAra (✉)
University of Edinburgh, Edinburgh, UK

© The Author(s) 2017

149

S. Armstrong et al. (eds.), *Reflexivity and Criminal Justice*,
DOI 10.1057/978-1-137-54642-5_7

In this chapter, I develop the argument by exploring in more detail three interrelated implications of this local history: (i) what it tells us about statecraft, namely the nature and operation of the power and right to punish; (ii) what it tells us about the limits of criminological influence and impediments to impact; and consequently (iii) what it suggests about the future of criminology as an applied and policy-relevant discipline. In doing so, I am going to reflect on my own role as researcher–participant within Scottish criminal justice, tracking and commenting on the spatial and temporal context of knowledge production.

I begin with an overview of the Edinburgh Study and the main policy implications of the findings as they emerged over a period of some 18 years. The chapter then explores the challenges posed by the nature and operation of political power as deployed over the same time frame and, in particular, how pathways to impact were shaped and sometimes blocked by the variant modes of 'statecraft' deployed. I conclude with a critical review of the 'impact imperative' as a mechanism by which the worth of research is assessed.

The Edinburgh Study

The Edinburgh Study is a longitudinal programme of research on pathways into and out of crime for a cohort of around 4300 young people, who started secondary school in the City of Edinburgh in 1998.[1] A key objective of the Edinburgh Study is to use the findings to support the development of more effective policies for tackling the problems presented by young people who come into conflict with the law.

Multiple data sources about the cohort have been collected including: self-report questionnaires (six annual waves up to age 18 for the whole cohort, and one follow-up wave at age 24, for those young people who had been referred to the juvenile justice system and two matched groups); official records (school, social work, juvenile justice, criminal convictions); a pastoral teacher survey (when cohort members were aged 13); a parental/main caregiver survey (when cohort members were aged 14);

[1] This work was supported by the Nuffield Foundation; The Scottish Government; and the Economic and Social Research Council (R000237157; R000239150).

and finally a geographic information system (based on census and police-recorded crime data) (further details about the Edinburgh Study can be found at McAra and McVie 2012).

Situating the Cohort

Importantly, the Edinburgh Study cohort has grown to maturity over three distinct policy phases in juvenile justice in Scotland. They were born in the mid-1980s and reached the age of criminal responsibility (age eight in Scotland) in the early 1990s, a point immediately prior to devolution in Scotland.[2] This was during the high point of welfarism in juvenile justice: predicated on the Kilbrandon philosophy, juvenile justice was characterised by a needs-based focus, with institutions being committed to the promotion of social welfare (see preamble to the Social Work (Scotland) Act 1968). The cohort reached the peak age of self-reported offending (age 14/15) in the early 2000s during the Scottish New Labour/Liberal Democrat coalition years when juvenile justice was characterised by a more punitive turn (with the then Cabinet Secretary for Justice stating that punishment was a key part of the youth justice process, McAra 2006). Members of the cohort reached the age of 21 at the start of the Scottish National Party (SNP) government years (from 2007 onwards) which saw the implementation of a more 'compassionate' phase of justice, predicated on prevention (through early and effective intervention) and maximum diversion (see McAra 2016).

Key Findings and Policy Implications

The findings from the Edinburgh Study present a number of challenges for policy makers primarily because they suggest that the most effective way of tackling serious and persistent offending by young people is through enhancing educational and economic opportunity, with maximum diversion from criminal justice. The Study has evidence that

---

[2] The UK Government ceded substantial self-governing powers to Scotland through the Scotland Act 1998 which established the modern Scottish parliament. This was a manifesto commitment of the UK Labour Government which took office in 1997.

a group of young people—the usual suspects—are recycled into the juvenile justice system again and again, with many making the transition into the adult criminal justice system by age 16. This is the product of the long-standing working cultures of key gatekeepers to formal systems of justice (including the police, the Reporter to the children's hearing system and the procurator fiscal)[3] which differentiate between categories of young people on the basis of class and suspiciousness (McAra and McVie 2005, 2012). These working cultures have been impervious to the changing policy terrain described above: highlighting an unacknowledged disjuncture between political discourse and institutional practice over many years (McAra 2016).

Whilst it is impossible to predict from a young age whether a person will become a serious and persistent offender by their mid-to-late teenage years, the findings of our research show that early system contact runs the risk of labelling and creating a self-fulfilling prophecy. Indeed early experience of residential care is one of the strongest predictors of whether a youngster will end up in prison by age 24 (McAra 2014). The findings also show that critical moments during the teenage years are key to understanding criminal conviction pathways. In particular, school exclusion is associated with significantly raised odds of obtaining a conviction (McAra and McVie 2010). In the mid-teenage years, system contact appears to have a stigmatising effect, inhibiting the normal process of desistance from offending which begins at around age 14/15 for the cohort as a whole (McAra and McVie 2007). Rather than lifting the usual suspects out of poverty or opening up opportunity, system contact serves instead to entrench poverty and adversity, thereby reproducing the stigma that drives systemic referral processes (McAra 2016).

---

[3] The children's hearing system deals with young people in need of care and protection from birth up to age 16, and young offenders from age eight (the age of criminal responsibility in Scotland) to 16. Cases are referred to the 'Reporter' who investigates whether or not there is a prima facie case that one of the grounds for referral to a hearing has been met and the child is in need of compulsory measures of care. The hearing is a lay tribunal and disposals include residential and non-residential supervision requirements. In Scotland, social workers deliver probation and through care services and are responsible for community-based disposals such as community service orders. The procurator fiscal is the prosecutor.

Taken together, the findings highlight the need for a holistic approach to service delivery running counter to the more segmented character of extant policy portfolios and suggest that the significant resource accorded to criminal justice would be more effectively deployed elsewhere. Moreover, they remind us that the policy phases which young people live through all have a sequential effect on life chances and developmental pathways: something which policy evaluation rarely takes into account when assessing what works. In this case, the labelling effects from a young age have continued to impact on the identity of young people and their institutional processing, an impact which increases exponentially over time with further systemic processing. When encountering a new mode of intervention, the young people are therefore carrying the baggage of all previous encounters (see McAra and McVie 2012). Importantly, the longitudinal nature of the research itself has meant that the Edinburgh Study 'narrative' has developed incrementally and cumulatively over time. Just as there are period effects which are required to be explored within longitudinal data (Blanchard et al. 1977), so too are there period effects in knowledge production and impact: and it is to these that the next section turns.

Knowledge Production and Impact: Situating the Researcher–Participant

As was noted, a key objective of the Edinburgh Study is to utilise our findings on crime pathways to support the development of practical and effective approaches to the delivery of justice for young people. However, the influence of the Study has been somewhat uneven and any success hard won. It has required experimentation with a multiplicity of engagement strategies over the 18 years in which the Study has been in existence, and it is only in the past five years that the Study team has gained major applied policy traction. In this section, a discussion of the Study team's strategies of impact, and their effects or not, are organised chronologically in two parts and covering three key themes of youth policy identified earlier.

(i) The early years (1998–2006): from welfarism to the punitive turn

I joined the University in 1995 from the Scottish Office Central Research Unit: gamekeeper-turned poacher! With David Smith, I began planning the Edinburgh Study. Susan McVie subsequently joined the research team, also a former member of the Central Research Unit. Our strong belief was that the lessons learnt from our time in government (commissioning and managing research and providing research-based policy advice to Ministers) would stand the Edinburgh Study in good stead in terms of policy influence and impact. In particular, we recognised the importance of producing short, sharp reports which distilled complex findings and their policy importance in plain English. We also brought insider-knowledge about how to network effectively across government and the wider criminal justice system, and with whom to network for maximum influence. And we had a strong belief (based on our practical experience) that good and robust science could and usually would over-ride populist political imperatives.

As a point of reference, we interpreted the term 'policy engagement' as a mode of influencing, and acting as a critical friend to, politicians and the relevant policy divisions within the civil service. Policy, as object of analysis, was loosely conceived. For the purposes of our research it could take the form of government documents, legislation, and variant modes of communication including Ministerial briefings and speeches. The team also recognised from the outset of the Study that to make a real difference to the lives of young people meant tracking the flows from policy into practice (rather than simply looking to influence policy), acknowledging thereby the need to interrogate the facilitators and impediments to real-world change for young people (and to make this part of the research design).

In the period up to 2005, the team was very proactive in providing policy briefings for government (publishing 14 bespoke policy digests) and networked and collaborated in this regard with key civil servants in the separate divisions with responsibility for education, criminal justice and children and families. We gave over 100 applied policy seminars for a range of audiences (including the civil service, the police, schools, social work, children and families services and the Scottish Children's

Reporter Administration); we responded to requests for information, undertook short life bespoke analyses on demand, and generally purposed the research team as an 'on call' service for those seeking research-based evidence. We also contributed to public consultations on policy where relevant, and gave evidence as witnesses to Parliamentary committees (as e.g. on the proposed anti-social behaviour legislation in 2004) and disseminated press releases to accompany all publications.

However, all of these tactics had very limited effect on government and very limited impact on institutional practices across the system (McAra 2016). Indeed, we were told by a senior civil servant that when she had brought the Edinburgh Study findings to the Minister's attention, highlighting why the government's proposed youth justice measures (relating to anti-social behaviour and the targets set for reductions in the number of persistent offenders) would not be effective, the Minister responded: 'I don't care'. We were locked out.

(ii) The later years (2007 to the present): from the punitive turn to prevention and early intervention

In response to lock out, the research team reviewed and then diversified its impact strategy. A minority government (SNP) took office in 2007, and the team made major efforts to ensure that the new administration were appraised of Study findings in more informal ways (including arranging to share a platform at a community event with the new Cabinet Secretary for Justice in his very early weeks in office, with the explicit aim of 'bending his ear'). We also began to campaign more actively and collaboratively with NGOs, human rights groups and third sector agencies, bringing critical research-based evidence to debates on strategic issues such as the age of criminal responsibility, and the need to change the stigmatising ways in which disclosure of information on childhood convictions was routinely released to future employers. We also took opportunities to organise and participate in seminars hosted by Members of the Scottish Parliament (MSPs) at the Parliament.

In the most recent phase of fieldwork (completed in 2011), we negotiated a series of secondments from Scottish Government for their analysts to work on the Study, supporting the evolution of the questionnaire, contributing to fieldwork and undertaking analysis. This had three benefits: it supported the personal development and training of government analysts in survey design and methodology, thus ensuring a knowledgeable and receptive landscape for future quantitative research; it increased government confidence and trust in the way the design evolved; and the principal seconded acted as Study 'champion' on return to government and was able to bring Minsters' attention to the research findings in ways which would have been impossible without the benefit of an insider.

And finally, we explored more creative modes of policy and public engagement including a fringe show ('Hug a Thug' in 2015), drama and photography (the Story Telling Project, McAra 2014); and co-production with the Scottish Storytelling Centre to support collaborative leadership development across the criminal justice system.

Impacts on Policy

At face value, the diversified modes of engagement developed post 2005 met with some success. Here I pick out three highlights:

The first of these is the *Whole System Approach,* a comprehensive youth justice policy aimed at diverting young offenders away from formal systems to meaningful community based services. This was piloted and then rolled out across Scotland in 2011 and has become a flagship policy for the SNP government. The Edinburgh Study provided the principal evidence base for this policy. Full roll out of the policy has been accompanied by dramatic reductions in convictions amongst young people in Scotland (for example offence referrals to the Scottish juvenile justice system have fallen by 83 % from the period prior to implementation to 2014/15, rates of conviction for 16 year olds have reduced by 76 % and custodial sentences for young people under the age of 21 have reduced by 60 % over the same period). A maximum diversion approach is now influencing other areas of criminal justice policy, including new approaches to dealing effectively with vulnerable women who come into conflict with the law and extending the Whole System Approach to all under 21s.

Secondly, Study findings have formed the evidence base to changes in the law relating to disclosure of criminal convictions for the purposes of employment. This was the result of a collaboration of team members with the Scottish Human Rights Commission, the Office of the Scottish Children's Commissioner, the Scottish Child Law Centre and independent consultant Maggie Mellon. Changes to the Children's Hearing (Scotland) Bill in 2011 now mean that offences admitted to by young people in the hearings system (with the exception of the most serious offences) count as alternatives to prosecutions (rather than convictions), and, as such, are no longer disclosable to future employers. This change has opened up employment opportunities for young people who were formally in conflict with the law and better protects the rights of children who are referred on offence grounds to the Reporter.

Finally, the findings from the Study have underpinned new interventions, led by Apex Scotland, aimed at increasing school inclusion (the 'Inclusion Plus Project'). These interventions have been piloted across the Fife and Dundee areas of Scotland, with some evidence already suggesting that they have led to a significant reduction in permanent exclusions. For example, over the period of implementation of Inclusion Plus across the Fife area, the rate per 1000 population of pupils in secondary education being excluded has dropped by 68 %; in contrast to the national rate of school exclusion which has dropped by only 33 % over the same time frame (Scottish Government 2015). There is recent evidence too that the significance of educational inclusion highlighted by the Edinburgh Study has informed the new regime being rolled out in Scotland's young offender institution (predicated on a vision entitled: 'creating a learning environment').

From a period of lock out in the mid-2000s, there is now anecdotal evidence that the findings from the Edinburgh Study have gone 'viral'—to the extent that they are being used as evidence for interventions or informing practice by a vast range of agencies, which we have not been able to track nor fully document. Was this transformation in knowledge uptake simply the product of a more imaginative approach to engagement with policy and practice? How far and to what extent are researchers really in control of the pathways they construct for maximum impact? To answer these questions requires a more detailed review of the wider context of knowledge production.

Impediments and Facilitators of Impact: Statecraft as Context

In this section, I'm going to suggest that the principal factors which impede or facilitate research impact are not always under the control of researchers. Rather opportunities for impact arise out of particular configurations of political and institutional practices, opportunities which can be capitalised upon by those scholars who position themselves as 'policy entrepreneurs' (see also Fishwick in this volume). Fundamentally, research will only be picked up if it 'makes sense' according to the dominant narratives of policy and practice at key time points. Within Scotland, political discourse and institutional practices have both exhibited a self-referential, even at times autopoietic, character; achieving some form of dynamic equilibrium by constantly reconstructing the social world within their own terms (Canaris 1969; Luhmann 1986). Thus external referents (such as academic research) become absorbed by policy and practice only where they already accord with dominant narratives or where they can be remade and reconstructed into their tropes. In contrast, other referents are 'noise' and generally ignored. To explore how these dynamics have shaped the uptake of criminological knowledge, I review first the relationship between politics and knowledge production over key policy phases already mentioned, and second, the nature and function of institutional practices and the limits of academic influence over the same time frame.

Politics and Knowledge Production

Paradoxically, the political cycle means that systems of knowledge often operate in a somewhat stochastic manner, with the tendency of new governments to position themselves against the former dominant narratives and to refresh and to remake system predicates. The very nature of political discourse and the will to power that animates particular modes of governance, thus acts as a potential barrier to the ready uptake of research knowledge, as demonstrated by the Scottish case.

(i) The dominance of welfarism: a golden age?

The Edinburgh Study formally began in 1998 towards the end of what might be characterised as a golden age for evidence-based policy in Scotland. Policy discourse, in the area of youth and criminal justice, was under the control of key elites including networks of senior civil servants, the judiciary, representatives from crown office, directors of social work, and the social care inspectorate (McAra 2016). Academics were part of this elite group, supported and sponsored by the Central Research Unit of the then Scottish Office, which, in addition to commissioning research, also undertook its own primary research. Policy elites were well known to each other, often educated at the same schools and universities and 'doing business' at conferences including the then Scottish Association for the Study of Delinquents conference (a key networking event). Crucially, these elites shared a similar world view, which shaped the dominant policy narrative around penal welfare values. As a government researcher in the early 1990s, I was part of these networks (albeit it a fairly junior one), and I witnessed at first hand the uptake and absorption of research which accorded with these precepts: not least the integration of knowledge from the 'what works' literature into policies aimed at the better rehabilitation of the 'young adult offender' (McAra 2000).

The dominance of penal welfare narratives in Scotland was sustained by pre-devolutionary constitutional arrangements which opened up both a physical and conceptual space for progressive policy ideas to flourish. Scotland had always had a great deal of autonomy from the UK national government, retaining its own education and legal systems and, in the Scottish Office, had a set of departments located at arm's length from Westminster (see Paterson 1994) . This 'quasi-state' gave imprimatur and locus to the ambition and values of the policy networks just described. This enabled differentiation from the more punitive discourses which abounded south of the border in England and Wales over that time frame from the early to late 1990s (McAra 2011), and enabled the construction of penal welfarism as a distinctly Scottish approach to dealing with children and young people who came into conflict with the law (McAra 2011).

(ii) The punitive turn

The post-devolutionary period from the late 1990s to early 2000s saw an abrupt end to the modalities described above, as the new Scottish labour, liberal democratic coalition government grappled with the levers of power. This period saw the demise of the Central Research Unit, with government researchers being replaced by analysts who no longer undertook primary research. Many research contracts were now let to survey companies, rather than academics, and the research output tended to be flat and descriptive in orientation.

More fundamentally, the category of youth was deployed more negatively across policy narratives in the service of polity building—with a new and punitive narrative gaining traction across government and one which was quickly taken up by the media. The 'persistent young offender' became a central part of this narrative—set up in opposition to suffering victims and fractured and failing communities—and juvenile justice was reconfigured in order to protect the public from this new folk devil with tight targets and fast-track systems (Hill et al. 2005). In establishing their power to punish, the new Scottish administration post-devolution embarked on a massive programme of institutional construction—over 100 new institutions linked to juvenile and adult criminal justice were created, many with overlapping competencies (McAra 2011). This emergent institutional landscape broke up extant penal elites positioning them into advisory roles (rather than policy drivers) and enabling Ministerial command and control over discursive framings. From being policy insiders, key academic researchers (with the exception of a very tiny minority of those who were co-opted as special advisors) were largely cut adrift. Whilst lip service was paid to consultation, results from research were generally ignored in favour of more populist imperatives—as for example, the anti-social behaviour legislation (2004) where the contributions of academics to committee evidence gathering were completely overlooked.

Under these particular discursive and institutional framings, it becomes easier to see why traditional modes of policy engagement as adopted by the Edinburgh Study team would have little resonance, particularly as our published results suggested that government juvenile justice policy would not work. As government became closer to the populace, through the devolved settlement, so too did Ministers construct their policy narratives around the needs of an imagined set of publics. In a context where responses to youth crime became suborned in service of polity building, and academics challenging these responses were viewed with increasing suspiciousness, the Minister's statement ('I don't care') makes 'sense' from her perspective.

(iii) Prevention and early intervention

The SNP administration which followed (from 2007 to 2011 as a minority administration and from 2011 as a majority one), positioned itself in opposition to much of the former punitive policy rhetoric. Building on a narrative of early intervention, it embarked on a rationalising and centralising programme, as well as adopting the theme of compassionate justice as a distinctively Scottish approach to crime control and penal practice (McAra 2016). The 'at risk child' now replaced the 'young persistent offender' in policy narratives linked to youth justice. By placing greater emphasis on front-end informal modes of intervention to nip problems in the bud, policy narratives became less emotive. Terms such as inclusivity began to find their way into key documents and the national performance framework for government included commitments to create safer and more cohesive communities in which all young people could flourish (Scottish Government 2009). In developing this policy framework, government began to look to research to support its ambition. The Scottish Crime and Justice Research Centre and the Scottish Institute for Policing Research became two particular points of contact for government with the academic world (see, respectively, Blaustein and Henry in this volume). These Centres flourished in a new and more receptive policy environment (McAra 2011). Moreover, the dynamics of a minority administration also meant that the government had to listen to other views to get their programme through the Parliament. This pivotal moment created opportunities for researchers to inform, advise and co-produce. And the relationships thus reborn and remade continued to gain purchase in policy narratives in the second, now majority, government of the SNP from 2011 onwards.

The Edinburgh Study findings published over this time frame high-lighted the significance of diversionary measures and systems management to building effective practice (McAra and McVie 2007, 2010). These findings chimed with dominant policy narratives and in particular, the rationalisation of the institutional infrastructure undertaken by government. The multiplicity of engagement strategies evolved by the Study team over this phase of Government did bring the findings to the attention of key user groups, but, arguably, these findings would not have had such purchase had they not been in accordance with extant political planning and ambition.

Institutional Practice

Turning then to institutional practices: across the variant phases of policy described above, there is evidence from the Edinburgh Study that the cultural practices of key institutions within the juvenile and adult criminal justice systems have exhibited a high level of continuity rather than change. Indeed, it has been the exception rather than the rule (until very recently) that these day-to-day practices have been directly shaped by political discourse or affected by criminological knowledge. Here, I differentiate between the practices of institutional leaders (such as the Chief Executive of the Scottish Prison Service, the Principal Reporter, or the Lord Advocate) and those of practitioners who deal on a routine basis with the cases of young people who come into conflict with the law (e.g. police officers, the Reporter and prosecutors).

As has been published elsewhere (McAra 2016), the key drivers of decision-making have created a degree of inertia across the gatekeeping institutions linked to youth justice. At different time points and across the variant policy phases, police decisions to warn or charge have been driven by the same rules of troublemaker recognition, including being known to the police from previous years and low socio-economic status. Similarly, the key predictors of being brought to a hearing or to court remain static over time, with early adversarial police contact and low socio-economic status again featuring strongly in decisions. (Indeed, they remain predictors even when controlling for serious offending, including violence.) These drivers of decision-making have become subsumed within institutional folkways and customary practices, taking on an autopoietic quality, a self-referential dynamic which belies the shifting political context.

The longevity of these institutional cultures has become further entrenched at times where statecraft is exercised through the reconfiguration of institutional structure rather than by tackling working cultures. Thus, the hyper-institutionalisation of the Scottish labour/liberal democratic coalition governments from the late 1990s to mid-2000s failed to transform the extant practices of the youth justice institutions which remained intact (McAra 2016). Similarly these practices continued long into the SNP minority government years, until political efforts focused on changing decision-making practices via the systems management dynamic of the Whole System Approach.

By placing decision-making practices under greater scrutiny, and by forcing institutions to work more closely together to support the diversionary dimensions of the policy, a critical alignment was possible between criminological knowledge, policy narrative and institutional practice leading to better outcomes for the many of the young people caught up in the system (Murray et al. 2015). However, whilst there is evidence of greater diversion from youth justice as a result of this policy, it is unclear whether the selection criteria for institutional processing has in fact changed that much. There is some evidence that whilst fewer youngsters are referred into the system, those that are referred continue to be drawn from the most deprived communities; and once in the system, they continue to be recycled, as the stigma of suspiciousness attaches. This is demonstrated by the continued high reconviction rates of those who are sucked furthest into the system. Similarly research on the stop and search tactics of Police Scotland also suggests a disproportionate focus on young people from deprived communities (Murray 2014). It should be noted that the Whole System Approach is applied only to children and young people. Members of the Edinburgh Study cohort are now in their late 20s and there is strong evidence that the usual suspects from this age group have yet to escape the institutional gaze: for example, the peak age of conviction has risen within Scotland from age 18 in 2005 to the late twenties in 2014/15 (Scottish Government 2016). As long as these cultural practices prevail, then the uptake and influence of research is likely to be limited and short-lived.

Concluding Reflections on the Impact Imperative

As the above section indicates, pathways to impact are shaped by the vagaries of the political and institutional environment which can work in tandem (as with the Whole System Approach) or more often in opposition. I use this final section of the chapter to reflect on the implications of the Scottish case for scholars who are aiming to bring their research knowledge to bear on policy and practice.

Within the UK, a key measure of the worth of research is its impact (see Introduction to this volume). Being able to demonstrate impact can result in increased income flows through the Research Excellence Framework, and pathways to impact are a core part of research grant applications. The Scottish case problematises this construction of 'worth'. As demonstrated, the politics of knowledge production confound a linear conception of research into policy and practice. Pathways to impact are not always under the control of the researcher, and once knowledge is taken up by policy makers, researchers often lose control of the ways in which it is deployed. Under these circumstances, researcher agency is generally compromised.

Impact most often will occur where research findings accord with dominant political narratives. In this regard, governments seek out research to support a view already taken, rather than critically engaging with a wider field of knowledge (some of which may contradict or confound political perception). The evidence from the Scottish case highlights the challenges in prompting transformations in political discourse where policy is at odds with research findings. At times of lock out, because of the self-referential dynamics of policy narratives, research will simply not gain traction. It becomes an external referent and an aspect of wider environmental 'noise'.

Turning to institutional decision-making practices, these are not easily touched or shaped by political discourse and, as was noted, have tendencies to inertia. It is somewhat ironic that governments have utilised responses to youth crime as a mechanism through which to build political capacity when in practice, their control and direction over youth justice institutions is only ever partial and very rarely complete. The rules of recognition which underpin institutional cultural practices are long standing and as with political narratives not always receptive to the lessons from research.

In this chapter, I have tracked a sometimes very personal history of efforts to engage policy and practice with research and considered the time points at which some success has occurred. Youth justice systems are segmented phenomena, containing a multiplicity of institutional framings and shifting policy narratives. For academics to influence policy and practice, we need to learn the rules of engagement, build the necessary networks, communicate our findings widely at all levels and wait for the moment in which conduits for influence open up. We need to act as policy entrepreneurs.

A danger for our discipline is that the allure of impact and its rewards (in terms of grant income and associated career kudos) create temptations to compromise on research integrity and sidestep robust and critical engagement with potential user groups. To avoid this, we must put reflexivity at the heart of all that we do and put critical energies into understanding and researching the politics of knowledge production. Fundamentally, we need to recognise that criminologists can sometimes make history, but this is generally not under circumstances of their own making!

References

Blanchard, R., Bunker, J. and Wachs, M. (1977) 'Distinguishing aging, period and cohort effects in longitudinal studies of elderly populations', *Socio-Economic and Planning Sciences* 11(3): 137–146.

Canaris, C. (1969) *Systemdenken und Systembegriff im der Jurisprudenz*, Berlin: Duncker and Humblot.

Hill, M. Walker, M., Moodie, K., Wallace, B., Bannister, J., Khan, F., McIvor, G., and Kendrick, A. (2005) *Final Report of the Evaluation of the Fast Track Children's Hearings Pilot,* Edinburgh: Scottish Government.

Howard League (2013), *Justice for young people: Papers by the winners of the Research Medal* https://d19ylpo4aovc7m.cloudfront.net/fileadmin/howard_league/user/online_publications/Justice_for_young_people_web.pdf

Luhmann, N., (1986) The Autopoiesis of Social Systems. In Geyer, F. and Van der Zouwen, J. (eds.) *Sociocybernetic Paradoxes: Observation, Control and Evolution of Self-Steering Systems,* Beverly Hill California: Sage.

McAra, L. (2016) 'Can Criminologists Change the World? Critical Reflections on the Politics, Performance and Effects of Criminal Justice', *British Journal of Criminology,* advance access: doi: 10.1093/bjc/azw015.

McAra, L. (2014), *Crime and Justice: A Vision for Modern Scotland, Apex Annual Lecture* (2 September), Edinburgh, Scotland.

McAra, L. (2011) The Impact of Multi-Level Governance on Crime Control and Punishment. In A. Crawford (ed.) *International and Comparative Criminal Justice and Urban Governance: Convergence and Divergence in Global, National and Local Settings,* Cambridge University Press, Cambridge: 276–303.

McAra, L. (2006) Welfare in Crisis? Youth Justice in Scotland. In J. Muncie and B. Goldson (eds) *Comparative Youth Justice,* Sage: London: 127–145.

McAra, L. (2000) *Parole in the Penal System: Towards a Relational Theory of Penalty,* Doctoral thesis, University of Edinburgh.

McAra, L. and McVie, S. (2012) 'Negotiated order: Towards a theory of pathways into and out of offending', *Criminology and Criminal Justice* 12(4): 347–376.

McAra, L. and McVie, S. (2010) 'Youth Crime and Justice: Key messages from the Edinburgh Study of Youth Transitions and Crime', *Criminology and Criminal Justice,* 10(2): 179–209.

McAra, L. & McVie, S. (2007) 'Youth justice? The impact of system contact on patterns of desistance from offending', *European Journal of Criminology* 4(3): 315–345.

McAra, L. and McVie, S. (2005) 'The usual suspects? Street-life, young people and the police', *Criminal Justice* 5(1): 5–35.

Murray, K. (2014) *Stop and Search in Scotland,* Doctoral Thesis, University of Edinburgh.

Murray, K., McGuinness, P., Burman, M. and McVie, S. (2015) *Evaluation of the Whole System Approach to Young People Who Offend in Scotland,* Edinburgh: Scottish Government.

Paterson, L. (1994) *The Autonomy of Modern Scotland*, Edinburgh: Edinburgh University Press.

Scottish Government (2016), Criminal Proceedings in the Scottish Courts, Statistical Bulletin, Edinburgh: Scotland. http://www.gov.scot/ Publications/2016/02/6001

Scottish Government (2015*), Summary Statistics for Schools in Scotland*, Edinburgh: Scotland. http://www.gov.scot/Resource/0046/00465732.pdf

8

Reflexive Academic–Practitioner Collaboration with the Police

Alistair Henry

Introduction

Reflexivity in the understanding and practice of research is not just something to be cultivated amongst researchers. Particularly as models of collaborative research develop—models which tend to already work with a reflexive understanding of research—there is a growing need to think about the reflexivity of the researched. This chapter characterises research as ultimately being about learning across the (recognised) boundaries of social worlds (the academy or, in this case, the police being distinctive social worlds). It will argue that reflexive practice on the part of social researchers, in that it challenges some of the myths about scientific social research, might itself play an important role in encouraging reflexivity on the part of practitioners (or 'the researched'), and that reflexivity on the part of practitioners will encourage challenge of some of the myths about their practice, fostering a more realistic understanding and ownership of research that sees it not in narrow instrumental, credibility-

A. Henry (✉)
University of Edinburgh, Edinburgh, UK

© The Author(s) 2017   **169**
S. Armstrong et al. (eds.), *Reflexivity and Criminal Justice*,
DOI 10.1057/978-1-137-54642-5_8

enhancing terms, but as something relevant and to be learned from, even where—perhaps especially where—it is critical of extant practice. However, local demands of practice, external politics, and interests in maintaining public relations also make reflexive engagement with research a challenge.

I begin by sketching out what I term a new praxis of research—the sustained academic–practitioner collaboration—doing so with reference to knowledge transfer and exchange (KTE) literatures, to my own conceptualisation of it as brokering communities of practice, and to a particular example, The Scottish Institute for Policing Research (SIPR), an ongoing attempt to build a sustained and multi-disciplinary dialogue between Scottish Universities and the police with which I have worked since its formation in 2007. In the section that follows, I draw on some foundational theory on reflexivity to examine its role in demystifying both researchers and research in ways that I think are promising for opening up a more credible dialogue around research. I conclude by returning to the conceptualisation of academic–practitioner collaboration as the brokering of communities of practice to emphasise some of the risks and challenges to both researchers and the researched inherent in such processes, and to emphasise the possibilities and impediments thus far characterising attempts to cultivate reflexive academic–practitioner collaboration.

Academic–Practitioner Collaboration: A New Praxis of Research?

Even though recent emphases of UK Research Councils and the Research Excellent Framework (REF) have sharpened interest within the social sciences in having research impact on practice, the desire to inform policing through research evidence is far from new (Fleming 2010; Engel and Henderson 2013: 218; see also Lumsden, this volume), and work on the reflective use of knowledge in problem-solving within professions (Schön 1983), and on the transfer, exchange, and mobilisation of knowledge (KTE) and research evidence within fields as diverse as medicine and health (Mitton et al. 2007), education (Davis 1999), social work (Sheldon and Chilvers 2000), and throughout public services (Nutley et al. 2007) is extensive and growing. Numerous common challenges to informing or shaping practice through evidence are found across all of the different disciplines, an in-exhaustive list of which would include: the incongruence of research and practice organisations, including in relation to the timelines for doing and acting upon research; the need for personal trust relationships to be forged, and how this constantly needs to be renegotiated as people move roles; uncertainty about the 'message' of bodies of research evidence; and different value placed upon different kinds of research and the purposes for which it is being under-taken (for a brief overview see, Henry and Mackenzie 2012: 318–321). What runs through all of these challenges is the fact that academics and practitioners occupy different worlds of work, each of which has its own distinctive, and not always compatible, ways of understand-ing and doing things. By 'worlds of work', I refer to the institutional, professional, and organisational domains which organise and validate recognised activity within them through the evolution of defined and tacit frames of reference. They are 'epistemic communities' in which members' shared understandings of what they do make sense to them, and which are recognised in numerous anthropological and sociologi-cal literatures on institutions (Douglas 1986), the 'worlds' of the arts (Becker 1982), sciences (Kuhn 1996), and law (Fish 1989). Crossing the boundaries of these epistemic communities or 'worlds of work' is, in theory, difficult and the problem of knowledge exchange is thus often a problem of distorted communication across the boundaries of the acad-emy and the work worlds of practice where the products (research) of the former are either incomprehensible to, or likely to be largely reinter-preted within, the latter.

I have argued elsewhere (Henry 2012; Henry and Mackenzie 2012) that Wenger's communities of practice perspective (Wenger 1998) is a helpful framework for understanding this problem and for think-ing about research as necessarily involving the crossing of boundaries. Communities of practice refer to the social relations and attendant ways of thinking about the world that evolve through people's everyday social interactions in collective activities. They are ubiquitous in that they exist in all such activities—families negotiating everyday routines, our pur-suit of hobbies, or within more formal activities like work (whether that be academic work or the work of a police officer). In pursuing collective activities, we build tacit and sometimes explicit shared knowledge and understandings of the world, and think about ourselves, who we are, and what we know, in relation to the multiple overlapping communities of practice in which we participate (Wenger 1998: 45). Because communities of practice are so entwined throughout our personal and professional lives we are constantly negotiating the boundaries of them and in this way the brokering of these boundaries is a very necessary and natural concept for Wenger (1998: 108–113). However, communities of practice can become very 'deep'—where the shared knowledge, language, routines, and skills of members become a distinctive/primary dimension of their identities that differentiates them from non-members. So, for example, the talk and practice of lawyers or technicians in the IT department will often be difficult to fully comprehend by those who are not members of communities of practice within those occupations. For Wenger, if organisations want to harness knowledge from the numerous deep communities of practice that constitute them then there has to be brokering across them, carried out by people who cross the boundaries of different communities of practice with sufficient membership of them to be able to appreciate their practice and to interpret and translate it for other communities of practice in the organisation. An example of a broker in Wenger's work is the supervisor of a claims processing unit within an insurance company, located on the boundaries between communities of practice of both managers and claims processors. An analogous example in the police would probably be the Sergeant. In both cases, mere occupation of the formal role does not itself make the incumbent an effective broker, in the same way that not all researchers are necessarily as good at appreciating and interpreting the worlds they study.

It is useful to think about research and academic–practitioner collaboration in these terms. Crossing the boundaries of communities of practice is essentially what reflexive social researchers are doing as they seek to understand and interpret the worlds and practices of others. As they translate those worlds to be comprehensible within their own communities of practice in the academy there is an element of brokering, although until recently there was usually only brokering into the academy with little engagement going back to the world of practice. Academic–practitioner collaborations probably represent the most sustained attempts to rectify this, fostering ongoing brokering between academic and practitioner communities of practice.

'Collaborative' models of research influenced much of what is now viewed as academic–practitioner collaboration. Here practitioners are recognised as coproducing new knowledge not only through their participation as the subjects of research, but also through their wider participation and involvement in the whole research process from formulation and design, to implementation, analysis, and practical application. The paradigm example of such an approach, in methodological terms, is participatory action research in which the research process is very much conceptualised as a 'collective' enterprise between researchers and practitioners (McIntyre 2008). Not dissimilar, in that it involved researchers being situated within the field of practice concerned, in this case a Youth Offending Service in Swansea, is the reflective friend research developed by Case and Haines (2014). Case and Haines argue, drawing on Wenger as I do, that collaboration involving researchers being situated within the field, responding to emergent questions and findings from the research context, engaging in dialogue with collaborators, and sustaining this kind of relationship with them, itself allows researchers 'a means of producing better quality (in the sense of a closer and more accurate description of social reality) research' (2014: 60–61). It is a key argument of proponents of such approaches that collaboration in the research process itself allows a deeper and richer 'appreciation' of the research field to emerge (see also, Henry and Mackenzie 2012: 320–321), through which sharper, critical research questions can be identified that otherwise would have been hidden or, to use my favoured terminology, incomprehensible to a researcher who had not sufficiently crossed the boundary of the community of practice being studied. The key charge against such collaboration (also commonly made against ethnography), however, is that the researcher becomes too immersed in the field, inured to what is sociologically interesting about it or what is critical or problematic about practice in which they have themselves become invested as participants. In short, the criticism tends to be that the researcher 'goes native' and so lacks a critical distance and independence from it.

This is also a noted challenge of boundary work explicitly recognised by Wenger, effective brokers being those who avoid 'capture' by particular communities of practice (Wenger 1998: 108–110; Henry 2012: 421–422). As we'll come to in the following sections, claims to independence and freedom from bias within positivist sociology are themselves not unproblematic (Gouldner 1970: 54; Case and Haines 2014: 58–59). However, criticisms around independence should nonetheless also be acknowledged in relation to the more structural manifestation of collaboration that goes beyond individual ad hoc projects, specifically, institutional collaboration arrangements between Universities and practitioner organisations. Arguably the police have been at the vanguard of forging such relationships, initially in the USA through pioneering work at the University of Berkeley at the beginning of the twentieth century. Nowadays, there is evidence of such work in many (albeit largely 'western') jurisdictions (see, Johnston and Shearing 2009). I am going to focus my observations largely on my direct experience of working within SIPR.

The Scottish Institute for Policing Research

SIPR was established as an inclusive partnership between twelve independent Scottish Universities, the Scottish Further and Higher Education Funding Council, and, at the outset, all eight of Scotland's regional police services, since amalgamated into a single service called Police Scotland. SIPR has aspired to engage the police and the academy in ongoing dialogue around research in a sustained way in order to cultivate a broader 'culture of engagement' (Fyfe and Wilson 2012: 311), rather than focusing on individual projects per se. SIPR does have a modest budget to fund small projects—whether new research or projects to disseminate existing evidence—but these are generally viewed as 'seed corn' funding designed to support work that might inform the design of larger project bids to UK and/or EU funding councils. SIPR does not 'monopolise' policing research, which continues to be sustained by individual academics working in independent Universities. Given that it seeks to forge collaboration across a diverse set of disciplines (including social sciences, psychology, international relations, geography, health sciences, education, law, forensic sciences, and management studies) this would in any case be impossible, as well as undesirable. Rather, its more modest aspiration has been to act as a hub and facilitator for academic–practitioner collaboration. It has developed a multifaceted approach to this end, using standard activities such as conferences, events, workshops, small project grants, and the use of a website as an information and contacts hub for users alongside attempts to foster collaboration and relationships at different levels throughout the academy, the police, and partner agencies. Examples include (also see, Fyfe and Wilson 2012: 309–311):

* an Executive Committee of academics and practitioners meeting regularly to maintain an overview of its activities, identify and facilitate important strategic areas of work, and connect SIPR to wider UK and international collaborations to ensure that it avoids becoming parochial;
* a Practitioner Fellowship scheme whereby practitioners work with an academic mentor on fashioning a project relevant to their practice but also informed by substantive research evidence and sound research practice and ethics;
* a blended-learning Master's degree in Policing Studies, administered by the University of Dundee, works closely with the Scottish Police College to ensure academic input into its continuous professional development programmes for serving police officers;
* an Executive Sessions programme pairing up senior police officials (not always from Scotland) with academics to work together on using research evidence to engage with 'wicked issues';
* themed 'sandpit' events bringing police, partner agencies, and academics together to generate conversations on issues of mutual interest that might be developed into KTE or research projects; and
* active engagement of PhD researchers with an interest in policing, broadly defined, initially through some funded scholarships, latterly through away days, workshop events, and poster presentation competitions, which interested practitioners attend and are involved as respondents (there are also serving police officers undertaking PhD degrees).

In short, SIPR is playing a long game, incrementally exposing police practitioners throughout the organisation to research and the process of producing research evidence. It has to be acknowledged that this remains a work in progress. However, although recent scholarship on reflexivity already identifies many of the challenges and opportunities facing the researcher within this more collaborative praxis of research (Case and Haines 2014), less has thus far been said about the reflexive practitioner and how reflexivity on their part might also be something to be cultivated. Experience in SIPR suggests it is worthwhile, but that it comes with limitations.

Reflexive Research and Reflective Practice

Reflexivity in research practice is not just about researchers being transparent about their standpoints, biographies, and biases that naturally shape their research choices, although this does flow from it. More fundamentally, reflexive research in the social sciences (theoretical and empirical) is about the researcher being cognisant of the fundamentally social process of interpretation through which knowledge is produced and given meaning, their role in that process, often in collaboration with others (the researched), and of the ways in which this process is inherently political because it implicitly or explicitly gives credence to some perspectives over others, either challenging or validating the status quo, extant practice, and/or interests (Alvesson and Skoldberg 2009: 10–12). This insight—that research is an interactional, interpretive, and appreciative activity in the lived world in which the researcher is a participant, and that reflection and study of that activity itself forms as appropriate a focus of social scientific investigation as much as the worlds of work of 'lay' practitioners—may have been long-coming (Gouldner 1970: 54), but it certainly has arrived. Importantly, it emphasises that the researcher should not be distinguished from the researched as being the only active participant in research.

In the social interactions and interpretations that lie at the heart of research, knowledge is coproduced and collective rather than the individual creation of the researcher alone, even though the traditional reified outputs of research (the report, article, monograph) tend to be represented as such (see, Becker 1982: 1–39 on art as collective activity). It is therefore to *both* the researcher and the researched (actually with an emphasis on the latter) that I want to turn in my own observations on reflexivity and its resonance for thinking about academic–practitioner collaborations as brokering communities of practice. In doing this, I will highlight two related insights gleaned from Giddens' and Gouldner's foundational work which informs my sketch of the reflexive practitioner. I will note in conclusion a distinction to be made between that and the 'reflective' practitioner.

Reflexive Research Is Credible Research

One of the staunchest criticisms of collaborative research (and of 'funded' research more generally) is that it lacks, or has a tendency to lose, the independence of objective positivistic science (Engel and Henderson 2013: 230–231). This is a vitally important issue for research, and I will come on to argue that acknowledgement of the boundaries between academic and practitioner fields remains crucial precisely because it gives cognisance to the issue.

However, there is a problem with the positivist claim, one that reflexivity towards the interactive process of research guards against:

> When sociologists stress the autonomy of sociology – that it should (and, therefore, it can) be pursued entirely in terms of its own standards, free of the influences of the surrounding society – they are giving testimony to their loyalty to the rational credo of their profession. At the same time, however, they are also contradicting themselves as sociologists, for surely the strongest general assumption of sociology is that men are shaped in countless ways by the press of their social surround. (Gouldner 1970: 54)

In this formulation, sociologists' claims to independence from fields to be objectively scrutinised ultimately reflected the trammels, culture, and recognised methods of a profession rather than a reality. For Gouldner, the idea of the social scientist free from any bias or prior assumption was a presentational affectation designed to bolster the professional credibility and distinctiveness of the scientist. In fact, he argued, social scientists, like all human beings in society, exercised their 'freedom' to choose their topics of interest and the methods to study them within 'the press of their social surround', which included accepted theoretical and methodological resources within the communities of practice of sociology, as well as elements of their personal biographies. Sociologists' failure to acknowledge themselves as socially constructed, and as making political decisions in their choice, method, and dissemination of sociological work, framed by professional and personal assumptions, became internally visible within the discipline as these assumptions became dissonant with those of newcomers to the field who recognised them as such—assumptions and biases rather than neutral, true, or incontestable ways of seeing society (see, Gouldner 1970: 39)—and with whom such theorising lost credibility.

Gouldner's insight lies at the very heart of current theorising of reflexivity which sees acknowledgement of the researcher as part of the field of study, their interpretations of it framed within their own professional and personal identities, as simply more credible than the positivist 'myth' of the independent social scientist, standing above a field of study, ready to provide the objectively 'right' answer in relation to it. For researchers, this debunking can be liberating and suggests a need to be honest, humble, and realistic about what their work can do (see also, Blaustein, this volume). The skills and resources of their communities of practice (subject to their own competence) allow them to provide credible understandings of issues grounded in an explicitly articulated academic rigor, with due attention being given to its limitations, but do not imbue them with the mythical power of finding incontestable truth. Such a myth itself (one I still see in practitioners' expectations from researchers) creates a distance between researcher and researched and a denial of the ways in which research processes do (whether reflexively recognised or not) involve a coproduction of knowledge through interaction, appreciation, and interpretation. Researcher reflexivity provides a good starting point for cultivating practitioner reflexivity by narrowing this distance and acknowledging the collective and collaborative nature of the process, giving practitioners purchase on this more realistic enterprise. Further, the nature of researcher reflexivity, drawing into view issues of bias, professional, personal and political standpoint, and presumption plausibly cultivates similar reflection on the part of collaborators. Being transparent about their interests in the research, and how it might be used, is beneficial if it can lead to a transparent engagement around the research with the researcher in the first instance (see, Case and Haines 2014), but also raises potentially more thorny issues reflecting the real issues of power implicit in collaborations, from narrowly focused agendas seeking to validate and 'rubber stamp' 'successful' initiatives that do not challenge the status quo (Henry and Mackenzie 2012: 321), to questions of organisational reputation and practice deemed beyond contestation (see the discussion of stop and search below). I will argue in the final section that brokering captures the fact that these issues are unlikely to go away but also that rendering them transparent provides a more likely condition for the kinds of sustained collaboration necessary to challenge them.

Social Scientific Research Does Not Have 'The Answers'

This point was alluded to above, where credible research was characterised as research that does not claim to have 'the answer'. It is a common finding in KTE research that practitioners often place particular value on research that they feel will provide an answer to an instrumental question (Nutley et al. 2007: 36), or worse, which will enhance their legitimacy (Boswell 2009). In the field of policing, the rise of 'crime science' and 'what works' are cases in point. It is dangerous for social science to claim to have the 'right answer' as the reality of research and analysis, even in what might seem like very technical areas such as crime mapping and profiling, tends to be messy and rather less 'scientific' than is presented (Innes et al. 2005). Of course, the more reflective proponents of crime science emphasise incremental learning through ongoing research, not bald claims to truth, but such claims, and the associated aspiration that answers are indeed what research can provide, still persist and are detrimental to the maintenance of any serious research collaboration. They are detrimental because they reflect another myth about social science, one that reflexivity dispels. For Giddens, the institutional formation of the social and natural sciences was guided by the Enlightenment's aspiration that the incremental accumulation of knowledge would ground society in reason, stability, and proof, a belief which still lingers. However:

> Science depends, not on the inductive accumulation of proofs, but on the methodological principle of doubt. No matter how cherished, and apparently well established, a given scientific tenet might be, it is open to revision – or might have to be discarded altogether – in the light of new ideas or findings. (Giddens 1991: 21)

The answers provided by science are subject to revision and refutation and are not, even within the worlds of natural scientists, stable and incontestable. In the more mundane contexts of academic–practitioner collaboration and KTE further question about extracting an answer or a coherent message from what might be an extensive, even multi-disciplinary, body of research also arise (Henry and Mackenzie 2012: 320 and 324–325). Not only are individual pieces of research not 'the answer', systematic analyses of whole bodies of research do not necessarily contain a single message, rather being contested, contradictory, or incompatible. One issue this raises for SIPR is that it has to be very clear that it does not 'represent' any particular 'research community view' because there generally is no single agreed 'view' within the research community.

This further demystification of research and 'evidence' again, when made explicit, provides for more realistic, credible, modest, and necessarily qualified engagement between collaborators. Of course, there might be a risk of the researched taking the demystification to mean that research tells them nothing, but this would be a mistake. Paraphrasing David Smith somewhat (2007: 302), people generally trust doctors not because they can cure them but because doctors work to professional standards, are of good character, have a duty of care, and draw on the best (but imperfect) evidence-base that they have to help people. The doctor who says 'trust me, I can cure you' should be avoided. Similarly, I would suggest that trust between researchers and practitioners is not on a firm foundation if the researchers' trust-claim is 'I can give you the answer'. More plausible might be to claim to work to professional standards, to be of good character (which might be extended to include reflection on standpoint) and subject to a duty of care (research ethics), and to draw on the best evidence-base (substantive and methodological, both imperfect) available, to provide rigorous, critical interpretations of a problem or field. This demystification wrought by reflexivity on the part of researchers invites reflection on the part of research collaborators by opening up research as something that can be engaged with, even challenged, not something that happens elsewhere, probably in a locked laboratory. It sees research characterised more as a resource to prompt and open deliberation, not as an 'answer' that closes it. If research is not merely a search for answers this suggests questions for practitioners: what might research be for?; what ought it to be for?; and, are the right questions even being asked? Whether such questions necessarily evidence reflexivity or reflection is a matter of degree as there is an important distinction to be made between the two.

Reflection in practice is what people do and is certainly a pre-requisite of professional practice (Schön 1983). Schön's work provides examples of architects, psychotherapists, planners, and scientists, amongst others critically reflecting on and evolving their practice through using, applying, and stretching the intellectual tools of their worlds of work to negotiate emergent problems or new cases to be dealt with. Police officers very clearly do this in applying (or not) their legal powers and craft skills to meaningfully carry out tasks in ways that are coherent with the frames of reference of their jobs. This professional creativity and skill in using professional resources demonstrates reflection in practice, in much the same way that a researcher applying the methodological skills of their discipline to the design of a new project does. Reflexivity, however, implies not only competence within a particular community of practice/world of work but an ability to see oneself within it, and to peer beyond it. Reflection is within a community of practice and reflexivity takes you beyond its trammels.

Academic–Practitioner Collaboration as Brokering Communities of Practice

Thinking about academic–practitioner collaboration as brokering communities of practice sits well with a reflexive understanding of research and suggests possibilities for cultivating reflexivity in practitioners that serves to challenge, or at least unsettle, the sometimes narrow trammels of their communities of practice.[1] In this section, I draw out and emphasise two recurrent themes of the discussion so far—that research itself involves appreciation across boundaries and that collaborations are best conceptualised as ongoing processes of brokering and learning—before concluding with a third point, that recognising boundaries also acts as a healthy reminder of the importance of independence (academic research is valuable precisely because it tests police communities of practice) and of the limitations of cultivating reflexivity towards research in practitioners who are ultimately beholden to many internal and external pressures that make learning from research a challenge to them.

Research Involves Appreciation Across Boundaries

Research into social groups and what they do involves crossing the boundaries of communities of practice. The reflective researcher, using the tools of their trade, whether observation or interviews, but also if drawing upon the artefacts of a community of practice (which could be the data it routinely collects or the documents and reports it produces), is (to greater or lesser degrees) making another world comprehensible to them and their academic communities of practice through their interpretation of it. Of course, the reflexive researcher explicitly recognises that their interpretation is not 'neutral' but is framed by the professional and personal assumptions they bring to the study from the communities of practice in which they are immersed (Alvesson and Skoldberg 2009: 10–12). Recognising these boundaries, and the unfamiliar char-

---

[1] It should be acknowledged that many police officers in Scotland were already reflexive and outward looking prior to SIPR, indeed some of them were instrumental in establishing the collaboration.

acter of communities of practice to non-members behind them, acts as a reminder to the researcher that they don't necessarily know from the outset what the most important research questions are. It is by starting with a critical appreciation of the field, an engagement with the communities of practice that comprise it, that researchers are more likely to identify research questions that talk to the issues that matter within it, that are comprehensible to those working within it, and so which forms the basis of research which better reflects the lived experience of participants, and so which stands a better chance of communicating across academic and practitioner communities of practice, the perennial problem of KTE where the importance of the boundary has not been so heeded (see also, Case and Haines 2014: 60–61). Crossing boundaries of communities of practice seems to me to be an accurate descriptor of the reflexive research process and the active negotiation of academic and practitioner frames of reference, values, and interpretations implied by it. For the researcher, the promise of a reflexive approach to research is thus better research that meaningfully grapples with the lived world. For the researched, reflexive research demystifies and makes accessible the research process. However, cultivation of deeper practitioner reflexivity lies beyond individual research projects and through learning within more sustained brokering of communities of practice.

Research Collaborations Are Processes of Brokering and Learning

The aim of SIPR has been to create a 'culture of engagement' (Fyfe and Wilson 2012: 311) around research through sustained interactions with the police involving diverse academic disciplines, and at different levels, from the strategic development of the Institute through the Executive Committee, to its broader role as an information and contacts hub, to its more grass-roots engagement through events, practitioner fellowships, research and KTE collaborative small grants, training and CPD, and through the nurturing of a growing community of doctoral researchers. The reflexive demystification of researchers and the 'messages' of research have lain (sometimes more implicitly than they should have it must be

said) at the heart of these various efforts to allow practitioners to feel
that they have a stake in the research process, that it is something that
necessarily involves them, and in which they ultimately contribute to the
generation of new knowledge valuable both as academic output and as
aid to practice.

Cultivation of a culture of engagement and deliberation around
research, perhaps particularly with the police where the values, tacit
knowledge, and craft of communities of practice are notoriously deep
(Loftus 2009), is not an overnight task. We are not there yet but there are
some promising signs. The sheer diversity of police research emerging in
Scotland since 2007—covering fields including criminology, law, politics,
forensic science, psychology, education, health studies, geography, social
policy, and business studies—has only been made possible by active police
engagement across all of these fields. This has itself exposed the police to
the point that there is no single, simple message to be gleaned from 'the
research', a healthy outcome in itself. The sheer variety of research is also
worthy of note because it alludes to the inclusive understanding of 'policing' within SIPR (not an institute of 'police' research) which is of interest
and importance to agencies beyond the police themselves. Through its
work, SIPR has drawn in and connected with a broad set of agencies with
policing interests, including local government services and third sector
agencies, an unspoken benefit of which is that it decouples policing from
just the police, offering opportunities to expose the police to non-police
knowledge and data about policing, challenging traditional, often dearly
held, 'police views' of the world (yet more boundary crossing of course).
All of this has been to cultivate a kind of reflexivity in police collaborators, to help them see outside the parameters of their own communities
of practice to problems and challenges that they simply might not have
recognised. In particular, I think that it has been about trying to cultivate
two things: the asking of more diverse questions from research; and, the
insight that 'critical' research is to be welcomed not feared.

As noted previously, there are documented tendencies for practitioners
(not just the police) to value and seek research that provides answers
to instrumental concerns, or which can be used tactically to validate
existing practice (Nutley et al. 2007: 39; Boswell 2009). The aspiration of sustained brokering is to challenge both. On the first, there is

evidence of such reflexivity amongst some police officers in Scotland who have actively sought to ask questions about ethics, human rights, social and demographic trends, concepts of procedural justice, and community engagement, all of which look beyond the traditional focus of the police and demonstrate an understanding that research can inform and challenge values and commitments, as well as evaluate initiatives and practices. In short, the police are beginning to ask a more diverse set of questions from research than the instrumental. On the second, the fear of the 'critical' remains something of a concern.[2] It's true that the asking of broader questions and the engagement with non-police perspectives already indicates critical thinking and awareness that the status quo may need challenging. There is probably quite a lot of understanding within the police that it is critical research that drives innovation and creativity. Engel and Henderson (2013: 230) demonstrate that critical research is far from something that the police should fear, given that now well-accepted developments in police practice (they give Goldstein's problem-orientated policing as a key example, others might include more enlightened approaches to domestic violence and greater probity in the recording of interviews etc.) emerged out of research that was critical of extant practice. Evidence of real appreciation of the value of 'critical' research, as something to be learned from, will be evidence of practitioners seeing beyond the parameters of their own communities of practice and engaging in their own research reflexivity. However, the interests, responsibilities, and liabilities of researchers and the researched are not identical. There are real boundaries between them and different priorities given to research within them.

Boundaries Are Real

Recognising boundaries talks to issues of independence, the value of critical research that questions the status quo, and wider internal and external influences on practitioners' receptivity to research. Academics and

---

[2] Here I'm not using 'critical' to denote critical theory as such (although it might of course produce very important, albeit challenging insights for practitioners), rather I'm using it in a general way to refer to research that does not merely validate extant practice.

practitioners occupy different communities of practice and this is precisely the point of their collaboration. Both collaborators have different skills, expertise, and interests, and although sustained brokering may see a negotiation and mutual acceptance of these that can be of benefit to the research process (Case and Haines 2014), the differences and the boundaries between them remain of value (see, Henry and Mackenzie 2012: 324–325) and are brought into stark relief when there is controversy about research. In Scotland, the clearest recent example of this has been in relation to Murray's research on stop and search. The research was funded as a PhD by the Scottish Centre for Crime and Justice Research (SCCJR), a sister collaboration to SIPR covering wider criminal justice issues, and supervised through both SCCJR and SIPR, both of which supported its subsequent dissemination (Murray 2014a, 2014b). The study was published into what was already becoming a politicised climate around policing following the 2013 amalgamation of Scotland's eight regional forces into Police Scotland. Amongst other things it demonstrated that use of the tactic was substantial, that it was disproportionately used against young people and children, and that it lacked adequate legal regulation (Murray 2014a).

Over the longer term, the result has been largely positive where research that uncovered problematic police practices that had developed over a long period of time (certainly before the creation of Police Scotland), seemingly under the radar of researchers, government, and the police themselves, created much-needed formal deliberation about those practices. The police established an internal working group—inviting academics, including Murray, to sit on it—to 'improve' practice drawing from reviews that had swiftly been undertaken by the Scottish Police Authority (the body which formally oversees Police Scotland) and Her Majesty's Inspectorate of Constabulary in Scotland. Interest was such that The Scottish Government also established an independent review convened by a leading Human Rights lawyer, one of its tasks being to explore the drafting of a Code of Practice to clarify and regulate stop and search (see, Advisory Group on Stop and Search 2015). Then the Criminal Justice (Scotland) Act 2016 was recently given Royal Assent and provides a statutory basis for a stop and search Code of Practice, as well as explicitly removing police powers to conduct 'consensual' searches without a legislative basis. So far so good. Thus far the narrative sounds like a success for collaborative research, with public deliberation and legislative reform following critical research, but this is only part of the story.

In the concluding sections of her thesis, Murray (2015) documents difficulties she faced pursuing and disseminating the research, including Police Scotland and the Scottish Government running their own event justifying stop and search to coincide with (and presumably take attention from) the initial publication of her findings with SCCJR. Unsubstantiated claims regarding the tactic's role in contributing to Scotland's declining experience of knife crime, collaboration with an academic willing to place a positive spin on the tactic, and a series of uncomfortable meetings before the Justice Committee of the Scottish Parliament, including a bizarre and embarrassing scene involving admission that 20,000 stop and search records had been 'lost' through the pressing of the wrong button on an IT system (Ellison 2015; Hutcheon 2015) are but some of the less edifying chapters in the wider story of Police Scotland's initially defensive response to the concerns about their practice uncovered by Murray (such tactics not being new, see, Henry 2007).

Conclusion

Even in a context where considerable progress has been made in cultivating a culture of engagement around research, and in which many police collaborators do show a reflexive interest in challenging the status quo of their practice, there are necessary limits to academic–practitioner collaboration that relate to the boundaries between collaborators. Murray's research was useful to the police (even if it was not at first viewed this way) precisely because it was independent, rigorous, and did not shy away from findings that challenged extant practice. The boundaries between the academy and the police were tested by the coordinated police resistance to them, but they were maintained and the research was published (2014a, b), duly informing the independent review of stop and search. It is disappointing that the police did not initially respond more constructively to the research as a prompt for internal critique and an opportunity for learning, but it is naive to assume that research will necessarily be the primary focus for practitioners. It is difficult to know exactly what prompted their initial response, but unreflective internal commitment to the practice, coupled with the public relations challenge of a politicised external environment in which the media and the Scottish parliament were increasingly willing to challenge them, seem to have been the norm. Ultimately it is the external political pressures on the police, rather than the research itself, which resulted in more positive engagement with the issue in this instance. Certainly it is to be hoped that SIPR's ongoing efforts to foster a culture of engagement and more reflexivity towards research from practitioners might result in more measured responses to uncomfortable and critical research findings in the future, responses characterised more by deliberation than defensiveness. Indeed, it is when findings are critical of the present that opportunities for learning and improvement truly arise. Such opportunities are more likely when the boundaries between the academy and the world of practice—so necessary to maintain critical distance and independence—continue to be recognised and respected even as we work to negotiate and broker between them. This—like all good academic–practitioner collaboration—will be an ongoing project.

References

Advisory Group on Stop and Search (2015) *Report of the Advisory Group on Stop and Search,* Edinburgh: The Advisory Group on Stop and Search.

Alvesson, M. and Skoldberg, K. (2009) *Reflexive Methodology: New Vistas for Qualitative Research,* 2nd edn, London: Sage.

Becker, H.S. (1982) *Art Worlds,* Berkeley and Los Angeles: University of California Press.

Boswell, C. (2009) *The Political Uses of Expert Knowledge: Immigration Policy and Social Research,* Cambridge: Cambridge University Press.

Case, S. and Haines, K. (2014) Reflective friend research: the relational aspects of social theory. In K. Lumsden and A. Winter (eds) *Reflexivity in Criminological Research: Experiences with the Powerful and the Powerless,* Basingstoke: Palgrave Macmillan: 58–74.

Davis, P. (1999) 'What is evidence-based education?', *British Journal of Educational Studies* 47(2): 108–121.

Douglas, M. (1986) *How Institutions Think*, Syracuse, New York: Syracuse University Press.

Ellison, M. (2015) 'Police lost 20,000 stop and search records after "wrong button pressed"', *BBC News Website* (19 February). URL (accessed on 14 May 2016): http://www.bbc.co.uk/news/uk-scotland-31525040.

Engel, R. and Henderson, S (2013) 'Beyond rhetoric: establishing academic-police collaborations that work'. In J. Brown (ed), *The Future of Policing*, London: Routledge: 217–236.

Fish, S. (1989) *Doing What Comes Naturally: Change, Rhetoric and the Practice of Theory in Literary and Legal Studies*, Oxford: Oxford University Press.

Fleming, J. (2010) 'Learning to work together: police and academics', *Policing* 4(2): 139–145.

Fyfe, N.R. and Wilson, P. (2012) 'Knowledge exchange and police practice: broadening and deepening the debate around research-practitioner collaborations', *Police Practice and Research* 13(4): 306–314.

Giddens, A. (1991) *Modernity and Self-Identity: Self and Society in the Late Modern Age*, Cambridge: Polity Press.

Gouldner, A.W. (1970) *The Coming Crisis of Western Sociology*, London: Heineman Educational Books Ltd.

Henry, A. (2012) 'Situating community safety: emergent professional identities in communities of practice', *Criminology and Criminal Justice* 12(4): 413–431.

Henry, A. (2007) 'Looking back on Police and People in London'. In A. Henry and D.J. Smith (eds), *Transformations of Policing*, Aldershot: Ashgate: 1–23.

Henry, A. and Mackenzie, S. (2012) 'Brokering communities of practice: a model of knowledge exchange and academic-practitioner collaboration developed in the context of community policing', *Police Practice and Research* 13(4): 315–328.

Hutcheon, P. (2015) 'Revealed: Police Scotland and Scottish Government tried to hamper research into stop and search', *Herald Scotland*, 22 February.

Innes, M., Fielding, N. and Cope, N. (2005) '"The appliance of science?": the theory and practice of crime intelligence analysis', *British Journal of Criminology* vol. 45(1): 39–57.

Johnston, L. and Shearing, C. (2009) 'From a "dialogue of the deaf" to a "dialogue of the listening": towards a new methodology of policing research and practice', *Police Practice and Research* 10(5–6): 415–422.

Kuhn, T.S. (1996) *The Structure of Scientific Revolutions*, 3rd edn., Chicago: University of Chicago Press.

Loftus, B. (2009) *Police Culture in a Changing World*. Oxford: (Clarendon) Oxford University Press.

McIntyre, A. (2008) 'Participatory action research', *Qualitative Research Methods Series 52*, Thousand Oaks, Cal: Sage.

Mitton, C., Adair, C.E., Mckenzie, E., Patten, S.B. and Perry, B.W. (2007) 'Knowledge transfer and exchange: review and synthesis of the literature', *The Milbank Quarterly* 85(4): 729–768.

Murray, K. (2014a) 'Stop and search in Scotland: an evaluation of police practice', *SCCJR Report 01/2014*.

Murray, K. (2014b) 'The proactive turn: stop and search in Scotland', *SIPR Annual Report 2013*, 24–25.

Murray, K. (2015) *The Proactive Turn: Stop and Search in Scotland (A Study in Elite Power)*. Unpublished University of Edinburgh PhD Thesis.

Nutley, S., Walter, I. and Davies, H.T.O. (2007) *Using Evidence: How Research Can Inform Public Services*, Bristol: The Policy Press.

Schön, D.A. (1983) *The Reflective Practitioner: How Professionals Think in Action*, New York, NY: Basic Books.

Smith, D.J. (2007) New challenges to police legitimacy. In A. Henry and D.J. Smith (eds), *Transformations of Policing*, Aldershot: Ashgate: 273–305.

Sheldon, B. and Chilvers, R. (2000) *Evidence-Based Social Care: A Study of Prospects and Problems*, Lyme Regis: Russell House.

Wenger, E. (1998) *Communities of Practice: Learning, Meaning and Identity*, Cambridge: Cambridge University Press.

9

The Shifting Legitimacy of Knowledge Across Academic and Police/Practitioner Settings: Highlighting the Risks and Limits of Reflexivity

Karen Lumsden

Introduction: Reflexivity and Criminology

The value of reflexivity is now largely accepted by qualitative researchers (Alvesson and Sköldberg 2011; Lumsden and Winter 2014), and has helped to address the sanitized nature of research accounts typically featured in methods textbooks. Although criminology has a less prominent legacy of producing 'reflexive accounts' than in sociology or anthropology for instance, recent publications such as this edited volume, the chapters in Lumsden and Winter's (2014) *Reflexivity in Criminological Research*, and the writings of others such as Jupp et al. (2000), Jewkes (2012) and Liebling (1999), demonstrate the growing recognition amongst criminologists of the value of reflexivity, in addition to feminist criminologies (Gelsthorpe 1990). Reflexive accounts can also be found in classic sociological studies of crime and deviance, which highlight the dangers faced in the field, and questions of research ethics (Whyte 1943; Polsky 1967; Adler 1993[1985]; Hobbs 1988). Reflexivity is valuable in that

K. Lumsden (✉)
Loughborough University, Loughborough, UK

© The Author(s) 2017
S. Armstrong et al. (eds.), *Reflexivity and Criminal Justice*,
DOI 10.1057/978-1-137-54642-5_9

it draws attention to the researcher as part of the world being studied, while reminding us that those individuals involved in our research are 'subjects', not 'objects' (Lumsden and Winter 2014). By being reflexive we acknowledge that social researchers cannot be separated from their autobiographies and will 'bring their own values to the research and their interpretation of the data' (Devine and Heath 1999: 27).

As Finlay (2002) points out, the question in the social sciences is no longer whether to be reflexive but: *how do we go about 'doing' or practicing reflexivity?* Despite raising this question more than a decade ago, we appear to be no closer to understanding, debating or critiquing how we *practice* reflexivity. In addition, the opening of this Pandora's box appears to have created a new 'hierarchy of speaking positions' (Adkins 2002), with the related danger that reflexivity (and reflecting on 'particular' aspects of identity) becomes a 'tick-box' exercise for justifying the production of our social accounts, or an exercise in naval-gazing by focusing primarily on the researcher's experiences while overshadowing the role of the researched in the co-production of knowledge. Equally, little is said regarding the actual *process* of reflecting, and which experiences and observations we might consciously reflect on while doing our research, which we may discount or not disclose publicly, and also the value of 'retrospective reflexivity' beyond the lifespan of a research project (Lumsden 2013). As Bourdieu points out, reflexivity acknowledges 'the limits of knowledge specifically associated with the analyst's membership and position in the intellectual field' (Wacquant 1992: 39). This includes not just the social origin and coordinates of the researcher, but also taking account of their position in the 'academic field' and the 'intellectualist bias which entices us to construe the world as a spectacle, as a set of significations to be interpreted rather than as concrete problems to be solved practically' (Wacquant 1992: 39).

In this chapter, I use my experience of researching/engaging with police in order to highlight the issues encountered when attempting to 'do' reflexivity, and the risks and limits of adopting a reflexive approach. Studies have highlighted the difficulties researchers face when they encounter the often 'hidden' world of policing (Rowe 2007; Norris 1993) and the challenges of partnership work with police (Bradley and Nixon 2009; Fleming 2011, 2012; Fyfe and Wilson 2012). We also now have access to reflexive accounts from criminologists researching 'up' or 'with' other 'powerful' groups such as policy makers, politicians, government officials and lawyers (Lumsden and Winter 2014). Williams (1989: 254) reminds us that the chance to 'study up' will not be provided by powerful groups themselves, but instead 'will emerge only if social scientists are prepared to consider their dealings with the powerful as part of the research agenda'.

I focus on the value of reflexivity for understanding not just the actual 'doing' of research, but 'doing' public engagement or as it is often referred to—'public sociology' (Burawoy 2005) or 'public criminology' (Loader and Sparks 2010), or in the case of research which focuses on the needs of the research users, a form of sociology which Burawoy (2005) terms 'policy sociology'. Burawoy (2005) is particularly critical of this form of sociology, highlighting the danger of the sociologist becoming merely a 'servant of power' by sacrificing their scientific integrity. As engagement and relationships with various 'publics' and 'research users' become increasingly important for academics in relation to research 'impact' and the enterprise university, I argue that reflexivity must also extend to interrogation and analysis of these encounters. The discussion reflects on knowledge transfer, in the form of the strategic development of academic and police partnerships, focusing on the case study of funded enterprise project work with forces in England. The current emphasis on evidence-based policing in the police context, and the emphasis on enterprise, stakeholder engagement and impact on the academic side, sets the context for the shaping of police–academic partnerships, which it will be shown can be mutually beneficial. However, the chapter reflects upon how certain forms of social scientific knowledge are contested or deemed less legitimate in certain settings, while highlighting the risks and limits inherent in a 'reflexive approach' in work with stakeholders. Two main challenges are reflected on: (1) power and privilege associated with the evidence-based movement in policing and the related definitions of legitimate forms of knowledge (and research); and (2) questions of academic freedom. These examples help to demonstrate both the benefits and the risks that a reflexive approach can present, the possibilities that participatory approaches can offer to academics and police, and the unintended consequences of reflexivity.

Policing Research and the 'Evidence-base'

Police and Academic Partnerships

The social sciences have a legacy of generating seminal studies of policing, particularly ethnographies of police culture from academics (Banton 1964; Manning 1977; Bittner 1967; Fielding 1995) and 'insider' police researchers (Holdaway 1983). Reiner (1989) points to four stages categorizing policing research in the UK from the 1960s to 1980s which include 'consensus'; 'controversy'; 'conflict'; and a 'contradictory' stage emerging in the late 1980s which involves academics and police working more closely. Although these studies have been pivotal in paving the way for future research on policing, their impact on policing policy and practice itself has been minimal (Fyfe and Wilson 2012), highlighting a need to pay more 'systematic attention to evidence about the effects of what is delivered' and make better use of previous research (Tilley 2009: 135).

The past decade has witnessed a proliferation of writing on police–academic collaborations (Fleming 2012; Murji 2010; Johnston and Shearing 2009; Fyfe and Wilson 2012). The relationship between police and academics has been conceptualized as 'two worlds' consisting of a 'dialogue of the deaf', which can be understood as a 'mutual misunderstanding that negatively impacts on the police-academics relationship' (Bradley and Nixon 2009: 423). Academics can be criticized for failing to engage with the complex demands of policing resulting in 'a lingering cultural mistrust between police and academia that can hinder research partnerships' (Wilkinson 2010: 147). To overcome these barriers, Bradley and Nixon (2009: 423) call for a third model of research which goes beyond the either/or of the 'critical research' and 'policy police research', allowing academics and police to work in 'close and continuous collaborative relationships'. Police and researchers have also drawn attention to the benefits of co-produced research for shaping successful police–academic collaborations and research agendas (Fleming 2012; Foster and Bailey 2010; Wood et al. 2008). Bradley et al. (2006: 190) suggest that academics and police need to come together in a 'policing research network' to help address a deficiency in 'knowledge generation, validation, diffusion and adoption', while Henry and Mackenzie (2012) draw on the concept of 'communities of practice' (Wenger 1998) as a fruitful means for advancing knowledge transfer work with police. The focus has therefore shifted from doing research 'on' police, to doing research 'with' police.

Evidence-based Policing

The political context in which UK[1] policing currently operates can be said to include an increased emphasis on evidence-based policing, imported from the USA in the work of Lawrence Sherman (2003), and gaining increased popularity and political support in the last decade. Evidence-based policing is defined as:

> a method of making decisions about 'what works' in policing: which practices and strategies accomplish police missions most cost-effectively. In contrast to basing decisions on theory, assumptions, tradition or convention, an evidence-based approach continuously tests hypotheses with empirical findings. (Sherman 2013: 377)

'Robust' or 'good' evidence is assessed on a five-point scale, based on the Maryland Scale of Scientific Methods. This scale ranges from statements about 'what works' at the top, to statements about 'what's promising' and then statements about 'possible impact'. Systematic reviews demonstrate 'what works' and thus are placed at the top of the scale, followed by randomized control trials (RCTs) (College of Policing n.d.). Police resources are guided by what Sherman (2013: 3) refers to as the 'triple-T' of 'targeting, testing and tracking', involving the use of statistical evidence to proactively guide and manage police resources. He calls for social science to become more 'experimental', as when used properly experimental methods can 'control bias better than observational methods' (Sherman 2003: 10), and for greater education of the 'consumers' of social science research in order to defend 'against misleading evidence of all kinds' (Sherman 2003: 6).

---

[1] Within the UK, there have always existed important differences between policing in England and Wales, and policing in Scotland. These differences are even starker after reforms including the creation of a national police force in Scotland in April 2013 (see Fyfe 2014).

The growth of the evidence-based policing movement coincides with the increased financial cuts to police post-2008 recession. The years following the Conservative–Liberal coalition government formation in 2010 have witnessed substantial cuts to police forces across England and Wales as a means of reducing the fiscal deficit. From 2010–11 to 2015–16 there was a 25 per cent real-terms reduction in central government's funding to Police and Crime Commissioners (PCCs),[2] and from March 2010 and September 2014 there was a 36,672 reduction in the size of the police workforce (National Audit Office 2015: 4). The growing professionalization of policing is reflected in the creation of the College of Policing in 2012, a professional policing body which has a 'mandate to set standards in professional development, including codes of practice and regulations, to ensure consistency across the 43 forces in England and Wales' (College of Policing 2015). It promotes the use of knowledge and research to develop an evidence-based approach to policing, for instance hosting the 'What Works Centre for Crime Reduction'. There is emphasis on police officers not only having access to the latest research evidence, but also being provided with the necessary skills to undertake their own research and evaluations, working with academics to address research priorities and build an evidence-base.

The focus on evidence-based policing has implications for the co-construction of knowledge, understandings of research by officers and staff, how academics understand evidence-based policing, and also which forms of academic research and methodologies will be viewed as appropriate. Hammersley has provided a detailed critique of evidence-based research in education and medicine, and many of his observations apply to evidence-based policing:

> its privileging of research evidence over other considerations in the decisions of policymakers and practitioners, and of a particular kind of research evidence at that; the assumptions made about the nature of professional

---

[2] In 2010, the government changed how police forces in England and Wales are governed by introducing elected PCCs in 41 of the 43 police forces. PCCs are responsible for setting out in an annual police and crime plan the objectives they will address, allocating the funds needed to achieve them and holding police forces accountable on behalf of the electorate (National Audit Office 2015).

practice and about the 'transmission' of evidence to practitioners; and the connections between calls for evidence-based practice and managerialism in the public sector (2013: 16).

Bullock and Tilley (2009) highlight barriers to the implementation of evidence in policing as including: difficulties in discerning what counts as 'evidence' of effective practice; the availability of evidence; and organizational constraints. Hope (2009: 130–131) is critical of Sherman's experimental design for policing research, which focuses on crime 'hot-spots', noting that: 'Rather than a promise, there is as much a threat to liberty posed by offering the RCT as a tool for the powerful to legitimize their actions'. Tilley argues that the current understanding of evidence-based policing risks 'stifling heterodox alternative methodologies rooted in critiques of the RCT' (2009: 143).

In what follows, I focus on two challenges encountered during knowledge transfer and research with police forces in England: (1) the power and privilege associated with the 'evidence-based movement' in policing and the related definitions of legitimate forms of knowledge (and research); and (2) questions of academic freedom. These examples help to demonstrate both the benefits and the risks that a reflexive approach can present, the possibilities that participatory approaches can offer to academics and police and also the unintended consequences of research and reflexivity.

Reflections on Police–Academic Collaborations

The Project: 'Doing' Enterprise Work with Police

The discussion is based on the author's experiences while Principal Investigator of a one-year-funded Enterprise Project Grant[3] (2014–2015) that focused on developing academic partnerships and conducting knowledge transfer with police forces in England. The proj-

---

[3] Funded via an Enterprise Project Grant from the Higher Education Innovation Fund (HEIF). There is no individual award number for this grant.

ect involved the full-time Senior Research Associate, in a role similar to what might otherwise be termed a Knowledge Transfer Manager, spending seven months seconded to police forces, while also liaising with other relevant stakeholders. The aim was to strategically develop a university partnership with police forces, showcasing research in the social sciences (and cognate disciplines), which was applicable to policing, and further develop research collaborations. This included identifying research projects already completed, with an application for policing; researching within the context of the police forces themselves what their research needs were; and how these could be addressed within future research. In addition, we conducted a small piece of qualitative research into police officers' perspectives of research and evidence-based policing.

Fifteen semi-structured interviews were conducted with staff and officers who had key roles in relation to the utilization of 'research evidence' or had experience of undertaking research themselves and/or collaborating professionally with academics. The perspectives are also based on data collected via observations during the setting-up and reviewing of the collaboration(s); observations and notes taken during attendance at relevant meetings and at research fairs; informal conversations with a variety of police personnel including from probationary Constable level to Assistant Chief Constable level; and shadowing of officers on response, in a custody suite and in a control room. The above constitute a 'purposive' rather than a 'representative' sample. For the purpose of ethics the identities of the police forces, individual police officers and staff in question have been fully anonymized. In no way did the project entail the assessment of the practices or policies of police organizations, officers or staff.

The Shifting Legitimacy of Knowledge and Evidence-based Policing

In partnership work with police we were presented with a situation in which 'instrumental knowledge' was more important than 'reflexive knowledge' (Burawoy 2005: 17), reflecting notions of research as a 'product', with 'off the peg' solutions to problems. According to Nutley et al. (2007: 34), 'instrumental' uses of research are most often focused on in the current evidence-based policy and practice agenda, despite the reality that 'research is often used in much more indirect, diverse and subtle ways'. This latter use of research has been termed 'conceptual use' (Nutley et al. 2007: 36). This focus on instrumental use posed challenges in terms of how we could demonstrate to research users that there were benefits of the research which went beyond financial benefits, one of the key political rationales guiding evidence-based policing—'doing more, with less'. As a member of staff working in policy development explained in relation to evidence-based policing:

> I would assume that what we're talking about is that on the basis of some of their decisions and some of the activities, that we'd at least look at what research has been conducted in that particular area to... inform the decision-making. If there isn't any research... perhaps we should be considering commissioning some (Interviewee 1 – police staff).

A Temporary Chief Inspector (Interviewee 7) echoed the point about saving the force money observing that 'austerity is a huge driver' for partnerships with academics. Interviewees also highlighted the way in which strategic force and Police Crime Commissioner priorities were informing the research agenda:

> For (academic-police partnerships) to really work, the individual force needs to be clear about where its priorities lie so that you know where to focus (Interviewee 2 – police staff).

When asked about knowledge transfer, interviewee 1 in a more cynical tone responded:

> I would try to avoid it becoming part of the Force agenda, part of the higher management agenda... We've got Strategic Objectives – and if you look at strategic objectives... essentially what we're talking about are straplines, that we're sort of thinking, 'this is a good message to sell', oh, you know 'Keeping People Safe' – well, you know... you're a police force! Isn't that what it's about? (Interviewee 1 – police staff)

Knowledge transfer risks becoming a means of reaffirming organizational decisions. Our activities and engagement with police officers and staff could 'end up reinscribing the very power geometries' that criminology should question (Browne and Bakshi 2014: 56). Performance measurement was also an important driver guiding what academic research would be 'useful' to research 'consumers':

> at the moment, when our crime figures go down, [senior managers] get a big pat on the back, they get a bonus, but when they go up, they don't know what happened for it to go down, so they can't actually progress that downward trend – so it's all sat there at the vagaries of statistical variance (Interviewee 1 – police staff).

As well as the police force, one officer referred to the input of the Home Office and the College of Policing in putting Police–academic partnerships on the agenda:

> If the College of Policing have got to have results that are based on professionalizing… the service, then they need the help of academics – and police to work together and so the push has come from, jointly between the Home Office and the College (Interviewee 10 – Chief Inspector).

Police officers' understandings of research in the current evidence-based policing context presents challenges for social sciences, arts and humanities researchers, whose methodologies and critical standpoints might be at odds with the randomized control trials and crime science discourses that evidence-based policing promotes. We were struck by the extent to which for police officers, research or academic research had been incorporated and was increasingly understood under the evidence-based mantel. For instance:

> I've just used it personally, in my studies. I'm a member of the Society for Evidence Based Policing. I've got a bid in about doing some… work (Interviewee 7 – Temporary Chief Inspector).

He also cites the impetus for evidence-based policing as linked to the following:

Well you've got the Chief Constable of the College, Alex Marshall; Larry Sherman, Professor of Criminology at Cambridge and Larry runs the Masters... a number of superintendents go on that from around the country... and then at the last conference, you had the Commissioner of the Met, Chief of Thames Valley, Chief of West Mids, Chief of Greater Manchester – they're the biggest forces in the country – if they're advocating it, there's got to be some impetus behind it (Interviewee 7 – Temporary Chief Inspector).

We also encountered some scepticism amongst police officers with regard to evidence-based policing, as the below quote demonstrates:

I think it's the new buzzword that we've currently got (laughs) because I've sat through what seems like an awful lot of presentations about it. And it usually involves a ladder of a kind – 'this is a study which doesn't really have much academic robustness'... and then at the top you've got this kind of sampling... which is very, very robust...'(Interviewee 5 – Temporary Inspector).

There were examples of officers referencing the need for research which would not fit the 'evidence-based' gold standard of RCTs and systematic reviews. At a continued professional development event on victims and the criminal justice system organized as part of the knowledge transfer project, officers during a mapping exercise referred to the need for more research on victims' experiences of police and criminal justice, but of a kind that particularly focused on stories or narratives of victims. Officers cited the need for qualitative research which would help glean further insight into the needs of victims. Officer and staff analyses of what research might offer also included a better understanding of the causes of the crimes they were trying to tackle and an opportunity to participate in the design and delivery of effective interventions. The implication is that a multi-factorial mixed-method approach is needed. Not everything can be measured in a positivist sense, and there is a need to recognize the 'social construction' of phenomena and the importance of context (Thacher 2001):

If I put something in place – a youth group – how do I know that's been successful? We measure everything – do you measure that against what we project the anti-social behaviour (ASB) figures should be in 5 years' time? And then if they're lower than that, it's a success? Or, that isn't really a good measure because actually there might be fewer young people in that areas, therefore there's probably going to be fewer ASB? (Interviewee 4, police staff)

Gaining a better understanding of what lies behind crime figures before engaging in any kind of intervention, knowing how to define success, and working out how to evaluate the effectiveness of efforts was a common theme among officers working more and more in partnership with other agencies across health, education and welfare. While they referred to the evidence-based 'gold standard' when explicitly asked about 'research' and 'evidence', there was an implicit dichotomy between the dominant model of research in current discourses of evidence-based policing and the kinds of research they reported as usefully informing their own practice, also highlighting the focus for some officers on 'conceptual' or 'tacit uses' of evidence (Nutley et al. 2007).

A further question was: *how to transfer research evidence and knowledge into policing practice?* This was the constant 'elephant in the room' and a question which tended to be 'swept under the carpet', rather than acknowledged as an issue which needed discussion:

> In terms of barriers – not setting specific aims and objectives at the beginning of projects. That's one. So therefore, when we come to evaluate, what are we evaluating? There's a number of times I get, 'Will you look at this and see if it worked?' What does 'worked' mean? (Interviewee 4 – police staff)

Interviewee 5 also commented on the organizational barriers to translating research findings into practice, and in supporting academic research:

> I think there would be barriers and again I think that's not from individuals, we're currently going through austerity and a lot of people are focused on the here-and-now, the austerity and the pressure that we are under and I think this just comes from the top all the way down (Interviewee 5 – Temporary Inspector).

We encountered misconceptions from some stakeholders as to what academic research entailed and the turnaround time of a research project and implementation of findings. Forces and staff often wanted 'quick fixes' and they would conflate academic research with consultancy work. The timescales they would anticipate in terms of turnaround were often unfeasible and/or their attention had moved to another policing issue, highlighting the often 'reactive' nature of policing. As Wilkinson (2010: 147) notes: 'Police often bemoan research losing "currency". By the time it is published, events may have driven policing agendas to change or the policing environment had moved on to focus on other priorities'.

Ozga (2011: 218) highlights the construction work which policy makers engage in, and how elites can 'seek to control, manipulate and manage the research process'. We found ourselves engaging in 'boundary-work', which is a 'stylistic resource for ideologies of a profession or occupation' (Gieryn 1983: 791). We tried to expand our authority and expertise into the domain of policing which was gradually becoming 'claimed' by the evidence-based policing movement, in addition to engaging in 'boundary' creation between practitioner-based 'working theories' (Hammersley 2013) and social scientific knowledge.

Academic Freedom

A further challenge we encountered relates to the question of academic freedom when those we research or engage with have a vested interest in the 'outcome' of activities. For example, one of the gatekeepers required organizational vetting of any publications or conference papers, before their delivery or submission. Here, we had to refer to a clause included in the original project collaboration agreement drafted between the university and the force, in which it was stated that senior police officers had permission to comment on publications (within a three-month period of submission) if requested, but not, in doing so, to interfere with academic freedom or scientific inquiry. Our experience was similar to Aldred (2008: 899) in that '…"academic freedom" is contested and its virtue far from guaranteed. It may be used as a managerial defence of privilege'.

We were conscious of the need to be sensitive to the reputation of the police forces involved, and individual members of the organizations, but equally, we had a responsibility to tell the stories of the individuals who had given consent to the interviews, while also adhering to the principles of intellectual freedom and critical inquiry. This was a sensitive and often conflicting line which we had to negotiate at key points of the project (cf Wilkinson 2010). We faced unanticipated challenges in meeting the requirements and needs of various levels of the organization, while negotiating individual personalities and the police (workplace) culture (Marks et al. 2010). Therefore, 'personal and professional relationships can become entangled... with the consequence that feelings of loyalty towards individuals inform a sense of loyalty towards the organizations within which those individuals are based' (Smith 2010: 185). Here, there is a risk posed by public reflections, in that claims by research users regarding what is published or disclosed also constrains space or potential for reflexivity.

Discussion and Conclusions

This chapter focused on experiences of engaging and researching with police officers and staff from forces in England as part of an enterprise project. The discussion centred on two challenges encountered: (1) the power and privilege associated with the 'evidence-based movement' in policing and the related definitions of legitimate forms of knowledge (and research); and (2) questions of academic freedom. By examining these experiences, we learn more about the shifting nature of the police organizational culture in the context of economic cuts and professionalization, and the impact (or not) of the evidence-based policing movement on police organizations, officers and staff. We gain insight into the power dynamics and privilege(s) created via the evidence-based policing movement, which risks overshadowing or discounting as legitimate, certain forms of social scientific knowledge and research methodologies (particularly qualitative research, work in the arts and humanities, and critical sociological accounts of policing), which can help to inform policing strategies and crime prevention. In many cases, what police officers claimed they 'needed' as 'evidence' (such as narratives and stories of victims of crime) was at odds with the RCTs and systematic reviews that the evidence-based policing movement promotes. What was needed was an enhanced understanding of the causes of crime in order to inform programmes of intervention. The police face a 'broader range and a more ambiguous mix of values' (Thacher 2001: 391) than the instrumental incarnation of evidence-based policing, espoused by the College of Policing, is able to address.

It is well recognized that police and academic collaborations have the potential to challenge narrow conceptions of research and enhance understandings of university and police cultures for the respective participants (Bradley and Nixon 2009). Our experience was that knowledge transfer activities which can 'showcase' the myriad research projects conducted in/across various disciplines can be advantageous in this sense, and in challenging narrow 'what works' conceptions of research. However, there is a related risk that when faced with the methodological and disciplinary variations, and/or when 'promised' research fails to deliver, police will return to basing decisions on 'craft knowledge' and practitioner-based theories. As Nutley et al. (2003: 128) note: 'Tacit knowledge is valuable but can also be built around custom and practices that are not effective, and this, combined with its deeply embedded nature, makes it a potential barrier to EBP implementation'. It is important to acknowledge how practitioners understand and conceptualize 'academic research', and how their 'practice theories' (Curnock and Hardiker 1979) and professional judgements are assessed and utilized alongside or in addition to research recommendations. This has direct implications for how, or if, there is willingness to implement findings in practice. As Nutley et al. (2003: 129) argue, in evidence-based practice 'there is a need for far greater emphasis to be placed on know-about, know-how, know-who and know-why as opposed to the current emphasis on know-what'. Different, multiple and overlapping 'epistemic communities' also exist within and across police forces and:

> may well interpret knowledge, its value and its potential uses in different ways, so 'evidence' that is transferred from one to another may be reinterpreted and attributed a different value in the recipient (Henry and Mackenzie 2012: 320).

The same can be said for the means of implementing research evidence into policing practice, where different groups, such as front-line officers, middle management, senior officers and civilian staff (working within varying capacities and roles), interpreted the drivers, facilitators and barriers in different ways. It also depended on their experience of conducting research, sometimes 'in-house'.

Reflexivity must therefore extend to interrogation and analysis of our experiences with practitioners such as police and policy makers, and general 'publics'—the latter encompassing those myriad social groups which criminologists and sociologists engage with as part of both research and public engagement (including generating research 'impact'). In contributing to understandings of how we interact and engage with groups typically defined as 'powerful', such as the police, I raised questions as to what it tells us about the expectation to be reflexive in these encounters. It is important to note that power as fluid, situational and slippery means that certain individuals within organizations will be powerless in certain situations, and so might the researcher. As Williams (1989: 254) notes, organizations typically deemed to be 'powerful', such as the police, are not 'homogenous bodies, with a single ideology, directed from the top by a small, elite group'. Power is subject to situational and contextual circumstances, in addition to the personalities of key players in the organization (Marks et al. 2010).

Instances in which certain forms of academic knowledge and research methodologies were discounted for not 'fitting' into the evidence-based policing mould of systematic reviews and RCTs can create dissonance and uncertainly on the part of the academic in their interactions with police, and also the requirement to balance the research needs of the 'users' or 'consumers' of research, with an intellectual and critical 'criminological imagination' (Young 2011) on the part of the academic, which challenges the labels and definitions of the powerful. The need to defend academic freedom against the requests and demands of those we research or publicly engage with is an uncomfortable experience which demands further debate, particularly in the age of greater user involvement in research, and public engagement, in addition to requests from funding agencies and universities for more 'impactful' research. As Wacquant observes, the 'science-politics nexus in criminology' is forged via the:

hierarchical articulation of the academic field, of which the criminological domain is a sector, the bureaucratic field, the political field and the journalistic field – in short, by the changing location and uses of justice scholarship in the patterned space of struggles over instruments of rule that Bourdieu calls the field of power (2011: 441–442).

In addition to the academic 'field' of criminology, the risk here is that (as hinted above) the 'field' of policing is becoming defined and shaped by the acceptance of evidence-based policing and the 'what works' agenda (in addition to normative and positivist criminologies). Has the tide already turned too far, as the institutions of government, individual police forces, and the recently established College of Policing have embraced the tenets of 'evidence-based policing' as the status quo for those conducting research with/on policing? If so, there are clearly challenges ahead for criminologists who wish to work with police on critical research agendas, or use particular (qualitative or ethnographic) methodologies, which fall outside the 'gold standard' of RCTs and systematic reviews. For instance, it is important to recognize the legacy of the ethnographic studies of policing in the 1970s, which paved the way for future research, and the value of this method for shedding light on police organizational transformations and police cultures (Marks 2004; Manning 2005).

According to Fyfe and Wilson (2012: 38): 'In developing researcher–practitioner collaborations in policing, there is… a need to engage with this full spectrum of knowledge requirements and embrace a degree of eclecticism in relation to theoretical frameworks, methodological approaches and types of empirical data'. As Manning (2005: 23) notes, policing researchers can also be confronted with 'tensions between public pressures for short-term funded research and theoretically grounded scholarship'. Therefore, reflexive accounts of these experiences shed valuable insight into our interactions and engagement with groups such as the police, and the challenges faced in the co-production and definitions of (legitimate) knowledge by police and academics themselves. One means of empowering internal police voices that are interested in aspects other than that which crime science offers, is via more participatory models of research and knowledge exchange (Foster and Bailey 2010; Marks et al.

2010; Fleming 2012). However, there is also a question as to what extent this engagement or empowerment might percolate to different ranks/ levels in the policing context? As Wood et al. (2008: 72) argue it is only possible to advance police theory and research when police officers are 'actively involved in the research process and in finding solutions to practical problems'. The focus should be on a fragmented, micro-level view of police culture instead of a 'broad brush depiction of police culture' (ibid.). This includes taking account of the experiences of 'rank and file' police (Birzer 2002) as well as those in middle management and senior leadership positions.

The often uncomfortable way in which we might publicly reflect on and share our accounts of 'doing' research or public engagement with groups deemed to be 'powerful', such as the police, tells us a great deal about the mechanisms by which reflexivity operates in a disciplinary sense in sociology and criminology, those settings in which 'researcher privilege' is most prevalent and in which we are more comfortable sharing our reflexive accounts of social groups—such as those in more powerless positions. As Barbara Hudson (2000) notes, 'of all the social sciences, criminology has the most dangerous relationship to power'. The process of reflexivity itself can therefore via its unintended consequences (Lumsden 2013) ironically risk reproducing the power imbalances and privilege, which a 'reflexive approach' aims to address. Adkins (2002: 345) alludes to this when she claims that 'reflexivity' privileges a 'hierarchy of speaking positions', the inscription of which is disguised through claims that reflexivity is 'good' and 'progressive' with regard to the gender politics of social research. Thus, we need further debate on the ways in which these forms of disciplinary critique and judgement treat reflexivity as a 'tick-box' exercise rather than engaging in inquiry into the actual practices of reflexivity, its theorizing, and how we teach reflexivity to our students. May and Perry (2011: 38) argue that:

> Reflexivity might work as a sensitizing device bringing into view those elements of research that remain hidden by the limitations of such approaches, but when it works to produce yet another social scientific hierarchy through which to judge the adequacy of results about the social world, it easily slips into undermining, as opposed to positively contributing to, dialogue and representation.

We need a stance which recognizes that 'knowledge is situated' and is 'produced from social subjects with varying amounts of capital, located in a nexus of power relations' (Skeggs 1997: 28). Critical reflections in studies where the researcher is in an underprivileged position, such as those involving powerful groups can make public reflections difficult, and raises questions as to how researchers avoid becoming 'servants of power' in doing 'policy sociology' (Burawoy 2005). Reflexivity is valuable, but it also presents risks to the researcher and the researched. In cases such as this, participatory models of partnership working offer clear benefits for academics and police to overcoming misunderstandings with regard to research and knowledge transfer, and ensure that researchers also keep the needs of users in mind when designing, conducting and disseminating research. Reflexivity can allow for mitigation and awareness of the process of partnership working, and the drivers and barriers encountered along the way. It permits awareness of the ways in which research can impact directly on practice and in this instance the potential for police powers to exclude, harm or marginalize—and the danger that unreflexive criminological research and user engagement lends credence to potentially harmful practices (see also Blaustein, this volume). There is a need to be sensitive to the potential and unintended consequences of research and knowledge transfer work in our attempts to work more closely with groups such as the police.

References

Adkins, L. (2002) 'Reflexivity and the Politics of Qualitative Research'. In T. May (ed.) *Qualitative Research in Action*, London: Sage: 332–348.

Adler, P. (1993[1985]) *Wheeling and Dealing: An Ethnography of an Upper-Level Drug Dealing and Smuggling Community*, 2nd edn, New York: Columbia University Press.

Aldred, R. (2008) 'Ethical and Political Issues in Contemporary Research Relationships', *Sociology* 42(5): 887–903.

Alvesson, M. and Sköldberg, K. (2011) *Reflexive Methodology: New Vistas for Qualitative Research*, 2nd edn, London: Sage.

Banton, M. (1964) *The Policeman in the Community*, London: Tavistock.

Birzer, M.L. (2002) 'Writing Partnerships Between Police Practitioners and Researchers', *Police Practice and Research: An International Journal* 3(2): 149–156.

Bittner, E. (1967) 'The Police on Skid Row: a Study of Peacekeeping', *American Sociological Review* 35(5): 699–715.

Bradley, D. and Nixon, C. (2009) 'Ending the "Dialogue of the Deaf": Evidence and Policing Policies and Practices. An Australian Case Study', *Police Practice and Research* 10(5/6): 423–435.

Bradley, D., Nixon, C., and Marks, M. (2006) 'What Works, What Doesn't Work and What Looks Promising in Police Research Networks'. In J. Fleming and J. Wood (eds) *Fighting Crime Together*, Sydney: University of New South Wales Press: 170–194.

Browne, K. and Bakshi, L. (2014) 'Participation Beyond Boundaries? Working as, with and for Lesbian, Gay, Bi and Trans Communities'. In Y. Taylor (ed.) *The Entrepreneurial University: Engaging Politics, Intersecting Impacts*, Basingstoke: Palgrave Macmillan: 43–60.

Bullock, K. and Tilley, N. (2009) 'Evidence-Based Policing and Crime Reduction', *Policing* 3(4): 381–387.

Burawoy, M. (2005) 'For Public Sociology', *American Sociological Review* 70(1): 4–28.

College of Policing (2015) 'About Us'. URL (accessed 15 May 2015): http://www.college.police.uk/About/Pages/default.aspx

College of Policing (n.d.) 'Evidence Based Policing: What's All This Then?' URL (accessed 21 June 2015): http://www.excellenceinpolicing.org.uk/wp-content/uploads/2013/09/3-2_Evidence-Based-Policing.pdf

Curnock, K. and Hardiker, P. (1979) *Towards Practice Theory: Skills and Methods in Social Assessments*, London: Routledge & Kegan Paul.

Devine, F. and Heath, S. (1999) *Sociological Research Methods in Context*, New York: Palgrave.

Fielding, N. (1995) *Community Policing*, Oxford: Clarendon Press.

Finlay, L. (2002) 'Negotiating the Swamp: the Opportunity and Challenge of Reflexivity in Research Practice', *Qualitative Research* 2(2): 209–230.

Fleming, J. (2011) 'Qualitative Encounters in Police Research'. In L. Bartels and K. Richards (eds) *Qualitative Criminology*, Sydney: Hawkins Press: 13–24.

Fleming, J. (2012) 'Changing the Way We Do Business: Reflecting on Collaborative Practice', *Police Practice and Research* 13(4): 375–388.

Foster, J. and Bailey, S. (2010) 'Joining Forces: Maximizing Ways of Making a Difference in Policing', *Policing* 4(2): 95–103.

Fyfe, N.R. (2014) 'A Different and Divergent Trajectory? Reforming the Structure, Governance and Narrative of Policing in Scotland'. In J. Brown (ed.) *The Future of Policing*, London: Routledge: 493–506.

Fyfe, N.R. and Wilson, P. (2012) 'Knowledge Exchange and Police Practice: Broadening and Deepening the Debate Around Researcher-Practitioner Collaborations', *Police Practice and Research* 13(4): 306–314.

Gelsthorpe, L. (1990) 'Feminist Methodologies in Criminology: A New Approach or Old Wine in New Bottles?' In L. Gelsthorpe and A. Morris (eds) *Feminist Perspectives in Criminology*, Milton Keynes: Open University Press: 89–106.

Gieryn, T.F. (1983) 'Boundary-Work and the Demarcation of Science from Non-Science: Strains and Interests in Professional Ideologies of Scientists', *American Sociological Review* 48(6): 781–795.

Hammersley, M. (2013) *The Myth of Research-Based Policy and Practice*, London: Sage.

Henry, A. and Mackenzie, S. (2012) 'Brokering Communities of Practice: a Model of Knowledge Exchange and Academic-Practitioner Collaboration Developed in the Context of Community Policing', *Police Practice and Research* 13(4): 315–328.

Hobbs, D. (1988) *Doing the Business: Entrepreneurships, the Working Class, and Detectives in the East End of London*, New York: Oxford University Press.

Holdaway, S. (1983) *Inside the British Police*, Oxford: Blackwell.

Hope, T. (2009) 'The Illusion of Control: a Response to Professor Sherman'. *Criminology & Criminal Justice* 9(2): 125–134.

Hudson, B. (2000) 'Critical Reflection as Research Methodology'. In V. Jupp, P. Davies and P. Francis (eds) *Doing Criminological Research*, London: Sage: 175–192.

Jewkes, Y. (2012) 'Autoethnography and Emotion as Intellectual Resources: Doing Prison Research Differently', *Qualitative Inquiry* 18(1): 63–75.

Johnston, L. and Shearing, C. (2009) 'From a "Dialogue of the Deaf" to a "Dialogue of Listening": Towards a New Methodology of Policing Research and Practice', *Police Practice and Research* 10(5/6): 415–422.

Jupp, K., Davies, P. and Francis, P. (eds) (2000) *Doing Criminological Research*, London: Sage.

Liebling, A. (1999) 'Doing Research in Prison: Breaking the Silence?' *Theoretical Criminology* 3(2): 147–173.

Loader, I. and Sparks, R. (2010) *Public Criminology*, London: Routledge.

Lumsden, K. (2013) 'You Are What You Research: Researcher Partisanship and the Sociology of the Underdog', *Qualitative Research* 13(1): 3–18.

Lumsden, K. and Winter, A. (eds) (2014) *Reflexivity in Criminological Research: Experiences with the Powerful and the Powerless*, Basingstoke: Palgrave Macmillan.

Manning, P.K. (1977) *Police Work*, Cambridge, MA: MIT Press.

Manning, P. (2005) 'The Study of Policing', *Police Quarterly* 8(1): 23–43.

Marks, M. (2004) 'Researching Police Transformation: the Ethnographic Imperative', *British Journal of Criminology* 44: 866–888.

Marks, M., Wood, J., Ally, F., Walsh, T., and Witbooi, A. (2010) 'Worlds Apart? On the Possibilities of Police/Academic Collaborations', *Policing* 4(2): 112–118.

May, T. and Perry, B. (2011) *Social Research and Reflexivity*, London: Sage.

Murji, K. (2010) 'Introduction: Academic-Police Collaborations – Beyond 'Two Worlds', *Policing* 4(2): 92–94.

National Audit Office (2015) *Financial Sustainability of Police Forces in England and Wales*, London: National Audit Office.

Norris, C. (1993) 'Some Ethical Considerations on Field-Work with the Police'. In D. Hobbs and T. May (eds) *Interpreting the Field: Accounts of Ethnography*, Oxford: Clarendon Press: 122–143.

Nutley, S.M., Walter, I. and Davies, H.T.O. (2003) 'From Knowing to Doing: a Framework for Understanding the Evidence-into-Practice Agenda', *Evaluation* 9(2): 125–148.

Nutley, S.M., Walter, I. and Davies, H.T.O. (2007) *Using Evidence: How Research Can Inform Public Services*, Bristol: Policy Press.

Ozga, J. (2011) 'Researching the Powerful: Seeking Knowledge About Policy', *European Educational Research Journal* 10(2): 218–224.

Polsky, N. (1967) *Hustlers, Beats and Others,* Chicago: Aldine Publishing Co.

Reiner, R. (1989) 'The Politics of Police Research in Britain'. In M. Weatheritt (ed.) *Police Research: Some Future Prospects*, Aldershot: Avebury/Police Foundation.

Rowe, M. (2007) 'Tripping Over Molehills: Ethics and the Ethnography of Police Work', *International Journal of Social Research Methodology* 10(1): 37–48.

Sherman, L.W. (2003) 'Misleading Evidence and Evidence-Led Policy: Making Social Science More Experimental', *Annals of the American Academy of Social and Political Science* 589: 6–19.

Sherman, L.W. (2013) 'The Rise of Evidence-Based Policing: Targeting, Testing and Tracking', *Crime and Justice* 42(1): 377–451.

Skeggs, B. (1997) *Formations of Class and Gender*, London: Sage.

Smith, K. (2010) 'Research, Policy and Funding – Academic Treadmills and the Squeeze on Intellectual Spaces', *British Journal of Sociology* 61(1): 176–195.

Thacher, D. (2001) 'Policing is Not a Treatment: Alternatives to the Medical Model', *Journal of Research in Crime and Delinquency* 38(4): 387–415.

Tilley, N. (2009) 'Sherman vs Sherman: Realism vs Rhetoric', *Criminology & Criminal Justice* 9(2): 135–144.

Wacquant, L.J.D. (1992) 'The Structure and Logic of Bourdieu's Sociology'. In P. Bourdieu and L.J.D. Wacquant *An Invitation to Reflexive Sociology*, Cambridge: Polity Press.

Wacquant, L.J.D. (2011) 'From "Public Criminology" to the Reflexive Sociology of Criminological Production and Consumption', *British Journal of Criminology* 51: 438–448.

Wenger, E. (1998) *Communities of Practice*, Cambridge: Cambridge University Press.

Whyte, W.F. (1943) *Street Corner Society*, Chicago: University of Chicago Press.

Wilkinson, S. (2010) 'Research and Policing – Looking to the Future', *Policing* 4(2): 146–148.

Williams, K. (1989) 'Researching the Powerful: Problems and Possibilities of Social Research', *Contemporary Crises* 13: 253–274.

Wood, J., Fleming, J., and Marks, M. (2008) 'Building the Capacity of Police Change Agents: the Nexus Policing Project', *Policing & Society* 18(1): 72–87.

Young, J. (2011) *The Criminological Imagination*, Cambridge: Policy Press.

10

The Politics of Establishing Reflexivity as a Core Component of Good Policing

Dominic A. Wood and Emma Williams

Introduction

This chapter presents an argument favouring reflexivity as an important component in establishing what it means to be a good police officer. The term reflexivity is used here to denote a fully developed and enhanced reflective practitioner as presented within Schön's (1991[1983]) seminal contribution. We see an officer's reflexivity improving the more he/she reflects upon a wide range of variables when dealing with policing matters. This includes reflecting upon past experiences and performance, but also legal knowledge, awareness of force policy, appreciation of socio-economic and demographic circumstances and other factors that frame the professional practice contexts in which the officer is operating.

Reflexivity is currently, as Christopher (2015a) notes, largely absent in the policing literature. We counter this neglect with recommendations as to how it could become embedded within normative statements about

D.A. Wood (✉) • E. Williams
Canterbury Christ Church University, Canterbury, UK

© The Author(s) 2017
S. Armstrong et al. (eds.), *Reflexivity and Criminal Justice*,
DOI 10.1057/978-1-137-54642-5_10

215

the primary purposes of policing. We refer to literature that addresses the democratic deficit within policing, in terms of both the internal organisation of police services (Sklansky 2008) and the broader question of the police's democratic mandate within society (Manning 2010; Reiner 2013). We also draw upon our own professional reflections developed over time from working with the police as a researcher within a police service and/or as an academic teaching in a university on policing degrees. This equates, between the two of us, to an aggregated period of more than 20 years of teaching on a policing degree and a further 10 years of researching and evaluating within a police service. The chapter also makes references to the initial findings of a survey and follow-up interviews conducted with serving police officers who had undertaken a degree programme in policing.

From Reflective Practice to Reflexivity: How Do We Define a Good Police Officer?

The idea of reflective practice is widely established within different professional areas, to the point that it can be accommodated uncritically as unthinking 'sloganizing' (Halpin 2015: 133). However, Kinsella (2007) argues that Schön's (1991[1983]) articulation of the reflective practitioner draws heavily on the philosophical insights of Michael Polanyi and Gilbert Ryle in offering important insights into understanding 'the notion of *an embodied mode of reflection*' in conceiving 'of reflective processes in professional life' (Kinsella 2007: 408)[1]

It is worth reminding ourselves that Schön (1991[1983]: 5) was motivated by a crisis in the professions and in particular a growing perception of 'the amoral, irrelevant, or coercive aspects of professional education.' He presents the idea of the reflective practitioner as an alternative to what he presents as the 'Technical Rationality' model of professional knowledge, which involves 'the application of scientific theory and technique to the instrumental problems of practice' (Schön 1991[1983]: 30). Schön's (1991[1983]) insight is that knowledge is not simply something that is

---

[1] Kinsella (2007) identifies especially Polanyi (1967) and Ryle (1949).

established in the abstract, and then applied in practical contexts, but rather that there is something called knowing-in-action. Kinsella (2007: 401–2) summarises Schön's development of Michael Polanyi's notion of tacit knowledge in the following way:

> ... we know more than we can say ... this knowing is revealed in our actions and ... by observing and reflecting on our actions we can sometimes formulate constructions that account for the tacit knowledge revealed in what we do.

From the idea that we can know in action, Schön (1991[1983]) establishes that we can also reflect in action. He develops his thinking further by situating knowing and reflecting in action within a concept of professional practice, producing the notions of *knowing-in-practice* and *reflecting-in-practice* (Schön 1991[1983]: 59–61). Whilst this provides the basis of reflective practice, it remains potentially narrowly framed and of little importance within professional contexts. This is recognised by Schön (1991[1983]) when he notes that a practice involves repetition and therefore a practitioner can easily fail to recognise the frame within which a practice is performed. Awareness of frames is important in developing the critically reflective capacity of practitioners (Kinsella 2007) and allows for a greater reflexive capacity to transform a professional practice. This is crucial in understanding how reflexivity informs good policing.

However, establishing what it means to be a good police officer is not that straight forward. Policing, as Reiner (2015) notes, is what Gallie (1956) describes as an *essentially contested concept*. There are, and always will be, very different ideas of the purpose of policing and what police officers should be doing routinely. Despite repeated assertions that police officers are crime fighters there are alternative perspectives (Chan 2003; Reiner 2010) and there is a long-term evidence base to show that police officers do relatively little crime fighting and are much more likely to be involved in conflict resolution within communities (Muir 1977; Punch 1979). Indeed Roach (2002) shows that the modern police in the UK were primarily established as an order maintenance body with the explicit exclusion of any crime detection function.

Establishing reflexivity as a core attribute of a police officer likewise highlights the contention surrounding performance measures within policing. There exist target-oriented approaches to measuring police performance (Cockcroft 2013; Guilfoyle 2013), despite sustained criticism of targets, especially when they prioritise the crime fighting view of policing at the expense of non-crime policing functions (Cockcroft and Beattie 2009; Guilfoyle 2013). Assessing police performance is not necessarily problematic. However, it becomes so the more we ignore the literature on procedural justice (Tyler 2003; Myhill and Bradford 2011; Bradford 2014) and focus exclusively on outputs at the expense of processes. Exclusively quantitative measures make it particularly difficult to establish *being reflexive* as an important component of what it means to be a good police officer.

Being a Reflexive Police Officer

As Christopher (2015b) notes, police officers are routinely placed in nuanced and complex situations that require professional judgement, interpretation and reflection. This makes policing a necessarily reflexive occupation and is reflected in the focus on discretion within the police ethics literature (Kleinig 1996; Davis 2002; Delattre 2011). The ideal of autonomous police officers empowered to make discretionary, professional judgements is expressed within the concept of the office of constable (Police Federation 2008), and is reaffirmed within the Policing Protocol 2011 (Winsor 2013). It is also underpinned by the notion of the moral agent found within professional ethics contexts that requires the good police officer to be 'morally responsible' (Hill et al. 1978: 33). The moral agent does not abdicate responsibility or offload it to 'someone else, or the role' (Hill et al. 1978: 34). However, in practice, an officer's power to exercise discretion is curtailed, especially at the rank of constable (Rowe 2015), when considered against the dominance of risk aversion (Westera et al. 2016). Indeed reflexivity is discouraged by top-down regulation (Sklansky 2008).

The retreat from discretion and the failure to develop reflexivity can lead to what Rowe (2015) refers to as 'accurate misrepresentations.' Rowe

(2015) uses this term to describe a routine instance of police practice he observed as part of an ethnographic research project. He reports seeing officers carry out a stop and search that was in full accordance with force policy that provided an accurate account of the instance. However, Rowe (2015) was left feeling that this account was nonetheless a misrepresentation of what happened and the instance demonstrates that there is no scope within the process for measuring the decision-making capacity of the officer. Instead, the officer simply provides documentation to show that procedures have been followed. But a more representative account of the stop and search encounter, which would enable a much richer measurement of the officer's ability to assess a situation and respond in an appropriate and proportionate manner, is lost.

Reflexivity as a Feature of Democratic and Human Rights Values

This deficit becomes more problematic, the more we consider policing in terms of societal aspirations espoused, for example, through the concepts of democracy and/or human rights. As Manning (2010) notes, policing is never judged against democratic norms or values. We do not assess the police in terms of the extent to which they have upheld, or indeed advanced, human rights. At best democratic principles and human rights act as a constraint on policing when it is deemed to be excessively intrusive or inappropriately coercive. But this puts democracy and human rights, alongside reflexivity, at the margins of police work rather than at its core.

Human rights and democratic sentiments are firmly established as core values within British society, notwithstanding the Conservative Party's (2014) stated intention to scrap the Human Rights Act 1998. Human rights are presented as 'the *lingua franca* of liberal democracy' (Neyroud and Beckley 2001: 216), and what is true for human rights is arguably more so for democracy (Zakaria 2004; Fukuyama 2011). Democracy is accepted even more readily as a good thing, and whilst there may be different accounts of what democracy is and/or should be (Wood 2014), democratic sensibilities nonetheless pervade all aspects of society. They have been normalised as routine measures for virtually everything that we do and it is therefore hard to see how they are not embedded more within policing ideals as suggested by Manning (2010) and Reiner (2013). Police officers need to embed democratic and human rights considerations within decision-making processes and the ability to do this requires a high degree of reflexivity.

A particularly pressing issue is the extent to which the police fail to be organised internally in ways that conform to democratic expectations and norms (Sklansky 2008). The fostering of reflective practitioners within policing demands democratic structures that allow for appropriate levels of dissent, diversity of thought and questioning. This is problematic within an organisation that has a defined and authoritative rank structure (Silvestri 2003). However, the failure to allow for the kind of reflexivity that makes conscious the frames within which police practice operates results in police organisations missing out on challenges to unexamined assumptions, and the exploration of more innovative ways of working (Vickers cited in Silvestri 2003: 182). There is a danger here of exaggerating the importance of hierarchical necessity within policing and, in particular, of insisting that this is a consistent feature across all aspects of police work.

There are opportunities to enhance the internal democracy of police services through organisational justice measures (Sklansky 2008; Haas et al. 2015), and doing so encourages a more engaged and motivated workforce within the police. Officers are more likely to carry out their duties in a procedurally just and reflexive manner, the more that they feel they have been treated fairly and justly within their police organisation (Bradford 2014). Such findings resonate with the key messages that emanate from our own small research project. This shows frustrated officers who feel the personal time and expense invested in a degree programme is largely ignored. There are positive experiences but these are contingent upon supportive line managers rather than on routine or systematic processes.

This frustration has been manifested recently within the National Student Survey (NSS) results from final year students on the degree programme we run at our University. Our 'in-service' policing degree has tended to receive exceptional levels of satisfaction from students on this programme. However, in the most recent NSS results from the past three years, we have witnessed a fall in the satisfaction rates under personal development. This was at 80 % in 2013, 74 % in 2014 and 61 % in 2015. Over the same time period, the satisfaction rate relating to teaching on the programme has gone up from 88 % in 2013, to 94 % in 2014 and to 97 % in 2015. The personal development of students on this programme is largely located within their employment situation. We suspect that officers are demonstrating unfulfilled reflexivity potential here by voicing dissatisfaction at the lack of recognition their learning receives within the police service. The personal development of the officer does not equate to any professional development and consequently, the opportunities to be reflexive are limited. The degree programme has reflexivity embedded as a core component running throughout all modules. Officers are thus able as individual practitioners to reflect as a consequence of undertaking the programme, but when they try to apply this in practice, it is within a constrained context that allows little scope for going beyond the narrowly oppressive frames within which their broader professional practice operates. Overcoming these limitations requires better understanding and collaboration between universities and police services but importantly, as Hallenberg (2012) states, unless senior leaders within the police are supportive, any positive outcomes are likely to be lost. Indeed, even where support is forthcoming from senior police leaders, there are still strong cultural barriers that need to be overcome.

Where Are We Now? A Snapshot of Developments Within UK Policing and the Prospects for Reflexive Practice

We have spoken about an idea of policing that has at its heart the notion of a critically reflective police practitioner. Reflexivity has been identified as a core attribute required of officers operating within democratic contexts that aim to foster a culture and ethos of human rights. Here we consider the future prospects of establishing a more reflexive work force within the police services of England and Wales.

A positive note to begin with is the emergence of the College of Policing. The College came into being following the demise of the National Police Improvement Agency (NPIA) at the end of 2012 and was formally launched with Alex Marshall at its helm in February 2013. The College has been given a clear mandate to professionalise the police and to establish itself as the professional body for policing. It has begun to do this by establishing a code of ethics for policing, which it sees as an essential requirement of any profession, and it has promoted the idea of evidence-based policy and practice through the support and promulgation of evidence-based policing (EBP) and the *What Works Centre*. In 2015, the College awarded research funds to 14 successful bids totalling £10 million in conjunction with the Home Office and the Higher Education Funding Council for England (HEFCE). It has also launched a global policing database, a research map to help facilitate research projects across the country, research surgeries to offer support to police services from the researchers based at the College and a programme for developing leadership skills and integrity across the service. Most recently, the College has begun a consultation process regarding establishing graduate entry requirements into the police service. These initiatives portray a level of intention that far surpasses what the NPIA was able, and/or willing, to do.

There are concerns that the College is potentially pursuing a narrow interpretation of what constitutes evidence within academic research (Wood and Bryant 2015; Heaton and Tong 2015), especially given the extent to which the Police Knowledge Fund has the potential to become the only source of funding for police researchers going forward (Fleming 2015). It is also not entirely clear the extent to which the College will be able to force the hand of Chief Officers and/or overcome resistance for the Police Federation, especially when it comes, for example, to establishing more rigorous entry requirements into the police service. Despite a lingering perception that the College is the NPIA by another name, we feel this underestimates both the College's determination to do things differently, and the support it has to do this within, and outside of, the police service. Nonetheless, there is more to be done to establish reflective practice within policing as a norm and expectation.

The survey and interviews we undertook were aimed at asking officers to reflect upon the extent to which completing the degree had enhanced their understanding of policing, but also the extent to which this learning was acknowledged and/or utilised by others within the workplace. The results suggest that resistance to the kind of reflexivity we feel should be a core component of good policing remains. In the next section, we address this enduring resistance.

Resistance to Education Within Policing

We have discussed reflexivity as an attribute in a way that hopefully makes resistance to it seem unusual. Why would anyone not agree that reflexivity is core to good policing if it equates to the ability to interpret and read situations, coupled with knowledge about the different legal, social, political, moral and demographic contexts within which the police operate. Likewise, understanding reflexivity as a necessary feature within the context of the democratic sensibilities and expectations of contemporary society is well established. However, it is not the increasingly complex nature of policing or the demands this places on officers that is contested. The resistance emerges at the point we associate these qualities with a university education. It is equating reflexivity to attributes commonly associated with a university education, rather than the attributes per se, that seems to be objected to most of all.

Readers will not be surprised to find university lecturers arguing in favour of academic attributes, and the education implications that follow. We do not pretend to ignore the obvious benefits for our own degree programmes arising from the elevation of these attributes within policing. However, too often we feel that the debate about reflexivity as an attribute is easily lost because of an unhelpful fixation on qualifications.

Talk of turning police organisations into all graduate employers understandably creates anxieties given the extent to which entry into the police has largely been characterised by a lack of any formal educational attainment requirement (Neyroud 2011; Winsor 2012). Those currently employed within the police without academic qualifications will naturally feel at the very least somewhat overlooked in this discussion, if not insulted. Indeed, the response in the news to the College's proposals regarding degrees and recent traffic on social media has high-lighted just this. It is easy to understand how officers could feel under-valued and angered by a discussion that implies they are inadequate because they lack an academic qualification, one that was not required when they joined the police. Furthermore, it is highly probable that they will know an officer without a degree who they consider to be a first-rate officer, just as it is likely that they will know an officer with a degree who they feel is less than adequate in at least some aspects of their duties.

It is important for this reason that we focus on reflexivity as a core component of good policing rather than giving the false impression that having a degree will in and of itself make someone a good police officer. We need to be more explicit in recognising that having a degree does not guarantee someone a job. There are further application processes through which employers assess whether they think a given applicant meets the particulars of the job. Having a degree might demonstrate abilities that meet necessary requirements of a given role; for example, research sug-gests that police graduates are better at using discretion, being empa-thetic, utilising communication skills and providing a more thoughtful range of solutions (Meese 1993; Worden 1990). But a degree is never going to be sufficient in evidencing everything that an employer seeks. We should avoid polarising the debate around academic qualifications. It is nonsense to suggest, on the one hand, that having a degree will automatically make someone a good police officer. But at the same time being awarded a degree should tell us something about the suitability of a person's ability to be a police officer, even if it is nothing more than a starting point.

We also need to give much more thought to how we deal with the thousands of serving police officers who do not have a degree. Again our argument rests upon establishing what makes someone a good police officer. We acknowledge that this is contentious but at the same time we need to establish ideas of what good policing looks like and corresponding measurements that allow us to assess performance. This does not mean that these measures need to be crudely set as targets, nor does it mean that they should be established as universal measures for all time. But we can establish core components, such as reflexivity, in determining what it means to be a good police officer. Unfortunately, the focus on qualifications, rather than attributes, makes this more difficult.

We need to focus on the attributes that we think are important rather than fixating on qualifications, which are a secondary, and potentially arbitrary, factor. We are in no doubt that there will be many serving police officers who do not have the latter but are more than capable of demonstrating the former. The important point is that police organisations need to be supported, and to have supportive mechanisms in place, that allow officers to have their attributes formally recognised. There need to be opportunities for officers without degrees to attain academic credits through work-based activities alongside dedicated and protected time for learning. This would necessarily also require a meaningful time frame for existing officers to demonstrate attributes in a way that would result in academic attainment. This would require, for example, something like a ten year strategy (Bryant et al. 2013) along the lines of that adopted in Northern Ireland following the Patten Report (1999). Importantly, it would need to include developmental time for those not immediately meeting the expectations of the service.

Furthermore, it should not only be those without academic qualifications who need to demonstrate the required level of reflexivity. Many who have joined the police with a degree have done so without the degree having been of any significance in their recruitment. The distinction between those who have entered the police with a degree and those who entered without a degree has been for the most part insignificant. The academic attainment of those with degrees has been of little importance in terms of why they have been employed and/or how they have been subsequently utilised. Moreover, in most professional contexts, there is a continuing professional development requirement. Even where a degree is taken as evidence of reflexivity at the point of employment, there remains a need for ongoing demonstration of this attribute.

Austerity as an Exacerbating Factor

The resistance that comes from officers feeling disenfranchised by the qualifications debate is exacerbated further by a more general level of resistance to any change in policing at the moment. It has been a sobering experience for us that even officers who have chosen to complete a degree in their own time and at their own expense will express resistance to the idea of an all graduate police profession, despite speaking favourably about their own experiences on a degree programme. This again is understandable given the scope of an ongoing process of change that has been accelerated through the austerity programme of the Coalition Government since 2010. The election of the Conservative Government in 2015, with a clear intention to extend cuts within policing, weighs heavily in the minds of many police officers. The sense of a never-ending police reform process, which generates changes that seem inevitably to lead to more demands on officers, appears to be having a draining impact on police morale.

We were conscious of this in the timing of the survey and the interviews we conducted. This is an unsettling time for police officers and the frustration of having to deal with spending cuts and the broader austerity measures comes through in officers' responses. The preoccupation with these concerns is understandable and it produces a distraction away from discussions about the importance of reflexivity within policing. We should not assume that this kind of distraction necessarily equates to opposition to change. The degree of uncertainty amongst officers is tangible and it is understandable that officers are focused on matters that have a more pressing and personal presence. The question of establishing and embedding reflexivity as a core policing attribute lacks the immediacy of the next Comprehensive Spending Review, which renders other matters insignificant and trivial. Indeed, the speed with which many changes are already occurring in policing has created a perception amongst officers that they are under attack, which in turn triggers a defence mechanism that is expressed as resistance to change.

It is only natural that officers will find it difficult to look for positives and opportunities if and when all seems to be collapsing around them.

Within the current climate, this kind of resistance is perhaps inevitable and almost impossible to counter. It is above all else an emotional level of resistance that is largely immune to reasoned debate. It needs to be understood and acknowledged as a constraint on what is possible. We cannot overcome this form of resistance completely without being able to offer a tangible level of stability and security to officers.

The Prevalence of an Anti-intellectual Bias Within Policing

Although difficult, the current climate does offer an opportunity to focus the debate more on the frames within which professional police practice operates. This is a good moment to return to the understanding of the reflective practitioner found in Schön (1991[1983]) and the possibility of policing becoming a more critically reflective practice (Christopher 2015a, 2015b). However, this requires a firm stance against the anti-intellectual form of resistance that opposes any suggestion that police officers need to be educated.

One argument against educating officers makes reference to the Peelian notion of police as *ordinary* citizens. From this, it is suggested that a compulsory educational hurdle unnecessarily excludes people looking to join the police. This argument conflates the Peelian ideal of a police officer with the real men, and later women, that actually joined the police. The presentation of the police officer as *ordinary* was designed to allay fears amongst the ruling elite who saw the 'New Police' as a threat to the liberties of free born English men (Emsley 2009). The designate *ordinary* was aimed at disarming those critical of introducing a standing body of professional police by downplaying its significance. The ideal of the police officer as *ordinary* citizen was a deliberate attempt to imply continuity of tradition over radical change despite the symbolic magnitude and momentous, historical importance of what was being proposed and brought into being (Waddington 1999; Reiner 2010). In reality, police officers have never been ordinary citizens. They have always been aspirational and have had to meet exceptional requirements at different times during the history of the police, for example, in the form of unusually high levels of intrusion into the private lives of officers or in terms of not being able to join a trade union. There is nothing ordinary about having to seek approval from your employer when choosing a spouse or deciding where you want to live. There is nothing ordinary about giving up the right to strike.

Furthermore, the public service ethos underpinning the police role was anything but ordinary in the first half of the nineteenth century. Likewise, the appeal to the rule of law and the establishment of democratically legitimised political institutions are largely normalised in today's society in a way that they were not in the nineteenth century, and indeed for much of the twentieth century (Wood 2014). Police officers have performed *extraordinary* duties in helping to establish the kind of democracy we have today, often in ways that make policing inherently problematic (Waddington 1999). If the police did nothing more than what ordinary citizens are willing and able to do, it would be much easier to make the cuts in the police favoured by the current government. But this implies the kind of idealised big society imagined by David Cameron that has proven difficult to achieve. The stark reality is that the police are needed to do the things that ordinary people do not want to do. This places demands upon police officers that make them anything but ordinary citizens.

A recurring argument against educational entry qualifications for police officers is that it would preclude the 40-year-old plumber from switching jobs mid-life. We favour allowing people to come into policing later in life and recognise the different perspectives that such individuals can bring to police work. But we need to be wary of the suggestion that anyone can do policing; that the only qualification required to be a police officer is the motivation to sign up. We should apply the same kind of qualifying criteria to the 40-year-old plumber who wants to become a police officer that we would to the 40-year-old police officer who wants to become a plumber. If a police service wants to recruit a 40-year-old plumber, then they need to support such an individual by providing opportunities for her to change careers and join the police. This would be something for police services to consider, and to invest in, if they wish to benefit from having recruits who offer a different perspective than typically younger recruits. But this should not result in opening the recruitment gates to anyone. Applicants should still need to demonstrate apposite attributes before being unleashed on the general public, and in our mind, this includes the kind of reflexivity discussed above.

A second problem with the ordinary citizen argument is the implication that there is something extraordinary about undertaking a degree programme. This is simply no longer true. As the President of the Police Superintendents Association Irene Curtis (2015) noted, in a candid presentation in which she acknowledged her own prejudices against academia, nearly half of school leavers are now going to university. University education is no longer exceptional. It is becoming increasingly normal, to the point that graduates are now underrepresented within police recruitment (Curtis 2015). Higher education is no longer the preserve of an elite minority. It is attended by the kind of 'ordinary' people who would have traditionally joined the police. They are not ordinary but rather aspirational individuals who are willing to be subjected to additional demands. Furthermore, despite the fact that police officers often seem to revel in their own ordinariness, this is not how they are perceived within society. Indeed, within the Higher Education Statistics Agency (HESA), the charitable company that provides the UK Government with different data sets regarding universities, employment in the police at sergeant and below is categorised under the heading of 'associate professional and technical occupations' under the broad umbrella of professional, as opposed to non-professional occupations. Similarly, Police Community Support Officers fall under the same category. This means that these roles are recorded by universities as graduate employment within the annual Destination of Leavers from Higher Education (DLHE) survey. It is hardly surprising therefore that school leavers wishing to join the police see it as natural to undertake a policing degree before joining the police in a way that would have been unimaginable ten years ago. Recognition of the extent to which going to university has been normalised is missing from the debate within policing about higher education. To this end, Curtis' (2015) honesty is a welcome development.

It is quite remarkable to see how animated officers become on the matter of diversity in the police when it comes to educational hurdles. The argument that raising the entry requirements for police excludes ethnic minorities has been largely dropped, because it is evident that universities are more ethnically diverse than police organisations. The debate about diversity has moved from ethnicity to class. But again, how genuine is this argument? Whilst universities could do more to extend opportunities to people from disadvantaged backgrounds, much has already been done to widen participation within higher education. Universities are still attended by privileged, wealthy individuals but there is a broad base of students from a wide variety of backgrounds at higher education institutions across the UK. We certainly do not see a discernible difference between the students on our pre-service and in-service policing programmes. The reality is that the police have a poor record on diversity. The current arguments around class amount to little more than the protection and preservation of the historical homogeneity of the force. Such arguments ultimately seek to maintain the privileged status of an idealised typical officer and have little to do with a genuine desire to make the police service more diverse.

There is no reason why an educational entry qualification should exclude suitable candidates for the police, especially those from disadvantaged backgrounds. The police might need to take more responsibility for ensuring that they recruit from wider sections of society and this is where working with universities could be beneficial. One thing the police could do, for example, would be to help debunk the myth about university 'fees.' Currently, the vast majority of undergraduate students do not pay university fees, but rather draw upon loans that are only repayable if and when the student starts earning above £21,000. If the student is earning £30,000 per annum that would require paying back £67 a month (Student Loans Company 2015). For someone from a disadvantaged background, the prospect of a gross £2500 monthly salary from a respectable, secure, professional occupation, is truly life transforming.

Experience Versus Education

Another common argument that needs to be addressed is one that posits experience *against* education in establishing how police officers become good at their jobs. For us, it makes no sense to see experience and education as opposites in this way. Instead, our understanding of reflexivity as an enhanced and developed form of the critically reflective practitioner is such that it requires both to operate in a mutually reinforcing manner. Reflexivity understood in this way draws upon a quality recognised within Ancient Greece through the work of Aristotle as *phronesis* (Grint 2007). *Phronesis* draws upon both technical and academic understandings to produce a third kind of understanding, which is manifested as a practical wisdom that informs the kind of professional decision-making required of police officers (Wood and Tong 2009). The question should not be whether experience is better than education or vice versa but rather that experience is an integral part of the educative process in producing *phronesis* or practical wisdom, especially within professional contexts.

Education has to be presented to officers not simply as training but as part of a wider array of knowledge that can be utilised and drawn upon within professional judgements and discretion. Professionalism should be seen here as a multifaceted and dynamic concept (Chan 2003), which is rarely static (Holdaway 2015). Moreover, different understandings of professionalism are found within and between police ranks and roles (Chan 2003). There is a danger of professionalism being utilised as a means of establishing particular controlling behaviours that will be met with scepticism and resisted accordingly (Chan 2003). Chan (2003) draws upon Illich in concluding that structures to make organisations more professional do not always result in a more effective service. Indeed top-down processes to define professional agendas can result in 'systematic disabling of clients' (Chan 2003: 6).

Fleming (2015) has noted that her ongoing research in this area demonstrates that police officers remain very wary of academic research as a starting point for developing their understanding of a given policing problem. They feel much more comfortable reflecting upon their own experiences. Significantly though, they are also willing to explore the experiences of colleagues from near and far to broaden their own understanding. This is a really important step towards academic learning. It demonstrates a willingness to go beyond personal experience and to recognise the limitations of one perspective. Academics need to be mindful of this and much more prepared to build upon the willingness of police officers to explore alternative perspectives. Academic research can often come across as either being a long winded way of establishing what we already know or, alternatively, of producing operational outputs that are so counter intuitive and at odds with the experiential perceptions of the officers, that they are simply rejected. Academics need to be much more mindful of the extent to which policing lacks the kind of research awareness that has been developed over time in other areas of professional work such as in education or nursing (Wood and Bryant 2015).

As academics, we need to be much more prepared to support officers in their endeavours to understand the professional world in which they operate. The experiences of practitioners can be an important starting point from which to develop appropriate research questions and the generating of data that are directly and readily meaningful to officers. As Fleming's (2015) preliminary findings show, whilst officers express a wariness and scepticism towards academic research, they are eager to refer to peers in order to learn about others' experiences. This is an important step towards establishing a reflexive, critical approach to learning from incidents and practices, as opposed to simply experiencing them.

Concluding Remarks: The Importance of Reflexivity as a Core Attribute of Officers We Need Today

The extent to which democratic norms, underpinned by human rights, inform contemporary society, demands police officers who can demonstrate the kind of reflexivity that we have presented within this chapter. This demand is given further weight, the more we see the College of Policing's embedding of a police code of ethics and a sound knowledge base underpinning all aspects of police work. These demands require officers to be reflective and thoughtful. It is unfortunate that debates about professional policing tend to get mired in polemical disagreements about qualifications and the relationship between universities and police organisations. These are undoubtedly important political factors that need to be addressed and resolved but it is our belief that they will only be resolved if we can find a degree of consensus on what we want and expect from our police officers. In our minds, policing that is unreflective is simply not tenable within complex democratic societies that demand more transparency, responsiveness and accountability. The contexts within which a police officer operates today places demands upon the intellectual capacity of the officer that truly require a degree of reflexivity that equates to the kind of practical wisdom found within the Aristotelian concept of *phronesis*. The police officers we need today are far from ordinary. They need to be decidedly practical, socially adept, ethically minded problem solvers who are above all else highly reflexive. In short, they require heroic, extraordinary and aspirational qualities. If we can agree on this, then the qualifications, recruitment processes and organisational justice matters begin to look after themselves.

References

Bradford, B. (2014) 'Policing and Social Identity: Procedural Justice, Inclusion and Cooperation Between Police and Public', *Policing and Society* 24(1): 22–43.

Bryant, R., Cockcroft, T., Tong, S., Wood, D., (2013) Police Training and Education: Past, Present and Future. In J. Brown (ed) *The Future of Policing*, Abingdon: Routledge: 383–397.

Chan, J. (2003) *Fair Cop: Learning the Art of Policing*, Toronto: University of Toronto Press.

Christopher, S. (2015a) 'The Police Service Can Be a Critical Reflective Practice... If It Wants', *Policing: A Journal of Policy and Practice* 9(4): 326–339.

Christopher, S. (2015b) 'The Quantum Leap: Police Recruit Training and the Case for Mandating Higher Education Pre-entry Schemes', *Policing: A Journal of Policy and Practice* 9(4): 388–404.

Cockcroft, T. (2013) *Police Culture: Themes and Concepts,* London: Routledge.

Cockcroft, T., and Beattie, I. (2009) 'Shifting Culture: Managerialism and the Rise of "Performance"', *Policing: An International Journal of Police Strategies and Management* (32) 3: 526–540.

Conservative Party (2014) *Protecting Human Rights in the UK. The Conservatives' Proposals for Changing Britain's Human Rights Laws*, London: Conservative Party.

Curtis, I. (2015) Key Note 2. *POLCON 6: 6th Annual Conference of The Higher Education Forum for Learning and Development in Policing.* Staffordshire University, September 2–3, 2015.

Davis, M. (2002) *Profession, Code, and Ethics: Towards a Morally Useful Theory of Today's Professions,* Aldershot: Ashgate.

Delattre, E. J. (2011) *Character and Cops. Ethics and Policing,* 6th Edition, Lanham, Maryland: Rowman & Littlefield.

Emsley, C., (2009) *The Great British Bobby: A History of British Policing from 1829 to the Present,* London: Quercus.

Fleming, J. (2015) Key Note 4. *POLCON 6: 6th Annual Conference of The Higher Education Forum for Learning and Development in Policing.* Staffordshire University, September 2–3, 2015.

Fukuyama, F. (2011) *The Origins of Political Order: From Prehuman Times to the French Revolution,* London: Profile Books.

Gallie, W.B. (1956) 'Essentially Contested Concepts', *Proceedings of the Aristotelian Society,* 56: 167–198.

Grint, K. (2007) 'Learning to Lead: Can Aristotle Help Us Find the Road to Wisdom?', *Leadership* 3(2): 231–246.

Guilfoyle, S. (2013) *Intelligent Policing: How Systems Thinking Eclipse Conventional Management Practice,* Axminster: Triarchy Press.

Haas, N.E., Van Craen, M., Skogan, W.G., & Fleitas, D.M. (2015) 'Explaining Officer Compliance: The Importance of Procedural Justice and Trust Inside a Police Organization', *Criminology and Criminal Justice* 15(4): 442–463.

Hallenberg, K.M. (2012) *Scholarly Detectives: Police Professionalisation via Academic Education.* PhD thesis, University of Manchester.

Halpin, D. (2015) 'Essaying and Reflective Practice in Education: The Legacy of Michael de Montaigne', *Journal of Philosophy of Education* 49(1): 129–141.

Heaton, R. & Tong, S. (2015) 'Evidence-Based Policing: From Effectiveness to Cost-Effectiveness', *Policing. A Journal of Policy and Practice* doi: 10.1093/police/pav030.

Hill, P.H., Bedau, H.A., Chechile, R.A., Crochetiere, W.J., Kellerman, B.L., Ounjian, D., Pauker, S.G., Pauker, S.P., & Rubin, J.Z. (1978) *Making Decisions: A Multidisciplinary Introduction,* Reading, MA: Addison-Wesley.

Holdaway, S. (2015) *The Re-Professionalisation of the Police in England and Wales.* Lecture presented at Canterbury Christ Church University, 17th April 2015.

Kinsella, E.A. (2007) 'Embodied Reflections and the Epistemology of Reflective Practice', in *Journal of Philosophy of Education* 41(3): 395–409.

Kleinig, J. (1996) *The Ethics of Policing,* Cambridge: Cambridge University Press.

Manning, P.K. (2010) *Democratic Policing in a Changing World*, Boulder: Paradigm Publishers.

Meese, E. (1993) 'Community policing and the police officer', *Perspectives on Policing*, Vol. 15, Washington, DC and Harvard University, Boston, MA: National Institute of Justice, p. xx.

Myhill, A. & Bradford, B. (2011) 'Can Police Enhance Public Confidence by Improving Quality of Service? Results from Two Surveys in England and Wales', *Policing and Society: An International Journal of Research and Policy* 22(4): 397–425.

Muir, W. (1977) *Police: Streetcorner Politicians*, Chicago: The University of Chicago Press.

Neyroud, P. (2011) *Review of Police Leadership and Training Volume One*, London: Home Office.

Neyroud P.W. & Beckley A. (2001) *Policing, Ethics and Human Rights*, Cullompton, Devon: Willan.

Patten, C. (1999) *A New Beginning: Policing in Northern Ireland. The Report of the Independent Commission on Policing for Northern Ireland* (Patten Report). London: HMSO.

Polanyi, M. (1967) *The Tacit Dimension*, London: Routledge.

Police Federation (2008) *The Office of Constable. The bedrock of modern day British policing*, Leatherhead: Police Federation of England and Wales.

Punch, M. (1979) 'The Secret Social Service' in S. Holdaway (ed) *The British Police*, London: Edward Arnold.

Reiner R. (2010) *The Politics of the Police*, 4th Edition, Oxford: Oxford University Press.

Reiner, R. (2013) 'Who Governs? Democracy, Plutocracy, Science and Prophecy in Policing', *Criminology and Criminal Justice*, 13(2) 161–180.

Reiner, R. (2015) 'Utopia in one institution? Can policing be democratic in an unjust society?' presented at *Policing and Democracy in the 21st Century*, The International Criminological Research Unit, Liverpool University, 17th September 2015.

Roach L.T. (2002) 'Detecting Crime Part I: Detection and the Police', *Criminal Law Review*, May 2002: 379–390.

Rowe, M. (2015) 'Police! Camera! Lay observation!' presented at *Policing and Democracy in the 21st Century*, The International Criminological Research Unit, Liverpool University, 17th September 2015.

Ryle, G. (1949) *The Concept of Mind*, London: Hutchinson.

Schön, D. (1991[1983]) *The Reflective Practitioner: How professionals think in action*, Avebury: Ashgate.

Sklansky, D. A. (2008) *Democracy and the Police*, Stanford: Stanford University Press.

Students Loan Company (2015) *Loan Repayment*. Available on-line, accessed 15/10/15: http://www.slc.co.uk/students/loan-repayment.aspx

Tyler, T. (2003) 'Procedural Justice, Legitimacy, and the Effective Rule of Law', *Crime and Justice* 30: 283–357.

Silvestri, M. (2003) *Women in Charge: Policing, Gender and Leadership,* Devon: Willan Publishing.

Waddington, P.A.J. (1999) *Policing Citizens,* London: UCL Press.

Westera, N. Kebbell, M., Milne, B and Green, T. (2016) 'The Prospective Detective: Developing the Effective Detective of the Future', *Policing and Society: An International Journal of Research and Policy* 26(2): 197–209.

Winsor, T. (2012) *Independent Review of Police Officer and Staff Remuneration and Conditions Final Report – Volume 1* (March 2012) Cm 8325-I. London: The Stationery Office.

Winsor, T. (2013) Operational independence and the new accountability of policing. John Harris Memorial Lecture to the Police Foundation, available at: http://www.hmic.gov.uk/media/hmcic-tom-winsor-john-harris-memorial-lecture.pdf (accessed 20 March 2014).

Wood, D.A. (2014) 'The Importance of Liberal Values Within Policing: Police and Crime Commissioners, Police Independence and the Spectre of Illiberal Democracy', *Policing and Society: An International Journal of Research and Policy*. DOI: 10.1080/10439463.2014.922086.

Wood, D.A. & Tong, S. (2009) 'The Future of Initial Police Training: A University Perspective', *International Journal of Police Science & Management* 11(3): 294–305.

Wood, D.A. & Bryant, R.P. (2015) 'Researching Police Professionalism' in M. Brunger, S. Tong & D. Martin (Eds) *Introduction to Policing Research: Taking Lessons from Practice,* Abingdon: Routledge.

Worden, R.E. (1990) 'A Badge and a Baccalaureate: Policies, Hypotheses, and Further Evidence', *Justice Quarterly* 7: 565–92.

Zakaria, F., (2004) *The Future of Freedom. Illiberal Democracy at Home and Abroad,* London: W.W. Norton & Company.

11

Getting In, Getting Out and Getting Back: Conducting Long-term Research in Immigration Detention Centres

Mary Bosworth and Blerina Kellezi

Introduction

In this chapter, we document challenges we face in conducting ongoing research on everyday life in immigration removal centres (IRCs) many of which relate to the highly contested nature of these sites. Immigration detention is frequently in the news, yet rarely the topic of independent academic scrutiny. The Home Office and the private companies who manage these sites of confinement hardly ever allow researchers into them, leaving most of those who write about such places dependent on NGOs, former detainees or evidence gleaned from conversations in the visits halls. We are the exception to the rule, having obtained and retained permission to enter IRCs to conduct independent academic research in 2009. In this chapter, drawing on interviews and field notes with and

M. Bosworth (✉)
University of Oxford, Oxford, UK

B. Kellezi
Nottingham Trent University, Nottingham, UK

© The Author(s) 2017
S. Armstrong et al. (eds.), *Reflexivity and Criminal Justice*,
DOI 10.1057/978-1-137-54642-5_11

about staff, we explore some of the tensions inherent in maintaining a working relationship over a long period of time and in these complex research sites. Though aspects of our experience are specific to IRCs, some will apply to other, long-term research projects in custody.

The research on which this chapter is based took over a year to arrange. In autumn 2009, after numerous discussions, proposals and appointments with men from the custodial sector in Britain, Mary finally met the civil servant who had the power to decide whether or not she could conduct her long-planned study of everyday life in immigration detention centres. Nobody had ever been given permission from the Home Office, she was warned; she was certain to be turned down.

Understandably nervous, Mary was taken aback to realise that, unlike the senior custodial staff who had been assisting her up to that point, the man in charge of the decision was her own age. Expecting to negotiate with an older, more suspicious, man, she immediately felt more optimistic. Indeed, the young, and friendly, civil servant had already made his decision. She was welcome to start whenever she liked and he looked forward to hearing more about her findings. His one caveat, to which we shall return below, "we don't want your research to embarrass us." (Home Office, senior civil servant).

Since that date, Mary has been conducting research inside immigration detention centres, free from scrutiny, and, despite producing a series of critical reports, articles, blog posts, conference papers, and a research monograph, without interference (see, for example, Bosworth 2012, 2013, 2014). The first study has led to a number of other projects, deploying a range of methodologies from surveys to photography. The original civil servant has long since moved on (to the private sector). Not all of his replacements have been as enthusiastic about facilitating academic research yet none of them have terminated it either. They maintain a wary acceptance.

In July 2010, Mary was joined by Blerina, who for 18 months, worked alongside her in three IRCs: Yarl's Wood, Tinsley House and Brook House. Mary is currently heading a five-year research project on immigration detention, and has a number of students who are conducting research in and on these centres. Blerina continues to collaborate on some of these projects (Bosworth and Kellezi 2012, 2013, 2014, 2015).

This chapter describes our work together, focusing on the first portion of our research into 'quality of life' in IRCs, in order to explore the ramifications and nature of conducting work in secretive, politicised sites like these. While we are grateful for the research access we enjoy, we reflect on the possible costs of the permission we have been given, as well as the challenges we have encountered in maintaining it. Whereas researchers are accustomed to negotiating consent with participants, they spend rather less time discussing the role of institutional gatekeepers in facilitating their projects. As a result, research access, if it is discussed at all, is often cast as a one off arrangement, granted or withheld.

When projects stretch over some years, as ours has, matters are not so straightforward. Relationships with gatekeepers evolve and shift. The top-level decision-makers themselves rarely stay in post, yet the institutions remain. The researchers publish findings, which, in sites like these, are rarely positive. They may also develop new areas of interest, and wish to move on from their original focus. Impression management attempts that may be made in one or two meetings, to disguise or deflect questions about personal opinions and intent are unsustainable over the long term. Researchers have to, at least in part, show their true colours.

While the Home Office has continued to support projects associated with the first one they authorised, they have not extended the same openness to other academics. Under these circumstances, thinking reflexively about access is urgently needed. In so doing, we hope not only to assist others seeking entry to the field but also to contribute to academic understanding of immigration detention itself. As we will argue below, methodology and the research process illuminate and are structured by quite fundamental aspects of daily life in detention that, in turn, connect to, and may shed light on, wider questions about their purpose and effect.

The Research Context

Immigration detention centres are relatively new sites of criminological inquiry (Bosworth 2014; Aas and Bosworth 2013). In the UK, there are around 4000 people held on any one day in one of 11 IRCs. Over the course of a year nearly 40,000 people pass through these sites of confinement.

IRCs are concentrated in the South East of the country, with four situated adjacent to Gatwick and Heathrow airports. Though a national system, each institution is contracted out to a private custodial company or to the prison service. These custodial organisations run the IRCs on behalf of the Home Office according to the Detention Centre Rules, 2001.

Although not part of the criminal justice system, detention centres share many characteristics with more familiar penal institutions. They are, for the most part, built to Category B prison design, or are former prisons that have been converted into IRCs. They are staffed by uniformed 'detention custody officers' (DCOs) and 'detention custody managers' (DCMs), who are overseen by a small non-uniformed 'senior management team' (SMT). All centre managers are former prison governors and many in the Home Office have previously worked in the National Offender Management Service (NOMS, the merged agency for prisons and probation in the UK) or in the Ministry of Justice. In addition to the custodial officers, each IRC houses a complement of onsite Immigration Officers, whose job is to communicate with the off-site Home Office case-workers who make all the immigration decisions concerning the detainees.

IRCs are inspected by the same groups that monitor prisons: HM Inspectorate of Prisons (HMIP), the Independent Monitoring Board (IMB) and the Prison and Probation Ombudsman (Bosworth 2007). A number of detainees have served prison sentences, sometimes for immigration-related offences, but often for more 'everyday' criminal matters like armed robbery or drugs. A handful of them are on multi-agency public protection arrangements (MAPPAs), having been convicted prior to detention of serious violent or sexual offences. Finally, daily life in these closed institutions is shaped by a series of instruments and tools from detention custody orders to room share and risk assessment policies all of which originated in prisons and have merely been adjusted for their new population and setting.

These similarities assisted Mary in her initial bid to enter IRCs as she was able to draw on existing research relationships in the prison service to find a pathway into the Home Office. A retired prison governor introduced Mary to a centre manager and the head of a custodial company, both of whom, after one meeting, recommended her project to the Home Office. Like her original contact, the centre manager and the CEO, had previously been prison governors too. All had reservations about how IRCs were operating. They believed in the 'Decency Agenda' of the prison service and hoped it could somehow be transposed to detention centres. All were aware of and supported the prisons research centre at the University of Cambridge, which has worked for many years alongside prison staff to understand and ameliorate prison life. Perhaps Mary, at Oxford, could achieve a similar goal in detention, they proposed.

Like our early gatekeepers, when we began our project, we expected to draw on tools and ideas from prison sociology (Bosworth 1999; Liebling 2004; Crewe 2009; Philips 2010). Not only did we expect to find an environment in which regime and relationships were important, but we thought we could rely on similar methodologies and concepts to explain them. One of the strategies that had proved useful in gaining access, proposing to design and implement a new survey, the *Measure of the Quality of Life in Detention* (MQLD) (Bosworth and Kellezi 2013, 2015), was explicitly modelled on Alison Liebling's *Measure of the Quality of Prison Life* (MQPL) (Liebling 2004) which has been adopted by the prison service. Both instruments draw on extensive qualitative research with staff and the incarcerated. Both seek to quantify aspects of daily life to assist with progressive policy development.

As we will detail below, however, matters did not always work out as we had anticipated. While some ideas and techniques could be easily adjusted, others did not translate at all. The surveys have ended up being quite distinct while the process of gathering a meaningful sample in these uncertain sites remains extremely challenging.

Such methodological issues intersected with and were often amplified by the absence of an existing body of literature on these places as research sites. The lack of experience among staff and detainees as research subjects sat uneasily alongside the politicisation of the sites in which they were found. We were often the very first academics anyone had actually met. Explaining our ideas and the purpose of study, under these conditions, was difficult, and raised uncomfortable questions about our capacity to gather informed consent. What were people agreeing to? And why would they participate? Paradoxically, the lack of a research culture was also, at times, liberating. Few staff or detainees had preconceived ideas or expectations about us. As a result, once we had obtained research access, we had considerable flexibility in what we could do, where we could go, and the kinds of questions we could ask.

Getting In

Research access is made up of a series of interactions, of which 'getting in,' in a formal sense, is only the first. Once inside, researchers must attract participants. They also need to understand the site they have entered. In custodial research, these tasks, of engagement and comprehension, can be particularly challenging due to the well-known and extensively documented power differences among the confined and those who secure them (see, inter alia, Sparks et al. 1996; Bosworth 1999; Crewe 2009; Philips 2010). Each side may be wary of cooperating with a researcher. In detention, matters are made still more complicated by the sheer array of staff and detainees and by the distinct and still largely unfamiliar nature of these establishments.

In contrast to the long tradition of prison sociology, very little academic work has been conducted inside detention centres (Hall 2010, 2012; Bosworth 2012, 2014; Bosworth and Kellezi 2014). Instead, for the most part, academic scholarship on detention is either purely theoretical (De Genova 2010; Silverman and Massa 2012), is based on interviews with former detainees (Klein and Williams 2012) or relies on information gleaned from social visits (Griffiths 2014). Before we began there was little other than reports from NGOs and the government to prepare us for what detention was like (HMIP 2002; Phelps 2009). Until 2010, when Alexandra Hall published an article on her doctoral research with staff in a British detention centre, there was nothing at all about detention as a research site (Hall 2010; see also Hall 2012).

While all of this scholarship contributes to our understanding of the impact, nature and justification of border control, the growing distance between the interior life world of these sites of confinement and the academic and political debate over them raises some uncomfortable questions. While it is clearly not the case that only empirical accounts can explain carceral institutions, without any systematic, independent scrutiny, our understanding of them is inevitably limited. At the same time, there are also risks and costs associated with institutional studies. Asking people to reflect on traumatic experiences while they are still undergoing them can be painful. Some might argue that entering these sites could, however unintentionally, legitimate them (see also Armstrong and Lam, and Harding, this volume). How bad can they be, people may ask, if researchers are able to visit?

Such queries demand a response. Institutional ethnographies cannot uncover the 'truth' but they can illuminate hidden spaces and the experiences of those within by gathering testimonies, describing day-to-day activities and bearing witness to life inside. Without such detail, theoretical and political debate becomes unhinged from the very lives it seeks to understand or improve. 'Bearing witness,' as Emma Kaufman (2015) observes, is a form of recognition. In sites like IRCs, which are designed to expel, face-to-face encounters are inherently political. It is no wonder, then, that the state is so unwilling to allow outsiders entry.

On a more personal level, the absence of scholarship placed us, in the beginning at least, in an uncertain position. The politicization of these sites can be disorienting, as it is difficult to separate research from normative questions about the morality of locking up people on the basis of their immigration status. Confusion about these sites and concerns about their legitimacy weighed heavily on us at all stages of the project, and continue today. In these uncomfortable feelings, we glimpse what it might be like to enter or work in IRCs as those within are also often unclear and anxious about them.

Even today, six years into the research field, entering detention centres is unsettling. Although there is some variation in their architectural design and levels of security, they are all ringed with razor wire and CCTV cameras. Researchers, as well as staff and visitors, may be searched on entry. They are only allowed to bring in with them certain pre-authorised items Fig. 11.1.

Natural light in most IRCs is restricted. Hallways stretch, lined with locked, or at least closed, doors. Sections of the building end suddenly with barred doors. The institutional smell of cleaning fluids pervades. In certain sections, often the legal corridor where meetings about deportation occur, the odour of nervous sweat can be overwhelming (Fig. 11.2).

Fig. 11.1 External image of Campsfield House

Fig. 11.2 Housing block (Morton Hall)

As in prisons, sound is both muffled and occasionally piercing. Detention centres ring with the jangling of keys, slamming doors and, sometimes, raised voices. Some of the institutions we visited used a tannoy system to call individuals to meet immigration officers, lawyers or visitors, although most have subsequently ended this practice. In the more highly secure facilities, corridors linking the housing units and activities areas can be over-run with men or women as they move during specific periods of the day, but otherwise sit silent, with all the activity occurring behind heavy metal doors that block the noise.

Unlike prisons, mobile phone ringtones punctuate the day. So, too, the chatter of voices and snatches of melody are rarely in English. In Brook House, when we conducted our research, the area outside the centre shop[1] was particularly raucous as men sat playing dominoes, crashing their pieces together loudly and shouting. Those institutions situated alongside or adjacent to Gatwick and Heathrow airports vibrate with noise from the runway, as plane after plane takes off or lands, reminding those within of the state's intention for them.

In sites of research, these issues matter. Not only are some of them difficult to navigate but they also reveal important qualities of daily life. Most obviously, our ability to communicate with those confined was attenuated in an environment designed to hold foreigners. While most people in detention speak some English, few are fully fluent. On occasion, we brought in interpreters or drew on our own foreign language skills. Yet, due to the logistics of research access which made it difficult to bring in interpreters, we conducted most of our interviews and administered nearly all the surveys in English, using our own foreign languages where possible.

Elsewhere we have written at some length about the impact of such matters on understanding as well as their effect on immigration detainees (Bosworth and Kellezi 2012, 2014; Bosworth 2012, 2014). As we observe in those publications, detainees are, on the whole, anxious and depressed, confused and alarmed. These are deeply problematic institu-

---

[1] Each centre runs a shop in which detainees can purchase everyday products as well as lodge mail orders for Argos. The shop is usually staffed by 'civilian' officers (i.e. not DCOs). IRCs vary in what they say they do with the profit; some invest it back into the centre, others do not.

tions, with few clear objectives and much, however unintentional, torment many of those they house.

For as long as the British government, like so many others, remains stubbornly attached to detaining foreign citizens as part of their attempts to manage asylum and immigration, it is important to reiterate their deleterious effects on those who are locked up. Detention centres hurt those within them, their families and their friends. In the rest of this chapter, however, we want to focus on the implications of IRCs for custodial staff and for our ability to engage with and understand them.

Staff are affected by the uncertainties of detention and by the built environment in which they work. They are also not immune from the uncertain status and legitimacy of these sites. Many find the politically contested nature of IRCs particularly upsetting, and feel frustrated with their negative depiction in the media. Nobody wants to believe they are actively engaged in harming others. Some articulated considerable ambivalence about their job, worrying about its morality and ethical foundations.

Such matters raised distinct challenges for engaging staff in the research project. Like detainees, officers could be mistrustful. Many felt alienated from their colleagues, particularly the senior management team. Under these circumstances, staff participation and perspective was often hard to predict.

Some of the challenges we faced sprang from participants' unfamiliarity with academic research. While a handful of officers and detainees had university degrees, for the rest we were usually the first academics anyone had ever met. They were unsure why we were interested in their stories, nor, what we would do with the information they told us. Often, this circumstance worked in our favour as neither group knew what to make of us nor had much of a sense of the nature or purpose of academic research. At the same time, however, such ignorance about applied research and publishing made it difficult to obtain informed consent and also to explain our role and responsibilities as scholars. It also made some people suspicious.

Some believed our research would make things better. Senior officers, who had worked in prisons, were particularly enthusiastic about our plans to design and administer a survey on the 'quality of life.' Those who were familiar with the MQPL, believed, as a senior member of staff at IRC Colnbrook put it, that the MQLD, had '*huge value for detainees.*' (SMT, Colnbrook), and would help them improve their 'service delivery.'

Others were rather more modest in their view of us, believing that our interactions with detainees might simply alleviate some of the anxieties of those in their care. By spending time with detainees, some believed we made officers' jobs a little easier. For this alone, some DCOs offered grudging approval. "At the beginning," one DCO confessed in IRC Tinsley House, "we were very suspicious of you but then we saw you were really interested in talking to the men so I hope something good comes out of it…" (Barry, DCO, TH).[2] As in previous projects, the aspirations of research participants were hard to live up to (Bosworth et al. 2005). Our goal was to understand. Yet, those we interviewed and observed hoped for more. They wanted our research to make things better.

Some officers were clearly uneasy around us. Like the detainees, they sought to know why we had been allowed in to study these secretive sites, when so many others had failed. Unwittingly echoing the words of detainees,[3] Tim confronted Blerina in the library of Tinsley House, demanding suspiciously "who are you? You are some kind of a spy. You work for UKBA" (DCO, TH). In Brook House, Slade was just as blunt, telling Mary in no uncertain terms that "If it were up to me, I wouldn't let you in here" (SMT, BH).

Rather than simply ill-tempered suspicion, these testimonies capture the uneasy relationship between the Home Office and custodial staff and the lack of clarity many officers felt about the nature of their job. While their concerns were articulated against us, they revealed considerable mistrust and uncertainty within the structures of everyday life and governance in these institutions, at odds with the dominant official representation of such places. Like the civil servant who agreed to the project, staff and detainees were prepared to participate, but they were not entirely sure they trusted us, or anyone else in detention.

---

[2] This is not his real name. All participants cited in this article have been given pseudonyms.

[3] "'Why are you here?' Jamil challenged Mary. 'Who let you in? Maybe you're from UKBA and everything I tell you, you will go and tell them. I know how the system works. Why should I talk to you?'" (Uganda, BH, in Bosworth 2014: 59).

Permission to conduct research in IRCs can only be granted by the Home Office. Requests to individual centre managers must be passed onto them. Unlike the NOMS, there is, as yet, no structure for reviewing applications. Instead research requests are managed in an ad hoc fashion, by the head of detention services. This highly individualised and discretionary approach to research access mirrors the immigration system more broadly, where decisions to detain and deport are made on a case-by-case basis. It is currently under review.

In making their decision to allow research, the Home Office do not have to consult the private contractors. However, in the early stages of her project, Mary was invited to pitch ideas to a meeting of the centre managers. She has subsequently returned and reported on some of her findings to this collection of senior staff. They remain among the most vocal supporters of research in detention, happier to open the doors of their establishment than their public service 'customer.'

Neither centre managers nor the Home Office consult DCOs or detainees in determining research access. These people, who will have the most contact with researchers, are rarely forewarned. While some centres circulated information about the original project and subsequent activities in advance, DCOs were and often remain unaware of our plans. In each site, reflecting the high turnover of employees, there will always be staff new in post. Others will not have read the email. Still others may have missed a briefing due to their shift pattern. Whatever the reason, in practical terms, we can never rely solely on our formal permission, but rather have had to negotiate and renegotiate our research access in each site.

Staff control and may block our access to and within the centres in a number of ways. Sometimes they refuse entry to the establishment altogether, claiming a lack of proper instructions. More commonly, those on the gate merely delay our entry insisting on confirmation from management before letting us proceed. On one occasion, in Brook House, after a 90-min drive from Oxford, Mary was not permitted to enter and had to go next door to Tinsley House instead. An irritable field note describes what happened:

I am meant to be at Brook House but not a single member of SMT or UKBA there. So nobody knew who I was and wouldn't let me in. (Fieldnote March 2011)

They also have subjected us to varying levels of security inspection, sometimes waving us through, at other times searching our clothes, mouths and possessions for contraband. Digital recorders, which are authorised, are often queried. Some places have made us wear badges to identify us as visitors, others have let us wander around without them.

Once within the walls of the centres research access still has to be managed. Fairly early on in the project, we took the decision to carry keys, to reduce our burden on the establishment and to facilitate our freedom of movement. However, this is not always possible, leaving us dependent on DCOs to lock and unlock doors. Even with keys, DCOs and onsite Home Office staff occasionally challenge us directly, querying our presence, intention and viewpoint in front of detainees or colleagues, demanding our opinion of detention or an account of ourselves. A few have refused to participate altogether, abandoning prearranged interviews, into which their senior management had 'volunteered them' once we informed them that under the University ethics requirements they were free to refuse to participate. Others just kept putting us off, agreeing to be interviewed, but then constantly rescheduling.

Often their reluctance springs from quite mundane sources. DCOs are busy. Time spent with us takes them away from their responsibilities. Yet their reticence is rarely purely pragmatic. Many feel considerable anxiety about their job, its purpose and its security.

While those in senior management sometimes express corporate pride, many uniformed officers feel precarious, complaining frequently about working conditions, pay and scheduling. Few have deliberately sought out a career in detention custody. Most have fallen into it simply as a means of paying their bills. Many work at more than one job, badly paid and vulnerable in each. Some, like Todd, a DCO in Yarl's Wood, struggle to cope,

I have worked here many years. It is really hard work. I had a nervous breakdown 5 years ago … They don't appreciate how hard the work is here.

> It was much worse when men were here because they were aggressive. But the women are much better. You can make friends with a lot of them. There are rarely any fights. These working hours don't go with family life. Any relationship would break really quickly.

Perhaps for this reason, custodial companies were initially far more concerned about the participation of their staff than they were about us surveying, observing and interviewing detainees. Unlike the questions we posed to detainees, the schedule for formal staff interviews had to be authorised before we could invite officers to participate. While informal interactions with staff were not, to our knowledge, scrutinised, we cannot be sure that staff were not counselled to monitor their behaviour with us.

Such matters took us by surprise. While we had braced ourselves for staff suspicion about our interactions with detainees, we had not been prepared for concerns about including officers. We had also not given sufficient thought before we entered the field about how such institutional mistrust would make us feel.

Given our commitment to the research project and the considerable emotional burden it placed on us, small examples of inefficiency or suspicion could often feel more upsetting than perhaps they were intended. In Yarl's Wood, for instance, Mary's field notes reveal her irritation with staff coupled with her anxiety about whether she was actually doing the research properly:

> I left the dining hall to find loo and go somewhere to write up notes, I was accosted by a staff member: the gatehouse hadn't made me a visitor's badge and he was clearly worried about who I was. As at Campsfield House nobody seems to have been told about me or about my work. Instead I'm just dropped into this. (Field note, June 2010)

While it is tempting to dismiss such events as personal, these examples capture the wider uncertainty and lack of trust that characterises IRCs. Documented by scholars, activists and government agencies, such uncertainty is not only a distinctive characteristic of detention but also profoundly corrosive (Bosworth 2014; Griffiths 2014; HMIP and ICIBI 2012). Staff and detainees struggle in this environment of low trust, unsure what to make of themselves and others. It should not be surprising that this backdrop shaped people's willingness to participate in our research.

In a lengthy excerpt from one interview with a DCO in Tinsley House, we see how this officer's uncertainty about us intersected with and amplified his conflicted view of detainees and how to treat them. "At the beginning," Barry told Blerina, "everyone was wondering how you got access from the back door." Why were we there, they wondered and to whom were we actually reporting? Over time, however, such concerns ebbed; "I think you have been the most positive influence here. I don't want to say bad things about other people there but you seem to have fitted in here very well" (DCO, TH).

The difference, he noted, was that we were able to spend time with the detainees to garner their trust. "We try not to get too close to them." Barry observed a little regretfully. "You must get much more because you seem willing to hear them talk about anything. We get only parts of the stories and it is understandable they are less willing and trust us less than they trust you." Though seemingly wanting a closer relationship, at least with some of those in his care, Barry made it clear that, trust and openness were simply not possible in his line of work. Maintaining a level of mistrust and distance, he said, "is one way for us to deal with this job. If we get too close to them it would be very difficult. Like with (name of detainee). Because of how interesting, gentle and nice he was it was very difficult not to like him. So I feel sad for what he had to go through" (DCO, TH).

Constantly enjoined to maintain emotional distance from detainees, officers like Barry were often unsure who or what to believe (Bosworth 2014; Hall 2010). This 'culture of mistrust' was exacerbated and underpinned, by the steep hierarchy of custodial posts, in which uniformed 'DCOs' are positioned at the bottom and non-uniformed 'SMT' at the top. It also occurred in the context of tense working relationships in many centres between custodial and Home Office staff, and within an environment in which a limited number of outsiders from charities and voluntary organisations, the medical professions and visiting MPs make occasional appearances (Bosworth and Slade 2014). No wonder then that some officers were not keen to speak to us.

According to Patenaude (2004), prison staff, administrators and prisoners mistrust researchers because they cannot control what each group can say of the others. In detention, trust has an additional dimension since those who are detained are individuals whose story has not been believed. Mistrust under these circumstances is both generalised and particular. Individual detainees attempt to persuade the Home Office their claims are true, while knowing they are part of a group that is constituted by an official view that their claim is groundless.

Staff often claimed skills in differentiating fact from fiction. While they accepted that some detainees told the truth, they were keen to tell us that we would not be able to determine which ones were to be trusted. "It takes a while," Tim said breezily, "but then you learn to see through the lies. It will take some time before they learn to trust you. We have seven guys who have been here for many months and you will get to talk to them quite frankly. Some of the stories are horrific. You will learn to tell the true ones, some are just buried in the truth and some aspects made up" (DCO, TH).

Others simply discounted everything the detainees told them, as the conversation below reveals. After some weeks in detention, Abdi had succeeded in persuading the Home Office he had been tortured and was, as a result, immediately released. Notwithstanding the efforts undertaken to make the legal case, and significant physical evidence of this man's suffering, one of the officers, charged with this man's care, Tom stubbornly refused to believe his story, steadfastly denying the evidence put forward. Suzan, a female DCO, was much more sympathetic towards Abdi's case:

Suzan: "Did you hear that (detainee name) was released? There are people like him who should have never been kept in here, and others that probably should be here. Did you see the signs of physical torture he had in his body?"

Tom: "How do you know he did not do that to himself? Or he could have got one of his friends to do it for him. Don't they do that kind of stuff in their pilgrimage things"?

Suzan : "No. There is no way he could have done that to himself. He had scars on all his body and broken arms and everything. I have never seen anyone with worse scars on their body than him. It was really bad".

Tom: "Well, you must ask yourself what he has done to deserve that and why they did that to him? He must have done something really bad."

Suzan: "Actually in Iran, if nowhere else it is the place where you don't need to do anything wrong to get that done to you. You have no idea what they do to people there."

While Tom's refusal to believe Abdi's claim seems distinct from Barry's regretful distance from detainees, in practice such matters are often connected. Urged by their senior officers to 'empathize,' but not 'sympathize,' many officers reported, like Barry, that they avoided learning too much about people's immigration cases and dwelling on the wider, global inequalities these people often represent. "I understand why they do it [come to the UK]" Sam admitted (DCO, TH).

But there is to be a limit. There are not many resources in this country and some of them are a big burden to the system. Like one of the guys who has got problem with this blood, he can't stop bleeding. The doctor had to get an injection for him and he told us that the injection costs more than a family car. I don't know how much that is but it sound like a lot of money. This person might die if he goes back but there needs to be a limit. This country is overloaded anyway. A lot of them come from poor areas where the whole village needs to pay for them to come here and then they pay the village back. I don't blame them for doing it. There are areas people are so poor you see them selling three tomatoes on the side of the road to get some money.

As the first systematic study of everyday life in detention, it was important to include staff perspectives as well as detainee accounts. Yet, these kinds of statements, in which humanity is denied and social injustice glossed over, are hard to witness without intervening. At such times, it was important to remind ourselves that staff were also research participants. We were not there to adjudicate, but rather to document in order to understand. Considered in this light, their perspectives may be viewed as accounts of estrangement (Ahmed 2000), words that render powerfully and persuasively the difficulties inherent in and violence of forcing people out of the country (Bosworth 2014). Less conceptually, they show the personal nature of working in coercive environments designed to expel, raising urgent questions about the ethics and costs of this form of confinement.

Getting Out

While gaining access to conduct research and persuading people to participate can be difficult, so too is leaving. Whereas quantitative colleagues aim for a particular sample size, such matters in qualitative research are notoriously fuzzy. Numbers will not provide the clue, but we depend on rather less well-defined concepts like 'saturation' or 'understanding.' The challenges, in articulating such matters, are manifold, and encompass practical and emotional concerns. When it is time to leave? More intimately still, how does a researcher say goodbye? Do we stay in touch?

As this was the first project of its kind, we were keen to include as many sites as possible. Indeed, whereas Mary had first envisaged just two or three institutions, by the end of the first two years, she had spent considerable time in six detention centres. Six years on, the numbers of IRCs in our research continue to grow (Bosworth and Turnbull 2015).

Sometimes, external factors determine the end point of research. The first site in this project was IRC Campsfield House, just outside Oxford. Mary began working there in November 2009. She moved on in January 2010, when another centre, IRC Colnbrook asked to be included after hearing Mary present her ideas at a meeting of the centre managers. A former prison governor, this centre manager hoped research could improve how her establishment ran. Familiar with prisons research, she hoped that a similar body of work on the detention estate might be harnessed to ameliorate conditions and improve governance.

Anxious to gain as much experience across the detention estate, Mary felt it was important to take up any and all offers within the two years of funding she had available, even though she remained doubtful about the possibility of meaningful reform in the sector. She also sought to include examples from all the custodial providers, and to determine whether there were any substantial differences among them.

Fieldwork in the final site of Morton Hall had to be fitted into a new colleague's summer research plans, before he took up a new post abroad (Bosworth and Slade 2014; Bosworth et al. 2012). Blerina had stopped, not just because of funding, but also because of pregnancy. Such factors have little methodological justification, and may even complicate best-laid plans. Yet, they often characterise the hidden aspects of the research process which usually proceeds alongside other aspects of academic and personal life, such as teaching, family responsibilities, health and holidays.

Even as the research continues, there are internal endpoints. While ethnography invites ongoing interactions, a survey can only be completed once. Hemmed in by funding and short time scales, even unstructured interactions can be focused. Despite appearances, the researcher is often quite deliberate in her encounters. This is not always easy to do as Blerina acknowledged in her field notes, "What I am finding hard now is the sense that once I know their story I don't make much of an attempt to approach them. I have their stories already" (YW, August 2010).

The emotional demands of fieldwork can, sometimes, be overwhelming and may also become grounds for moving on. Both of us occasionally left early, unable to absorb any more pain, suspicion, confusion or hostility. Crying detainees, intolerant staff, and an unwelcome environment took their toll. During the research period and some months thereafter, we both suffered emotional and physical effects from sleeplessness to anxiety and palpitations. It was difficult to find a way of discussing the research, let alone analysing the findings, without feeling emotionally overwhelmed.

At the same time, however, we both expressed ambivalence about departing. We were worried about losing contact with people with whom we had forged a connection and worried that we had not done enough to help them. Above all, we felt guilty. Blerina worried about such matters almost from the beginning, noting, just six weeks into the project that, "It is strange but I am feeling anxious and sad about the time when I will stop coming to YW. I will have no way of knowing what is going to happen to all these people and I find some of them really special" (BK, YW, August 2010). As her time at Yarl's Wood started to draw to a close, she noted her guilt. "I feel like I am abandoning them. I don't feel that I have been helping them anyway, as I watch powerless while people are being deported. But I feel like I am abandoning them" (BK, YW, November 2010).

Such concerns spring from the emotional weight of this particular research project and the unhappiness we witnessed. They raise broader questions, however, about the purpose of academic study that scholars rarely publically acknowledge. Leaving is hard when you are unsure what you have achieved and when it is not clear what you should be trying to do. What can and should academics do if we fundamentally do not believe that the institution we are studying is justified? Is it possible to influence progressive reforms? In a long-term project, other issues arise. Given the initial warning 'not to embarrass' the Home Office, as the first stage of fieldwork came to an end, Mary wondered what that meant. Would she be allowed back in, once she published?

Getting Back

While some researchers may finish a project only to turn to another quite different topic, it is more common to maintain some level of consistency across an academic career. In thinking about research access, therefore, it is important to reflect on the feasibility of return. How can return be secured and what might put it at risk? Can criticism be communicated without alienating gatekeepers?

Such questions direct our attention to the, often thorny, relationship between the government and the academy, and, particularly to questions about criminology and the state. As British universities become urged to provide evidence of 'impact' beyond the academy, studies like this, with its scope for influencing policy, practice and public debate, are increasingly promoted by administrators. Yet, as criminologists know all too well, impact on policy matters can be elusive. It may also have unintended consequences. The Border Observatory, at Monash University, for instance, who created the first list of border deaths in Australia, were horrified to find their statistics cited by the government of Tony Abbott as justification for the success of their scheme to 'turn back the boats.' As the number of deaths at sea fell on the Observatory's list, the Prime Minister's office pointed to it as evidence of his humanitarianism.

There are many examples of narrowing research, particularly in the field of custody (Wacquant 2008; Simon 2000; Hannah-Moffat 2011). Prisons in the USA are notoriously difficult to access, as they have become in Canada. Whereas the UK has a long and robust tradition of prison sociology, IRCs remain, for most, inaccessible. Instead, and notwithstanding a burgeoning field of study on immigration control, asylum and refugees (Bhatia 2014), researchers find it difficult to enter these sites.

There is no straightforward explanation of or strategy for maintaining access. This project proceeded according to the usual tenets—an intensive period of fieldwork followed by a longer time devoted to writing. With no restrictions on publication, we were able to produce a range of outputs aimed at different audiences. Early on, acknowledging the institutional interest in the MQLD survey, we presented the research findings to centre managers and civil servants, as well as produced a statistical report for them (Bosworth and Kellezi 2012). We did not give feedback directly to the DCOs or detainees.

At a rather more sedate pace, we have also published a number of academic outputs (see, for example, Bosworth 2012, 2013, 2014; Bosworth and Kellezi 2014). These accounts cover a wide range of issues and formats. While ostensibly in the public domain, they are likely to be rather difficult for those outside the academy to locate and access.

During the time it took Mary to publish her research monograph (Bosworth 2014), the civil servant in charge of removals and enforcement changed three times. This personnel turnover has effectively erased any direct chain of responsibility for the decision to permit the original study. Rather than weakening her position in the field, the erasure has probably strengthened it, as incumbents can deny responsibility for her findings. At the same time, sufficient senior members of staff in the Home Office and in the custodial companies remain, offering an important line of continuity so that research relationships do not have to be fully recreated each time.

The mixed methodology has also been successful in establishing continuity. The MQLD survey is widely approved. Staff understand that a quantitative tool requires lengthy qualitative research, and have been patient in our requests to return and revisit their institutions.

From the very beginning, we benefited from the importation of research culture from the prison service among staff throughout the detention estate. Whatever our own doubts about the possibility of reform in this sector, such contacts have been extremely useful. Anecdotally some centre managers have told us our research has inspired them to expand their provision of welfare services in IRCs, and to pay more attention to staff morale.

Acknowledging the discretionary nature of decision making in the immigration system, we have expended a lot of effort in maintaining collegial relationships with centre managers and civil servants. Centre managers have often been our biggest champions, encouraging the Home Office to allow us in, and permitting a range of additional projects on art and craft, and photography with staff as well as detainees. Charged with the complicated job of confining those awaiting expulsion, these individuals appreciate the potential of academic scholarship, aware of the role it has played in the prison service, hopeful it could be as useful in their line of work. Some civil servants do as well. They too, on occasion, express reservations about their job, distinguishing between their personal beliefs and the expectations of their job, acknowledging inefficiencies or individual cases. Mindful of the limited opportunity for critique, and the close scrutiny of MPs, members of the Home Office on site and further afield also, sometimes, evidently hope our work may help them make matters better.

Conclusion: Academic Research and Policy Impact

At the best of times, custodial research is emotionally and ethically challenging. Conducting research in highly politicised and hidden sites like IRCs is even more difficult. The varied expectations and aspirations surrounding our research often feel overwhelming. The relationship between understanding and reform is not a simple one.

While we aspire to 'make a difference,' we are mindful that academic scholarship is neither purely policy oriented nor produced on the same time frame. So far, we have managed to act as 'critical friends' thereby perhaps not straying as far from prison studies as we had thought, notwithstanding our far more limited scale of research (Liebling 2010). As the rhetoric and law surrounding migration control continues to harden, however, questions remain over how long this kind of relationship will last.

It is not at all clear that IRCs are sites that can be improved. To do so, would be to accept they are justified, which we do not. So many of the challenges staff and detainees face stem from border control more generally and the exclusionary politics they embody and promote. To this challenge, we have no easy answer. While some might argue that our presence legitimates the structure, or worse, due to our disciplinary home, that we exacerbate them, both charges overstate the role and impact of academic research. IRCs and border control will continue irrespective of our presence for as long as they are politically expedient. Our role remains, after all these years, primarily to understand them.

Through documentation, bearing witness and describing them, we gather evidence of their nature and effect. Working alongside the staff and detainees, we look for explanation and detail, pointing out their uncertainties, contradictions, pains, and occasional moments of joy, creativity and compassion. The details we gather reveal over and over again, the contested, painful and uncertain nature of these sites. They also demonstrate our shared humanity with those within. Such accounts, in the current political climate, may not seem like much. Yet, this surely is the task of academic research: documenting, interpreting and analysing in order to understand. We may not be able to force change, but we certainly can and must argue for it where possible.

References

Aas, K. F., and Bosworth, M. (Eds.) (2013) *Borders of Punishment: Migration, Citizenship and Social Exclusion*, Oxford: Oxford University Press.

Ahmed, S. (2000) *Strange Encounters: Embodied Others in Post-Coloniality*, London: Routledge.

Bhatia, M. (2014) Researching 'Bogus' Asylum Seekers, 'Illegal' Migrants and 'Crimmigrants'. In K. Lumsden and A. Winter (Eds.) *Reflexivity in Criminological Research: Experiences with the Powerful and the Powerless*, London: Palgrave: 162–177.

Bosworth, M., Campbell, D., Bonita, D., Ferranti, S.M. and Santos, M. (2005) 'Doing Prison Research: Views from Inside', *Qualitative Inquiry*, 11(2): 249–264.

Bosworth, M. (2014) *Inside Immigration Detention*, Oxford: Oxford University Press.

Bosworth, M. (2013. Can Immigration Detention be Legitimate? In K.F. Aas and M. Bosworth (Eds.) *Borders of Punishment: Migration, Citizenship and Social Exclusion*, Oxford: Oxford University Press: 149–165.

Bosworth, M. (2012) 'Subjectivity and Identity in Detention: Punishment and Society in a Global Age', *Theoretical Criminology* 16(2): 123–140.

Bosworth, M. (2007) Immigration Detention in Britain. In M. Lee (Ed.), *Human Trafficking*, Collumpton: Willan Publishing: 159–177.

Bosworth, M. (1999) *Engendering Resistance: Agency and Power in Women's Prisons*, Aldershot: Ashgate Press.

Bosworth, M. and Kellezi, B. (2015) *Quality of Life in Detention: Results from the MQLD Questionnaire Data Collected in IRC Campsfield House, IRC Yarl's Wood, IRC Colnbrook and IRC Dover, September 2013 – August 2014*, Oxford: Centre for Criminology.

Bosworth, M. and Kellezi, B. (2014) Citizenship and Belonging in a Women's Immigration Detention Centre. In C. Phillips & C. Webster (Eds.) *New Directions in Race, Ethnicity and Crime*, Abingdon: Routledge: 80–96.

Bosworth, M. and Kellezi, B. (2013) 'Developing a Measure of the Quality of Life in Detention', *Prison Service Journal* 205: 10–15.

Bosworth, M. and Kellezi, B. (2012) *Quality of Life in Detention: Results from the MQLD Questionnaire Data Collected in IRC Yarl's Wood, IRC Tinsley House and IRC Brook House, August 2010 – June 2011*, Oxford: Centre for Criminology.

Bosworth, M., Kellezi, B. and Slade, G. (2012) *Quality of Life in Detention: Results from Questionnaire Data Collected in IRC Morton Hall*, Oxford: Centre for Criminology.

Bosworth, M. and Slade, G. (2014) 'In Search of Recognition: Gender and Staff-Detainee Relations in a British Immigration Detention Centre', *Punishment & Society* 16(2): 169–186.

Bosworth, M. and Turnbull, S. (2015) Immigration Detention and the Expansion of Penal Power in the UK. In K. Reiter & A. Koenig (Eds.) *Extreme Punishment: 50*, London: Palgrave.

Crewe, B. (2009) *The Prisoner Society*, Oxford: Oxford University Press.

DeGenova, N. (2010) The Deportation Regime: Sovereignty, Space and the Freedom of Movement. In N. De Genova and N. Peultz (Eds.), The Deportation Regime: Sovereignty, Space and the Freedom of Movement, Durham, NC: Duke University Press: 33–68.

Griffiths, M. (2014) 'Living with Uncertainty: Indefinite Immigration Detention', *Journal of Legal Anthropology* 1(3): 263–268.

Hall, A. (2010) 'These People Could be Anyone: Fear, Contempt (and Empathy) in a British Immigration Removal Centre', *Journal of Ethnic and Migration Studies*, 36(6): 881–898.

Hall, A. (2012) *Border Watch: Cultures of Immigration Detention and Control*, London: Pluto Press.

Hannah-Moffat, K. (2011) Criminological Cliques: Narrowing Dialogues, Institutional Protectionism and the Next Generation. In M. Bosworth & C. Hoyle (Eds), *What is Criminology?*, Oxford: Oxford University Press: 440–455.

HMIP. (2002) *An Inspection of Campsfield House Immigration Removal Centre*, London: HMIP.

HMIP and ICIBI. (2012) *The Effectiveness and Impact of Immigration Detention Casework: A Joint Thematic Review*, London: HMIP & ICIBI.

Kaufman, E. (2015) *Punish and Expel: Border Control, Nationalism, and the New Purpose of the Prison*, Oxford: Oxford University Press.

Klein, A. and Williams, L. (2012) 'Immigration Detention in the Community: Research on the Experiences of Migrants Released from Detention Centres in the UK', *Population, Space and Place* 18(6): 710–714.

Liebling, A. (2010) Being a Criminologist: Investigation as a Lifestyle and Living. In M. Bosworth and C. Hoyle (Eds.) *What is Criminology?*, Oxford: Oxford University Press: 518–529.

Liebling, A. (2004) *Prisons and Their Moral Performance*, Oxford: Oxford University Press.

Patenaude, A. L. (2004) 'No Promises, But I'm Willing to Listen and Tell What I Hear: Conducting Qualitative Research Among Prison Inmates and Staff', *The Prison Journal*, 84(4 suppl): 69S-91S.

Phelps, J. (2009) *Detained Lives: The Real Cost of Indefinite Immigration Detention*, London: LDSG.

Philips, C. (2010) *The Multicultural Prison*, Oxford: Oxford University Press.

Silverman, S. and Massa, E. (2012) 'Why Immigration Detention is Unique', *Population, Space and Place* 18(6): 677–686.

Simon, J. (2000) 'The "Society of Captives" in the Era of Hyperincarceration', *Theoretical Criminology* 4(3): 285–308.

Sparks, R., Bottoms, A.E. and Hay, W. (1996) *Prisons and the Problem of Order*, Oxford: Oxford University Press.

Wacquant, L. (2008) 'The Curious Eclipse of Prison Ethnography in the Age of Mass Incarceration', *Ethnography* 3(4): 371–397.

Part 3

Positionality, Power and the Reflexive Imperative

12

Cartel Biographies: The Researcher as Storyteller and the Preservation of the Research Wilderness on the Inside of the Subject

Christopher Harding

Introduction: A Third Person Consideration of Discursive Context

What follows here as an exercise in reflexivity is primarily a contemplation of the researcher's constitution and construction of the subject of the research, and the dilemma of the independent identity of the latter. Does the subject of any research exist in an autonomous way, 'out there', 'in the real world', or is it the product of a particular 'external' narrative, the researcher's story telling? This question can be located in the field of scientific and academic discourse as 'the fundamental problem of anthropology, that of the relations between the ethnographer and authochthonic subject'.[1] As an aspect of researcher reflexivity the discussion

---

[1] The question as summarised by Mieke Bal, *Narratology: Introduction to the Theory of Narrative* (3rd ed, University of Toronto Press, 2009) at p. 185. Bal draws at this point on the argument of Clifford Geertz, "'From the Native's Point of View": On the Nature of Anthropological

---

C. Harding (✉)
Aberystwyth University, Aberystwyth, UK

© The Author(s) 2017
S. Armstrong et al. (eds.), *Reflexivity and Criminal Justice*,
DOI 10.1057/978-1-137-54642-5_12

here connects with that twentieth into twenty-first-century element of self-reflection in social science concerning the role of social inquiry and its methods in the 'enactment' of social reality and the social world.[2] Summarising their argument that social scientific research methods are 'performative', Law and Urry state:

> ... the disciplines of the social are themselves social practices that simply form another part of the social world ... the argument made by Anthony Giddens and others is that the social sciences can be understood as an expression of – and a reflexive moment in – the continuing elaboration and enactment of social life ... this has become more important in high modernity with its apparently increasing commitment to 'reflexive modernisation'.[3]

The significance of this line of argument is that social scientific research methods are not innocent, and then to some extent enact what *they* may describe *into reality*, so becoming a matter of 'ontological politics'.[4]

The focus of the present discussion is a particular kind of outlaw or law-breaker, whose conduct and identity are described, discussed and in a sense then constituted as outlaw activity via a narrative account, or rather a number of such accounts, including a summative account, or meta-narrative, presented finally by a researcher-story teller. But the discussion will also point out an irony in this process of narration: the fact that the 'heart' of the subject matter, the research subject's own autobiographical narrative, remains problematically accessible, driven into a kind of wilderness domain of story telling by the dominating force of the other

---

Understanding', in *Local Knowledge: Further Essays in Interpretive Anthropology* (Basic Books, 2000), at p. 55.

[2] For a valuable critical review of this role of social scientific research, see: John Law and Jon Urry, 'Enacting the Social', Department of Sociology and Centre for Social Sciences, Lancaster University, On-Line Papers, 2003.

[3] *Ibid.,* at p. 2. See also Thomas Osborne and Nikolas Rose, 'Do the Social Sciences Create Phenomena? The Example of Public Opinion Research', (1999) 50 *British Journal of Sociology* 367, and their argument that 'social sciences have played a very significant role in making up our world, and the kinds of persons, phenomena and entities which inhabit it', at p. 368.

[4] Law and Urry, note 2 above, at pp. 9–10.

external narratives. In such a way, therefore, does the ethnographer as scientific storyteller find elusive the subject of that telling.

Social scientific ethnographers may then strive for a closer acquaintance and experience of that subject of their own construction—what Mieke Bal has described in her own work as the usefulness of an 'integration of anthropological eagerness for understanding real otherness and a narratological discipline of structural textual analysis'.[5] This is no easy task, and the challenges should not be underestimated. It is a matter of the researcher-investigator being able to shake loose from a preferred self-image of what Geertz has described as the 'myth of the chameleon fieldworker, perfectly self-tuned to his exotic surroundings, a walking miracle of empathy , tact, patience, and cosmopolitanism'.[6] But the central point of argument for the reader of the discussion in this chapter to bear in mind is the *crucial role of narrative and story telling* in the ethnological and criminological study and discussion of an outlaw situation.

Hopefully, what has been said so far will serve to locate the following discussion in some kind of academic and disciplinary landscape. In particular, it should serve to acknowledge a debt to narratology and cultural anthropology, as much as to more mainstream ethnological method and theorising in the context of criminology. Having said that much, the present author will now self-consciously shift from a third person narrative presentation to an autobiographical first person telling of a research story. Thus 'Harding' becomes 'I myself'.

Reflection: Narrative, Autobiography and Biography

I shall start this reflection on researcher role and my account of a particular episode of research activity, appropriately enough, with some autobiographical musing, and emphasise in the first place that this is

---

[5] Bal, note 1 above, at p. 186.
[6] Geertz, note 1 above, at p. 55.

being written in the first person.[7] Also, at this point, I can clarify for the reader's benefit my use of a referencing style which is determinedly unsocial scientific, that is to say I am avoiding the 'Harvard', author-date style of referencing. This is partly because I feel that it simply does not work in an autobiographical account. But it is also because I am deliberately distancing myself from a method of narration which cloaks itself in a spurious objectivity of data collection and argument.[8]

In the following discussion, I shall use as an example a recent research project[9] in which I had a major role, and the methodology of which naturally led to some reflection on my own (and others') role as a researcher and writer in relation to that research subject. To put it briefly, the research was concerned with an evaluation of the impact of legal sanctions used to deal with prohibited business cartels and set out to examine the actual historical use of such sanctions in relation to a significant sample of completed cases over a recent 30-year period. The method was therefore retrospective, considering an established (and in many ways a full and reliable) body of historical data and drawing conclusions and interpretations from what had happened in the 'real' world of actual legal enforcement. In that sense, it was a departure from and self-conscious distancing from a favoured approach of academic economists and criminologists in relation to such a subject and research question, which is predictive—for instance, working out an 'optimum penalty' on the basis of an assumption of how actors will behave as rational actors. In short, my main role as a researcher was to collect a body of historical data and

---

[7] Here is a first point of reflexivity: how do researchers talk and write about their own activity in a professional context—in the first or the third person? This is sometimes seen as mainly a matter of style, or cultural and professional preference. For instance, it might be observed that American researchers, editors and publishers seem happier with the use of the (subjective ?) first person narration, compared to a British preference for (more objective, detached and rigorous ?) third person accounts. In an English-speaking context, most universities urge their students to write in the third person, although increasingly note that this trend may be changing as exercises in self-reflection are now more favoured. On further consideration, it is more than just a matter of style, but does indeed relate to the researcher/writer's own sense of role, intention, and indeed degree of self-awareness.

[8] This is not to mention a further objection to the 'Harvard' method—that it is uninformative and even lazy while giving an impression of full and deep research—it simply does not make clear the precise connection between the source and the statement in the text.

[9] Harding and Edwards, Leverhulme funded project, *Explaining and Understanding Business Cartel Collusion*, 2012–14.

interpret and analyse that evidence. I needed to and did reflect on that role in designing and implementing the methodology, noting in particular that as the researcher/writer I would be carrying out important tasks of selection, interpretation and narration. None of those tasks could, on reflection, be considered wholly objective or uncontestable—as the researcher/writer, I was very much involved subjectively in forming the subject, and this has been acknowledged in the writing up of the research findings and argument.[10] The approach being used in this research was very consciously described as 'biographical', referring frequently to the compilation of 'cartel biographies', so that a number of methodological parallels were considered as between biographical writing and the writing up of this research.

The method adopted for the project therefore from the beginning embodied some reflection about an active and determining role for the researcher, not just as an investigator but also importantly as a narrator. This perception of research activity enables some shift in understanding how research is carried out, by casting some doubt on the idea of the disinterested and objective investigator (the 'examining magistrate' model) and recasting the researcher as a kind of storyteller who at the end of the day will relate just one out of number of possible narratives. The researcher as storyteller (the 'troubadour' model) will concede his or her provenance, culture and heritage, in accepting that such a background may determine the questions which prompt the search for information, which in turn will be selected so as to fashion a largely pre-determined narrative, itself a product then of purpose, selection and interpretation.

This emphasis on the narrative aspects of research activity was not especially new to me in my own role as a researcher and writer. I had already made some use of this approach in the same field of research activity. In my earlier research collaboration with lawyer/enforcement agent Julian Joshua[11] in which we sought to report on, explain and anal-

---

[10] See in particular, the research project website (http://www.aber.ac.uk/en/law-criminology/research/research-clusters/global-commerce/cartel-collusion), and the cautionary note struck in 'Cartel Stories'; see also some of the discussion in Christopher Harding and Jennifer Edwards, *Cartel Criminality: The Mythology and Pathology of Business Collusion* (Ashgate 2015).

[11] A biographical note. Julian was successively an official with the European Commission, undertaking a leading role in the investigation of suspected illegal business cartels, and then a lawyer

yse the development of anti-cartel regulation in Europe,[12] we had sought
to close our discussion by employing the conceit of a number of parallel tellings (for instance, the 'prosecutor's tale', 'the economist's tale') of
what might in research terms be seen as a single line of narrative derived
from the same body of evidence—although that kind of meta-narrative
was probably what we tried to convey in our book, in order to present
that as an 'authoritative' account which should then command attention
as such. Already, then, I was in the business of exploding the myth of a
master version of a research account, and warning that differing disciplinary or political perspectives could affect the way in which the same
subject is understood and then presented to the rest of the world. And the
individual researcher is part of that narrative diversity, although perhaps
prone to a belief in his or her own disinterested and objective standpoint
and role.

By the time the project on the impact of anti-cartel sanctions was
under way,[13] myself and my co-researcher on the project, Jennifer
Edwards, were enthusiastically playing with the idea of different and
competing narratives. On the project web pages,[14] we provided a number of illustrations of different cartel stories which could be drawn
upon—read, interpreted and retold—for purposes of constructing
our own 'cartel biographies'. Thus, in working out and explaining our
methodology, we discussed the biographical method, the role of anecdote and vignette, we discussed the story-lines emerging from different informational formats—maps, tables, different types of graphic,
our research database of cases, statistics, quotations, glossaries, cinema
and documentary film, political cartoons, academic studies as compared with politicised campaigning statements and accounts, and legal
reporting of case law. In relation to presentation of research and argu-

---

advising companies on their legal position in relation to cartel activity. Our research collaboration
started in the later 1990s when we sought to combine insider (official and lawyer) and outside
(academic researcher) perspectives in a research and writing synergy.

[12] See: Christopher Harding and Julian Joshua, *Regulating Cartels in Europe: A study of Legal Control
of Corporate Delinquency* (Oxford University Press, 2003), the first edition, and the same authors,
Regulating Cartels in Europe (Oxford University Press, 2010), the second edition.

[13] In 2012, the main research activity was funded for the period 2012–14.

[14] See note 10 above.

ment, we considered the differing narratives which may emerge from power point based lectures, posters or single story boards. And we showed how a particular 'non-conventional medium', poetry, could be used effectively and concisely to tell two different versions of the same cartel biography, in the case of the well-known European Soda Ash Cartel: [15]

'Page One Thousand' as a poem narrating an 'analytical history' of cartel behaviour and anti-cartel enforcement

Page One Thousand,
Wrote some bold entrepreneurs
Back in Nineteen Forty Five,
To celebrate many days of good fellowship -
Thriving days of yore,
Many dollars in the corporate chest.
And, hey lads,
Good times are here again!
The arguments are over,
We can recover our smart project,
Peace will revive our wealth.
Page One Thousand,
That's code for the bond we shall not sever,
Let's renew our trust for ever,
And ever.

Page One Thousand,
Discovered in a dusty document
In Nineteen Ninety One,
An indictment of too many days of bad fellowship -
Thriving days to be sure,
Many dollars in the corporate chest.
And hey lads,
Look what we have here!

---

[15] Indeed, we went on to use the example of the Soda Ash Cartel extensively in our research and book. We considered that there was rich material there—a longstanding cartel arrangement and a saga of legal proceedings enduring for over twenty years. It became a favourite story for us. I say 'well-known case', although that really means well-known to cartel cognoscenti.

The search is complete,
We can recover our good repute,
And their wealth will rest in peace.
Page One Thousand,
That's code for conspirators' play,
Now proof for their judgment day.[16]

Thus, the cartelists' story, followed by the regulators' story. This was all exciting as methodology, and with this discussion there also developed an increasing awareness of our own role in fashioning the subject, and in turn a greater consciousness of whom we were as researchers—our own provenance, role and particular ambitions.

Researcher Reflexivity and Researcher Autobiography: Profiling the Researchers

And so, some autobiography might prove instructive at this point: from provenance to recent conduct.

In early January 1973, I recall, two postgraduate students, Christopher Harding and William Allan, met at Waterloo Station, London, to exchange a library copy of a book, written by the German lawyer and expert on competition law, Arved Deringer.[17] It was the only copy of the work then available to them, borrowed from the University of Exeter Library. That was how research was carried out in those days. In the summer of 2010, the same two were walking up and down Bill's garden in London, talking about my idea for a research project (as mentioned above). By then, I was a Professor of Law at Aberystwyth University and had been researching cartel regulation for some time, and Bill had been a leading practitioner in the field of competition law and was now

---

[16] Christopher Harding, 2001. 'Page One Thousand' was the code name for the cartel plan, as revived in 1945 and then used as the basis for cartel activity involving the companies Solvay and ICI until the 1980s.

[17] Arved Deringer, *The Competition Law of the European Economic Community* (Commerce Clearing House, 1968). This was one of the earliest English language publications on the subject. By the way, reader, why I have slipped into the third person at this point?

a part-time member of the UK Competition Appeal Tribunal. It was a useful conversation which, looking back, was to inform the development of the project (and Bill would later be 'interviewed' by Jennifer and myself as an expert legal advisor within the subject matter of the research). My concept of the project—its more exact scope, objectives and method—crystallised while walking around the centre of Brussels[18] in early 2011, having just had a research-interview meeting with a specialist competition lawyer based in Brussels. The project was assisted and shifted into top gear by a favourable decision from the Leverhulme Trust to fund much of the work and enable the appointment of a full-time postdoctoral research officer, Jennifer Edwards, to work with me for a period of two years. So we entered a period of research, writing and publication, as partly described above. As the main researchers, we were based in the Department of Law and Criminology at Aberystwyth University and drew upon our training and experience in those two disciplines—by provenance, both originally socio-legal scholars, working in particular towards a book which would self-consciously describe itself as a (pioneering?) criminology of cartel and business collusion,[19] and employing sources and methodology which were widely interdisciplinary in character. In the course of the research, we met with a number of people, largely in the role of 'expert witnesses', such as lawyers, those connected with the enforcement activity, and subject specialists with different disciplinary perspectives. It would not be accurate to describe these meetings as semi-structured interviews, so beloved in social scientific research. They were more free-wheeling in character. My reservation about the semi-structured interview is that it still plays very much to the interviewer's agenda, and is the nature of a puppet-master managing a marionette.

It was one of these latter meetings which would prompt some particular reflections on the aims and method of our research, by identifying a more empty space or 'wild' area as I would like to call it, at the heart of the research activity. Jennifer and myself met with Melanie

---

[18] It literally may happen in that way, the moment of revelation, the flashing light bulb thought balloon above the thinker's head, as then retold in popular anecdotes, such as Einstein's moment of realisation as he travelled in a streetcar past the large clock in the centre of Bern.

[19] *Cartel Criminality*, note 10 above.

Williams, a Professor in the Law School at the University of Exeter. Melanie, with expertise in both Criminal Law and 'law and literature' methodology, was a member of the project's advisory board, and acted as a sounding board for our use of and adventures with the narrative method. During this conversation, some year or so into the main research, Melanie reflected: 'There is something in particular which may be missing here, something I'm not hearing very much about – the view and experience of the business cartelists, as the subject of this process of legal control.' This struck us as an important observation, albeit difficult to act upon (more of that later). But as an observation and argument, it was very much an outcome of a particular perspective, which approached the subject matter of the research as a collection of different and perhaps competing stories and voices. And what was emerging more explicitly in this conversation was an issue of a missing, or lost, or elusive voice. To put the matter more in social science speak, we may have been actively 'triangulating' the evidence from enforcement prosecutors, defence lawyers and economists, but had not done much to triangulate the testimony from those witnesses and that which might have been presented by the defending parties, as rule-breakers within the system. In terms of a narrative method, it might be assumed that at the heart of a cartel biography there might be found a cartelist autobiography. By its nature, the latter may well be elusive and then, when found, difficult to interpret. And admittedly this is likely to prove a problem for a good deal of criminological research into many areas of illegal and criminal conduct. But it is well to bear this in mind, when happily taking the evidence from other more accessible voices and sources.

The purpose of this short autobiographical statement is not just to set the scene for some reflexive discussion of a research episode,[20] and introduce some of the *dramatis personae* in that episode, but also to explore something of the provenance and culture of the process of research design, its underlying ideas and how it was carried out. Since this is *my* reflexive experience, I, Harding, naturally enough appear as

---

[20] By using the word 'episode' I am of course selecting some arbitrary limits to the subject matter of this discussion, so side-stepping the question, when does particular research begin and end?

a protagonist in this account, and others then more or less, according to their role. So the reader of this account may gain some idea that this protagonist is a male British researcher of a certain age and era, while his main co-researcher at the time was younger, of a different era, female, although also British and with a similar disciplinary background and academic training. We (myself as reflexive author and you as readers of this account) may in due course reflect on the significance of any of this. But it will have had some impact on the outcome of the research.

Constructing the Cartel Biographies: Whose Evidence?

In conventional research discussion, this is the question of our sources. Where did we seek information, impressions and ideas? Or, to personalise that question, who did we consult for that purpose, whether those persons be deceased or alive, remote or in person?

In the first place, as a natural starting point in academic research, we considered the body of writing which comprised information, expert commentary and opinion on the subject, which provides the sensible point of access, although indirect as a source—the 'secondary literature'. It would be relevant to note that this source material comprised legal scholarship, and also the work of economists, political scientists and historians, and is thus multi-disciplinary. Moreover, it may be said that over time its provenance has evolved, although broadly speaking maintaining a 'law and economics' character. One striking feature of this literature one hundred years ago was its burgeoning as a kind of scientific writing in Germany, where the resonant description 'das Kartellproblem' was applied.[21] Also at that time, there was some notable political and campaigning literature, especially in the USA, directed against the phenom-

---

[21] For a summary description and analysis of this distinctive Germanic contribution, see: David J Gerber, *Law and Competition in Twentieth Century Europe: Protecting Prometheus* (Oxford University Press, 1998), although Gerber identifies a set of ideas articulated in Fin-de-Siècle Austria 'as the original core of the European competition law tradition' (at p. 43).

enon of business trusts and monopolies there.[22] More recently, by the late twentieth and early twenty-first centuries, the secondary literature may be fairly described as comprising conventional academic expertise, distributed across a spectrum of legal and economics scholarship, but also involving a significant intervention on the part of practitioners— economists for hire, (defence) legal advisors to business, and lawyers and investigators working for competition enforcement agencies—and also governmental and intergovernmental policy formation writing. Indeed, an interesting reflexive exercise would be to take an example of a substantial bibliography of a contemporary book dealing critically with the subject of business cartels[23] and allocate the sources listed therein to those categories of provenance listed above. Those categories may not be hard and fast in their boundaries, but it would nonetheless provide an instructive survey of how some of the main storytellers may be identified. And, indeed, a reading of these various sources is likely to reveal some different and contesting accounts of the subject.[24] But finally, it may be noted that criminology does not appear as a significant provenance of this secondary literature, and hence our sense of pioneering activity and new perspective.

But the reference just above to contesting accounts takes us closer to the original sources, emanating from the main actors in the drama[25] of cartel activity as a business activity and anti-cartel enforcement as a legal activity. Viewed in that way, three main protagonists emerge: the businesses (companies and individuals working for the companies), the regulators who take legal action against anti-competitive business practice

---

[22] At the time sometimes referred to as 'muckraking' literature. A notable example would be the work of Ida Minerva Tarbell, *The History of the Standard Oil Company* (McClure, Phillips & Co, 1904). But this body of critical commentary also comprised a rich source of political cartoons published in magazines and newspapers.

[23] Being both reflexive and self-serving, takes as an example the bibliography in the second edition of Harding and Joshua, note 12 above, at p. 392 *et seq,*

[24] For an example of an academic study which considered contesting 'defence bar' and 'enforcement oriented' interpretations of the course of cartel regulation, see: Christopher Harding and Alun Gibbs, 'Why go to court in Europe ? An analysis of cartel appeals 1995–2004', 30 (2005) *European Law Review* 345.

[25] The term drama is deliberate and closely descriptive; if we are honest about this kind of discussion, it is a narrative as a drama that we are interested in probing.

such as that involved in cartels, and the legal advisors who support and defend the companies in advance or in the event of some actual enforcement action.

It is the nature of the process of legal control and regulation that the latter two sources are likely to be more forthcoming[26] than the first, especially in the context of any actual formal enforcement process which may be documented and reported for purposes of a public record. In the European context, there is an especially rich and easily accessible published source relating to proceedings taken by the European Commission against cartelists infringing the EU competition rules. This source is amplified by the high rate of appeals against Commission decisions, resulting in extensive reporting of the evidence of cartel activity and its legal evaluation in the *European Court Reports*, which contain reports of *all* cases dealt with by the European Courts (Court of Justice and Court of First Instance/General Court).[27] This provided a rich source for the European part of our project database. Most importantly, data from such a source can provide a wealth of detailed evidence of business and legal practice, the veracity and reliability of which has been carefully tested in the legal process itself. For anybody seeking detailed cartel stories and biographies, there are thousands of pages in the European Court Reports which provide just such reading.

But, while these may be detailed accounts, they are not full accounts but a selective rendering of the full stories.[28] According to their objectives and intentions, all historians and biographers provide a selective account, but this kind of legal documentary source is selective in a particular way,

---

[26] And indeed willingly forthcoming to researchers and to the public, save a certain amount of redaction when some claims of confidentiality, secrecy and anonymity are respected on legal grounds.

[27] Unusually in case law, the *European Court Reports* provide an authoritative report of every case taken through to a judgment or ruling by any of the EU Courts (and so now run to thousands of pages). Underlying this judicial documentation, the Commission, in its competition enforcement role, provides detailed formal decisions in its cartel cases (published in the *Official Journal of the European Union*), and also shorter press releases.

[28] The term 'full' is used advisedly here. To talk of a full story suggest an agreed starting and finishing point in the narrative and an agreed amount of detail. This is an inherent problem in any narrative. For instance, we had decided in our research accounts to provide some 'pre-history' of actual cartel operations, to provide a fuller account and understanding of the origins and business culture of the cartel in question.

recording only information which is relevant to the legal process, and in any one case that will be partly determined by the strategies employed by the parties to the proceedings. The significance of this element of selection may be nicely demonstrated from our own research in comparing the kind of data available from comparable US and EU law reporting documentation. Part of the richness of the EU source arises from the preference and tendency in that European context to engage in appeals on as many grounds as possible, thereby multiplying legal argument and evidence. This is broadly speaking a matter of European and EU legal culture.[29] In the USA, there is a contrasting preference, especially in federal criminal cases, for a pre-trial settlement, often through plea and charge negotiation, and avoiding a fully contested jury trial.[30] This is also a matter of legal culture, with the result of much less documentation of evidence and argument, since a deal is cut more discreetly and without the publicity of evidence testing before a jury in open court. In fact, this also results in a dramatic foreclosure of the story-telling since it prevents the defendant and defence lawyer from providing a fuller and more embellished account aimed at a jury's reading of the matter. The contrast is vivid. In the EU system, the Court as the reader of the story, is saying in effect to the parties: 'Tell as much as possible to enable us to gain a full picture in order to decide the case.' In the American system, the prosecutor says in effect to the defence in private: 'We have agreed on the legal outcome, so stop right there and say no more to anybody, since that legal outcome depends on the agreed version of events that we have just worked out'. We shall return to this point of comparison later.

From a researcher's point of view, the rich, long story or 'saga' version of cartel activity and proceeding in the EU context is very tempting. In that respect, we embarked on the research with a kind of jubilant shout, that we had 30 years' worth of ample material, as much as we needed,

---

[29] An interesting point in itself, reflecting a highly developed European culture of legal entitlement and rights assertion. For further discussion, see Harding and Gibbs, note 27 above, especially at pp. 349–53. Those authors describe the EU appeals process as 'a major legal industry'.

[30] For some critical account of the development and operation of this aspect of American criminal justice, see, for instance: Angela J Davis, *Arbitrary Justice: The Power of the American Prosecutor* (Oxford University Press, 2007); Mary E Vogel, *Coercion to Compromise: Plea Bargaining, the Courts and the Making of Political Authority* (Oxford University Press, 2007).

especially if supplemented a little by conversation with some of those responsible for managing the process on each side (the enforcers and the lawyers). It enabled a quick construction of a database, easy access to a large body of information taken from a reliable and authoritative source, and so ensured the feasibility of a research project funded for a limited period of time. There would be some imbalance between the extent of the European and American material, but our selected biographies would for the most part comprise large international cartels dealt with in both jurisdictions, so that the European element would compensate in providing the underlying cartel story. On the one hand, to be fair to ourselves, we were able to provide detailed accounts and much food for thought in our narratives. On the other hand, on reflection we need to concede that these accounts were largely driven by the narrative agenda established by legal process. And although the cartelist or cartelist company at the heart of this process may have been able to determine to some extent that agenda of legal process, that would have been in a strategic rather than fully-fledged cartelist role. At the end of the day, our biographies were largely narratives written from a law enforcement perspective.

Melanie's point: we might have been writing cartel biographies of a certain kind, but we were not providing the reader with cartelist autobiographies.

Inside Looking Out: The Search for True Cartelist Autobiography

As already stated, the missing inside picture or outlaw's[31] own account of what happened during a criminal or rule-breaking career or episode, is a general phenomenon and so is a wider challenge in criminological research, especially in so far as the latter seeks a more informed understanding of offender motivation and personality. There are a number of

---

[31] I am using this term 'outlaw' now carefully and deliberately, in order to avoid more obviously value-laden terms such as 'offender', 'law-breaker' and in particular 'criminal', and stress that in using 'outlaw' I am being descriptive and not pejorative. In my use of the term, an 'outlaw' is literally somebody who, for whatever reason, finds him or herself outside lawful activity and in breach, or allegedly in breach of rules.

more obvious reasons for the elusiveness of the outlaw's own account, not least the natural disincentive to talk openly about involvement in outlaw activity on account of the legal, moral and occupational risks in doing so. But it is also important to be aware of the impact of legal process itself on the provision of a full autobiographical account of rule-breaking activity. Strategic and evidential considerations may be inhibiting, as already discussed in relation to foreclosure following a guilty plea, but also arising for instance from procedures and tactics relating to confidentiality, anonymity,[32] decisions for a variety of reasons not to call the defendant to give evidence in court,[33] or the tactical withholding of certain evidence. To some extent, therefore, the less complete autobiographical inside story is to be expected.[34]

Therefore, a fuller account of the outlaw's own story must be sought in other ways, and both journalists and researchers may eagerly pursue such versions by talking directly to offenders and those associated with them. Sometimes, after the event and after the imposition of sanctions, an individual may provide a full retrospective account in interviews and in writing. We can usefully summarise some of the main forms and some examples of such autobiographical reports and musings.

Recorded and/or Published Interviews, Whether Academic or Journalistic

There are some examples in relation to convicted cartelists, most notably in my view the substantial interview carried out by lawyer Michael O'Kane with the convicted Marine Hose cartelist Bryan Allison and

---

[32] In the context of cartel proceedings, the resort to leniency programmes to gain evidence, and the resulting interest in anonymity for the leniency applicant/informer will result in the redaction of some evidence relating to a significant member of the joint illegal enterprise.

[33] At the recent (June 2015) Galvanised Steel Tanks Cartel case before Southwark Crown Court, it was decided in the end not to call the two defendants to give evidence before the Court, for good tactical reasons, but thereby denying to the jury the chance to hear directly from these major protagonists their own account of what happened.

[34] It is also interesting to speculate on the impact of such legal strategy and procedure on the defendant's own internal recollection of events: whether the effect of such legal process may be to suppress memory or alter the personal interpretation of the actor's own history—an area for further investigation and research.

published as a full transcript in *The Antitrust Bulletin*.[35] There are a number of other statements and brief accounts from convicted (and usually imprisoned) cartelists available from internet sources such as trade journals.[36] These accounts may contain suggestive and possibly revealing facts and statements, but of course remain essentially subjective and anecdotal as research evidence.[37]

Biographical and Autobiographical Published Works

Certain kinds of criminality, including areas of organised crime, have become the subject of detailed literary presentation, in works of reportage, biography and more exceptionally autobiography. Again there are some examples in recent years of books of this kind dealing with some high-profile business cartels and individual cartelists, notably for instance Kurt Eichenwald's *The Informant* (dealing with the Lysine Cartel in the USA),[38] Christopher Mason's *The Art of the Steal* (dealing with the Sotheby's–Christie's Art House Auctions Cartel),[39] and as an example of autobiography, Alfred Taubmann's *Threshold Resistance* (a robust and unrepentant apologia from a leading player in the Art House Auctions conspiracy).[40] Predictably enough, the research value

---

[35] Michael O'Kane, 'Does prison work for cartelists?—The view from behind bars', 56 (2011) *The Antitrust Bulletin* 483. Michael O'Kane is Head of the Business Crime Practice at Peters & Peters, London, and a good example of a practitioner who is also a writer and commentator in this field.

[36] For example: Eric Larson, 'Ex-BA Executive Shares Prison Tales to Sway Violators', Bloomberg, 22 October, 2010, commenting on ex-businessman Keith Packer's new career advising businesses as a cartel pundit; 'Interview: Mark Whitacre – Lysine Cartel Whistleblower on Price Fixing and Rebuilding his Life After Prison', *FeedInfo News Service*, 13 January 2009, dealing with the afterlife of Lysine cartelist Mark Whitacre – both containing revealing quotations.

[37] But see our discussion of the value of anecdote in the research project web page 'Anecdote, Vignette and Quantification: A Biographical Dilemma', note 10 above.

[38] Kurt Eichenwald, *The Informant: A True Story* (Portobello Books, 2009). This detailed journalistic account provided the basis for a feature film, directed by Steven Soderbergh and released in 2009 (sometimes described as a 'biography-comedy-film). It is possible then to compare three tellings of the Lysine Cartel story, through legal documentation, the book and the film.

[39] Christopher Mason, *The Art of the Steal: Inside the Sotheby's – Christie's Auction House Scandal* (Putnam Publishing, 2004).

[40] Alfred Taubmann, *Threshold Resistance: The Extraordinary Career of a Luxury Retailer Pioneer* (Harper Business, 2007).

of such works is variable, ranging from the meticulously researched to the flagrantly self-serving, although even the latter can be instructive in some ways.[41]

Documentary, Journalistic and Published Monograph Accounts of Criminal Careers and Episodes, and Industry Histories

There may be some overlap between such works and the biographies referred to above, but more generally this category has a more general, less individualised and contextual scope and coverage. Examples over time in relation to anti-competitive practices would include Ida Minerva Tarbell's *The History of the Standard Oil Company*,[42] Stocking and Watkins' *Cartels in Action*,[43] or Birgit Karlson's 'Cartels in the Swedish Forest Industry'.[44] The range of work here spans political campaigning (Tarbell) and rigorous academic investigation (Karlson), but usefully may provide a longer term and historical perspective.

Naturally enough, in our research, we sought out and made use of these sources, while conceding the subjective and anecdotal quality of this kind of data.[45] Our own limitations of time and resources precluded any direct and systematic interrogation of cartelist themselves, even assuming much availability and willingness on the part of the latter to engage with researchers. Overall, in the end it was the competition agency's voice and the lawyer's voice which predominated in our own story-telling, and indeed I would say that this is true of much criminological and socio-legal research. After all, most criminologists

---

[41] Taubmann's subsequent autobiography, which is arrogantly unrepentant and boastful, provides revealing evidence of the personal impact of sanctions such as imprisonment, at least in that particular business and cultural milieu.

[42] Note 25 above.

[43] George W Stocking and Myron W Watkins, *Cartels in Action: Case Studies in International Business Diplomacy* (The Twentieth Century World Fund, 1946).

[44] Birgit Karlson, 'Cartels in the Swedish forest industry in the interwar period', Chap. 13 in Sven-Olof Olsson (ed), *Managing Crises and Deglobalisation* (Routledge, 2010).

[45] Research Project web site, note 10 above, 'Anecdote, Vignette and Quantification: A Biographical Dilemma'.

will start their enterprise with a view of crime as a social problem and pose questions from the outside society perspective about the ways in which crime, as a problem, should or can be addressed. Or, to put this point another way, do 'insider' accounts by a relatively small number of high-profile criminals, such as John McVicar's *McVicar by Himself*,[46] qualify as criminological research and writing? Sure enough, many criminologists interrogate offenders or would-be offenders in large sample surveys, systematically and working to a pre-set agenda. But the semi-structured or free-flowing more personalised interview ('tell me everything about it from your point of view') is rarer, often for reasons of resources and ethical misgiving.[47] And then it is left to novelists and filmmakers to try to penetrate this inside world through essays in criminological imagining. Take, for example, Peter Carey's *True History of the Kelly Gang*,[48] a work of fiction dealing with historical characters, presented as an autobiographical account and written in the 'real' nineteenth century vernacular language of north east Victoria, and purporting in its title to be a *true* account—such a book raises the question of how we, as observers and readers, may most effectively gain access to and try to cohabit an 'inside' outlaw domain.[49]

---

[46] John McVicar, *McVicar by Himself* (Artnik, 3rd revised ed, 2000). McVicar, a convicted and imprisoned bank robber, subsequently studied for a degree in Sociology while in prison, and later became an articulate commentator on crime and criminal justice and also the subject of a feature film, directed by Tom Clegg and released in 1980, so adding to the tellings of that story.

[47] It is interesting to reflect on occasional but substantial encounters between researcher and criminal, or ex-criminal. See, for instance, Sally Vincent, 'How We Met: Laurie Taylor and John McVicar', *The Independent*, 22 August 1993.

[48] Peter Carey, *True History of the Kelly Gang* (University of Queensland Press, 2000).

[49] Or through music? For instance, there is the song 'Outlaw Pete' by Bruce Springsteen (from the album *Working on a Dream* (2009) and described by Springsteen as a story which 'flows from many sources' and as the narrative 'of a man trying to outlive and outlast his sins'. It is an interesting example of an 'artistic' attempt to penetrate the outlaw domain, now also supplemented by a short book co-authored by Springsteen and artist-cartoonist Frank Caruzo, *Outlaw Pete* (Simon & Schuster, 2014). Fictional and musical investigations of the outlaw domain would certainly qualify as 'troubadour' accounts, the Springsteen example classically so. In discussing fictional and artistic attempts to enter the criminal domain and criminal mind, Lisa Rodensky's study of the handling of criminal responsibility in nineteenth century novels is of considerable interest: *The Crime in Mind: Criminal Responsibility and the Victorian Novel* (Oxford University Press, 2003).

Perspective, Story-telling and Researcher Collusion: 'I'm Outlaw Pete! Can You Hear Me?'[50]

And so I return reflexively to this question of my own research, and the little-investigated wild or inaccessible outlaw space at the centre of my research subject, and confront my own collusion in maintaining that space in that form. It has been alleged often enough that social scientists may collude in the enactment of a preferred, sometimes 'official' reality, and I agree that it is important for us, as researchers, to be continuously reflective and reflexive about such possibility.

Why do I present it as a matter of collusion? This is partly to reflect on the way in which social scientists, responding to research exigencies, are tempted to rely on accessible and 'easy' sources for a quick and convincing result, then perhaps at the expense of other important sources. And I think it would be fair to admit that as researchers we were to an extent seduced by the availability and richness (in some respects) of our European documentary sources. In that way, we have then been guilty of reinforcing the obscure nature of that internal outlaw zone of the subject, of privileging the external regulators' and lawyers' account of the subject, and not trying hard enough to hear the voice of Outlaw Pete. But, of course, we had limited time, in terms of the period of employment of the main researcher, and deadlines for the writing of a book and other outputs, and in terms of the expectations of our funders, both external and the University. And in some defence, I can say that we became more aware of this hole in the research field, especially following the conversation with Melanie, and did at least try to pick up some traces of the outlaw voice.[51] So, at the present moment, I have a feeling not so much of shame, but of a lesson well taken on board.

That lesson will now provide my conclusion to this discussion. All research can be viewed as a process of reading and listening to a number

---

[50] Bruce Springsteen (2009), note 49 above.

[51] Indeed, we can also point to some earlier smaller attempts to engage with the insider view and mind set, for instance in the first part of the 'Page One Thousand' poem, above.

of stories, and researchers need to consider very carefully which accounts they examine and which voices they listen to (and to remember that their own subsequent report and discussion will become one further account, and one more voice). In that perspective, it is striking that one of the voices which may not be heard easily or fully is that of the main subject of interest in the research, especially if the research is criminological, focussing on the collusive behaviour of businesses and the reaction of the latter to legal sanctions. A priority for such research, therefore, should be to find ways of gaining access to the outlaw domain and hearing properly the outlaw voice on those issues.

As stated near the opening of this discussion, that that may be more easily said than done, it is not on the other hand an impossible ambition. It is an ambition that deserves some further reflection on both method and objectives.

On the method, we should note the past and existing attempts by researchers to engage fully and directly the inhabitants of the outlaw domain, or even more generally a group of people or culture which is the subject of sociological enquiry. Thus, anthropologists and then criminologists have engaged in that way with different kinds of social groupings through ethnographical approaches. More specifically, criminologists such as Laurie Taylor have engaged with subjects such as John McVicar,[52] and lawyers such as Michael O'Kane engaged with a Marine Hose cartelist.[53] At the same time, the problems and limitations of ethnomethodological research are well recognised[54] and the problems arising from Taylor's ambitious attempt to understand the London professional crime domain via his connection with John McVicar are instructive.[55] Even with the best contacts and open discourse within the outlaw domain, how easily may the researcher shake off a voyeuristic

---

[52] See in particular: Laurie Taylor, *In the Underworld* (Basil Blackwell, 1984).

[53] See O'Kane, 'Does prison work for cartelists?', note 34 above.

[54] For a useful critical overview of the ethnomethodological approach in criminology, see: Katherine S Williams, *Textbook on Criminology* (Oxford University Press, 7th ed, 2012), at pp. 428 *et seq*. In particular, Williams notes that one of the reasons why some criminologists do not favour an ethnomethodological approach is that 'the reflexive need to question their own research is both awkward and time-consuming' (at p. 432).

[55] Taylor, *In the Underworld*, note 52 above, at p. 11. See also: Peter Bramham, review of *In the Underworld*, 36 (1985) *British Journal of Sociology* 636, at p. 638

role? Certainly, researchers need to be aware of their own provenance (hence our own autobiographical notes offered above) and how that may affect their ability to engage with the subject of research. I very much suspect that in our case there was a greater natural empathy and ease of manner in dealing with lawyers and regulators than would have been the case in talking to business people. Specifically in my own case, I should admit that I can more comfortably talk with Bill Allan as a lawyer or even with an official working for the European Commission in Brussels (often a legal background again) than with a marketing manager working for an international producer and supplier of whatever commodity.[56] Perhaps we should bear that in mind when appointing researchers for particular projects.[57]

Despite the methodological difficulties, I am increasingly convinced that the objective is worthy and important.[58] As a researcher in this field, I want to hear Outlaw Pete and understand his position better and more fully. It is important to strive to do so in an area of contested policy and practice, since a matter such as anti-cartel enforcement is contingent on certain assumptions of ideology and policy (the perceived virtue of trade liberalisation and the 'open market') and also assumptions regarding the use of certain sanctions which should be critically reviewed. If the subject matter is contested in that way, then any tendency on the researcher's part to listen to the enforcer's voice rather than seek out the more elusive voice of the subject of enforcement, is a matter for critical self-reflection. As Williams has argued:

---

[56] For a caricature image with some basis in real world sensibility, think of an intellectual university-based, *Guardian*-reading researcher listening to a recording of an actual cartel meeting, at which the 'blokish' talk is as much about football as fixing prices. My thanks to Andreas Stephan of the Law School at the University of East Anglia for helping to craft this example.

[57] We sometimes did discuss in a strategic way the advantages and disadvantages of either Jennifer or myself, or the two of us together, taking part in meetings and interviews with certain people.

[58] For an interesting study and attempt at ethnographic penetration of a particular professional tribe—British policy-making civil servants—see: Alex Stevens, 'Telling Policy Stories: an ethnographic study of the use of evidence in policy-making in the UK', 40 (2011) *Journal of Social Policy* 237. The author explains in his conclusion (at p. 250): 'I have tried to shape a coherent narrative out of the messy business of policy-making. I have, however, tried to show my own methods and uncertainties so that readers can judge whether my narrative fits the reality of this process, or just the tropes and assumptions of academic discourse on policy-making.'

'the time when it is most dangerous to deny the individual position .... is when it should be used to challenge the way in which those in authority use their power to force individuals and actions into categorieswithout giving full weight to the meaning and explanations of the people who actually carry out the activity.'[59]

We should, then, recognise this as a matter of 'ontological politics' and understand the researcher's significant role in that respect.

---

[59] Williams, *Textbook on Criminology,* note 54 above, at p. 433.

13

Who Needs Evidence? Radical Feminism, the Christian Right and Sex Work Research in Northern Ireland

Graham Ellison

Introduction

This chapter describes my experiences of conducting research on commercial sex[1] in Belfast, Northern Ireland, which was conducted as part of a larger British Academy–Leverhulme Trust-funded study that examined the policing and legal regulation of commercial sex in Belfast (Northern Ireland) along with three other cities: Manchester (England), Berlin (Germany) and Prague (Czech Republic).[2] This study provided the first empirical analysis of commercial sex in the jurisdiction and was instrumental in shedding light on prevalence rates for

---

[1] I use commercial sex or sex work in preference to prostitution in this chapter since the former is arguably a more reflexive and less stigmatising term than the latter. However, where I refer specifically to legislation or official policy I use the term prostitution.

[2] The Policing and Regulation of Sexual Commerce: A Four-City Case Study, British Academy–Leverhulme Trust (2013). Graham Ellison was PI on the project, Ron Weitzer Was CI. Ellison was solely responsible for the data collection in Manchester and Belfast.

G. Ellison (✉)
Queen's University Belfast, Belfast, Northern Ireland

© The Author(s) 2017
S. Armstrong et al. (eds.), *Reflexivity and Criminal Justice*,
DOI 10.1057/978-1-137-54642-5_13

those involved in the industry as well as providing demographic information on the age, nationality and sexual orientation of sex workers along with the sector worked in, whether on-street or off-street (Ellison 2015). While academics and researchers are now well attuned to the varieties and differences in the organisation of commercial sex both within and between jurisdictions, what is less well studied and understood are the ways in which attitudes to commercial sex are deeply embedded in local political cultures (Ellison 2015; Zimmerman 2012). In the chapter, I consider my role as a researcher and highlight some of the difficulties that I experienced conducting what was seen as controversial research in the politically, socially and culturally conservative context of Northern Ireland. In this respect, I situate the discussion within the Northern Ireland Assembly's decision to legislate for Lord Morrow's (of the Democratic Unionist Party, henceforth DUP) *Human Trafficking and Exploitation (Further Provisions and Support for Victims) Bill* that included a number of provisions to provide support to victims of human trafficking but controversially also included specific provisions to make it a criminal offence to 'pay for the sexual services of a person' (Clause 15) in emulation of the so-called 'Nordic model' of criminalisation of demand.[3]

Clause 15 is modelled on developments that originally occurred in the Scandinavian jurisdictions (first Sweden in 1999, then later in Norway and Iceland) and which refers to what is called an 'asymmetric model of criminalisation' whereby the buyer not the seller of sexual services faces legal penalties (Levy 2014; Scoular 2004). According to its adherents, this model reduces the opportunities for commercial sex and by extension the potential for human trafficking for sexual exploitation (see generally, Ekberg 2004; Farley et al. 2009). However, for its opponents, the model has vastly increased the risks to sex workers and has impacted most severely on those migrant (female) sex workers who face deportation from Sweden (Levy 2014).

The chapter is structured as follows. I begin by providing a summary overview of the hotly contested theoretical terrain of sex work research

---

[3] The earlier terminology of the Bill was criticized for implying that only women sell sex. In the version that was legislated for the terminology adopted was more gender neutral.

before moving on to consider how a more reflexive research position can illuminate facets of commercial sex that are not necessarily made apparent in traditional neo-abolitionist research (e.g. see Ekberg 2004; Farley et al. 2009; Jeffreys 2008; Barry 1995). I then discuss the evidence base for the claims made by DUP Members of the Legislative Assembly (henceforth MLAs) and some advocacy organisations that sexual slavery and trafficking for sexual exploitation are rife in Northern Ireland which provided the rationale for introducing sex-purchase legislation. The chapter ends with a discussion of the difficulties that I and other researchers faced in researching such a sensitive topic in the Northern Irish context.

Theorising Commercial Sex

One of the most contentious research areas in criminology and the social sciences generally concerns that of 'prostitution' or 'commercial sex' (Dewey 2014; Ryan and Huschke 2015; Hammond and Kingston 2014; Shaver 2005). Indeed, as several commentators have noted the decision to engage with commercial sex as a terrain of research *also* means entering into a 'hotly contested political and ideological terrain' (Dewey 2014: 4). Even the terminology chosen—'prostitution' or 'commercial sex' —reflects the a priori ideological, moral or political standpoint of the researcher and as a consequence can lead to particular problems in how we engage reflexively with the subject matter. While space precludes a detailed overview, the landscape of sex work research is dominated by two broad but mutually exclusive positions. First, is a perspective rooted in a strand of radical feminism—what is termed neo-abolitionist feminism (Bernstein 2007)—that regards all aspects of commercial sex (to include pornography and all forms of adult entertainment) as exploitative and the embodiment of patriarchal domination and oppression. Indeed, this particular perspective has been termed the 'oppression paradigm' by Weitzer (2011). Commentators writing in this genre prefer the terms 'prostituted women' or 'women in prostitution' to signify a lack of agency whereby women (men and transgendered individuals are absent from these analyses) are coerced into prostitution, objectified and turned into a commodity to be bought and sold (Ekberg 2004; Farley et al.

2009; Barry 1995; Jeffreys 2008). For some prominent neo-abolitionists such as Melissa Farley, women cannot consent to commercial sex under any circumstances and as she suggests, 'To the extent that any woman is assumed to have freely chosen prostitution, then it follows that enjoyment of domination and rape are in her nature' (cited in Weitzer 2006: 34). While some feminist commentators in this genre regard *all* heterosexual sexual activity—what they term 'penis in vagina sex' (Jeffreys 2008: 327)—as exploitative, it is prostitution that represents the epitome of exploitation: Indeed, for the radical feminist Kathleen Barry, prostitution is '...the most extreme and crystallised form of all sexual exploitation' (Barry 1995: 9).

An alternative reading of commercial sex has been termed a 'polymorphous perspective' by Weitzer (2011). This perspective is considerably broader than the 'oppression paradigm' mentioned above insofar as it is anchored in a variety of theoretical positions (Rubin 1989; Weitzer 2011; O'Connell Davidson 2002; O'Neill 2010; Dewey and Zheng 2013; Sanders and Hardy 2014; Sanders et al. 2009). These include but are not limited to: the sociology of work and occupations whereby commercial sex is viewed as a kind of labour exchange relationship; third and fourth wave feminism (emphasising sexual rights and subjectivities) but also increasingly postcolonial or 'Third World' feminism (that points to the irrelevance in the global South of much feminist theorising) and where commercial sex is seen as a key route out of poverty for the women and men that participate in it (Kapur 2007; Doezema 2001; Agustín 2007). Other critical feminist commentators have pointed to the ways that traditional feminist discourse has been co-opted within neo-liberal apparatuses of governmentality around labour and work, migration and security (Fraser 2013; Bernstein 2007, 2010). Elizabeth Bernstein (2007), for example, argues that First World feminists have colluded in the maintenance of structures of control and domination exemplified in what she terms 'carceral feminism' which is a 'commitment of abolitionist feminist activists to a law and order agenda and a drift from the welfare state to the carceral state as the enforcement apparatus for feminist goals' (p. 143).

In general, those theorists who view commercial sex as a form of work argue that it is the moral and social stigma associated with commercial sex and its ambiguous legal status in a number of jurisdictions that makes it impossible for sex workers to work openly and without the threat of violence (see generally O'Neill 2010; Weitzer 2011). Consequently, these writers argue for sex workers' rights and statutory mechanisms that provide them with access to a range of state benefits such as health insurance and so forth. As Sanders et al. (2009) argue, this position opens up more possibilities for engaging reflexively with research subjects and for viewing commercial sex as a diverse range of practices that take place in a multitude of venues, with different opportunity structures and experiences of workers and clients. However, more fundamentally, it acknowledges that many workers in the sex industry exercise agency and choice, and while few researchers are blind to exploitation and abuse, these need to be put on a continuum of experience that varies with the particular sector worked in, whether street or indoor based and the degree of social capital between workers and clients.

Reflexivity in Sex Work Research

Several issues permeate sex work research that have important implications for reflexivity in the research process (Hammond and Kingston 2014; Dewey and Zheng 2013; Ryan and Huschke 2015). First, there is significant disagreement about the actual object of study. The bulk of research in this area continues to be directed towards those forms of commercial sex that result in the direct exchange of sexual services for monetary or other compensation. However, in reality, commercial sex spans a plethora of activities that include but are not limited to text, image and video pornography, live sex shows, strip and lap dancing clubs and other forms of adult entertainment (see Sanders and Hardy 2014).[4] Even within those forms of commercial sex that depend on the direct (physical) exchange of sexual services for monetary compensation there

---

[4] Since the legislation passed by the Northern Ireland Assembly is mainly geared to criminalising commercial sex between consenting adults this is the aspect of sexual commerce that I focus on in this chapter.

is a huge variation between and within particular sectors (Weitzer 2011; Shaver 2005). For example, that which occurs on-street and off-street, but also in relation to female, male and transgender sex workers (Maginn and Ellison 2014; Mai 2011). These issues are further complicated by the rise of the digital economy that has profound implications for both how we respond to and understand the nature of commercial sex in the twenty-first century (Sanders 2013).

Second, there is also the problem of how the narratives of sex workers are positioned to reflect their diverse experiences and voices (see Agustín 2007; Dewey and Zheng 2013; O'Neill 2010). While some in the neo-abolitionist feminist camp may well argue that they are engaging reflexively with research subjects and are giving voice to those women abused and traumatised by prostitution, it nevertheless remains the case that the full range of voices and the different experiences of workers across the various sectors are rarely elucidated. This lack of contact with sex-working populations is partly reflected in theoretical and conceptual approaches to commercial sex that have tended to focus on how the researcher *would like things to be* rather than *how things are.* In other words, this estrangement from the subjects of study has led to claims being made about many facets of commercial sex that cannot withstand empirical scrutiny. Some of these claims are refracted through the domain of neo-abolitionist feminism itself. For instance, these perspectives have tended to eschew reflexive analyses of a complex subject matter to focus on samples of sex workers drawn from one particular strata (on-street) that is estimated to comprise only around 15 per cent of the *total* sex-working population (Weitzer 2011). Critics, however, suggest that this body of research invariably self-selects the most extreme cases and constructs arguments against prostitution based on small samples of street-based sex workers who may have drug and alcohol dependency issues, experience high levels of violence from both clients and 'pimps' and who have multiple problems in their lives (Cojocaru 2015; Weitzer 2011).

The selection of particular cases designed to illustrate women's oppression means that neo-abolitionists are placed in an awkward and contradictory position. On the one hand, feminism seeks to give voice to all individuals and all sectors of society, particularly those that are marginalised in patriarchal social structures (Butler 1995; Rubin 1989) and in many ways it was feminist versions of reflexivity that first drew attention to the power imbalances between researchers and their research subjects (Finlay 2002). But on the other hand, selective inclusion only of those voices that align with the political position of neo-abolitionism undermines the reflexive impulse of feminism. Serious criticisms of unethical behaviour in dealing with (sex worker) research subjects have been levied at, for example, the prominent neo-abolitionist feminist Melissa Farley that resulted in a complaint being made to the American Psychological Association by a New Zealand sex workers' rights group (see Dewey 2014 for a full discussion of this case). It is not the intention here to single Farley out for particular attention since this is a perennial problem, with some studies promoted by anti-prostitution advocates demonstrating biases, the use of unrepresentative sampling frames, ethical flaws and methodological inconsistencies (O'Neill 2010; Weitzer 2011; Ellison 2015). Consequently, some researchers (Dewey and Zheng 2013; O'Neill 2010; Shaver 2005) and sex worker advocacy organisations (e.g. the Paulo Longo Research Initiative, the UK Network of Sex Work Projects) have argued for participatory action research that not only engages with the complex and diverse experiences of workers involved in all sectors of the industry and foregrounds the 'voice' of sex workers, but more generally advocates for 'ethical, interdisciplinary scholarship on sex work to inform activism and advocacy that will improve the human rights, health and wellbeing of sex workers' (Paulo Longo Research Initiative).

Finally, the issue of reflexivity is also problematised in terms of the *effects* of the research on the researcher. Some researchers have documented how studying commercial sex can take its toll on their sense of emotional wellbeing, their career and their professional reputation. For example, Hammond and Kingston (2014) point out that as female researchers studying commercial sex, they experienced what Goffman termed 'stigma by association' (Goffman 1963) that had a profound impact both in their personal and professional lives. Similarly, as I describe below, Susann Huschke has outlined her experiences of conducting research into commercial sex in Northern Ireland in terms of 'emotional labour' that generated intense feelings of betrayal, anger and frustration (Ryan and Huschke 2015). My own particular difficulties led to a high degree of cynicism about Northern Irish politics in general,[5] but also a sense of fatalism about the limits to which we as academics can ever hope to effect policy change.

Researching Commercial Sex in Northern Ireland

The difficulties that I experienced in researching commercial sex in Northern Ireland needs to be overlaid by two observations that go some way to contextualising the somewhat vitriolic response both to my own research and that of others (see Huschke et al. 2014).

The first concerns the relatively high level of church attendance and religiosity in the region generally (Tonge et al. 2014) and the permeation of religious moral values into most aspects of social, political and cultural life in Northern Ireland. For example, it is only relatively recently that pubs and shopping centres have been allowed to open on a Sunday while the first international football match ever played in Northern Ireland on a Sunday occurred as recently as 2015. The second aspect concerns the ways in which the women's movement in Northern Ireland has been influenced by the legacy of religious morality and social conservatism. This reflects the view that 'gendered subjectivities formed within conservative societies will tend to develop a women's agenda that reflects society's religious values' (Ashe 2006: 582). In Northern Ireland, the alignment of one of the largest women's organisations—Women's Aid—with the DUP around the issue of prostitution/commercial sex can at least be partially understood by the relative lack of a third or fourth wave feminist tradition (until recently) that focuses on sexual rights and agency (Ashe 2006; Fegan and Rebouche 2003).

The above section provides the broad context to how my research was eventually perceived, but my particular interest in researching commer-

---

[5] In something indicative of this, some political parties in Northern Ireland told me in the course of my interviews that Lord Morrow's Bill was deeply flawed, but also added that they would be voting for it anyway 'because there are no votes in prostitutes'.

cial sex was spurred while I was watching the early evening news in late 2012 when I saw the DUP's Lord Morrow talking eloquently about gender equality, sexual slavery and the human rights abuses of women who sold sex (men who sell sex have never been mentioned by the DUP). I was initially confused because the DUP had never shown any interest previously in commercial sex, nor arguably, in women's rights (Ritchie 2015). In fact the Rev Ian Paisley, one time leader of the DUP and the *Free Presbyterian Church* had previously denounced prostitution as 'an activity which is illegal, sordid, degrading and biblically sinful [along with] with homosexual groups, paedophiles and drug dealers' (cited in Meredith 2003). The DUP takes a particularly conservative line on a number of social issues including those affecting women and as the lawyer and feminist blogger, Wendy Lyon notes: 'The DUP remains one of the most socially conservative parties in Western Europe. It is fiercely opposed to abortion and LGBT rights, and advocates for the teaching of creationism in schools' (Lyon 2015: 42). I was even more surprised when I learned that the DUP had elicited the support not only of Women's Aid in Northern Ireland but also of the Swedish radical feminist, Gunilla Ekberg who has been involved in a number of anti-prostitution campaigns globally.

The debate around sexual commerce in Northern Ireland led me to apply for research funding from the British Academy - Leverhulme Trust to study the policing and regulation of sexual commerce in four European cities (Prague, Berlin, Manchester and Belfast). The grant application was successful and after ethics approval had been obtained from my University I began the data collection, which was undertaken between 2013 and 2014. Since the earlier part of the research in England, Germany and the Czech Republic had been conducted without incident I had naively assumed that the same would hold for Northern Ireland. What I had not anticipated, given how uncontentious and unproblematic my research in the other three jurisdictions had been, was the extent to which the research evidence I gathered in Northern Ireland would be filtered through an ideological lens.

The very nature of 'evidence' and 'research' around commercial sex in Northern Ireland and how it was constituted became a site of considerable struggle and contestation. Indeed, what emerged from the parliamentary and media debates were 'hierarchies of evidence' (Nutley et al. 2012) with particular 'victim narratives' (Cojocaru 2015; Andrijasevic 2007) and 'autobiographical survivor stories' (Ryan and Huschke 2015) based on the accounts of 'survivors of prostitution' (e.g. see Moran 2013) accorded a much higher status than evidence produced by researchers and academics. Unusually, in terms of what Becker (1967) termed a 'hierarchy of credibility' where those in power define the parameters of the debate, even 'evidence' from *official* sources such as the police and Northern Ireland Department of Justice was downplayed to favour that which was based on feeling and emotion, particularly from a number of advocacy groups. Lord Morrow had a very public spat with a senior Police Service of Northern Ireland (PSNI) officer claiming that he was 'meddling' after the latter gave a media interview in which he suggested that the proposed legislation would be impossible to enforce (Telford 2013). In another example, at one of the Justice Committee hearings the DUP's Mr Jim Wells bizarrely accused senior officials from the Department of Justice of having clandestine meetings with representatives of the sex industry in order to undermine Lord Morrow's Bill (Northern Ireland Assembly 2014: 14–16).[6] A cursory analysis of the *Hansard* parliamentary reports covering the debates in the Northern Ireland Assembly around Lord Morrow's Bill notes at least 16 separate occasions whereby various DUP MLAs made the claim that research evidence on the issue of commercial sex in Northern Ireland was not needed and as Lord Morrow himself suggested:

> I always said that additional research was unnecessary. The basic issue with which we need to engage is not more scholarship but answering the question, do we think that selling sex is ever an appropriate form of work in 21st century Northern Ireland. (Morrow 2014a)

For the uninitiated, this of course could be construed to mean that there was already a large pre-existing evidence base around commercial sex in Northern Ireland from which such a position could be legitimated. This

---

[6] A subsequent investigation revealed that Mr Wells' accusations against Department of Justice officials were entirely spurious.

would be untrue: no such empirical research existed. There were no data to indicate the size of the sex-working population, the demographics of sellers and buyers, the sexual orientation of sex workers, the role of migration into the sex industry on the island of Ireland facilitated by a porous land border, nor indeed about the changing topography of commercial sex due to the digital economy. Aside from an excellent historical account of prostitution in Belfast from the nineteenth century (McCormick 2009) there have only been two other academic studies of commercial sex in the region: one by myself (Ellison 2015) and the other commissioned by the Northern Ireland Department of Justice (Huschke et al. 2014). Both these studies elicited the views and opinions of those most affected by both existing and proposed legislation—sex workers themselves. In spite of Lord Morrow's stated concerns for the welfare of sex workers he did not actually speak to any to ascertain what the effects of his Bill might have on their lives (Meredith 2015).

Determining the Size of the Commercial Sex Sector in Northern Ireland

I have written elsewhere (Ellison 2015) that the debate about commercial sex and trafficking for sexual slavery in Northern Ireland bears all the hallmarks of a moral panic as famously articulated by Stan Cohen in his *Folk Devils and Moral Panics* (Cohen 1972). But to what extent are these public and media concerns about prostitution and trafficking for sexual exploitation justified? This is important because the 'evidence' marshalled by the DUP and other advocacy groups based their support for a sex-purchase ban on the fact that 'thousands' of women may be involved in the 'sex slave trade' and that trafficking for sexual exploitation was rife in Northern Ireland (Poole 2012). However, both my own research and that of Huschke et al. (2014) concluded that the commercial sex sector in Northern Ireland is comparatively small and certainly much smaller than other UK jurisdictions and internationally. Because of the violent sociopolitical conflict that erupted between 1968 and 1994 Belfast never had a particularly active street scene like some other UK cities such as

Glasgow, Birmingham, Manchester and Liverpool owing to the inherent dangers of using public space, particularly at night. From the start of the peace process in the mid-1990s, a small street sector once again emerged in Belfast, but the representative from the Belfast Health and Social Care Trust (that provides sexual health advice and screening to street-based workers) told me that there were only around 20–30 street-workers based mainly in Belfast, although fewer than five are available on a day-to-day basis (Ellison 2015; Huschke et al. 2014). Nearly all street-based workers are from Northern Ireland and their ages range from 30 to 55 years. A small number of male street-based sex workers also operate in Belfast in the vicinity of a number of gay bars and clubs (Maginn and Ellison 2014).

In terms of the indoor off-street sector, I was given access to ano-nymised data from one of Ireland's largest escort websites (Escort Ireland) for a five-year period (2009–2013). This data suggested that each year around 600 sex workers registered with Escort Ireland as providing sexual services in Northern Ireland. However, because some sex workers only work for specific periods and some tour between cities in Ireland and the UK, only around 40–60 are available in Northern Ireland on any given day. Of course, Escort Ireland represents only one of a range of potential escorting websites in Northern Ireland. In a separate study by Huschke et al. (2014), data scraping techniques were used to survey a number of free and commercial websites (Adultwork, Gay Swap, Backpage, Escort Ireland, Craigslist, etc.) on seven random days during a particular month. The researchers' concluded that when these numbers are aggregated around 300–350 female, male and transgendered escorts offer commercial sexual services in Northern Ireland on a daily basis.

Out of all the cities studied as part of my British Academy–Leverhulme Trust research study, Belfast had by far the smallest commercial sex sector, and I concluded that the on-street sector in Manchester (England) is as large as the indoor and on-street sectors *combined* in Northern Ireland. In relation to trafficking for sexual exploitation into Northern Ireland, there have only been two prosecutions for this offence since 2009 (though nei-ther case resonates with conventional media narratives around trafficking) and as Huschke et al. (2014: 127) suggest, 'we found that the number of trafficked victims into the Northern Ireland sex industry is low and that the majority of people selling sexual services are not trafficked.'

The Wrong Kind of Evidence

Many academics, the PSNI and the Northern Ireland Department of Justice were opposed to Clause 15 of Lord Morrow's Bill. Some activist groups were also opposed, including notably, the Belfast Feminist Network (BFN). The BFN is a recently established network of over 1000 feminist activists that seek to engage with broader questions of sexuality, sexual rights and the relationship between religion and gendered attitudes in Northern Ireland. In its written submission to the Northern Ireland Justice Committee, the BFN made clear its position that Lord Morrow's Bill would likely increase, not decrease the risks to sex workers and that the cartography of sexual commerce was much more diverse than that depicted by Lord Morrow and Women's Aid (Belfast Feminist Network 2013). In particular, the BFN raised issues that were not acknowledged by the DUP nor Women's Aid: namely that the debate about commercial sex in Northern Ireland has been heteronormative—focusing exclusively on *male* buyers and *female* sellers and that the Bill essentialised the purchase of commercial sex as a purely exploitative relationship.

While arguably the BFN represents a broader spectrum of female opinion in Northern Ireland, their evidence was not acknowledged by the DUP and it was only Women's Aid whose evidence on behalf of women was taken into account in the legislative process. For my own part, in 2013, I published a letter in the *Belfast Telegraph* (one of Northern Ireland's largest circulation newspapers) pointing out that Lord Morrow's Bill was incorrect in painting a direct link between commercial sex and human trafficking and on the basis of my preliminary research findings I suggested that there was no evidence that a sex-purchase ban would have an impact on human trafficking and that the legislation may well have downstream consequences in terms of increasing the risks of violence to sex workers. I did not at any stage suggest that abuse and exploitation were absent from the sex industry; rather, I suggested that working in the sex industry had to be viewed on a continuum of experience. I followed this letter up with a longer op-ed in the *Belfast Telegraph* where I expanded on some of my research findings in more detail. It is important to point out that at no stage did Lord Morrow or anyone else in the DUP contact me to speak about my research, and in fact, the Party did not reply to numerous telephone and email requests to be interviewed in connection with the study.

In September 2013, the Swedish anti-prostitution activist and radical feminist Gunilla Ekberg gave evidence in support of Lord Morrow's Bill to the Northern Ireland Justice Committee and sat alongside Lord Morrow and Dr Dan Boucher from Christian Action Research Education (CARE).[7] Ms Ekberg had been a frequent visitor to Belfast and had participated in several media appearances with Lord Morrow during the launch of his Bill. During the questioning session, Ms Ekberg claimed without citing any evidence that 'the academic world in the UK is particularly pro-prostitution compared to other countries' and that '97 per cent of women' were coerced or forced into prostitution (Northern Ireland Assembly 2013). Similarly, Dr Dan Boucher from CARE positioned the role of research as a simple matter of weighing up two positions and basing a decision on their moral worth; the moral worth in this case being on the side of those who oppose prostitution (Northern Ireland Assembly 2013). However, as O'Connell Davidson (2013) pointed out in her own written evidence to the Northern Ireland Justice Committee, Dr Boucher appeared not to understand:

> ...the relationship between theory, value and evidence in social scientific research... [and] oversimplifies the positions that different academics take on the issue of prostitution. It is possible to approach prostitution as both a form of work *and* a site of exploitation (p. 2. Italics in original)

For Weitzer (2010), the claims made by some advocacy groups and political actors in relation to the debate about commercial sex are based on what he terms 'prescientific reasoning' (p. 15). Such claims are made in the absence of evidence and more importantly cannot be demonstrated as falsifiable. In this sense, Dr Boucher neglected to consider the Popperarian dimensions to scientific/social scientific inquiry where research hypotheses are tested and where the research process is conducted not in line with some preconceived ideological driver or motivation but on the basis of the available empirical evidence (Popper 2002).

---

[7] A London-based fundamentalist Christian lobbying group.

Of course, none of this is to imply that there is necessarily some underlying 'truth' waiting to be discovered in the research process and indeed the notion of reflexivity has been used to good effect to challenge certainty in the social sciences, pointing to the vast array of meanings that people use to make sense of their lives (Alvesson and Sköldberg 2009). Nevertheless, some critics have suggested that reflexive research poses particular challenges as well as opportunities. Finlay (2002), for example, describes how researchers can navigate some of these difficulties since for her reflexive research can come to represent a kind of postmodern bricolage where researchers have to:

> ...negotiate the "swamp" of interminable self-analysis and self-disclosure... On their journey they can all too easily fall into the mire of the infinite regress of excessive self- analysis and deconstructions. (p. 212)

For Finlay (2002), researchers should strive to keep their focus on the research participants and consider the ways that their research can contribute to new knowledge and understanding. In this sense, it might be argued that if criminology and indeed other social scientific disciplines are to have any purchase outside of the academy, they must *also* have a relevance to policy formulation by adopting rigorous and appropriate methodologies, deliberating on and analysing various sources of data and presenting the evidence itself in a way that exposes a range of possibilities. What this means—and of course it is easier said than done—is that social scientists must strive to ensure that their research is comprehensive, reliable and adhere to the canon of replicability as well as demonstrating transparency in the research process.

The Religious Right Meets Feminism in Northern Ireland

The level of co-operation between Ms Ekberg and the DUP was striking, although not particularly unusual since several commentators have documented what they perceive as a growing conservative and right-ward shift by a section of the feminist movement in the United States (Bernstein

2007, 2010; Zimmerman 2012). I decided to send Ms Ekberg an email inquiring into the alignment of herself as a radical feminist with a party of the Christian right. I specifically asked whether she shared the DUP's view of homosexuality as 'repulsive'.[8] I was aware of the nature of the 'sex wars' in the United States, but I could not really see what feminism or the feminist movement stood to benefit or gain from this relationship given that this alignment appeared to privilege the Christian right more than radical feminists particularly in the case of Northern Ireland where the DUP hold significant political power and have used it in the past to limit women's rights and non-heteronormative relationships (Ritchie 2015; Meredith 2003, 2015).

My email to Ms Ekberg was intended as a personal not a professional one and its tone, on reflection, was a bit ill-considered. However, I was not hostile or rude to her and I pointed out that I would have more in common with radical feminists rather than the DUP on most social issues. I pointed out that the incessant homophobia emanating from the DUP created such an aura of stigma among lesbian, gay, bisexual, and transgender (LGBT) youth that it could potentially lead to suicide, a finding of a recent Northern Ireland study (O'Hara 2013), and I also pointed out that the DUP's atrocious record on women's rights. Ms Ekberg did not reply to my email but it nevertheless ended up in the hands of Lord Morrow and was to come back to haunt me at the Northern Ireland Justice Committee in January 2014 which I describe below.

The Spanish Inquisition

In 2013, I submitted written evidence to the Northern Ireland Justice Committee in respect of Lord Morrow's Bill while my colleague at Queen's University, Dr Susann Huschke did the same. Our submissions were based on our respective research into commercial sex in Northern Ireland. For my own part, I kept my submission as descriptive and factual as possible: I included prevalence figures for the size of the commercial

---

[8] Several DUP party members have made homophobic statements. For example, Ian Paisley Jnr famously claimed that he was 'repulsed' by homosexuality (BBC 2007).

sex sector (see above), demographic characteristics of sex workers as well as a short description of the role of the digital economy in purchasing and selling sex, as well as the difficulties faced in transposing a policy designed for one jurisdiction (Sweden) to another (Northern Ireland) given the vastly different social, political and cultural context of the latter.

In early January 2014, I was surprised to be telephoned by an official from the Northern Ireland Justice Committee asking me if I would give oral evidence to the all-party Justice Committee later that month. I had not expected to be asked to give evidence since I had already submitted a lengthy written submission. In hindsight, I feel that I was asked to attend the Committee hearing so that the DUP could produce my email to Ms Ekberg and creating a public opportunity to demonstrate my 'bias' and in so doing undermine the research that I had conducted. As it turned out myself and Dr Huschke presented our evidence at the same session. I spoke first and from the outset I was slightly irritated by the fact that most of the DUP members were not paying the slightest bit of attention to anything I had to say and were twiddling with their mobile phones, or browsing on their laptop computers. The floor was then opened up to the committee members and the DUP MLA Mr Jim Wells went first and produced the email that I had sent to Ms Ekberg. He claimed that I was anti-DUP (correct in the sense that I fundamentally oppose their social policies), and argued (less convincingly in light of later developments) that the party was not homophobic and that there was no relationship between anything the DUP said against the LGBT community and incidences of suicide among LGBT youth. One commentator described our experience thus: 'Researchers Graham Ellison and Susann Huschke were subjected to an interrogation so aggressive that a Sinn Féin member told them they "might know what the Spanish Inquisition was like by the time you leave here today"' (Lyon 2015: 43). The DUP questioned whether we were spokespersons for 'pimps' and 'traffickers' since both of us had used data from an online escort website (in determining prevalence figures). The Chair of the Committee, the DUP's Mr Paul Givan, also demanded that I name my interview respondents for the study, something which I refused to do. At the end of the session, Mr Givan told me that he was reporting me to my University for making negative comments about the DUP.

A month after the Justice Committee evidence hearing, two Freedom of Information Requests were lodged to access my email correspondence. The first was submitted to Queen's University asking for all my email correspondence for the period of one year that mentioned any of the following terms: Swedish Model, Prostitution, Human Trafficking, Sexual Trafficking, Commercial Sex, Sex Worker, Prostitute. This generated several thousand emails, but any email that related to my research or that was between myself and a respondent was redacted under the University's research governance regulations and the condition of anonymity and confidentiality granted to research participants. This was an extremely time-consuming exercise and meant that over a week was dedicated to sifting through email correspondence. The second was submitted to the Northern Ireland Department of Justice asking for all copies of email correspondence that I and other organisations and individuals had with them regarding Lord Morrow's Bill. In both cases, I felt that the Freedom of Information request was simply a fishing expedition to find out who I had interviewed for the study and that it was related to Mr Givan's request at the Justice Committee for me to name my respondents.

Laura Lee (a Glasgow-based sex worker) and Lucy Smith from UglyMugs.ie (an organisation that campaigns to end violence against sex workers) experienced by their own accounts extreme levels of hostility in their questioning by DUP members on the Justice Committee. As Ms Lee notes, the DUP's Paul Givan '…felt that it was appropriate to quiz me about my personal sex life, my relationship with my dad and he also alleged that I target vulnerable disabled men' (cited in Lyon 2015: 42). Ms Lee was also forced by Mr Wells to give her real name as opposed to her working name on the live video stream, while at other Committee sessions so-called 'survivors of prostitution' were treated to the privilege of in-camera hearings and given a guarantee of anonymity by the Justice Committee. Similarly, Lucy Smith was aggressively questioned on her connection to an escort website that Uglymugs.ie advertises on, and was not asked by any DUP members about sex worker safety or the potential implications of Lord Morrow's legislation for violence experienced by sex workers (Lyon 2015).

Given that the Committee session was being broadcast live via webcam, the media quickly became interested in my comments about homophobia in the DUP ignoring the point in my email questioning the consistency of a feminist/DUP alliance. In relation to the DUP's complaint[9] about me to my University, Queen's saw this as an issue of academic freedom and were fully supportive of me and at one point considered advising academics not to participate with Northern Ireland Assembly Committees if they were going to be subjected to the kind of questioning that myself and Dr Huschke faced. I was inundated with hundreds of emails of support from colleagues, students, young LGBT people who had left Northern Ireland because of homophobia, random members of the public and even DUP party members! I was contacted by a senior DUP official and told that Mr Wells and Mr Givan had been reprimanded, though I suspect more for their treatment of Laura Lee since even in the macho world of Northern Irish politics, the DUP has limits about so aggressively and publicly attacking a lone female. The senior party official told me that they 'wanted the story to die' since all Mr Wells and Mr Givan had managed to do was once again raise the spectre of homophobia within the DUP. The party hierarchy removed Mr Givan as Chair of the Justice Committee several months later for unspecified reasons, while Mr Wells was later forced to resign as Minister for Health following comments he made about homosexuality (Belfast Telegraph 2015).

I fully accept that my email to Ms Ekberg created the impression among the DUP that I was a biased source, and gave them the ammunition to attack me that they had sought all along. But had anyone in the DUP asked what my views on the party's social policies were I would have had no hesitation telling them. Nevertheless, at no stage during the Justice Committee hearing was I asked any questions about what my research had uncovered by the DUP members despite being at that time only one of two people in Northern Ireland who had spoken to sex workers about the possible effects of the sex-purchase legislation on their lives. Indeed, Susann Huschke, the only other researcher to have drawn in views of sex workers themselves, was later subjected to wide-ranging criticism from DUP politicians, Women's Aid and a section of the Northern Irish media following the publication of her own research into commercial

---

[9] From what I was told, a telephone complaint was made by Mr Givan to Queen's University's Director of Communications.

sex in Northern Ireland (see Huschke et al. 2014). Among other things Huschke was accused of being a member of the 'pimp lobby' and that her methods and analytical approach demonstrated 'judgemental bias' (Ryan and Huschke 2015: 9). Huschke has subsequently written of her experiences in terms of the emotional labour it demanded from her as a researcher but also as an individual. As she explains:

> The most frustrating part was trying to discuss this topic with people who very clearly do not know much about research and methodology—and why would they, it is not their area of expertise—but come up with the most unfounded accusations that aim to destroy the research by making it look unprofessional... There was no way of explaining our methods and the research process to people like Paul Givan and Jim Wells (DUP representatives in the Justice Committee). They had made their minds up a long time ago about what sex work is and what is to be done about it, and were not going to be swayed by anything that we found in our study, or by anything sex workers themselves had to say about it. (cited in Ryan and Huschke 2015: 10)

Conclusions

In this chapter, I have revisited my own experience and the general climate of conducting research into the highly controversial topic of commercial sex in Northern Ireland. Undoubtedly, this research would have been controversial in any event but it was made much more so because the research itself intersected with political debates around the introduction of sex-purchase legislation by the DUP. Consequently, my research was perceived by the DUP as a direct attack on the proposed legislation and every attempt was made to attack my credibility as someone who was hostile to the Party.

Developments in Northern Ireland call into question the nature of 'evidence' and the purposes for which it can be used and abused. The number of DUP politicians who claimed that evidence on the nature of commercial sex was irrelevant suggests that evidence-based policy is a long way from becoming embedded as a value in the political process in

Northern Ireland, which in part is due to the relative newness of the political institutions established there.[10] Empirical evidence from research into commercial sex was either ignored or treated as inferior to that conducted by a number of advocacy groups which was based normatively on feelings, emotions and particularistic moral stances. As Lord Morrow himself notes: 'For me, taking action was very much motivated by my Christian faith and principles. I am not ashamed to say so' (Morrow 2014b). I have no particular objection to Lord Morrow's Christian principles, but what I do have an objection to is the way in which these principles are accorded a particular status within the Northern Irish policy arena and to imply that other sources of evidence are significantly less worthy. There are a number of prominent DUP politicians who argue that laws should be formulated according to a literal interpretation of the Bible (Tonge et al. 2014: 10). However, it is debatable whether this is either a practical or an acceptable basis for policy-making in the twenty-first century.

However, a more fundamental concern relates to the alignment of a section of the feminist movement with the Christian right. I have suggested in this chapter that this alliance needs to be viewed problematically and has benefitted *more* the Christian right that women generally. In the context of Northern Ireland, it could be argued that the alignment of Ms Ekberg and Women's Aid with the DUP has however inadvertently, set back not advanced, the position of women in Northern Ireland and those from LGBT backgrounds. In particular, 'winning' this particular battle only served to embolden the DUP to tackle what they perceived as other longstanding issues: namely, that of abortion/reproductive rights and LGBT equality. No sooner had the ink dried on Lord Morrows Bill (it was passed in December 2014) that Mr Jim Wells was proposing amendments to the forthcoming Northern Ireland Justice Bill to tighten Northern Ireland's already restrictive abortion laws even further by imposing a mandatory prison sentence of ten years on a women who procured a medical abortion in a private clinic in Northern Ireland (Teggart 2014). Around the same time, the DUP's Mr Paul Givan also launched a campaign to introduce what he termed a 'conscience clause'

---

[10] While the political institutions were established in 1998, in reality, it is only since 2007 that they became operational when Sinn Fein decided to take their seats.

in LGBT equality legislation that would make it legal to discriminate against members of the LGBT community on the grounds of religious belief (Kane 2014). It is in this sense that I would caution a section of the feminist movement to be very careful in what you wish for.

References

Agustín, L.M. (2007) *Sex at the Margins: Migration, Labour Markets and the Rescue Industry*, London: Zed books.
Alvesson, M. and Sköldberg, K. (2009) *Reflexive Methodology*, London: Sage.
Andrijasevic, R. (2007) 'Beautiful Dead Bodies: Gender, Migration, and Representation in Anti-Trafficking Campaigns', *Feminist Review* 86: 24–44.
Ashe, F. (2006) 'The Virgin Mary Connection: Reflecting on Feminism and Northern Irish Politics', *Critical Review of International Social and Political Philosophy* 9(4): 573–588.
Barry, K. (1995) *The Prostitution of Sexuality*, New York: NYU Press.
BBC (2007) 'Row Over "Repulsive Gays" Comment', BBC News, Wednesday 30th May. Available: http://news.bbc.co.uk/1/hi/northern_ireland/6705637.stm (Accessed 8th April, 2016).
Becker, H. (1967) 'Whose Side Are We On?', *Social Problems* 14(3): 234–47.
Belfast Telegraph, (2015) 'DUP Minister Jim Wells Quits After Gay Abuse Controversy', 27th April. Available: http://www.belfasttelegraph.co.uk/news/politics/dup-minister-jim-wells-quits-after-gay-abuse-comments-controversy-31173893.html
Belfast Feminist Network (2013) *Evidence to Committee for Justice: Trafficking & Exploitation (Further Provisions and Support for Victims) Bill*, Belfast: Northern Ireland Assembly.
Bernstein, E. (2010) 'Militarised Humanitarianism Meets Carceral Feminism: The Politics of Sex, Rights and Freedom in Contemporary Anti-Trafficking Campaigns', *Signs: Journal of Women in Culture and Society* 36(1): 45–71.
Bernstein, E. (2007) 'The Sexual Politics of the "New Abolitionism"', *Differences: A Journal of Feminist Cultural Studies* 18(5): 128–151.
Butler, J. (1995) 'Contingent Foundations'. In S. Benhabib, J. Butler, D. Cornwell and N. Fraser (eds.) *Feminist Contentions: A Philosophical Exchange*, New York: Routledge: 35–58.
Cohen, S. (1972) *Folk Devils and Moral Panics*, St Albans: Paladin.

Cojocaru, C. (2015) 'Sex Trafficking, Captivity, and Narrative: Constructing Victimhood with a Goal of Salvation', *Dialectical Anthropology* 39(2): 183:194.

Dewey, S. (2014) 'Anthropological Research With Sex Workers: An Introduction'. In S. Dewey and T. Zheng (eds.) *Ethical Research with Sex Workers*, New York; Heidelberg; Dordrecht; London: Springer.

Dewey, S. and Zheng, T. (eds.) (2013) *Ethical Research with Sex Workers: Anthropological Approaches*, New York; Heidelberg; Dordrecht; London: Springer.

Doezema, J. (2001) 'Ouch! Western Feminists' "Wounded Attachment" to the "Third World Prostitute"', *Feminist Review* 67(1): 16–38.

Ekberg, G. (2004) 'The Swedish Law that Prohibits the Purchase of Sexual Services', *Violence against Women* 10(10): 1187–1218.

Ellison, G. (2015) 'Criminalizing the Payment for Sex in Northern Ireland: Sketching the Contours of a Moral Panic', *British Journal of Criminology*: DOI 10.1093/bjc/azv107.

Farley, M., Bindel, J. and Golding, J.M. (2009) *Men who Buy Sex: Who they Buy and What They Know*, Eaves: London.

Fegan, E.V. and Rebouche, R. (2003) 'Northern Ireland's Abortion Law: The Morality of Silence and the Censure of Agency', *Feminist Legal Studies* 11: 221–254.

Finlay, L. (2002) 'Negotiating the Swamp: The Opportunity and Challenge of Reflexivity in Research Practice', *Qualitative Research* 2(2): 209–230.

Fraser, N. (2013) *Fortunes of Feminism: From State-managed Capitalism to Neoliberal Crisis*, London: Verso Books.

Goffman, E. (1963) *Stigma*, London: Penguin.

Hammond, N. and Kingston, S. (2014), 'Experiencing Stigma as Sex Work Researchers in Professional and Personal Lives', *Sexualities* 17(3): 329–347.

Huschke, S., Shirlow, P., Schubotz, D., Ward, E., Probst, U., and Ní Dhónaill, C. (2014) *Research into Prostitution in Northern Ireland*, Belfast: Department of Justice Northern Ireland.

Jeffreys, S. (2008) *The Idea of Prostitution*, Melbourne: Spinifex Press.

Kapur, R. (2007) '"Faith" and the "Good" Liberal: The Construction of Female Sexual Subjectivity in Anti-Trafficking Legal Discourse'. In V.E. Munro and C.F. Stychin (eds.) *Sexuality and the Law: Feminist Engagements*, London: Routledge.

Kane, A. (2014) 'Paul Givan: Conscience Clause MLA – A Politician on a Mission', Belfast Telegraph, 20th December. Available: http://www.belfasttelegraph.co.uk/life/paul-givan-conscience-clause-mla-a-politician-on-a-mission-30850887.html

Levy, J. (2014) *Criminalising the Purchase of Sex: Lessons From Sweden*, London: Routledge.

Lyon, W. (2015) 'Ireland: Clause 6', Albertine, July. pp. 40–43. Available: https://www.academia.edu/15363926/Ireland_Clause_6

Maginn, P. and Ellison, G. (2014) 'Male Sex Work in Northern Ireland and the Irish Republic'. In V. Minichiello and J. Scott (eds.) *Male Sex Work and Society*, New York: Harrington Park Press: 426–461.

Mai, N. (2011) 'Tampering with the Sex of "Angels": Migrant Male Minors and Young Adults Selling Sex in the EU', *Journal of Ethnic and Migration Studies* 37(8): 1237–1252.

McCormick, L. (2009) *Regulating Sexuality: Women in Twentieth Century Northern Ireland*, Manchester: Manchester University Press.

Meredith, F. (2003) 'Fear and Loathing: The Religious Right's View of Women is Fuelled by Hatred', The Guardian, 3rd August.

Meredith, F. (2015) 'Strait-Laced DUP Has Always Been Funny About Sex', The Belfast Telegraph, 1st May.

Moran, R. (2013) *Paid For – My Journey Through Prostitution: Surviving a Life of Prostitution and Drug Addiction on Dublin's Streets*, London: Gill and Macmillan.

Morrow, Lord (2014a) 'Briefing Note: Briefing on Clause 6 – Full Response to DOJ Research' Belfast: Democratic Unionist Party: Belfast.

Morrow, Lord (2014b) Human Trafficking and Exploitation (Criminal Justice and Support for Victims) Bill: Final Stage, Belfast: Northern Ireland Assembly. Available: They Work for You: http://www.theyworkforyou.com/ni/?id=2014-12-09.4.1

Northern Ireland Assembly (2013) Official Report (Hansard), Human Trafficking and Exploitation (Further Provisions and Support for Victims) Bill, Briefing from Lord Morrow MLA, CARE, Former Swedish Government Special Advisor, 12th September. Belfast: Northern Ireland Assembly.

Northern Ireland Assembly (2014) Committee for Justice, Official Report (Hansard), Human Trafficking and Exploitation (Further Provisions and Support for Victims) Bill: Department of Justice, Minutes of Evidence, 6th March.

Nutley, S., Powell, A., and Davies, H. (2012) 'What counts as good evidence?', Research Unit for Research Utilisation (RURU), Available: https://www.nesta.org.uk/sites/default/files/what_counts_as_good_evidence_provocation_paper.pdf

O'Neill, M. (2010) 'Cultural Criminology and Sex Work: Resisting Regulation Through Radical Democracy and Participatory Action Research', *Journal of Law and Society* 37(1): 210–232.

O'Connell Davidson, J. (2013) 'The Human Trafficking and Exploitation (Further Provisions and Support for Victims) Bill, Written Evidence in respect of Clause 6. Available: http://www.niassembly.gov.uk/globalassets/Documents/Justice/human-trafficking-bill/written-submissions/Professor-Julia-OConnell-Davidson.pdf (Accessed 7th April, 2016).

O'Connell Davidson, J. (2002) 'The Rights and Wrongs of Prostitution', *Hypatia* 17(2): 84–98.

O'Hara, M. (2013) *Through our Minds: Exploring the Emotional Health and Wellbeing of Lesbian, Gay, Bisexual and Transgender People in Northern Ireland*, Belfast: The Rainbow Project.

Poole, A (2012) 'Sex Slaves Suffer rapes 300,000 times a year in Ulster', February 15th. The Daily Mirror (Irish Edition). Available: http://www.thefreelibrary.com/Sex+slaves+suffer+rapes+300,000+a+year+in+Ulster..+INVESTIGATES...-a0280054501 (Accessed 12th August, 2015).

Popper, K. (2002) *The Logic of Scientific Discovery*, London: Routledge.

Ritchie, M. (2015), 'Why a DUP Coalition Would be Dangerous for Women', The Telegraph, 30th April.

Ryan, P. and Huschke, S. (2015) 'Conducting Sex Work Research in a Politically Contentious Climate: Lessons from Ireland'. In I. Crowhurst, A. King and A.C. Santos (eds.) *Sexualities Research: Critical Interjections, Diverse Methodologies and Practical Applications,* Routledge: London.

Rubin G, (1989) 'Thinking Sex: Notes for a Radical Theory of the Politics of Sexuality'. In C. Vance (ed.) *Pleasure and Danger: Exploring Female Sexuality*, London: Pandora.

Sanders, T. (2013) *Paying for Pleasure: Men Who Buy Sex*, London: Routledge.

Sanders, T. and Hardy, K. (2014) *Flexible Workers: Labour, Regulation and the Political Economy of the Stripping Industry*, London: Routledge.

Sanders, T., O'Neill, M. and Pitcher, J. (2009) *Prostitution: Sex Work, Policy and Practice,* London: Sage.

Scoular, J. (2004) 'Criminalising "Punters": Evaluating the Swedish Position on Prostitution', *Journal of Social Welfare and Family Law* 26(2): 195–210.

Shaver, F. (2005) 'Sex Work Research: Methodological and Ethical Challenges', *Journal of Interpersonal Violence* 20(3): 296–319.

Teggart, G. (2014) 'It's Time Northern Ireland Put an End to the Climate of Fear Around Abortion', New Statesman, 28th November. Available:

http://www.newstatesman.com/politics/2014/11/it-s-time-northern-ireland-put-end-climate-fear-around-abortion (Accessed 7th April, 2016).

Telford, L. (2013) 'DUP Man Lord Morrow Hits Out at PSNI "Meddling" Over Prostitution Bill', *The Belfast Telegraph*, 23rd September, Available: http://www.belfasttelegraph.co.uk/news/northern-ireland/dup-man-lord-morrow-hits-out-at-psni-meddling-over-prostitution-bill-29598199.html (Accessed 7th April, 2016).

Tonge, J. Braniff, M., Hennessey, T., McAuley, J.W. and Whiting, S. (2014) *The Democratic Unionist Party: From Protest to Power*, Oxford: Oxford University Press.

Weitzer, R. (2011) *Legalising Prostitution: From Illicit Vice to Lawful Business*, New York: New York University Press.

Weitzer, R. (2010) 'The Mythology of Prostitution: Advocacy Research and Public Policy', *Sex Research and Social Policy* 7(1): 15–19.

Weitzer, R. (2006) 'Moral Crusade Against Prostitution', Society March/April. 33–37.

Zimmerman, Y. (2012) *Other Dreams of Freedom: Religion, Sex and Human Trafficking*, Oxford: Oxford University Press.

14

Insider? Outsider? Reflections on Navigating Positionality When Researching Restorative Justice Policing

Kelly J. Stockdale

Introduction

This chapter explores the issue of reflexivity and researcher identity, particularly in relation to the insider/outsider dichotomy in qualitative research. It is important to acknowledge that researcher's positions are not always stable, nor are they categorised purely by insider/outsider terms: there is a 'space between' insider/outsider research (Dwyer and Buckle 2009) and 'fluidity' to a researcher's identity (Thomson and Gunter 2011). This chapter uses my experience of conducting research on an organisation that I worked for, a police force in England and Wales. As an employee within the force, in some ways I held an 'insider' status. However, as a member of police staff, and not a police officer, I did not share the same subcultural bonds as those I researched and was

I would like to thank the editors, particularly Alistair Henry, for their detailed feedback on an earlier version of this chapter.

K.J. Stockdale (✉)
Northumbria University, Newcastle upon Tyne, UK

© The Author(s) 2017
S. Armstrong et al. (eds.), *Reflexivity and Criminal Justice*,
DOI 10.1057/978-1-137-54642-5_14

therefore also an 'outsider'. I argue that the reflexive praxis of a 'two-way street', whereby there is a mutual and continuous affect between the researcher and the researched (Alvesson and Sköldberg 2009: 79), may be better imagined as a frequently visited 'roundabout' for the insider/outsider researcher: one constantly enters, and often exits, each encounter in the field from different positions. It is important to recognise the influence this may have on the reflexive process. As Berger argues, 'reflexivity in qualitative research is affected by whether the researcher is part of the researched and shares the participants' experience' (2015: 219). Therefore, the fluidity of identity requires the researcher to constantly note the approach they are taking upon entering this 'reflexive roundabout'. It not only requires consideration of the ways in which the researcher is shaping the research, and the ways in which the research is shaping the researcher, but also an additional awareness that one's positionality is affecting the reflexive process itself.

The chapter begins by discussing the role of positionality within reflexivity before offering an attempt to define my research position. First, it considers the research project and my new role/status as a doctoral candidate. It then proceeds to examine my role as a civilian employee within the force before attempting to define whether I occupied an insider/outsider position or if, as police staff, I fell into the space between. The chapter then proceeds to offer some reflections on researcher positionality and argues that there is a need to expand beyond basic typologies and to recognise the fluidity of a researcher's position and status at different points in each social encounter.

Reflexivity and Positionality

There is a growing body of literature which highlights the importance of reflexivity as a key component not only in the research process, but also in the development of criminological knowledge (e.g. Lumsden and Winter 2014). Reflexivity in social and criminological research requires a focus on the way in which knowledge is produced; the reflective process is crucial for all elements of the research from the selection of a research topic to the dissemination of findings (Lumsden and Winter 2014: 2). It also requires the researcher to engage in 'continual internal dialogue and critical self-evaluation of [their] positionality as well as active acknowl-edgement that this position may affect the research process and out-come' (Berger 2015: 220). Researcher's positioning can be influenced by personal characteristics including race, gender, ethnicity, sexuality, social class, positions of power, and their relationship with respondents (Lumsden and Winter 2014: 3). Berger posits three areas whereby posi-tionality may influence research: first, in terms of access and sharing of experiences; second, it may affect the researcher-researched relationship and therefore the information a participant will comfortably share; and third, the researcher's background may influence the way they view a situ-ation and filter the information received (Berger 2015: 220).

Whilst the importance of reflexivity has been discussed in many areas, Berger (2015) argues there is a need for more research focused on the position of the researcher and the area being researched. Using her own experiences of researching the familiar, the unfamiliar and also the 'in between' position as she moved from an outsider to an insider position, she provides a useful account of the relationship between reflexivity and the position of the researcher. Often the researcher's position in relation to the area being researched is straightforward and known in advance, although sometimes events and changes in circumstance might bring about a shift. At other times, the shifts and changes might be constantly recurring: the reflexive process itself contributes to this as one has to adopt a self-critical role in relation to social processes, thereby considering not only how one views one's own position but how one is viewed by others. This chapter deconstructs my research experience and the fluid nature of my research position and in doing so demonstrates why 'researchers must continually ask themselves where they are at any given moment in rela-tion to what they study and what are the potential ramifications of this position on their research' (Berger 2015: 232).

Defining My Research Position: The Research

My doctoral thesis explored the implementation of restorative justice across a police force. The research itself adopted a qualitative-dominant multi-method approach and used one police force as an in-depth case study. The force had previously attempted to implement restorative justice in 2008 and was now attempting to 're-launch' and embed a new 'restorative approach'. The research was designed to explore police understandings of restorative justice, why the first implementation had not been as successful as the force hoped it would be, and to follow the re-launch process. In doing so, it would consider the barriers and opportunities to successful policy implementation. A mixed-methods approach was used: this incorporated focus groups to capture shared opinions amongst police constables and police community support officers (PCSOs), semi-structured interviews with higher ranking officers, and participant observation of meetings held by the 'steering group' who were tasked with implementing the '100 day' restorative approach plan. My research design considered the ethical implications relating to informed consent, data storage, as well as wider considerations of access, reliability, and ethical dilemmas (see Rowe 2007). The research process required a constant reflective interpretation in relation to some of these aspects, particularly in relation to participant issues and ethics, for example, questioning how able officers felt to opt-out of the study.

Having left the force on a career break to allow time to write up my thesis, I began to reflect on some of the wider issues I had faced. This reflexive introspection allowed me to recognise how the overarching research questions and areas of exploration were affected by my struggle to determine my own position: a struggle that I had not fully recognised at the time as I considered it to be a clear insider/outsider dichotomy whereby my research and professional life were mostly separate. This included my attempts to make a clear distinction between 'work' time and 'research' time, presuming there to be more of a clear divide between my two identities where I left my office and attended other areas within headquarters or at other police stations when doing my fieldwork. Indeed my central research question explored elements of the organisation that were unrelated to my role. The research design focused on different commands (Response, Crime and Justice, and Neighbourhoods) rather than my own command of Tasking and Coordinating. Considering my status and position in relation to data interpretation alone meant I had overlooked the overarching impact of conducting research within a wider organisation and particularly in relation to police organisational behaviour, police culture and the position of civilian staff within it. Yet, in retrospect, my positionality had affected all aspects of my research including, but not limited to: the overarching research question, methods used, and the ways in which I went about the reflexive process.

It is important to note at this stage that my initial research proposals, whilst on restorative justice, were not specifically related to policing and were conceived a number of years prior to starting my PhD and based on my experience as a trained restorative justice facilitator and my experiences working with victims and offenders. However, after formulating this proposal, I was unable to pursue my PhD due to illness, and shortly afterwards I started working for the force as a member of police staff instead. Over the following years, I witnessed the introduction of restorative justice within this force, noting the process and the results of the implementation with a passing interest. Four years later, the opportunity presented itself to embark on my doctoral journey. My proposed research would always involve criminal justice; however, I now worked in the criminal justice system and had to consider this insider/outsider dichotomy. My 'new' status as an 'insider' and working within the police force had not altered my research topic, and I did not wish to build on previous police ethnographies and research my experience within the police (Young 1991; Holdaway 1979). I was initially wary of combining my two roles and had hoped to keep my identities as researcher and employee separate. This has to be the starting point for discussing my research as it is clear now that from the very start of the project this desire to keep my two identities separate influenced my approach.

Despite my initial wariness, there were obvious benefits to conducting research within the force, including access to the field, an ability to appreciate the complexity of the force's re-implementation (Romano 1968) in addition to my prior knowledge of the subcultural language and terms used by participants (Hockey 1993). I had been employed by the organisation when the restorative justice initiative was first introduced and I was aware of new developments, including a 're-launch' or 're-implementation' of restorative justice, which was being re-branded as a 'restorative approach'. I also had an awareness of some of the broader issues surrounding policy implementation and with my academic background approached my time working with the police with a 'vigour of curiosity' (Hockey 1993). This included my prior knowledge of issues and language particular not just to policing but also to that force, for example, around computer systems and their capabilities and limitations, and around references to people and local procedures. However, I did not have complete 'insider' status as this was not part of my everyday policing role, and therefore I was mindful of the 'partialness' to my insider knowledge (Hockey 1993: 199).

With mixed feelings I had a series of meetings with the Chief Constable. The first of these was clearly a scoping exercise to 'sound me out' (Poulton 2014). The focus of the conversation was as much about my background, my children, my rationale for doing a PhD, and my experience as a restorative justice facilitator as it was about my research ideas. It included more unusual questions such as 'If I was chief constable for a day, what would I change?' At the time, I felt that this question was clearly directed towards me as an employee of the force, an insider. It was not a request for academic insight: an outsider's opinion. The second meeting indicated that the Chief Constable had accepted me. I was introduced to the superintendent who would be leading the restorative approach task force or implementation 'steering group' who was given a clear directive to aid the research. It was here that I was offered unlimited access and the freedom to explore any area/aspect of restorative justice I wished. However, I was adamant that I did not want to research certain areas, for example, the 'restorativeness' of policing practices, not least because that would involve observing, and potentially critiquing specific officer's actions and behaviours. My research proposal therefore concentrated on the policy implementation process—exploring the initial launch and subsequent re-launch of restorative justice across the force. Reiner and Newburn note that insider/outsider police researchers are more likely 'to have a policy focus rather than one concerned with developing a theoretical analysis of policing' (2008: 356). This is an interesting point, although they do not elaborate why this might be the case. Further research into civilian staff and their position within police subculture would clearly be useful to help unpack these issues.

Defining My Research Position: My Role

It is useful to consider in detail what my position within the police force was. I shall therefore start by offering more detail of my role and how, as police staff, I occupied a 'partial insider' position. As noted, as a civilian I did not belong to the police sub-cultures that are identified as existing within a police force (Reuss-Ianni 1983; Chan 1996; Farkas and Manning 1997) and was therefore not an 'insider'. However, as a member of the same organisation I was not technically an 'outsider' either. At the time of conducting the fieldwork, I worked as an intelligence analyst in tasking and co-ordinating command and on tasks unrelated to restorative justice. As there was little involvement with the implementation of restorative justice in my own command, I justified my decision not to conduct research within it, concluding that conducting fieldwork with my peers would not help me to answer the research question I had set. Although my role often involved consulting with other commands for my day-to-day work, as a large organisation my fieldwork rarely brought me into contact with anyone that I particularly knew or worked with.

Upon reflection it is clear that faced with the struggle of occupying a limited and partial insider status I pushed towards an outsider position, aiming to achieve a degree of independence. There is no doubt that there was a misguided belief at the very start of the research process that I was able to control my positionality; that insider/outsider research is a straightforward choice. By distancing my research topic from my employment and aligning myself in an outsider position, I mistakenly believed this would make me more objective in my research approach. Yet it was only when I began to reflect on and acknowledge the social and cultural constructions within the police force and my position within each social situation (both as staff and employee) that I was able to write up my research findings with integrity: research independence requires adopting a reflexive approach to all areas, including one's positionality, allowing the details to be exposed to scrutiny, it is only when this is done that high quality social research can be achieved (Case and Haines 2014: 59).

It is therefore important to note from the outset that my role as civilian staff in the police organisation is very distinct from that of police officers and as such I am not a true insider—this research is not an auto ethnography: I would not 'pass' as a native (Hayano 1979). Indeed whilst research distinguishes different police cultures that operate amongst officers, little attention is paid to police staff's role (Manning 1993; Chan 1996; Waddington 1999). Police civilian staff, including PCSOs, are part of an 'extended family' (Mawby and Wright 2012). Whilst they might share some of the same culture and language, they do not share the same cultural bonds. There has been little research into civilian police cultures; however, research into PCSOs' acceptance shows a certain amount of hostility to staff who are not sworn police officers (Caless 2007). The conflict and 'culture clash' between my role as intelligence analyst and police officers has been highlighted in other studies (Cope 2004). Cope (2004), for example, raises many pertinent issues about the role of intelligence analysts within a police force, including: their civilian status; the gendered nature of police organisations, particularly in relation to civilian staff; and issues surrounding hierarchy and status.

The issue of hierarchy in particular needs to be stated: my grade as police staff is difficult to compare to that of police officers' due to the difficulties of police hierarchical structures to fully reflect non-warranted police staff expertise and experience. Cope's (2004) findings suggest the role of intelligence analyst would be equivalent to a sergeant, due to my supervisory responsibilities. It is useful to reflect on this, as I conducted focus groups that were deliberately chosen with no ranks of sergeant or above. However, police staff 'rank' as such, was not important—whilst it exists in civilian police culture there was no conflict in that police officers or PCSOs (who are effectively two scales below my 'rank') did not consider my grade/rank or see me as anything other than an office worker. However, Cope raises the issue of the police staff role of intelligence analyst as being one that potentially encroaches on police officer's expert status (Cope 2004: 197).

These issues indicate a potential for conflict and tension between analysts and police officers. It was an important point for reflection: whilst I was an insider in some respects in terms of belonging to the extended police family, I was an outsider to police officers' cultures. It should be noted that reflecting on your status within an organisation, and the way in which you are viewed by your co-workers as part of the research process, has the potential to impact on one's working relationships too. I not only had to consider how I was viewed as a researcher but also how I was viewed by police officers in my civilian role too. My six years of employment were under scrutiny. I faced an irony as I was included (in my student role) in more steering group meetings than I possibly would have been had I been there in my analyst role. My acceptance as an 'insider' to the fieldwork led me to feel more of an outsider as an employee.

Reflections on My Research Position: The Opportunities

Being part of the extended police family did have many advantages, the majority of which match to the pros of conducting 'insider' research (Greene 2014) in terms of access to the research site. I was given unlimited access from the executive, and so had the freedom, ability, and relative ease (i.e. movement in police buildings, access to computer systems) to look at any aspect of restorative justice across the police force. Conducting interviews and focus groups was much easier than for an outsider. It was easy to obtain contact details for participants, book meeting rooms, and access police buildings. The settings were now familiar and after many years working in a police environment I was now comfortable and at ease. I can still vividly remember the culture shock I experienced in my first few months working both at a local police station, and again when I transferred to a busy police headquarters: the nauseating smell of cannabis in the lifts and hallways from drugs seizures; a strange, almost fearful reaction when confronted with a raft of uniformed police officers; trying to work out the rank structure and forms of address; and many more things that felt strange at first but to which I have now grown accustomed. This 'culture shock' is a potential research obstacle (Nash 1963), albeit one that quickly ceases (Aguilar 1981) and so whilst it would not necessarily prevent an outsider from conducting this research it did mean

that the fieldwork was quicker in that it did not require a period of accli-
matisation or learning.

In addition, the ease at which I was able to attend meetings helped
me to get a feel for all of the events and activities that were taking place.
Many steering group meetings were relatively informal and held in the
canteen and they were sometimes cancelled or rearranged. From the start
I was flexible and asked to be copied in on all emails. Being an insider
and available through force systems meant that those organising meetings
could see my availability. I was visible on the internal force messaging
system, and simple things such as passing people in corridors meant they
remembered to invite me to a meeting or to send me some information. A further advantage of my 'insider' status was my ability to blend
into these meetings and other research situations. Having access to the
building and not needing to be signed in at reception and escorted at
all times and wearing the same police force lanyard meant I was more
'invisible' and less likely to alter the research setting of a meeting or event
(Hockey 1993) compared to an outsider who would be required to wear
a bright red 'warning' visitor's lanyard.[1]

Reflections on My Research Position: The Barriers/Constraints

The opportunities outlined above match those documented in relation
to the 'insider researcher', but the main challenge involved juggling two
identities as an employee and as a researcher. Until I had reflected on my
research position and critically analysed the social implications of my status and position within the organisation, I was unable to move forward
in my research, yet my perception of my role and status was often tied
to experiences that were occurring outside of the field in my day-to-day
employment. Situations occurred out of the field that impacted on the
way I positioned myself in the research. Whilst small and often seem-

---

[1] Whilst seeming a small almost trivial thing we had all been trained to watch for these lanyards—
red signalled warning and we had to be prepared to challenge anyone wearing these lanyards if
unaccompanied.

ingly unimportant, there were various pressures to contend with—what answer to give when some colleagues and superiors would ask seemingly innocuous questions such as 'how's your PhD going?' was the most challenging (recognising that different people asked for different reasons, this often felt a very loaded question, the intention of which was very much dependent on our combined status in relation to both a workplace hierarchy and levels of academic achievement). I found that I developed a range of non-committal replies and often found myself being disparaging towards my research when among peers. When asked what I was doing I would respond, 'it's not very interesting, just about restorative justice and stuff'. This is not the typical 'elevator speech' PhD students are encouraged to practice[2] and it is in direct conflict with the outsider research role I was attempting to develop.

There was also the unmistakable impression amongst colleagues that, as a direct result of my doing this research, I was close to the executive. On various occasions my professional staff peers referred to me as 'having the ear' of the Chief Constable, which of course was not true. I often found myself taking pains to explain my thesis topic was something I had planned to do years ago, before working at the force. Even writing this chapter I include a section explaining how this was a topic I wanted to study before joining the police! My insider experience clearly (still) affects my writing and how I approached and justified my research topic and questions in order to show that I had not chosen to do the research to get closer to the executive.

I had not considered what my peers' reactions to my research and field-work would be before engaging in this research, nor had I considered how my reflective endeavours had oscillated between insider/outsider approaches. It was only when I had left the force on a career break to write up my findings that I was able to consider the positionality of civilian staff and the how this additional 'in between' space affected the focus of my reflexive endeavours. The remainder of this chapter will proceed to discuss this in more detail using excerpts from my fieldwork notes in order to demonstrate in more

---

[2] One of the many tips offered to PhD researchers is to practice a succinct explanation of your research in a few short sentences—as though you had the opportunity of sharing an elevator with someone of importance and only had a few minutes to 'sell' your project.

detail how these multiple status positions affected my interactions and how these interactions impacted on my perceived positionality.

Conducting Insider/Outsider Research

The lens through which narratives are analysed changes not only through the acquisition of new knowledge but as the result of the researcher's positionality (Berger 2015: 226). It is this insider/outsider dichotomy and the way in which I was entangled as a researcher and a practitioner when conducting criminal justice research that forms the basis of this next section. Using three excerpts, two taken from a participant observation in my researcher role, and the third from an incident that occurred in my employee role, I consider the way in which my insider/outsider status added a further element to my reflexive endeavours.

This first example uses two excerpts from a participant observation session of the new restorative approach training. This was an all-day event and these events happened in series over the course of the restorative justice re-implementation process. The different scenarios demonstrate how I constantly fluctuated between insider/outsider identities with each encounter:

> Sitting around the table, wearing my employee lanyard I felt part of (and accepted as part of) the steering group. Despite an initial 'round robin' at the start of the session where I had explained why I was there nothing particularly distinguished me as a researcher, as an outsider to the force: for this session everyone was wearing plain clothes, there were no uniforms and it had been made explicit that there was to be no differentiation amongst ranks everyone here was an equal member of the group (no one should use the terms Sir/Boss etc.). As the hours wore on it was becoming more and more difficult to remain an impartial observer as I was included in the group discussions, the only noticeable difference was that I was visibly making notes, although this had become so normal over the last few months I suspected I was being viewed as a meeting minute-taker ... over morning break, I was chatting to the Superintendent and in passing I men-

tioned that I was there on my day off, he was shocked by this and started to argue that I should be paid for attending, that it wasn't right for me to do this 'for free': he even went as far as to offer to sign my timesheets. I felt conflicted: I was flattered that a high-ranking officer was valuing my presence at the session, that I had been accepted as part of the steering group, as an 'insider' but I also wanted to stress that I was there independently in a research capacity. Somehow not being paid by the force to be there (even though my monthly pay from the force for my role as an intelligence analyst was my main source of income) made me feel like I was more independent. I felt worried about the offer to sign my timesheets, thinking about what my line manager would say. I felt like I was breaching some sort of policy; being absent from my paid employment but being considered as being 'at work' in another capacity. I had to remind myself that this had all been cleared, through the Chief Constable and through professional standards.

At the time I thought I had approached this day of training as a researcher—it was taking place away from headquarters and was completely focused on the implementation of the new restorative approach. I had introduced myself primarily by my researcher status (although I still wore my employee lanyard). However, I felt distanced from my employee role. My task that day was to gather as much information in relation to my research question as possible. This involved making notes about the various interactions between steering group members and also where I spoke. I was not recording the session so all notes were handwritten at the time and focused on the changes that were being made to the force training sessions. The encounter with the Superintendent highlights the fluidity of my role. My status was not just based on my own perception but the social construct of the situation.

Later during the lunch break from the training session I was in a little kitchen area. I could hear some officers talking at the door and then I overheard one saying he was being interviewed by 'some woman from the University tomorrow'. Whilst this was further confirmation that I was clearly viewed as an 'insider' and participants were talking freely around me, I worried that they had missed who I was and why I was there, and what did this mean in terms of active consent? At first I didn't know what to do. I felt a bit embarrassed that I was being talked about but also that I had overheard it. I decided to go and introduce myself, announcing myself as an 'outsider': that I was that woman from the University. In doing so I effectively stopped the conversation so I did not hear any further remarks. I felt awkward. It was a harsh reminder that I had another identity and I was being discussed and described based on a researcher identity alone. I had taken pains to be there in a research capacity yet was shocked that they had not put the two together and realised it was me, the person who had been at all the meetings. I was a faceless 'University woman'.

This experience forced me to recognise and acknowledge my dual identity. I was 'outed' as an outsider by overhearing a conversation that was only meant for insider ears. Whereas the earlier conversation with the superintendent had given me a sense of belonging, I now felt awkward and out of place. I considered what I had overheard and questioned whether I should have interrupted them or used the conversation as data: would I have reacted differently if I were an outsider researcher? This dual identity created this further layer to my reflexive endeavours: I had to revisit each interaction from multiple positions in order to understand the meanings behind them. I so fiercely tried to guard my 'independent research' status, to distance myself from my insider role that I did not appreciate how much my insider role, my acceptance by the group, and the cultural dynamics between myself and other officers, needed to be constantly worked in to my reflexive activities. Furthermore, it required consideration from numerous positions. I had to revisit each situation, each encounter from another direction: as an outsider, and insider, and someone in between.

Ultimately as the fieldwork progressed, I began to realise that there was no clear distinction between my role as an 'employee' and as a 'researcher'. Furthermore, as my research became less about restorative justice and more about police culture I had to question my role within the police: as staff I did not belong to the same sub culture as police officers. Whilst police staff culture is not comparable to that of officers, conducting this research did separate me from my peers. With a sense of irony it was noted that the more immersed I was in the research, the more of an 'outsider' I felt in my work role. This second example highlights how the insider/outsider roles collided not only when conducting research but when going about my daily work as an intelligence analyst too.

I arrived back at my desk with some lunch from the canteen to find a heightened level of activity in the office: a colleague informed me that the Chief Constable was on his way with the new Police Crime Commissioner (PCC). Abandoning my jacket potato I mirrored the actions of my colleagues and set up my computer so that some of my recent analysis was on the screen. We were given advice from our managers to remind ourselves of the force priorities and other key facts in case we were questioned about them. The tension in the office mounted: we could hear the visitors talking to another team located across the hallway so we all tried to look busy whilst listening for a sign as to when it would be our turn. My desk was directly behind the door, my back to anyone coming in. I wondered if they would come to me first or last: if I should risk eating some of my lunch, or let it get cold as we continued to wait.

Eventually they appeared and our line manager began to introduce the team and the range of work we did. As she was giving her introduction, the Chief Constable saw me and immediately came over, bringing the PCC with him (away from my line manager). I was introduced as someone 'incredibly intelligent' who was doing a PhD. The focus was immediately taken from the team to me personally and my doctoral research project. Shaking the PCC's hand he recognised my name. 'I am actually interviewing you tomorrow for my research,' I explained. Agreeing to speak with me further, the next day he was led away back to the task at hand to talk to other team members. Breathing a sigh of relief, I tried to surreptitiously sit back down at my desk; moments later the Chief Constable took up an empty seat opposite me: leaning back in his chair and putting his feet up on the table: he then proceeded to spend the entire 'office tour' asking me how my research was progressing. Feeling the eyes of my colleagues and line manager on me the whole time I was completely torn: the discussion with the Chief Constable felt inappropriate as I was there in my analyst role, but in this situation—as an employee—I was also powerless to change the topic. I felt under pressure to downplay my PhD and to steer the conversation back to the work the team was doing. Most of all I wanted the visit to end: my two roles had collided, I felt awkward, unsure of what to say, who to be. I wanted the whole situation to be over but I also realised a line had been crossed; a barrier had been created between my colleagues and myself.

This example reflects the difficulties of being and insider/outsider researcher and how different identities were both in constant conflict and simultaneously in danger of being merged. Throughout the research project I had begun to view reflexivity differently, it was more convoluted than the two-way street: the continuous influence between researcher and researched as described by Alvesson and Sköldberg (2009). I began to question not only which role I saw myself in, and which status I assigned to myself—but also which role and status was assigned to me. Furthermore, this was not only at times when I was 'in the field' but also across my working day. Just as insider and outsider positions are not dichotomous, there were multiple avenues of exploration. There was a need to rigorously reflect on new information that emerged concerning my identity as I would new information about the research topic. I had to approach each scenario from a different route: as a researcher, an 'outsider', as an employee, an 'insider', as a civilian and not an officer, somewhere 'in-between'. The introspective reflexivity required to conduct research that was ethical and reliable meant that all elements of my role and status were being rigorously probed.

Conclusion

It is frequently recognised that researchers are unlikely to fit into the neat categories of insider or outsider (Dwyer and Buckle 2009; Thomson and Gunter 2011; Berger 2015). In criminal justice research, the boundaries between researcher and practitioner are continually blurring and the professionalisation of the industry and the recent developments within the College of Policing are allowing more police officers and staff to conduct academic research meaning that the intersections of policy, research, and practice are continually at play. Furthermore, changes within criminal justice linked with privitisation, civilianisation, and restructuring of services mean that traditional roles and associated statuses are changing while new statuses have yet to be established. It is therefore important that the researcher recognises their position, and that they are able to continuously engage in reflexive practices, not only from and insider/

outsider perspective, but also from one that recognises the wide variety of positions that fall into the space between.

Understanding reflexivity as a two-way street between the researcher and the researched is a useful starting point (Alvesson and Sköldberg 2009) but it is important to recognise how positionality not only impacts the research, but also the reflexive process itself. This chapter has therefore demonstrated the importance of recognising that one's reflexive process not only changes when conducting 'insider', 'outsider', or a hybrid 'insider/outsider' research and that positionality is not only a consideration for each research project but for each moment within the research process, including the reflexive interpretation required when writing up the research findings. Incorporating researcher positionality as part of the reflexive process and recognising this position through the research journey from initial research questions, to fieldwork, to final text production the reflexive lens must constantly change focus in order to recognise the situated nature of their position. It is not enough to view the research process as a two-way street, one must consider which street, which status they are approaching the research at any given time. Like a roundabout, one might come out from this encounter at a different intersection and one must constantly revisit in order to ensure all avenues have been explored.

References

Aguilar, J. L. (1981) Insider research: An ethnography of a debate. In D. Messerschmidt (ed.) *Anthropologists at home in North America: Methods and issues in the study of one's own society*, Cambridge: Cambridge University Press: 15–26.

Alvesson, M., & Sköldberg, K. (2009). *Reflexive methodology: New vistas for qualitative research*, London: Sage.

Berger, R. (2015). 'Now I see it, now I don't: Researcher's position and reflexivity in qualitative research', *Qualitative Research* 15(2): 219–234.

Caless, B. (2007) '"Numties in Yellow Jackets": The nature of hostility towards the Police Community Support Officer in Neighbourhood Policing Teams', *Policing* 1(2): 187–195.

Case, S. and Haines, K. (2014) Reflective friend research: The relational aspects of social scientific research. In K. Lumsden and A. Winter (eds.) *Reflexivity in criminological research: Experiences with the powerful and the powerless*, Basingstoke: Palgrave Macmillan: 58–74.

Chan, J. (1996) 'Changing police culture', *British Journal of Criminology* 36(1): 109–134.

Cope, N. (2004) '"Intelligence led policing or policing led intelligence?" Integrating volume crime analysis into policing', *British Journal of Criminology* 44(2): 188–203.

Dwyer, S. C. and J. L. Buckle (2009) 'The space between: On being an insider-outsider in qualitative research', *International journal of qualitative methods* 8(1): 54–63.

Farkas, M. A. and P. K. Manning (1997) 'The occupational culture of corrections and police officers', *Journal of Crime and Justice* 20(2): 51–68.

Greene, M. J. (2014) 'On the inside looking in: Methodological insights and challenges in conducting qualitative insider research' *The Qualitative Report* 19 (29), 1–13.

Hayano, D. (1979) 'Auto-ethnography: Paradigms, problems, and prospects', *Human organization* 38(1): 99–104.

Holdaway, S. (Ed.) (1979) *The British police*, London: Edward Arnold.

Lumsden, K., & Winter, A. (2014) *Reflexivity in criminological research: Experiences with the powerful and the powerless*, Basingstoke: Palgrave Macmillan.

Manning, P. K. (1993) Toward a Theory of Police Organization: Polarities and Change International Conference on Social Change in Policing. Taipei.

Mawby, R. C. and A. Wright (2012) The police organisation. In T. Newburn (ed.) *Handbook of policing*, London: Routledge: 169–195.

Nash, D. (1963) 'The ethnologist as stranger: An essay in the sociology of knowledge', *Southwestern Journal of Anthropology* (1): 149–167.

Poulton, E. (2014) Having the balls: Reflections on doing gendered research with football hooligans. In Lumsden, K., & Winter, A. (eds.) *Reflexivity in criminological research: Experiences with the powerful and the powerless*, Basingstoke: Palgrave Macmillan: 77–89.

Reiner, R. and T. Newburn (2008). Police research. In R. King and E. Wincup (eds.) *Doing research on crime and justice*, Oxford, Oxford University Press.

Reuss-Ianni, E. (1983) *Two cultures of policing: Street cops and management cops*, New Brunswick, Transaction.

Romano, O. I. (1968) 'The anthropology and sociology of the Mexican American', *El Grito* 2: 13–26.

Rowe, M. (2007) 'Tripping over molehills: Ethics and the ethnography of police work', *International Journal of Social Research Methodology* 10(1): 37–48.

Thomson, P. and H. Gunter (2011) 'Inside, outside, upside down: The fluidity of academic researcher "identity" in working with/in school', *International Journal of Research & Method in Education* 34(1): 17–30.

Waddington, P. A. J. (1999) 'Police (canteen) sub-culture. An appreciation', *British Journal of Criminology* 39(2): 287–309.

Young, M. (1991) *An inside job: Policing and police culture in Britain*, Oxford: Oxford University Press.

15

Situated Perspectives on the Global Fight Against Torture

Andrew M. Jefferson

Introduction[1]

The contemporary global struggle against torture began in 1973 at a conference organised by *Amnesty International*. Almost a decade later the organisation now known as *DIGNITY—Danish Institute Against Torture* was founded as the first Centre set up to treat and rehabilitate victims of torture. This chapter builds on interviews with six members of DIGNITY staff. Their narratives draw on a rich and multi-textured set of experiences working to prevent torture in various parts of the world. The chapter does not endeavour to paint an organisational history. Rather, the aim is more modest, namely to draw out some central pivotal themes and consider the relationship between personal and institutional reflexivity.

---

[1] I'd like to thank the editors and reviewers for inviting me to be involved in this project and creating an opportunity to engage with some of my colleagues at DIGNITY in an alternative manner than usual. And thanks of course to those six colleagues who willingly and frankly shared their perspectives. May any liberties I might be perceived to have taken be forgiven.

A.M. Jefferson (✉)
Danish Institute Against Torture, Copenhagen, Denmark

S. Armstrong et al. (eds.), *Reflexivity and Criminal Justice*,
DOI 10.1057/978-1-137-54642-5_15

The narratives reveal a high degree of personal reflexivity, shown in overriding concerns with 'fit' within the organisation and concern about the organisation's ongoing trajectory and 'fit' within the broader discourses of international development and human rights. Drawing on previous work comparing institutional encounters between human rights NGOs and prisons in the global south, a notion of 'institutional agency' (Jefferson and Gaborit 2015) will be invoked and a suggestion made that more serious consideration of the institution's capability to think and act agentically might be a fruitful way to proceed with making sense of the apparent discrepancy between high levels of personal conviction and engagement in the anti-torture movement and more ambiguous levels of institutional identification.

Introducing and Situating DIGNITY

DIGNITY's vision is a world without torture and other forms of organised violence… Our goal is to ease human suffering after torture, to prevent torture and to be a global driving force in the development of new knowledge about torture and its consequences. (https://www.dignityinstitute.org/who-we-are/vision/)

By any account DIGNITY is a complex institution, working nationally and internationally with the rehabilitation of survivors of torture and the prevention of torture and organised violence through multiple forms of partnership and collaboration. Currently the work is divided around three primary themes: the rehabilitation of survivors, the prevention of torture in poor urban environments and the prevention of torture in places of detention. Through its prevention work, DIGNITY is directly caught up in the field of criminal justice. Criminal justice systems, law enforcement agents and other agents possessing public authority are targets of DIGNITY's interventions and knowledge generation efforts. Sometimes DIGNITY staff engage directly with state agencies but more often they work through locally based NGOs, supporting their activities financially and through capacity building and various kinds of technical support to ameliorate the effects of torture and/or campaign for and implement measures designed to prevent torture, for example, preventive monitoring of places of detention. The organisation is staffed by a range of professionals from a variety of disciplines (e.g. medicine, law, psychology, social work, international development studies, anthropology, accountancy, etc.).

DIGNITY seeks to affect policy, transform practice and generate knowledge. To make a link to the overarching theme of this volume one might characterise the torture prevention work as being the regulation and inhibition of state (and non-state) crime.

Theoretical Orientation: Towards 'History in Person' and 'History in Institution'

The material presented below could be subject to a Bourdieu-inspired analysis: it is about contestation, about diverse positions within a field of power, about, in effect, the differential distributions and influence of symbolic capital (see Bourdieu 1984, 2000). But notwithstanding the potential benefits of such a framing I prefer to lean on the theoretical work of anthropologist Jean Lave (2011). Like Bourdieu, she emphasises the significance of contentious local practice. But she works harder to overcome the dualities inherent in much post-Cartesian thinking. Together with Dorothy Holland (Holland and Lave 2001) she has invoked a notion of 'history in person' to capture the way in which intimate identities and enduring struggles coalesce in local contentious practices. Rather than accept structure and agency as discrete poles on a pre-given axis she advocates exploring how the *relations between* structure and subjectivity are produced by and in practice. I have elaborated on this source of theoretical inspiration elsewhere (Jefferson 2014; Jefferson and Gaborit 2015). For example, in a chapter on the situated production of legitimacy, I argued against the paradigm that analyses legitimacy in terms of power-holders and audiences, suggesting instead that we need to attend to the complex ways in which relations framed in such ways come into being.

In a book called *Human Rights in Prisons: comparing institutional encounters* based on a research project that examined encounters between NGOs and prisons in three different countries Liv Gaborit and I extended Jean Lave's idea of history in person to the level of institutions (see Jefferson and Gaborit 2015). Drawing most significantly on Mary Douglas (1986) but also on new work by Lorna Rhodes on prisons we experimented with the concept of institutional agency, the idea that institutions act and have effects of their own that are more than equal to the sum of their constituent human or non-human parts. And we wrote of history-in-institutions in an attempt to capture the way institutional identities and enduring material, political, discursive, local and global struggles produce each other through local institutional practices such as those of an NGO. In many ways this is what follows here, not an institutional history but a partial account of how particularly positioned subjects reproduce understandings of the NGO and the business of which they are a part at the same time as they make sense of their own changing roles and positions within social, institutional and working trajectories. The study that features in this chapter did not set out with theoretical ambitions in mind. It was first and foremost an empirical project. Nevertheless it can be framed as an attempt to make sense of the complex and multi-faceted positionings and self-perceptions of persons-in-practice (Jefferson and Huniche 2009) as they produce, through participation in social practice, reconfigurations of the structures in which they work and the subjectivity they desire. In doing so, it also offers food for thought in relation to history in institution and suggests that it might be worthwhile to pursue a further line of enquiry in relation to institutional reflexivity.

Methodology and Sample

This chapter traces and explores two specific and significant themes that emerged as interviewees shared their experiences of engaging in the fight against torture. The themes were significant for the interviewees but we will see that they also have broader significance for understanding institutional reflexivity, and the ways in which specific phenomena (in this case torture as a singular cause) come to organise practice. Adopting an inductive and interpretive approach based on loosely structured interviews that at times resembled conversations (though one part listened more intently than usual and the other shared more frankly) the chapter illuminates the central themes of *self and the organisation* on the one hand, and perceptions about *torture as a unique phenomenon* on the other. By doing so the analysis casts much needed light on an NGO understood as a living, breathing, situated institution as narrated via the perspectives of a selection of its employees.

The chapter is based on interviews with six members of DIGNITY staff whom between them have 104 years in the anti-torture business. They have worked for DIGNITY for an average of 17 years and have an average age of 56 (range 47–64). The author's career (15 years at DIGNITY) and the careers of the interviewees have overlapped considerably. We have, to some extent, occupied the same empirical world. We have watched the organisation develop, watched each other develop and contributed to each other's and the organisation's development.

Two of the interviewees can be roughly classified as occupying core administrative/organisational positions; two others are predominantly researchers; and two may be classified as interventionists or change agents, though with somewhat different approaches. Criteria for identification of these six persons included length of experience, not being the author's direct manager, being a manageable number and being representative of a range of positions. Four were female and two male. Three of the interviews were conducted in English and three in Danish. Translations are my own. The interviews were not transcribed in full but listened to repeatedly and significant sections then transcribed and subject to further analysis

Each interview began with a preliminary, open question about the significance of being part of a global struggle against torture before flowing in directions that the interviewee largely decided. Efforts were made to cover the following topics: the nature of the work, motives and driving force, the relationship with international partners, the significance of professional or disciplinary backgrounds and the challenges of interdisciplinarity, the direction of the anti-torture business and the risks of activities having unintended consequences. Each interview closed with a question about the cost of working against torture: is there a price to pay?

Emergent Themes

As I conducted and listened to the interviews and then read my notes and transcriptions, I was in search of rationales, motives, driving forces, contradictions, dynamics and clues about institutional trajectories. In the presentation and discussion that follows I try to bring the convergent and divergent perspectives into conversation with one another adding a meta-reflexive layer which strives to be not just one more situated voice but an analytic voice juxtaposing and questioning, hesitating and puzzling and seeking new questions and points of curiosity. (This is partly how I conceive of the role of research within the organisation.)

For the purpose of this chapter, I have identified only two themes to dwell on. The first relates to people's self-perceptions and views on what drives them. How do they see their 'fit' in the fight against torture? What values do they identify as meaningful to them? What matters to them and why? The second relates to perceptions of the anti-torture business, with particular focus on the uniqueness (or not) of the cause or its potential and actual embeddedness within the broader discourses of international development on the one hand, and human rights on the other[2].

These themes will be probed in exploratory fashion as one might explore a fault line or seam of ore sometimes delving deep, sometimes staying at the surface seeking out variations in appearance and substance.

Theme 1: Self and the Organisation

For a number of the interviewees, perhaps unsurprisingly, being part of the anti-torture struggle was about participation in a worthwhile cause and an expression of a commitment to values. One spoke explicitly of

---

[2] In the first version of this paper some space was given over to consideration of an additional theme, namely whether there is a price to pay for individuals engaged in anti-torture work. The consensus was basically that costs, if existent were minimal or worth it and could not be compared to the price paid by activists on the front-line. Despite what seemed like a reasonable hypothesis to me—that the fight against torture might leave its warriors marked in some way—interviewees were having none, or very little, of this.

the importance of being 'part of something bigger, part of something where you take a stand, have an opinion, where you desire something.' Others spoke of the intrinsic worth of human beings, of social justice, of a 'foundational belief in the good in people'. One, expressing a form of universal obligation, stated 'we cannot just close our eyes' invoking the idea of human suffering that cannot be ignored and referencing 'that responsibility we all have'.

While there was general consensus that a similar set of humanistic values informed the anti-torture movement at the global scale some concern was expressed about the tension between such values and the demands of running a top-professional, modern organisation. Changing external conditions and the expansion of the organisation from a handful of relatively like-minded individuals on a pioneering mission over three decades ago to a highly diversified apparatus with a relatively large portfolio of projects nationally and globally have from some perspectives resulted in a reorientation away from core person-driven concerns. Some were concerned with the risk that organisational modernisation, professionalisation and bureaucratisation might mean a dilution of the commitment to transcendent values like justice and equality and the desire to prevent human suffering. In different ways interviewees expressed the idea—more or less strongly—that as one put it 'I still have an activist in the belly'.

One interviewee recounted an exchange during which she was shocked to encounter a colleague whose values seemed at odds with her own, someone who seemed less interested in the sufferings of children in conflict and more interested in profiling the organisation. She expressed considerable dismay: 'I felt totally alienated' she said, as if her worldview had been fundamentally challenged. What this interviewee clearly expressed was that she was in the business not for DIGNITY's sake but for the sake of victims of torture. Her orientation was external not internal. And she was not alone in this.

In the light of the ongoing professionalisation of the organisation, some nostalgia was expressed for the early days referring, for example, to 'a fellowship of values' that informed those days. But the desirability of being part of a fellowship of values is not self-evident to all. One interviewee spent considerable time speaking about the gradual reconciliation of his academic integrity with his institutional position describing how it took some time to work out what it meant for him to be part of the anti-torture movement, part of a movement that 'puts one particular victim at the centre.' Over time he did figure out 'how to accept and embrace' his participation in the anti-torture movement. 'I've found my way' he said, 'but it was not evident or easy'. This contrasts somewhat with the ways in which others seemed to find the anti-torture movement as a natural expression of their values and convictions.

This interviewee is less driven by values and more by the opportunities to connect. As he put it in answer to a question about what drives him, what sustains him, what gives him strength: 'it's all about relationships isn't it, relationships with all different kinds of people.' He continued 'as you probably realise the first person I think about in the morning is not the torture victim in XX or XX. It's the relationships I have with people who are also interested (laughing awkwardly) in that world.' His laughter indicated a sense of unease about this identification-from-a-distance and he proceeded to provide what he called 'a more legitimate' account of what drives him, namely 'some sense of social justice'. Here it was values like equality, and fair distribution of resources that shone through the account laced with an almost visceral identification with people who have 'the odds stacked against them' and against the rich and the powerful. 'What legitimacy' he asked 'do the rich have for stealing?'... 'I can hardly breathe in their company' ... 'the world is an unfair world; I think the rich and the powerful are callous and shameless.' This identification with people who have the odds stacked against them or with people heroically fighting almost impossible odds was present in a number of the interviews.

For some, the encounter with victims of torture through their work at DIGNITY was their first introduction to a 'dark side' of which they were previously unaware. One interviewee referred to himself as being 'like an innocent traveler in the world' prior to his employment at DIGNITY. That quickly changed as he was exposed during an international mission to the 'horror show' of Inge Genefke, DIGNITY's founding mother. This 'horror show' took the form of a lecture that showed the evils of torture in all their graphic detail, designed to shock and evoke 'horror, anger, indignation... to catalyse emotions'

This interviewee is driven less by values than by the inspirational example of others though he expresses a strong belief in solidarity and support where possible: 'what matters to me is to show the solidarity and find ways to support the struggle, the everyday struggle for change somewhere very far away from my own safe environment.' He consistently situates the anti-torture struggle within a broader development discourse and he consistently downplays his own role compared with those who on far off shores 'had devoted their life to fight against torture... often based on their own experiences'. His own values and position are secondary to those of his heroes, to those on the front-line, to those who have experienced torture on their own bodies and struggled to resist and fight back in situ: 'Over the years (encounters with such people) matured me and gave me... empathy and a strong feeling of being honoured to get to know these people and learn about their work and offer my small contribution.'

The rift between this faraway world and his world creates a dissonance that seems in some ways to have informed his working life. He spoke of being driven by the 'opportunity to get a snapshot of these enormously courageous human rights defenders all over the world' without whom, ' our societies would be more inhumane'. He described them as heroes he admires and respects contrasting his own safe Danish context with their 'conditions of life and death'. He contrasted his personality type with theirs: 'I'm not a daring person. I am more like a disciple type' ascribing to himself the task of the 'messenger... bringing news across borders from one human rights defender to the other.'

Another interviewee spoke of the rare victories in the fight against torture but implied that encounters with 'terrible destinies and fantastic people' were likewise inspirational. The simplicity of torture prohibition as a fact (torture *is* prohibited) was appealing to her. No beating about the bush. No nuance. Thou shalt not torture. Full stop. She is not driven by 'fluffy' values or over-complicated rationales. Indeed, along with valuing people equally she values clear and simple communication. But first and foremost: 'what matters is that what I do has attitude.' I understand this in a deeper sense than its simple, literal meaning might bestow. What she implies is not simply that opinions are expressed, or that there are principles at stake but that there is an edge to the work and it involves a deliberate stance-taking. Informed by a sense of justice instilled in her while quite young she is committed to a basic core value of helping people and ensuring they are treated decently and she does this by keeping both feet on the ground and helping organise the organisation.

Another evoked a more action-oriented source of drive. What inspired her to find the opportunity to work at DIGNITY 'almost too good to be true' was the opportunity to be personally committed: 'it fitted with engaging myself in something I thought was important'. The cause had value; she identified with it from the beginning. And she is driven by being able to apply herself and her expertise often at the front-line working with DIGNITY's international partners enabling them to 'be better able to control their economy, so economy control can be positive and so one can best exploit the available resources'. This is a facilitative role that includes hands on contact with partners and plenty of travel. 'I am grumpy that I can't travel next week', she shared. Stereotypes of people occupying such roles within organisations abound. She does not buy them, does not accept them, and no longer gets offended by them. She doesn't know to what degree colleagues share her view of accounting systems as lenses onto context or her view of financial accounts as alternative forms of telling a story about resource use. She shares, 'I think some might call me pedantic, I call it attention to detail. Accounting is an art not an exact science'.

More or less abstract values or commitments to principle might drive some people. Others are driven by passion, and in such cases, distinctions between work (professional engagement) and private life are hard to maintain. One interviewee put it this way when asked about her thoughts on her role in the anti-torture business: 'it means everything to me, it means a whole lot. It's not limited to my professional engagement; it's very much part of who I am. It's very much linked to the basic values that I have in life.' She is driven, she says, by a 'fundamental belief in… the need to change things on this globe to prevent torture and make sure that one day we won't have torture anymore'. She is certainly able to articulate values associated with this core belief: 'respect for other human beings, equality between human beings, that everybody, not only those living in this country, should have freedom, freedom from want, freedom from fear'. But most striking during the interview was reference to the rage underpinning her engagement.

Her upbringing that included exposure to progressive attitudes towards the marginalised in society and to international conflicts and injustice paved the way for a commitment to the anti-torture struggle but it was encounters with victims that she credits with fuelling the rage that still today occasionally causes uncomfortable moments at dinner parties when the 'blood bubbles'. The rage, which is 'more than indignation' she said, is related to impotency: 'The rage is there because… you feel quite insignificant… You sit in front of a human being and you see what harm has been done to that person completely unjustified and of course you feel compassion in that close relation and then rage towards the wider community, rage towards those harm-doers… and you feel powerless'.

What is clear from the above is that the work matters to people but also that some effort is required to ensure an ongoing match between personal and institutional values under changing conditions. Whether driven primarily by values, convictions, emotions, or politics, fitting in, making a meaningful contribution and being able to make sense of one's contribution in the light of previous experience and ongoing development are all central aspects of being constituted as a subject and negotiating one's own role in the fight against torture. Each of our interviewees is driven by forces that keep them moving, keep them on their toes. What is also clear is that being embedded within DIGNITY creates an outlet, a means of expressing convictions, values and politics that is in part conditional on DIGNITY's survival as an organisation. Paradoxically DIGNITY enables people to 'do justice' while organisational survival strategies (professionalisation, in other words) are from some perspectives seen as inimical to the foundations of that 'doing' as we will learn more about below.

Theme 2: Torture – A Singular Cause?

Is torture 'the mother of all human rights violations' as one interviewee quoted one of his heroes as arguing or is it simply one violation among many? From the perspective of the international community, torture is acknowledged as a peremptory norm, a norm of *jus cogens*. It is universally prohibited.[3] But does torture's unique status demand a unique or a more integrated response?

DIGNITY was the first organisation of its kind to be supported by government money: 'it was totally unique at that time'. Its founders were pioneers responding to what they saw as a specific and unique problem. For some torture is unique because it is extreme in itself. But it is also, claimed one interviewee, an extreme attack on the core values with which she identifies, values like respect, and the intrinsic worth of the human being. It is therefore—because they are undermined by torture—that such values are vital cornerstones of the anti-torture business. For another, torture, and the lack of respect for bodily integrity it implies, is a basic threat to human thriving: 'for humans to be happy... one of the key barriers to that is torture'. The way in which torture 'totally takes power from people' was another reason one interviewee privileged the work against torture even while she recognised it might make tactical sense to join forces against other forms of oppression, for example, poverty.

So, torture can be seen as so extreme that it intrinsically justifies a movement in its name. But not everyone will be persuaded. Another interviewee noted that one of the challenges of occupying a unique terrain is the need to 'convince people that the most important thing is the anti-torture business.' There may be political leverage to be gained from granting torture a unique status but it may also be counterproductive to decontextualise and reify torture to an almost other-worldly form of crime, at least according to one interviewee who argued that perhaps it should be brought down by a notch or two in order to have more purchase in the real world: 'There is too much horror associated

---

[3] Janis and Noyes (2006) quote, for example, a much-cited appeals court judgement (in the case of Filartiga v. Pena-Irala) which stated how 'the torturer has become, like the pirate and the slave trader before him, *hostis humani generis*, an enemy of all mankind.' Further, Peter Kooijmans, the special rapporteur on torture writing in 1986 put it this way: 'Torture is now absolutely and without any reservation prohibited under international law whether in time of peace or war. In all human rights instruments the prohibition of torture belongs to the group of rights from which no derogation can be made... If ever a phenomenon was outlawed unreservedly and unequivocally it is torture.' (Kooijmans 1986).

with it so it has become inapplicable… By constantly talking about torture as the worst crime of all we do ourselves a disservice'.

Another interviewee engaged in an honest appraisal of his own position describing how he had previously believed that 'torture was a more noble cause than the work on other rights… but recently I may have begun to think differently'. He elaborated on how today he feels we may be better off forming alliances with other groups involved in the struggle for rights in order to avoid 'putting ourselves on a pedestal.' He gives the founders credit for aggressively pursuing early tactics to profile *the* cause but fears the risk of alienation from other rights groups and development organisations should the movement be too particularistic today.

Another interviewee feared the dilution of the cause due to what she perceived as a reorientation from people and values to administration and institutional survival. There may be an ease with which one can identify with a singular cause compared with the more tricky job of harmonising personal values with a more diffuse and administration-heavy modern organisation engaged in a variety of tactical alliances. Where personal identification with the cause is the strong driving force diffusion can be a demotivating factor. From this perspective, the organisation is never more important than the cause. And paying only lip service to the cause is clearly undesirable even if sometimes evident: 'sometimes the overarching goal of the fight against torture is reduced to mere words'.

Perhaps it is inevitable that an organisation seeking to consolidate, become increasingly efficient and adapt to changing conditions (financial and political) becomes more inward looking and self-referential, even self-absorbed? Some of the interviewees saw alarming signs that this was so and expressed this in unequivocal terms. For example, 'the new DIGNITY is only interested in DIGNITY' and 'We take care of our own skin'. At the same time, it would seem relatively natural that the place of a pioneering institution would fade in time as a movement develops around the issue which the organisation has been at the forefront of profiling. It seems to have been the case that as the anti-torture movement developed DIGNITY's role in it diminished. As one interviewee put it 'DIGNITY now is one of many organisations whereas in the start we were something quite unique'.

What is revealed above are some of the ways in which torture as a singular phenomenon serves to anchor and secure the organisation, perhaps more so in the early days. But also that torture's singularity does not go uncontested. Kelly et al. have shown how the claim to uniqueness of the phenomenon may have the unintended consequence of meaning the extent of torture (e.g. in poor urban neighbourhoods) ends up being 'under perceived' (Kelly et al. forthcoming). And similarly, Canning has illustrated how the desire to definitively pin down torture in legal terms results in the relative invisibility of some forms of torture, particularly sexual torture, to the detriment of service provision with regard to such incidents (Canning 2016). Whatever the merits or not of torture's relative singularity it is still true that the anti-torture movement has never stood totally alone. Below I consider the relationship between the anti-torture movement and the discourses of international development and human rights.

Torture, International Development and Human Rights

Today, the anti-torture movement is arguably more or less naturally allied with three main discourses: trauma discourse, human rights discourse and development discourse. One interviewee reported how a Norwegian specialised clinic for victims of torture was swallowed up within a University department dealing with broader trauma-related issues, articulating anxieties on behalf of DIGNITY's own specialised clinic.

DIGNITY's prime source of funding has, since very early on been the Danish Foreign Ministry, the funds coming from the international development aid budget. Today however, the clinic is funded separately as part of the state health-care programme. So, in this sense the organisation is inherently part of the complex and multi-faceted assemblage of the development business.

In interviews, different accounts were offered of the significance of development vis-à-vis torture. Two of the interviewees expressed particularly strong views on the importance of being schooled in 'development thinking' in order to be able to engage meaningfully with partners in the south. Another expressed an extremely strong sense of identification with partners from the south expressing that relationships with them were his preeminent raison d'etre: 'there is a new fault line in the organisation between those who think the [local] partners [working on the ground against torture] are the most important and those that think DIGNITY is the most important and I squarely identify with those who think the partners are the most important,' he stated.

For one interviewee the early realisation that torture is a condition of life for the poor informed his inclination to link the fight against torture with development politics. 'I realised it was something that was an everyday condition of existence for especially poor people.' He went on 'the poor were caught up, trapped, being put at risk because of their lack of voice and power... it was not only something hitting hard on political opposition or students at rallies but a condition of life for poor people'. According to this interviewee an orientation to development and the conditions of existence of poor people offers a broader point of departure than the lenses of law or medicine (dominant discourses in the movement) which all too easily run the risk of functioning as 'exclusive clubs' with vocabularies few can understand operating at a remote distance from realities on the ground. For this interviewee proximity, and an orientation to local needs and immediate action (when necessary) is important. While not wholly dismissive of medical or legal discourses he resents the exclusivity and remoteness of these paradigms and believes the value of local innovators and change agents is underestimated. He contrasted local organisations in the 'jungle of Calcutta' committed to local engagements for local improvements with the discourses dominating in 'Geneva or New York or Copenhagen'. Another interviewee also alluded to the richness of the *in situ* struggle and the relative poverty of 'parachuting in' providing technical input, maybe showing or declaring solidarity and making a relatively quick exit. The sceptical interviewee acknowledged nevertheless how the medical and legal professions each in their own way, according to their respective orientations have played a role in the spread of the anti-torture movement, a typical pattern being doctors heading clinics for victims, and lawyers setting up advocacy organisations and speaking vociferously on behalf of victims. Indeed, the historical significance of lawyers and doctors cannot be underestimated. And it is not surprising that two such historically powerful disciplines have played a key role. As one interviewee put it: 'they are the two most authoritative languages that exist around these kinds of things: one is the authoritative language of the body, the other the authoritative language of the law.' Evidenced here is what Bourdieu would identify as clashes over the right to define the field. Whose language, whose symbolic capital carries the most force? What drives the distinctive influence of particular privileged professions? From where does their legitimacy come?

Echoing these questions, one interviewee not surprisingly acknowledged the inevitable clashes between people representing different disciplines: 'there are professional clashes that derive from the fact that we look at the world differently... immersed in own discipline with the conviction that yes with these and these tools...'. She identifies core blindness and the inability to see from the perspective of the other, to hear and speak the language of the other as central causal factors in the inability to exploit the possibilities of transdisciplinarity more effectively.

While regretting the disciplinary compartmentalisation she also expresses some doubts about the close historical ties between the work against torture and for human rights. While recognising the way the anti-torture movement 'grew out of human rights discourse and is still anchored in human rights discourse', she questions what she perceives as a narrow focus on human rights norms recognising that torture thrives in dysfunctional societies and that such societies are not always ripe for the planting or harvesting of human rights norms. 'If you have dysfunctional societies, she claims 'human rights norms are worth nothing'.

Another interviewee approached the question of transdisciplinarity from a different angle asking rhetorically to what kind of sources different people go to seek out answers to questions: to the home page of DANIDA, or the World Bank, or to an academic database: 'When it works the best here all those different languages all those different registers, all those different communities are brought together in a productive way and when it works the worst it's the opposite' He spoke of relishing the diversity but being simultaneously frustrated by it: 'I really enjoy that but at the same time it is super frustrating... these different communities have their own moralities their own ethics... at its worst each epistemic community elevates its position to a position of truth... pretending there are no other ways of speaking for others than ours'.

Identification, Passion and Professionalisation

For whose sake does the anti-torture movement exist? Three of the interviewees aligned themselves very solidly with international partners, desiring to connect with them, support them, facilitate their processes. One went as far as to explicitly resist the imposition of specific systems on local partners claiming that would be imperialist. She perceived her job as enhancing their ability to engage in relations with us (as donor) that make sense for them. The ability of local organisations to navigate, manoeuver and translate the demands put on them from the outside was a source of inspiration for her: 'I am inspired by their way of approaching implementation, the amazing navigation they do, their ability to report to us in a way we are satisfied with at the same time as they have such terrible conditions.' Like an earlier-cited interviewee it is very clear that she perceives DIGNITY as existing for the sake of the partners rather than the inverse and she worries about the price that might be paid by partners by DIGNITY's drive to expand and about the underlying motives for expansion. She is committed to the organisational development of DIGNITY's partners and their establishment as independent, sustainable organisations: 'It's organisational development that is the most important. I say this often' she said. 'If one is good to systemise work one is better to develop. Being systematic is about learning. If one has the information and knows what one has done before, one has a bigger chance to learn. Informed decision making is so important.'

This is arguably one of the major rationalities behind DIGNITY's increasing professionalisation over the last decade or so. In the following quote, this is suggested but it also carries a warning:

> when it started DIGNITY was a health-based humanitarian organisation that had a good heart and did a lot of good stuff out of empathy and good feeling.... I think what has happened has been professionalisation and us being much more strategic about what we do… to some extent… at the expense of the passion … the human link, the compassion is still there but it's a little bit more buried than it was to begin with…

A basic split is implied between rationality and passion, between Plato and Dionysius. My sense is some of my interviewees would resist the purity of this split. One, however, reflected on the advantages of increasing professionalisation: 'I think it's about time… it speaks to me. The lines are becoming clearer and it's not so muddy as before.' She continued, 'we must act more professionally while staying aware that the world out there looks different. We must not be rigid, but fluid, flexible.' She was wary of the work becoming over-technical and too ego-driven. 'We don't have the necessary respect for each other's work. That is a shame especially in this work'. The result of unnecessary competition and posturing was to her mind too little decisiveness and too much stalling. At the same time, she was aware that such dynamics are likely common, if not inevitable, in most organisations.

Some interviewees miss a more activist line, a greater outspokenness and a tension does seem evident between experience and identification-based passion on the one side and rational professionalism on the other:

> Inge Genefke was the incarnation of DIGNITY in those old days and she was not driven by what is most sensible. She was driven by her indignation and her rage … we now tend to put our minds into the work much more which does I think paralyse this one side.

The move towards a more professional and robust organisation is deliberate and not accidental. As one interviewee put it 'I mean we obviously do it because we think it has greater impact'. She later added 'the movement needs both; I think we are moving increasingly in the one direction', namely the one of professionalisation where passion risks extinction.

Conclusion: Towards Institutional Reflexivity

In this chapter, so far we have considered two stand-out themes that emerged from interviews with six highly experienced campaigners from within the anti-torture movement. We have considered their sources of motivation, and their perspectives on their fit within the organisation and the fit of anti-torture work within other discourses. In this final concluding section, I begin by revisiting the methodology to consider the way it in itself invoked a degree of reflexivity which nonetheless does not detract from the high degree of reflexivity revealed by the interviewees. What, I wonder, might it mean for the reflexivity of the organisation if there were greater opportunities for in-depth exchanges in an arena of appropriate attunement? I end with some further reflections on why it might be worthwhile to subject the idea of institutional reflexivity to further interrogation.

During the interviews, I got a sense that it was significant that, as mentioned earlier, part of the trajectories discussed had been shared. We had travelled some of the same roads together albeit sometimes in different vehicles, sometimes pulling in the same and at other times in different directions. Some interviewees invoked our pre-existing relationship only implicitly by a tone of voice or a look as we discussed. Others were more explicit, for example, the interviewee who speculated with reasonable grounds 'probably like yourself' as he talked about his struggle to reconcile academic and activist rationales underlying his work. Later, while discussing Bourdieu's notion of the Parvenu (relevant to the prevailing theme of 'fit') he attempted to draw me further in 'I recognise that in other people... I recognise it in you as well'. Another colleague alluded to the self-evident in what he said as he discussed the way in which 'all professions come with their own concepts and vocabularies and therefore occupy a piece of the verbal reality of this whole anti-torture jargon' adding 'you know that very well', alluding to my own position in various debates and conflicts about how to define the anti-torture field and what languages and traditions are best suited to make sense of it and give direction. Another, while extolling the virtues of the quotidian, problematised theorising: 'There is too much theorising... *You* theorise too much'.

These different ways of drawing me into their own reflections signal the different kind of relationships we have had but also that as interviewer I was not a simple mirror or sponge. During the interviews, the weight of a shared history implicated us. All indicated they had enjoyed our talk either through direct responses to an email I sent expressing gratitude or in conversations with colleagues that I subsequently heard about. One of the interviewees suggested we should have more conversations such as these, without the recording, saying it was 'more like an intimate conversation than an interview' apparently not realising the role the interview as method plays in creating such an atmosphere. Adopting the role of curious, active listener clearly had an effect on the quality of the dialogue, and may even have reconfigured my relationships with the interviewees.

Thus, it is clear that I am a complicit participant in the contentious positionings under discussion in this chapter. It is likely that my sympathy for what Bourdieu would call spiritual authority rather than temporal authority, for 'authenticity' rather than 'order' (Emirbayer and Williams 2005), for passion rather than professionalism shows through however much I have sought to bracket my own dispositions. It has been a deliberate choice not to declare a position in the various debates raised. I have resisted the urge to add my own perceptions to the mix in any structured fashion. I have not interviewed myself! My position, or my display of symbolic capital if you will, is most vividly displayed by the fact of my having conducted this small study and drafted this chapter. Bourdieu would say this is a 'refraction' of a pre-existing structural tension between the 'holders of economic, political or social privilege on the one side, and of intellectual pre-eminence on the other' (Emirbayer and Williams 2005: 692) and that this chapter represents an act of subversion. I have chosen a particular form of reflexivity—the reflexivity of a book chapter—that involves the partial suspending of my own reflexivity. This irony may be of interest in itself to scholars of reflexivity. In the light of this practice—of withholding reflexivity—we see how reflexivity itself is caught up in the messy production of relations between structure and subjectivity within situated institutional practice.

What is of further significance in the subtle—and not so subtle—invocation of a shared institutional history above is the way it hints at the possibility of an institutional reflexivity that we might have in common but which is more than the sum of our individual reflexive competencies. If institutions are agentic or at least have agency attributed to them (Jefferson and Gaborit 2015) then surely they also have the potential to be reflexive? We might ask whether the doubts about the direction of the organisation alluded to in the above analysis are expressions of a frustration that the limits of the institution reflect the limitations of its component parts (i.e. the parts of which it is the sum) or we might ask more radically perhaps whether they express a forlorn hope that the institution itself ought to be able to think, learn and act agentically and reflexively but does not do so sufficiently. My suspicion is that the interviewees in this study would find the idea of institutional reflexivity desirable. What I would advocate would be the pursuit of a form of institutional reflexivity that is not overdetermined and technocratic but open-ended and organic, a form of reflexivity that frames, evokes and channels the drive, passion and commitment evidenced in these interviews, a form of reflexivity that acknowledges and respects difference.

One final remark: the perspectives shared in the interviews conducted in order to write this chapter are heterogeneous. And as mentioned in the introduction high levels of personal commitment and investment are indicated alongside more ambivalent gestures of institutional identification. How can we make sense of this? How does such a diverse collection of perspectives nevertheless hold together? Exploring the value of thinking about institutional and political practices in terms of assemblages John Allen (2011) has considered the paradox of things holding together *because rather than in spite of* the co-existence of diverse logics and practices and different levels of identifications. This state of affairs can persist, he argues, by virtue of 'relationships and things that jostle, co-exist, interfere and entangle one another' (2011: 154). Coherence and homogeneity are not to be expected. Non-coherence and tension are productive. An orientation to assemblages means attending to the way hanging together because—rather than in spite of—is a function of connections and relationships rather than top-down dictates or pre-determined goals. An implication of this could be that organisations like DIGNITY should try harder to reflexively and consciously exploit the productive potential of inevitable tensions, fault lines and conflicts that can be understood as the products of the complex interplay between ongoing histories-in-person and ongoing histories-in-institution.

References

Allen, John (2011) 'Powerful Assemblages?', *Area* Vol. 43(2): 154–157.

Bourdieu, Pierre (1984) *Distinction: A Social Critique of the Judgment of Taste*, Harvard: Harvard University Press.

Bourdieu, P. (2000) *Pascalian Meditations*, Cambridge: Polity Press.

Canning, V. (2016) 'Unsilencing Sexual Torture: Responses to Refugees and Asylum Seekers in Denmark', *British Journal of Criminology* 6 (3): 438–455.

Douglas, M. (1986) *How Institutions Think*, New York: Syracuse University Press.

Emirbayer, M. and Williams, E. M. (2005) 'Bourdieu and Social Work', *Social Service Review* vol. 79(4): 689–724.

Holland, D. and Lave, J. (2001) *History in Person. Enduring Struggles, Contentious Practice, Intimate Identities,* Santa Fe, NM/Oxford: SAR Press, James Currey.

Janis, M. and Noyes, J. (2006) *International Law: Cases and Commentary*, 3rd edn., New York: West Publishing.

Jefferson, A. M. (2014) The Situated Production of Legitimacy: Perspectives from the Global South. In J. Tankebe and A. Liebling (Eds.) *Legitimacy and Criminal Justice: An International Exploration*, Oxford: Oxford University Press.

Jefferson, A. M. and Gaborit, L. S. (2015) *Human Rights in Prisons: Comparing Institutional Encounters in Kosovo, Sierra Leone and the Philippines,* Basingstoke: Palgrave Macmillan.

Jefferson, A. M. and Huniche, L. (2009) '(Re)Searching for Persons in Practice: Field-Based Methods for Critical Psychological Practice Research', *Qualitative Research in Psychology* 6 (1 and 2): 12–27.

Kelly, T., Jensen, S., Anderson, M. K., Christiansen, C., Sharma, J. R. (forthcoming) 'Torture and Ill-treatment Under Perceived Human Rights Documentation and the Poor', *Human Rights Quarterly* (accepted 18 March 2016).

Kooijmans, P. (1986) *Torture and Other Cruel, Inhuman or Degrading Treatment or Punishment.* Research Report, UN Special Rapporteur UN DOC E/CN.4/1986/15.

Lave, J. (2011) *Apprenticeship in Critical Ethnographic Practice,* Chicago: University of Chicago Press.

16

Ethical Criminologists Fly Economy: Process-oriented Criminological Engagement 'Abroad'

Jarrett Blaustein

Introduction

Criminology has developed into a transnational discipline (Aas 2011; Aas 2012) and many criminologists, particularly those working at universities based in the 'Global North', increasingly find themselves engaging with policy makers and practitioners from different jurisdictions. They are sometimes approached for their topical and methodological expertise and the proactive among them work to situate themselves in transnational policy communities that allow them to maximise their research impact. They may feel prompted to engage in this manner by a combination of idealistic and opportunistic factors yet most criminologists also recognise that these activities can generate unanticipated harms. These harms can be understood in relation to their criminological, cultural and social consequences for recipient societies (see Bowling 2011; Blaustein 2014a) and, the disempowerment or marginalisation

J. Blaustein (✉)
Monash University, Melbourne, Australia

© The Author(s) 2017   **357**
S. Armstrong et al. (eds.), *Reflexivity and Criminal Justice*,
DOI 10.1057/978-1-137-54642-5_16

of alternative understandings of the criminal question. The implication is that there are many pitfalls awaiting Northern[1] criminologists undertaking or promoting their research abroad; however, this chapter proposes that it may still be possible to do so in an ethical and potentially beneficial manner.

The approach that is articulated in this chapter is grounded in the author's consideration of how ideas like 'democratic under-labouring' (Loader and Sparks 2010) and 'civic criminology' (Scottish Centre for Crime and Justice Research n.d.) might be extended to an international research context. Although overwhelmingly positive in its assessment, the chapter does acknowledge that criminologists should not ignore the existence of global asymmetries and power inequalities which serve to structure and constrain the international political economy of knowledge production and dissemination (Connell 2007). This implies that a universal ethos grounded in what are predominantly liberal values must be qualified by a critical and reflexive understanding of the globalising tendencies of Northern scholarly discourses, lest its representativeness and inclusiveness be overshadowed by its own imperialist or hegemonic aspirations as a meta-narrative.

The chapter proposes therefore that the moral and epistemological compatibility of this particular meta-narrative with post-colonial critiques of the international political economy of knowledge production is dependent upon the ability and the willingness of criminologists to exercise reflexivity and reasonableness while interacting with prospective research users. For the purpose of this discussion, reflexivity refers to the idea that '[t]here is no one-way street between the researcher and the object of study' (Alvesson and Skoldberg 2009: 78) while reasonableness implies an acknowledgement of the fact that criminological concepts and questions can legitimately be defined, constructed and interpreted in relation to a variety of discursive perspectives and theoretical traditions (Young 2000).

Criminologists may not agree with all of the viewpoints they encounter in the field and this chapter contends that they have a moral right to voice

---

[1] 'Northern criminologist' implies that the researcher is primarily affiliated with an academic institution that is located in the 'Global North'.

their concerns if the issue in question lies within their particular area of expertise. However, this critical imperative does not constitute a mandate for intentionally advancing their interests or viewpoints through formal or informal nodes of policy-making or practice. Rather, as a cultural and contextual outsider, it is argued that a criminologist seeking to generate impact through their research internationally might consider using their intellectual and social capital to facilitate deliberations with different stakeholders, both international and local, that are 'authentic, inclusive and consequential' (Dryzek and Niemeyer 2010; Blaustein 2016). This is referred to as *process-oriented* criminological engagement and it stands in opposition to those research activities that are designed to predefine or constrain deliberations about policy *outputs* and *outcomes*.

The chapter begins with a brief critical discussion of the terms 'Global North' and 'Global South' that are employed throughout this chapter. It then proceeds to reflexively account for the author's formative influences and experiences of completing a policy ethnography of an active community safety project in Bosnia and Herzegovina (BiH) which have since come to inform his call for restraint in the context of international research engagement.

'Southern' Terminology

The term 'Southern' is used by social scientists as a 'metaphor for the other, the invisible, the subaltern, the marginal and the excluded' (Carrington et al. 2015: 5). Concepts like 'Global North' or 'Northern' thus imply that certain parts of the world, often due to a legacy of historic colonial relations, enjoy a significant degree of economic, political, social and intellectual capital that enables them to preserve their hegemonic influence and advance their interests through their interactions with 'Southern', 'subaltern' or 'peripheral' regions (see Connell 2007). Parts of the world that are commonly ascribed 'Northern' status include: North America, Western Europe, 'economically developed' parts of Asia, Australia and New Zealand. Regions that are typically labelled 'Southern' include: large parts of South and Southeast Asia, sub-Saharan Africa, Latin America and in some cases, Southeast Europe (see Carrington et al. 2015: 5).[2] It must be recognised however that the distribution of economic, political, social and intellectual capital within both Northern and Southern societies is often highly uneven meaning that both contexts invariably feature their own metropoles and peripheries.

It is also important to consider that many countries simultaneously exhibit Northern and Southern attributes. A good example of this is Australia, a former colony that is home to a number of affluent and highly 'liveable' cities, as well as structurally marginalised and historically oppressed indigenous populations. This implies that categorising a country as 'Northern' or 'Southern' will inevitably serve to oversimplify its geopolitical positionality and thus, obfuscate the complex, empirical realities of power and resource distribution that characterise it, both internationally and domestically. The fluidity of these categories also implies that both the researcher's judgements and their research design can play an important role in determining whether a particular country is assigned the 'Northern' or a 'Southern' label. For example, in my book *Speaking Truths to Power: Policy Ethnography and Police Reform in Bosnia and Herzegovina*, I identify BiH as an example of a Southern society (Blaustein 2015a). Although Southeast Europe does not neatly fit the North/South binary, I believe that this characterisation was justifiable due to the asymmetric power structures that are widely associated with the country's post-conflict 'transition'. I also acknowledge however that there are other features of BiH that might more accurately be described as Northern, or at least which are incomparable with other so-called Southern societies. The point is that a researcher's decisions vis-à-vis their research questions and case selection process may play an important role in constituting the Northern or Southern identity of a particular context within academic discourse. This implies that research outputs including publications may inadvertently serve to reinforce or validate the Northernness or the Southernness of particular countries or even entire regions.

---

[2] Many of these criticisms also apply to the labels 'developed' and 'developing' or 'underdeveloped'.

Criminologists must make an effort to acknowledge these conceptual and methodological issues lest they employ the concepts of Global North and Global South uncritically. Nonetheless, I believe that these concepts are useful for the purpose of analysing criminological expertise as a product of an increasingly globalised higher education sector. As a general rule, universities that are located in what most would uncritically consider the Global North enjoy better reputations than those universities that are located in the Global South. This perception is validated by international benchmarking exercises like the Times Higher Education (THE) and QS World University Rankings on annual basis. Of course, the performance indicators that are used to rank universities around the world are modelled on Northern definitions of academic excellence including, as evident from the methodology for the THE World University rankings: 'the learning environment'; research 'volume', 'income' and 'reputation'; 'industry income', and 'international outlook' (Times Higher Education 2015). Lacking the resources and established reputations of their Northern counter-parts, many Southern universities struggle to compete when it comes to these ranking exercises and this may in-turn diminish the ability of their affiliated scholars to generate international impact, be it scholarly or 'real world', through their research. In some cases, it also leads to the privileging of international expertise locally. To this effect, it has long been the case that policy makers and practitioners throughout the Global South have turned to Northern criminological expertise as a resource for addressing their problems of order (see Blaustein 2016). Some criminologists, including leading American proponents of 'Broken Windows' policing and 'evidence-based crime prevention', have enthusiastically embraced these opportunities to promote their work abroad while others, including myself, have done so cautiously. The following section attempts to illustrate the importance of adopting a cautious approach by presenting a brief autobiographical account of my experiences as a policy ethnographer undertaking research with the United Nations Development Programme (UNDP) in BiH.

Expert Knowledge, Minus the Expert

I completed my doctoral research at the University of Edinburgh between 2009 and 2013 and my project focused on the dynamics of internationally driven security sector reform in BiH. My decision to utilise ethnographic methods to develop a multi-level account of active policy transfer processes in the context of this project was influenced by my exposure to what I identify as the civic and critical sensibilities of my supervisors and mentors including Richard Sparks whose contributions to the development of 'civic criminology' I review in the following section. For the purpose of this vignette, however, I will first discuss an important component of my fieldwork that involved conducting what I have elsewhere described as a 'participatory policy ethnography' of the UNDP's 'Safer Communities' project (see Blaustein 2015a). The policy ethnography was participatory in the sense that during a period of three months, I assumed the role of a project intern and thus achieved full albeit temporary membership status with the project.

My primary motive for undertaking this policy ethnography was to generate data that would enable me to complete my PhD before my funding ran out and I was weary of inadvertently contributing to unethical or undesirable policy outcomes or practices (see Blaustein 2014a). The idea that I could participate in an active policy environment without leaving a footprint was naïve but my minimalist aspirations reflected my acknowledgement of the fact that my knowledge of policing in BiH, and indeed my knowledge of BiH, was extremely limited. I therefore accepted that I was a contextual and a cultural outsider who had been afforded expert status and the opportunity to participate in an active policy deliberation process as a result of my aforementioned academic credentials and institutional affiliation. This status constituted a form of Northern intellectual privilege and a potential source of power and influence.[3]

---

[3] Naturally, the project received full ethical approval from the University of Edinburgh before I commenced my fieldwork. My supervisors also worked with me to develop protocols and procedures (agreed by UNDP) that proved valuable when it came to negotiating my involvement with the Safer Communities project and articulating my needs as a researcher.

Assuming this membership role was crucial for my research because it enabled me to develop a habituated empirical appreciation of the work of my colleagues and a critical understanding of the political economy of security sector reforms in this context. It also meant that I was required to actively contribute to the project's activities. My primary task involved working with the Project Manager and the Community Policing Advisor to identify a compelling narrative for marketing the project to prospect donors for the purpose of extending it beyond its pilot phase.[4] The idea was that the narrative would then serve as the basis for a concept note and ultimately, a project proposal. The challenge, which I have elsewhere written about at greater length (see Blaustein 2014b, 2015a), was that European donors were unlikely to recognise the value of the project which involved introducing a community safety partnership model to BiH unless the initiative could be linked to an appealing thematic issue. We toyed with various ways of communicating the prospective benefits of the model including combatting social exclusion, crime reduction and facilitating BiH's accession to the European Union. Ultimately, our discussions led us to accept the fact that the prospective benefits or outcomes of the project could not be pre-defined because this risked undermining its local orientation. The Safer Communities project was never actually extended but discursive elements, specifically the emphasis on the importance of local multi-agency partnership working, were subsequently incorporated into a UNDP disarmament project that lasted from 2013 to 2015.

It was about an year after I had completed my fieldwork, once I started applying for full-time academic positions, that terms like 'impact' and 'research engagement' entered my academic vocabulary. This was largely due to the fact that at this time, universities across the country were scrambling to clarify the meaning of 'impact' for strategic purposes. Henceforth, research performance would no longer be measured solely

---

[4] The pilot phase involved supporting the implementation of a community safety partnership model in five municipalities, rendering these partnerships sustainable, and subsequently promoting the model in other municipalities throughout the country. Initially, the project was funded by what is known as core funding (money with no strings attached); however, sustaining the project in the long run would require access to non-core funding (money with conditions attached; see Blaustein 2015a).

in relation to scholarly publication outputs. Rather, it would also be assessed using a selection of 'impact case studies' that would be used to assess the 'real-world' benefits of academic research. There was of course limited consensus amongst academics at this time about how the concept of impact should be defined and measured (see e.g.: Upton et al. 2014). Indeed, there was even some discussion as to whether or not it was actually possible to meaningfully distinguish between positive and negative impact given that the long-term implications of a research project are often impossible to gauge within a limited five-year period (see also McBride, this volume).

I do not believe that my research with the Safer Communities project was especially impactful. Nonetheless, my introduction to the politics of impact vis-à-vis my familiarity with REF 2014 has subsequently prompted me to reflect on the ethical and recursive implications of my doctoral research. In retrospect, I have come to appreciate the relative autonomy that my status as a funded-PhD student afforded me because I felt no professional pressures to demonstrate the social utility of my research for institutional benchmarking purposes and nor did I feel compelled to participate in any project activities that I believed to be harmful or ethically problematic.[5] The absence of any conditions attached to my doctoral funding and my lack of a long-term professional stake in the outcome of the Safer Communities project therefore allowed me to follow my ethical instincts and exercise humility and modesty as a researcher.[6] I felt comfortable and indeed compelled to actively limit the scope of my involvement with the Safer Communities project to that of participating in critical, informed and reflexive discussions and I sought to limit my contribution to activities designed to achieve specific outcomes unless I determined that they represented the interests of local stakeholders and were grounded in the best available evidence.[7] This privileged introduc-

---

[5] This is not to suggest that I had major ethical reservations about the goals of the Safer Communities team.

[6] From my experience and training as a postgraduate at the University of Edinburgh, I simply assumed that collaborating with policy makers and practitioners was the norm for criminologists, something that was indeed desirable, albeit problematic at times.

[7] It is of course questionable whether an outsider is actually capable of making contextually informed judgements about the suitability of certain activities.

tion to international criminological research thus helped me to conduct myself as a 'reasonable' participant in this deliberative setting. This is not to suggest that my individual contributions to the Safer Communities team's discussions were of any strategic value to my temporary colleagues or indeed, sensible. Rather, reasonableness implies that I was 'willing [and indeed eager] to listen to others who were able to explain to me why my ideas were incorrect or inappropriate' (paraphrasing Young 2000: 24). I was also able to provide my colleagues with critical, albeit constructive feedback because their habituated appreciation of UNDP's capacity development ethos also rendered them reasonable participants in this setting.

These formative experiences combined with my subsequent reflections on the ethics of criminological research engagement abroad (see Blaustein 2015b, 2016) provide the basis for the concept of *process-oriented criminological engagement* that is developed in the remainder of this chapter. The idea is simple. Ethical criminological engagement abroad, especially in Southern or peripheral societies, necessitates reasonable and reflexive interactions with potential research users. At a time when criminologists are increasingly being pressured to promote their research to external audiences, this means working to facilitate mutually accessible and responsive dialogues rather than drawing on one's expert knowledge or privilege in order to advance or promote a particular agenda that reflects the criminologist's interests. The concept is grounded in a set of ideals that are most closely associated with concepts like 'democratic under-labouring' and 'civic criminology' which are critically reviewed in the following section. The key question that emerges from this review is, can a liberal meta-narrative that provides an aspirational normative account of the production and dissemination of knowledge actually accommodate Southern discursive perspectives?

Travels of the 'Democratic Under-labourer'

Following the decline of the rehabilitative ideal, the demise of the welfare state, and the increased politicisation of crime, utility or rather a perceived lack thereof has emerged as an important source of ontological insecurity for many criminologists in the Global North. In the UK, for example, the once privileged role of criminologists as 'platonic guardians' in the 1950s and 1960s and their 'pragmatic, empirical, [and] humanistic concern' for rendering 'criminal justice and penal institutions effective and decent' have become increasingly superfluous to the work of policy makers and practitioners today (Loader 2006: 567). In response to their self-perceived waning relevance, a number of high-profile criminologists in Britain and the USA have recently turned to what Hammersley (1999) describes as 'moral gerrymandering' in the hope of re-invigorating the discipline's status as a public purveyor of knowledge and evidence. The neologism which encapsulates these attempts to render criminological research politically impactful is 'public criminology', a conceptual off-shoot of the idea of 'public sociology' which gained popularity following Michael Burrawoy's Presidential Address to the American Sociological Association in 2004 (see Burrawoy 2005; for a critique, see Wacquant 2011).

In a critical review of the public criminology literature, Turner (2013) identifies three distinct approaches to doing public criminology: 'fighting for truth' (e.g. Currie 2007), 'news-making criminology' (Barak 1988) and 'democratic under-labouring' (Loader and Sparks 2010). 'Fighting for truth' assumes that criminologists are 'in possession of a "truth" that is not being heard by the wider public' (Turner 2013: 150). Its proponents argue that a public criminology should aim to 'produce research that is more scientific, more relevant, more usable and less political' (Turner 2013: 152). Turner (2013: 153) is critical of this perspective because it fails to clarify 'where, how and by whom ['truth'] is to be found'. 'News-making criminology', a term which was initially coined by Barak (1988), recognises that criminological knowledge is constituted by a diverse array of competing discourses so it rejects the existence of a single, objective truth. Rather than valuing discursive pluralism, 'news-making criminol-ogists' advocate 'adopting the skills and tools of the journalistic trade, [and] capitalizing on the opportunities afforded by new media formats' for the purpose of 'disseminating criminological discourses in such a way that they have a chance to compete with established ways of rep-resenting crime and justice' (Turner 2013: 153–154). The limitation of this approach is that it assumes a privileged status for certain academic criminological discourses, specifically those which are favoured by 'news-making' criminologists', in the public realm. Critics suggest that it is conducive to neither humility nor modesty because it treats this knowledge as a public good yet neglects to consider that these privileged discourses may not resonate with public views and understandings (Loader and Sparks 2010; Turner 2013). At its worst, it is undemocratic.

The final construction of public criminology identified by Turner (2013) is that of 'democratic under-labouring' (Loader and Sparks 2010). This perspective is most consistent with the civic and critical sensibilities I encountered as a graduate student at the University of Edinburgh. I am admittedly biased towards this approach insofar as I understand it to be fundamentally inclusive and conciliatory with regard to its formative intentions. Of course, it is not without its criticisms.[8]

According to Loader and Sparks (2010: 116), 'democratic under-labouring' represents 'a sensibility or disposition' that is intended to guide criminologists in the course of their efforts to engage with 'public life'. It is not intended to provide a comprehensive 'agenda' for researching crime, justice or security nor a 'user's manual' for guiding the dissemination of criminological knowledge (Loader and Sparks 2010: 116). Rather, 'democratic under-labouring' constitutes a manner of modestly conducting oneself as a criminologist that 'involves recognizing and making apparent the particular orientations and skills that different actors bring when they assemble around crime and justice controversies' (Loader and Sparks 2010: 129; see also Henry, this volume). With

---

[8] A number of relevant criticisms that focus specifically on the idea of 'democratic under-labouring' can be found in 'A Symposium of Reviews of *Public Criminology?*' that was published in the *British Journal of Criminology* in 2011 (Christie et al. 2011). Nils Christie, for example, suggests that Loader and Sparks fail to articulate what they mean by a 'better politics of crime' while suggesting that the diplomacy inherent to the sensibility of 'democratic under-labouring' may itself be harmful if one accepts that 'our Western societies might be in need of *more* explicated internal conflicts, not less' (Christie et al. 2011: 709). In their reviews, Elliot Currie and Gloria Laycock both take issue with the humility that is advocated by Loader and Sparks and suggest that criminologists need to be more assertive in their attempts to generate impact through their research (Christie et al. 2011). In other words, whereas the inherently political nature of crime leads Loader and Sparks to question the privileged status of criminologists as experts when it comes to criminal justice policy and practice, Currie and Laycock view the politicisation of crime as a solid justification for capitalizing on this expert status for the purpose of fostering more moderate, evidence-based policies and practices. The problem with the latter view however is that it is often difficult for criminologists to anticipate or manage the ways in which their knowledge and evidence will be utilised by policy makers and practitioners, hence the risk that even well-intentioned attempts to influence policy and practice may contribute to unanticipated and unintentional harms.

respect to the issue of public engagement, this implies that criminologists should cautiously embrace public and political sites of deliberation, discursive contestation and societal transformation rather than abstain from them or abhor them.

Politics, observe Loader and Sparks (2010: 122), is the 'space for mediating claims for recognition, determining who belongs, who 'we' are and the terms we set for our coexistence'. For criminologists to attempt to by-pass or subvert the political in the course of their attempts to influence crime control policy-making and practice would thus undermine the democratic legitimacy of the policy-making process in question, as well as the outputs it contributes to. Thus, rather than attempting to draw upon their privilege or capital as academics for the purpose of discreetly influencing the work of empowered criminal justice decision makers, be they politicians, bureaucrats or practitioners, criminologists who subscribe to this approach may feel compelled to draw upon their intellectual and professional capital for the primary purpose of facilitating greater awareness amongst key decision makers of the best available evidence and theories (Loader and Sparks 2010). This means embracing competing approaches to constructing, interpreting and addressing issues relating to crime, justice and security and evaluating their relative strengths and weaknesses through transparent and accessible dialogues with prospective research users. The assumption is that policy makers and practitioners must be prompted to recognise this plurality of perspectives before they can arrive at rational and informed policy decisions (Loader and Sparks 2010).

The idea that democratic under-labouring seeks to facilitate conciliatory dialogues implies that that communications between researchers and research users should ideally constitute a two-way process. In other words, democratic under-labouring is not just about educating potential research users, but also about listening to them and learning from their experiences. In this respect, it can be described as a mutually reflexive process. Of course, not all decisions that relate to criminal justice policy are made in the public sphere. Thus, implicit in the work of Loader and Sparks (2010, 2013) is a belief that these deliberative dialogues must be discursively representative (Dryzek and Niemeyer 2010) if they are to be considered democratically legitimate (see also Rosanvallon 2011). According to political theorists John Dryzek and Simon Niemeyer (2010), it is not essential that every stakeholder is actually afforded the chance to take part in the deliberation or that they are formally represented within the process. Indeed, this would be impractical for many bureaucratic decision-making processes that take place behind closed doors. In this case, the emphasis is on ensuring that as many discourses as possible are accorded the opportunity to influence the decision-making process. The ideal of representation is therefore more important than that of participation and the representation of discourses is treated as morally superior to the representation of individuals given that individual preferences are continuously constructed and re-constructed in relation to a variety of discursive perspectives (Dryzek and Niemeyer 2010). Acknowledging this fluidity is therefore important for ensuring that the truths that inform deliberations, be they public or restricted, are not reduced to a single, hegemonic narrative (see also Annison, this volume).

For a deliberative process to qualify as discursively representative, it must be '*authentic, inclusive and consequential*' (Dryzek and Niemeyer 2010: 10). 'To be authentic,' writes Dryzek, 'deliberation ought to be able to induce reflection upon preference in noncoercive fashion' (Dryzek 2000: 68), and involve communicating in terms that those who do not share one's point of view can find meaningful and accept. Inclusivity implies that 'all affected actors (or their representatives)' can participate in the deliberative process (Dryzek and Niemeyer 2010: 10). Finally, consequentiality means that the 'deliberation must somehow make a difference when it comes to determining or influencing collective outcomes'. In certain circumstances, Northern criminologists may be able to promote these meta-values in the course of their interactions with key decision makers. Their success will often depend on the receptiveness of their research partners to these particular ideals. At a minimum however, process-oriented criminological engagement requires Northern criminologists to work to ensure that their activities do not undermine the authenticity, inclusivity or consequentiality of any deliberative processes they encounter. In a short essay that I recently contributed to the OUP Blog, I have even argued that the wilful neglect of this responsibility by researchers should be regarded as an ethical breach (Blaustein 2015b).

Reflexivity and Reasonableness

The ideals of 'democratic under-labouring' are also consistent with what British criminologists including Jon Bannister, Fergus McNeil and Richard Sparks have elsewhere described as 'civic criminology' (see Bannister 2014). Civic criminology refers more broadly to a vision for criminological engagement with various 'communities of interest' including, but not limited to: policy makers, practitioners as well as 'those on the receiving end of crime prevention, policing and justice' for the purpose of 'inform[ing] deliberation and decision-making about the multiple intellectual, practical and ethical challenges presented by crime and its control' (Scottish Centre for Crime and Justice Research n.d.). The normative, theoretical, methodological and practical dimensions of civic criminology have been most clearly articulated by the coordinators of the Scottish Centre for Crime and Justice Research on its website which highlights the need for civic criminologists to exercise reflexivity and reasonableness in the course of their interactions with different audiences in the field. In other words, for the civic criminologist to 'imagine alternatives', be transparent about their 'formative influences' and 'intentions', 'realise' the 'applied value and social impact' of their research and contribute collaboratively to the development of 'better ways of responding to problems of crime, justice and order', they must understand their contributions to knowledge co-production (paraphrasing Scottish Centre for Crime and Justice Research n.d.). They must then recursively adjust their research engagement activities in accordance with the ideals stated above. The capacity of the researcher to continuously maintain sight of this reflexive praxis can thus be described as their reflexive awareness. This constitutes an important mechanism of researcher self-accountability.

For criminologists to participate in or facilitate discursively representative policy deliberations, they must continuously exercise personal reflexivity and reasonableness. Reflexivity in this sense requires both an understanding of the criminologist's position within their field of study and of the extent to which their participation in this field may contribute to the validation and legitimation of some discursive perspectives as facts and the dismissal of others. The implication is that process-oriented criminological engagement as a conceptual off-shoot of democratic under-labouring and civic criminology is about more than merely facilitating healthy dialogues which can accommodate a plurality of perspectives; it is also about holding oneself and possibly others to account for their 'formative influences and intentions' (Collins and Evans 2008: 126). This underlying reflexive imperative is clearly acknowledged by Loader and Sparks who write:

> any discussion of the criminal question encodes in miniature a set of claims about the nature of the good society, and any attempt to answer it – however apparently 'dry' and technical, or limited in scope – carries and projects a possible world, a desirable state of affairs that a political or criminological author wishes to recover, preserve, or usher into existence. (Loader and Sparks 2010: 123)

Political theorist Iris Marion Young (2000: 24) adds that '[r]easonable participants in democratic discussion must have an open mind'. She writes:

> They cannot come to the discussion of a collective problem with commitments that bind them to the authority of prior norms or unquestionable beliefs. Nor can they assert their own interests above all others' or insist that their initial opinion about what is right or just cannot be subject to revision. To be reasonable is to change our opinions and our preferences because others persuade us that our initial opinions and preferences, as they are relevant to the collective problems under discussion, are incorrect or inappropriate. (Young 2000: 24–25)

Loader and Sparks (2010) present their sensibility of democratic under-labouring as inherently reasonable insofar as it is capable of accommodating a plurality of discursive perspectives but Turner (2013: 163) concludes that reasonableness in practice necessitates the rejection of what Latour (1993) describes as the 'modern Constitution' of knowledge in favour of a constructionist approach. In other words, Turner (2013: 162) proposes that a criminologist who assumes the sensibility of democratic under-labouring must reject the artificial Weberian distinction between 'facts' and 'values' and instead, recognise 'that what emerges as 'knowledge' in any given time, in any given place, is contingent upon the context within which such knowledge is produced'. Turner's critique of the overly accommodating nature of Loader and Sparks's (2010) arguments thus highlights its susceptibility to manipulation by those whose epistemological leanings restrict them from truly appreciating the importance of discursive representation and democratic deliberations.

A Global Civic Criminology?

It is important to acknowledge that ideas like democratic under-labouring and civic criminology were initially articulated as part of a vision for facilitating criminological research and engagement with *domestic* policy makers and practitioners in the Global North. Scotland, the context where a number of these ideas might be said to have originated, is a small and economically privileged nation, at least relatively so. At the time of writing this chapter, the Scottish National Party also appears to be at least outwardly receptive to progressive, evidence-based policies that arise from collaborations with academic researchers. This dynamic affords criminologists working in Scotland unique opportunities to draw upon their research for the purpose of building longstanding relations with policy makers and practitioners. As members of this political context, Scottish criminologists can be said to possess relevant cultural and contextual knowledge of this setting as well as a long-term stake in the outcomes of the contributions to knowledge co-production. I would argue that this provides them with a legitimate basis for engaging in outcome-oriented impact activities in this context so long as they do not undermine authentic, inclusive or consequential deliberations. Accordingly, civic criminology must be understood as a particular approach to doing criminology in a unique political context.

The first question to consider then is whether Northern criminologists also have a legitimate moral basis for exporting their knowledge to influence policy and practice abroad. Some criminologists might argue that legitimacy could be derived from universalist human rights discourse and this is supported by the general consensus amongst international lawyers that the protection of individual human rights trumps the preservation of cultural rights in cases where the two conflict. However, it must be recognised that the preservation of human rights does not serve as the primary driver for much of what constitutes criminological engagement abroad. Rather, what has become known as 'translational criminology' is primarily concerned with transplanting legislation, norms, models, mentalities and/or 'best practices' from the metropole throughout the periphery while simultaneously cultivating local political and practitioner support to sustain them. In other words, much criminological research engagement at an international level is driven by either a belief that the knowledge generated in the metropole is superior to that of the periphery or, by the entrepreneurial tendencies of Northern criminologists who are keen to construct a global brand for their research. In these instances, the protection of human rights may be invoked as a justification for these entrepreneurial activities or identified as a necessary condition for ensuring ethical research engagement. The risk remains however that episodes of translational criminology that do not outwardly interfere with the protection of human rights may still interfere with the cultural and political rights of local and indigenous populations. In some cases, this interference may even generate cultural and structural harms (Bowling 2011; Cohen 1988).

A second question relates to whether it is in fact possible to advance this civic agenda at a global level without hegemonising meta-deliberations that relate to the ethics of international criminological engagement. This concern arises from Connell's (2007: 9) observation that 'sociology [and all social sciences] was formed within the culture of imperialism, and embodied an intellectual response to the colonised world'. She adds, 'This fact is crucial in understanding the content and method of sociology, as well as the discipline's wider cultural significance.' Consider that the ideals underpinning 'democratic under-labouring' and 'civic criminology' are themselves grounded in a set of classical liberal assumptions concerning the relationship between knowledge and politics, as well as what constitutes legitimate and illegitimate forms of criminology engagement. Any attempt to universalise these values and establish them as the basis for a global ethos therefore exhibits hegemonic tendencies that risk marginalising and subordinating alternative, Southern approaches and ideals. Short of embracing a purely relativistic approach which risks prioritising the protection of cultural rights over those of individuals, this is unavoidable but I believe that the risk of disempowerment can be managed by criminologists who adopt a process-oriented approach to criminological engagement abroad.

Towards an Ethical Self Checklist

The final section of this chapter sketches out the contours of an ethical self-checklist that is designed to help researchers achieve a reflexive praxis and regulate their globalising tendencies for the purpose of facilitating discursively representative policy-making processes abroad. The checklist takes the form of a set of questions that researchers might regularly ask themselves.

Question 1: What are my primary reasons for engaging with this particular policy audience or setting? The purpose of this question is to prompt criminologists to reflect on whether their motives and intentions align with the needs of local partners and stakeholders or, whether they are in fact a product of the researcher's professional aspirations. I do not wish to suggest that altruism represents a necessary or achievable quality of ethical social research but rather, that criminologists must reflect on whether their activities will add any value to the lives of the intended 'beneficiaries' before deciding whether to proceed with their impact-generating activities. Answering this question requires honesty on behalf of the researcher, along with a reflexive understanding of the professional pressures that they face in their native research context. Simply, pressures to commodify research or to develop an outstanding impact case study do not constitute a sufficient ethical basis for 'internationalizing' one's research.

Questions 2 and 3: Do I enjoy privileged status relative to other members of this policy-making process or setting? Is this status merited? More often than not, academic criminologists with Northern institutional affiliations will answer yes to Question 2. This in itself is not problematic, so long as the answer to Question 3 is also yes. In practice, it is often difficult to differentiate between the privilege accorded to Northern researchers on the basis of their scholarly expertise and that which is accorded to them on the basis of their Northern identity and scholarly reputation. In truth, the researcher in question is probably the only individual who is capable of making this distinction which means that the onus falls on them to be transparent and forthcoming about the limits of their expertise, especially when it comes to questions of cultural and contextual fit. Although it may prove unpopular with criminologists and their research partners alike, the phrase "I don't know" is often the most ethical response to pleas for advice or guidance about adapting or implementing a particular criminal justice model, mentality or practice. I personally used this phrase quite a bit during my time with UNDP's Safer Communities project.

Questions 4 and 5: Am I capitalizing on this status to advance a particular discourse, agenda or outcome? Does this discourse, agenda or outcome resonate with the needs and understandings of the intended beneficiaries? The answer to Question 4 should be fairly straightforward, at least to the reflexive criminologist. The same can be said about the ethical implications of their response to this question in relation to the ideal of process-oriented criminological engagement that was articulated earlier in this chapter. To reiterate, advancing a particular outcome or agenda 'abroad' may be ethically problematic insofar as it risks undermining or interfering with policy deliberations that are receptive to subaltern discursive perspectives. However, the addition of Question 5 implies that there may be circumstances where championing a particular discursive perspective may be ethically justified in a particular context, perhaps even necessitated by the political economy of the policy-making process or setting.

Hypothetically, a researcher with longstanding ties to the setting or extensive local knowledge may recognise that a particular, often local, discursive perspective has been underrepresented or marginalised from the deliberation. Alternatively, the researcher may recognise during the course of a deliberation that the favoured solution or outcome risks generating harms or adversely affecting a particular group. In either instance, the researcher should at least consider whether their ethical obligation to avoid causing harm through their research might require them to take a more proactive approach to championing the idea of process-oriented criminological engagement. In this instance, the researcher may take it upon themselves to provide a voice to the underrepresented discourse or in cases where they lack the knowledge or cultural credibility to assume this role, advocate wider participation as being necessary for the fulfilment of the inclusiveness criterion. The risk is that personally assuming the role of the champion may obfuscate the boundary between process-oriented and outcome-oriented research and thus, the researcher must ultimately exercise restraint in cases where their efforts to promote inclusivity appear likely to fail. Arguably, the exception to this involves cases where the likely outcome of the deliberation risks depriving individuals of fundamental human rights. What constitutes a sufficient risk in this respect is a matter for future discussion, especially considering that a number of Northern criminal justice models that have been transplanted throughout the developing world have had a detrimental impact on the human rights of local populations (Cohen 1988). Nowhere is this more apparent than in Latin America where the 'war on drugs' and 'zero tolerance policing' have contributed to increased levels of police violence that have disproportionately affected the urban poor (Campesi 2010).

Conclusion

In the spirit of fostering 'a better politics of crime and its regulation' (Loader and Sparks 2010: 117), I have attempted to use this chapter to recursively take stock of the opportunities and pitfalls associated with criminological engagement in transnational fields of knowledge production and dissemination. However, as I present these ideas in the early days of the 2018 'Excellence in Research for Australia' initiative and the next iteration of the Research Excellence Framework in the UK, the extrinsic viability of a cautious, process-oriented approach to criminological research engagement may appear questionable, at least in relation to the growing emphasis on performance management which is an endemic and inescapable feature of the so-called 'neoliberal university' with its globalising aspirations.

In light of these reflections and in recognition of the opportunities[9] and pressures that exist for criminologists across the globe to engage with policy makers and practitioners at every stage of the research process, we must acknowledge that the structural imbalances which characterise the global economy of criminological knowledge production and dissemination may constitute a threat to the deliberative governance of crime and security. Northern criminologists may not be empowered to change this structural dynamic, but this does not mean that they must be complicit with it or capitalise on it for professional gain. Resistance is both necessary and possible. The ideals of discursive representation and process-oriented engagement along with the ethical self checklist proposed in this chapter are intended to provide Northern criminologists with some initial resources for negotiating these challenging issues in the field. In the spirit of deliberation, it is important to acknowledge that the arguments and sensibilities proposed in this chapter provide only a starting point for future discussions about the ethics of criminological engagement abroad, not the final word.

References

Aas, K. (2011) 'Visions of Global Control: Cosmopolitan Aspiration in a World of Friction'. In M. Bosworth and C. Hoyle (eds.) *What is Criminology?*, Oxford: Oxford University Press: 406–419.

Aas, K. (2012) 'The Earth is One but the World is Not': Criminological Theory and its Geopolitical Divisions', *Theoretical Criminology* 16(1): 5–20.

Alvesson, M. and Skoldberg, K. (2009) *Reflexive Methodology: New Vistas for Qualitative Research*, London: Sage.

Bannister, J. (2014) 'Crime Is A "Wicked Problem" – What Should Criminology Do About It?', Lecture. Transcript available: <https://www.hssr.mmu.ac.uk/2014/01/30/crime-is-a-'wicked-problem'---what-should-criminology-do-about-it/>

---

[9] The opportunities in question are by-and-large a product of both the expansion and internationalisation of academic criminology as a field of knowledge production since the late 1990s. This expansion has been facilitated in a broad sense by various dimensions of globalisation which have created a demand for policy learning and more specifically by the establishment of international academic networks (e.g. the European Society of Criminology, the World Criminology Conference and the International Police Executive Symposium to name but a few), and international journals (e.g. *Translational Criminology*).

Barak, G. (1988) 'Newsmaking Criminology: Reflections of the Media, Intellectuals and Crime', *Justice Quarterly* 5(4): 565–587.

Blaustein, J. (2014a) 'Reflexivity and Participatory Policy Ethnography: Situating the Self in a Transnational Criminology of Harm Production'. In K. Lumsden and A. Winter (eds.) *Reflexivity and Criminological Research*, Basingstoke: Palgrave: 301–312.

Blaustein, J. (2014b) 'The Space Between: Negotiating the Contours of Nodal Security Governance Through 'Safer Communities' in Bosnia-Herzegovina', *Policing & Society* 24(1): 44–62.

Blaustein, J. (2015a) *Speaking Truths to Power: Policy Ethnography and Police Reform in Bosnia and Herzegovina,* Oxford: Oxford University Press.

Blaustein, J. (2015b) 'The Ethics of Criminological Engagement Abroad', OUP Blog.

Blaustein, J. (2016) 'Exporting Criminological Innovation Abroad: Discursive Representation, "Evidence-Based Crime Prevention" and the Post-Neoliberal Development Agenda in Latin America', *Theoretical Criminology* 20(2): 165–184.

Bowling, B. (2011) 'Transnational Criminology and the Globalization of Harm Production'. In M. Bosworth and C. Hoyle (eds.) *What is Criminology?*, Oxford: Oxford University Press: 361–379.

Burrawoy, M. (2005) 'For Public Sociology', *American Sociological Review* 70(1): 4–28.

Campesi, G. (2010) 'Policing, Urban Poverty and Insecurity in Latin America: The Case of Mexico City and Buenos Aires', *Theoretical Criminology* 14(4): 355–375.

Carrington, K., Hogg, R. and Sozzo, M. (2015) 'Southern Criminology' *British Journal of Criminology* 56(1): 1–20.

Cohen, S. (1988) *Against Criminology,* Trenton, N.J.: Transaction Publishers.

Collins, H. and Evans, R. (2008) *Rethinking Expertise,* Chicago: University of Chicago Press.

Connell, R. (2007) *Southern Theory: Social Science and the Global Dynamics of Knowledge,* London: Polity Press.

Currie, E. (2007) 'Against Marginality: Arguments for a Public Criminology', *Theoretical Criminology* 11(2): 175–190.

Dryzek, J.S. (2000) *Deliberative Democracy and Beyond: Liberals, Critics and Contestations,* Oxford: Oxford University Press.

Dryzek, J.S. and Niemeyer, J.S. (2010) 'Representation' in Dryzek, J.S. *Foundations and Frontiers of Deliberative Democracy,* Oxford: Oxford University Press: 42–65.

Hammersley, M. (1999) 'Sociology, What's It For? A Critique of Gouldner', *Sociological Research Online* 4(3). Available: <http://www.socresonline.org.uk/4/3/hammersley.html>

Latour, B. (1993) *We Have Never Been Modern*, Edinburgh: Pearson.

Loader, I. (2006) 'Fall of the 'Platonic Guardians': Liberalism, Criminology and Political Responses to Crime in England and Wales', *British Journal of Criminology* 46(4): 561–586.

Loader, I. and Sparks, R. (2010) *Public Criminology?*, London: Routledge.

Loader, I. and Sparks, R. (2013) 'Unfinished Business: Legitimacy, Crime Control and Democratic Politics'. In J. Tankebe and A. Liebling (eds.) *Legitimacy and Criminal Justice: An International Exploration*, Oxford: Oxford University Press.

Rosanvallon, P. (2011) *Democratic Legitimacy: Impartiality, Reflexivity, Proximity*, Princeton: Princeton University Press.

Scottish Centre for Crime and Justice Research (n.d.) 'Civic Criminology'. Website. Available: <http://www.sccjr.ac.uk/about-us/civic-criminology/>

Times Higher Education. (2015) 'About'. Available at: <https://www.timeshighereducation.com/news/ranking-methodology-2016> [Accessed 04 January 2015].

Turner, E. (2013) 'Beyond "Facts" and "Values" Rethinking Some Recent Debates about the Public Role of Criminology', *British Journal of Criminology* 53(1): 149–166.

Upton, S., Vallance, P. and Goddard, J. (2014) 'From Outcomes to Process: Evidence for a New Approach to Research Impact Assessment', *Research Evaluation* 23(4): 352–365,

Wacquant, L. (2011) 'From "Public Criminology" to the Reflexive Sociology of Criminological Production and Consumption: A Review of Public Criminology? by Ian Loader and Richard Sparks', *British Journal of Criminology* 51(2): 438–48.

Young, I. (2000) *Inclusion and Democracy*, Oxford: Oxford University Press.

Index

Note: Page numbers with "n" denote footnotes.

© The Author(s) 2017   **381**
S. Armstrong et al. (eds.), *Reflexivity and Criminal Justice*,
DOI 10.1057/978-1-137-54642-5

Printed in the United States
By Bookmasters